# IRELAND AND THE GREAT WAR

# IRELAND AND THE GREAT WAR

## A Social and Political History

Niamh Gallagher

BLOOMSBURY ACADEMIC
LONDON • NEW YORK • OXFORD • NEW DELHI • SYDNEY

BLOOMSBURY ACADEMIC
Bloomsbury Publishing Plc
50 Bedford Square, London, WC1B 3DP, UK
1385 Broadway, New York, NY 10018, USA
29 Earlsfort Terrace, Dublin 2, Ireland

BLOOMSBURY, BLOOMSBURY ACADEMIC and the Diana logo are trademarks of
Bloomsbury Publishing Plc

First published in Great Britain 2020
Paperback edition published in 2022

Cover design: Terry Woodley
Cover image © Courtesy of Adrian Foley

A catalogue record for this book is available from the British Library.
A catalog record for this book is available from the Library of Congress.

ISBN: HB: 978-1-78831-462-6
PB: 978-1-35024-669-0
ePDF: 978-1-78673-620-8
eBook: 978-1-78672-614-8

Typeset by Deanta Global Publishing Services, Chennai, India

*For John. That 'story' is now finished.*

# CONTENTS

List of figures                                              ix
List of maps, tables and charts                               x
List of abbreviations used in the text                       xi
List of abbreviations used in the notes                     xii
Preface                                                     xiv
Acknowledgements                                             xv


Chapter 1
INTRODUCTION                                                  1
    Contradictions                        1
    Irish civil society                   6
    The evidence                          10
    Chapter outline                       13

Chapter 2
MEMORY, HISTORY AND THE GREAT WAR                            17
    Remembering and writing 1914 to 1918  17
    Politics, apathy, and Irish nationalism 20
    Reappraising the war                  26

Chapter 3
IRISH WOMEN AND WAR-RELIEF ON THE HOME FRONT                 31
    War-relief across Ireland             31
    War-work in Southern Ireland          37
    War-work in Ulster                    47
    An all-Irish endeavour?               52

Chapter 4
THE WAR AT SEA: ENCOUNTERING THE GERMAN 'ENEMY'             61
    Bringing Ireland within the war zone  61
    Rural Ireland and 'Black '47'         73
    Ireland's 'enemy'                     82

Chapter 5
GREATER IRELAND AND CATHOLIC LOYALISM                       91
    Moderate nationalism and the war      91
    Irish Catholic loyalism               98
    'Ireland's half million'             107
    Meeting Irish-Canada                 113

Chapter 6
IRISH CATHOLICS, BRITAIN AND THE ALLIES 131
 The 'death of innocence', 1914–15 131
 Home Rule, recruitment and Britain, 1914–16 140
 Politics, conscription and recruitment, 1916–18 148
 A righteous defence 157

Chapter 7
CONCLUSION: IRELAND'S WAR? 171

Chapter 8
EPILOGUE: BEYOND AMNESIA 177

Notes 185
Bibliography 231
Index 246

# FIGURES

| | | |
|---|---|---|
| 1.1 | Unveiling the Great War memorial in Cork, 1925 | 2 |
| 1.2 | Mourners surround cross dedicated to the 16th (Irish) Division, College Green, Dublin, Armistice Day, 1924 | 3 |
| 1.3 | Armistice Day, Market Square, Longford, 1925 | 4 |
| 3.1 | The Catholic Lord Mayor, Henry O'Shea, meets Belgian refugees in Cork, 27 September 1914 | 36 |
| 3.2 | Great grand-daughters of Daniel O'Connell serving in a nursing capacity, *IL*, 20 June 1915 | 40 |
| 3.3 | The Arklow and Avoca War Hospital Supply Depot, *IL*, 1 September 1916 | 42 |
| 3.4 | Kerry No. 4 VAD, *IL*, 12 October 1917 | 43 |
| 3.5 | Wounded men at the Dublin Castle Red Cross Hospital, *IL*, 5 January 1917 | 45 |
| 3.6 | Treating the moss at the RCS Central Depot, Dublin, *IL*, 26 July 1918 | 54 |
| 4.1 | *Irish Independent* artist's impression of the sinking *Lusitania*. The Union Jack is visible | 65 |
| 4.2 | Members of the Royal Irish Regiment dig graves in Queenstown. Also published in *II*, 10 May 1915 | 68 |
| 4.3 | The Catholic cemetery at Queenstown. The Bishop of Cloyne, Robert Browne, is the prelate in white | 69 |
| 4.4 | Children lay 'doll-like' in morgues | 69 |
| 4.5 | Unknown woman awaiting identification | 70 |
| 4.6 | The extensive line of mourners. The Union Flag covers the coffin on the first hearse | 71 |
| 5.1 | Archbishop Mannix accompanied by fourteen Irish-Australian VC winners, 17 March 1920 | 100 |
| 5.2 | Composite photograph of fourteen Irish-Australian VC winners, presented to Lieutenant John Hamilton VC by Archbishop Mannix on 17 March 1920 | 101 |
| 5.3 | Recruitment and 'unity' in Irish-Canada | 110 |
| 5.4 | His Eminence Cardinal Logue with Officers of the Irish Canadians | 119 |
| 5.5 | The Catholic Irish Canadians arriving at Armagh Cathedral, 10 February 1917 | 120 |
| 5.6 | The Irish Canadians in Belfast, *The Illustrated London News*, 10 February 1917 | 122 |
| 5.7 | The Irish Canadians in Cork | 123 |
| 5.8 | Large crowds welcome the Irish Canadians outside Cork City Hall | 124 |
| 5.9 | Large crowds observe the Irish Canadians in Limerick | 126 |
| 6.1 | Recruitment meeting in Cork, *IL*, 8 October 1915 | 144 |
| 6.2 | Protestant and Catholic Irish women dressed as the Allies in Ballinrobe, Co. Mayo, *IL*, 29 January 1915 | 147 |

# MAPS, TABLES AND CHARTS

## *Maps*

4.1    Ships sunk by German U-Boats from September 1916–April 1917        81
4.2    Ships sunk by German U-Boats, May 1917–January 1918               83
4.3    Ships sunk by German U-Boats in the Irish Sea,
       February–October 1918                                            86

## *Tables*

2.1    Recruits raised in Ireland and across Britain per six-month period    29
3.1    Number of *sphagnum* moss dressings collected by the
       RCS excluding Ulster                                             56

## *Charts*

4.1    Terms related to self-government and 'submarine' as reported
       in *The Irish Times*, 1913–18                                    79
4.2    Terms related to self-government and 'submarine' as reported
       in *The Irish Independent*, 1913–18                              80
4.3    Terms related to self-government and 'submarine' as reported
       in *The Freeman's Journal*, 1913–18                              80

# ABBREVIATIONS USED IN THE TEXT

| | |
|---|---|
| AIF | Australian Imperial Force |
| ANZAC | Australian and New Zealand Army Corps |
| AOH | Ancient Order of Hibernians |
| BMH | Bureau of Military History |
| BRCS | The British Red Cross Society |
| CCORI | Central Council for the Organization of Recruitment in Ireland |
| CCWPC | County Cavan Women's Patriotic Committee |
| CDB | Congested District Board |
| CEF | Canadian Expeditionary Force |
| CWGC | Commonwealth War Graves Commission |
| DATI | Department of Agriculture and Technical Instruction |
| GAA | Gaelic Athletic Association |
| INAVDF | Irish National Aid Association and Volunteer Dependants' Fund |
| INF | Irish National Foresters |
| INV | Irish National Volunteers |
| IPP | Irish Parliamentary Party |
| IRA | Irish Republican Army |
| IRC | Irish Recruiting Council |
| JP | Justice of the Peace |
| MEF | Mediterranean Expeditionary Force |
| NSW | New South Wales |
| OTC | Officers' Training Corps |
| POW | Prisoner of War |
| RAMC | Royal Army Medical Corps |
| RCS | Royal College of Science |
| RDF | Royal Dublin Fusiliers |
| RIC | Royal Irish Constabulary |
| RMF | Royal Munster Fusiliers |
| SJ | Society of Jesus |
| TCD | Trinity College Dublin |
| UCC | University College Cork |
| UCG | University College Galway |
| UIL | United Irish League |
| UILGB | United Irish League of Great Britain |
| UVF | Ulster Volunteer Force |
| UWUC | Ulster Women's Unionist Council |
| VAD | Voluntary Aid Detachment |
| VC | Victoria Cross |
| WNHA | Women's National Health Association |

# ABBREVIATIONS USED IN THE NOTES

| | |
|---|---|
| AAA | Archive of the Archdiocese of Armagh |
| AC | *The Anglo-Celt* |
| ANZAC | Australian and New Zealand Army Corps |
| AOH | Ancient Order of Hibernians |
| Australian DB | Australian Dictionary of Biography |
| AWM | Australian War Memorial |
| BMH | Bureau of Military History |
| BRCS | British Red Cross Society |
| Canadian DB | Dictionary of Canadian Biography |
| CAS | Catholic Archdiocese of Sydney |
| CCCA | Cork City and County Archives |
| CE | *The Cork Examiner* |
| CJ | *The Clare Journal and Ennis Advertiser* |
| CT | *Connacht Tribune* |
| CWGC | Commonwealth War Graves Commission |
| DATI | Department of Agriculture and Technical Instruction |
| DCA | Dublin City Archives |
| DDA | Dublin Diocesan Archives |
| DED | District Electoral Division |
| Cambridge DIB | Dictionary of Irish Biography |
| FJ | *The Freeman's Journal* |
| FJ (Sydney) | *The Freeman's Journal* (Sydney) |
| GAA | Gaelic Athletic Association |
| ICPA | Irish Capuchin Provincial Archives |
| II | *Irish Independent* |
| IJA | Irish Jesuit Archives |
| IL | *Irish Life* |
| IN | *The Irish News and Belfast Morning News* |
| INF | Irish National Foresters |
| INV | Irish National Volunteers |
| IP | *The Irish Post and Weekly Telegraph for Cavan and the Midlands* |
| IPP | Irish Parliamentary Party |
| IRA | Irish Republican Army |
| IRB | Irish Republican Brotherhood |
| IT | *The Irish Times* |
| IWM | Imperial War Museum |
| JWC | Joint War Committee |
| LL | *Limerick Leader* |
| LO | *Leitrim Observer* |

| | |
|---|---|
| MG | *The Montreal Gazette* |
| NA | The National Archives |
| NAM | National Army Museum |
| NFB | National Film Board of Canada |
| NLI | National Library of Ireland |
| NR | *Newry Reporter* |
| NSW | New South Wales |
| NUI | National University of Ireland |
| NW | *Northern Whig* |
| NZEF | New Zealand Expeditionary Force |
| Oxford DNB | Oxford Dictionary of National Biography |
| RIC | Royal Irish Constabulary |
| RCS | Royal College of Science |
| SHC | Somme Heritage Centre |
| UCC | University College Cork |
| UCD | University College Dublin |
| UIL | United Irish League |
| VAD | Voluntary Aid Detachment |

## PREFACE

This book explores Irish responses to the Great War on the home front in Ireland and other Irish diasporic communities. Its subject matter is those Irish Catholics who assisted the British and Allied war efforts in Ireland, Britain, Canada and Australia, and it argues that support for the Allies was rendered by individuals and civil society for longer than is commonly accepted across much of the existing literature. Contingent events as well as imagined scenarios helped to shape Irish reactions to the war, and the book reveals the significance of 1915 in developing attitudes towards the international conflict. It illuminates how Germany came to represent the ultimate despotic power, particularly through its campaign of submarine warfare, and it offers a new perspective on Catholic attitudes towards the British and Allied war efforts following the political complications which arose between the government and Irish nationalists after the Easter Rising and conscription crisis of 1918. The book reveals a surprising degree of cross-confessional cooperation throughout the duration of the conflict, which has gone virtually unnoticed in existing scholarly accounts, as groups of Irish women and men put their domestic political differences to the side to support an international cause they both believed in. By broadening the framework of analytical enquiry and by shifting the emphasis of Irish participation away from recruitment and the respective desires of unionism and nationalism onto the war effort itself, this book offers a radical new reading of Irish involvement in the world's first 'total war'.

# ACKNOWLEDGEMENTS

For years I have been replying 'almost' whenever asked, "Have you finished your book yet?" Indeed, this project has been some years in the making – around ten years by the time it arrives on the shelves – and in that time, the First World War has undergone something of a 'revolution' in Irish historical memory.

When this project began life as an MPhil dissertation, and later as a PhD thesis supervised by Professor Eugenio Biagini at the University of Cambridge, the memory of the Great War in Ireland was not as popular, or as uncontroversial a topic, as it is today. I remember starting my research in the National Library of Ireland, where I met a fellow PhD student studying at University College Dublin. Upon telling him that I planned to research Irish Catholic involvement in the Great War, his reply was something along the lines of 'Only the scum of Dublin and Redmond's lot were involved in that war. Sure it was Britain's war' – a sentiment which, though it has come to be challenged by historians, has not gone away in contemporary Ireland, or even within the academy.

This book aims to further challenge the view that the Great War was not 'Ireland's War'. Undoubtedly it is a conflict that occupies an unusual place in Irish historical memory, straddling watersheds and turning points that have shaped modern Ireland, both politically and socially, but it is its assumed relationship with the political developments after the Easter Rising of 1916 and the rise of a better organized alternative to the old Irish Nationalist Party that has made any reappraisal of its popularity among Irish Catholics an attack on the primacy of the national question. This book does not seek 'war' on this front; when it does consider the domestic political situation, it aims to further complicate the essential dichotomy between constitutional nationalism and support for the war effort, and radical nationalism and anti-war sentiment, to provide a more nuanced and sophisticated understanding of the complex feelings, opinions and behaviours that many Irish Catholics felt and expressed towards the war during this formative moment in the history of national development.

Researching this project took me around the world. As a result, there are probably people who have helped me in some capacity within the last decade who I have forgotten to mention here. Please do contact me and I will ensure your contributions will be noted in future editions.

First and foremost, I would like to thank my former supervisor, Eugenio Biagini, for his meticulous eye for detail and for the helpful 'red pen' that has made this book stronger and more sophisticated. I will never know how you manage to unfailingly read draft after draft and still find areas to improve upon. Thank you for your diligence and for always being willing to give feedback. I am also grateful to Jon Lawrence and the late Keith Jeffery, who were my PhD examiners and whose encouragement convinced me to turn my thesis into a book.

For those people who helped me during my research, I wish to thank Patrick Hugh Lynch, Adrian Foley, Gerry White, Mark Cronin, Jean Prendergast and the members of the Cork Western Front Association; Noelle Dowling and the Dublin Diocesan Archives; John and the Wanderers' Football Club; Niall Cummins; Damien Burke and the Irish Jesuit Archives; the archivists at the National Library of Ireland, PRONI, the Somme Heritage Centre, Cork City and County Archives, the Armagh Diocesan Archives, and Jonathan Maguire and the Royal Irish Fusiliers Museum. In Britain, my thanks to the staff at the British Library and Newspaper Archive, Cambridge University Library, the Imperial War Museum, the National Archives, the National Army Museum and the Red Cross archives.

'Down under' I wish to thank Jeff Kildea for acting both as tour guide and as an encyclopaedia on the Irish-Australian contribution to the war; Julie Craig and Helen Russell for allowing me to dig through the archive at Maitland-Newcastle and for so graciously hosting me and showing me the sights, including, not least, the Hunter Wine Valley; the staff at the Australian War Memorial and the Sydney Archdiocesan Archives and Alison Bashford for the fantastic recommendation to visit Manly (a former quarantine station), where the *Lusitania* docked in 1895 and its crew inscribed their signatures on the adjacent cliff; and to the Lindsay family for putting me up and making me feel so welcome in Melbourne.

Many people helped to read drafts of chapters and sections of this work. I simply cannot thank you enough. Your feedback was highly valuable. In particular, I wish to thank William Norman, Louise Armstrong, Rosie Germain, Colin Barr, Alvin Jackson, Christopher Clark, Senia Pašeta, Tim Lindsay, Trisha Kessler, Christopher Kerr, Lucy Delap, Richard Evans and Christine Corton.

This book contains some fantastic images, and I am especially grateful to Colin Higgins and the team at St. Catharine's College Library for advising me and reproducing a number of them. My sincere thanks for all of your help. I would also like to thank the National Library of Ireland, *The Irish Examiner*, British Pathé and Reuters, the Irish Newspaper Archives, The Collins Press, Getty Images, the National Library of Australia, the Australian War Memorial and the Imperial War Museum for granting me the relevant permissions for the images in this book. Every effort has been made to trace the copyright holders of these items and to ensure the accuracy of their captions. This publication has been made possible by a grant from the Scouloudi Foundation in association with the Institute of Historical Research.

I would also like to thank my publishers, Bloomsbury, and especially the editorial team, including Joanna Godfrey and Olivia Dellow.

Finally, I would like to offer both sincere gratitude and my apologies to those friends and family who have lived with this book almost as much as I have for the last decade. Thanks for putting up with me while I squirrelled away at every opportune (and inopportune) moment, and thanks for listening to me while I harped on about my findings and tried to make sense of them. Special thanks go to my parents, Laurine and Seamus, especially for the unlimited taxi services to and from train stations and archives and for supporting me throughout this project; my sister, Bronač, for hosting me in Belfast and for reminding me of the value of this work; and my wonderfully patient partner, William, who offered valuable feedback and who is responsible for more commas than this book would have had otherwise. I'm forever grateful.

None of this, however, would have been possible without the advice, help and support of my uncle, John, to whom this book is dedicated. That 'story' is now finished.

# Chapter 1

## INTRODUCTION

### *Contradictions*

In April 2013 I was fortunate to meet an inspiring group of soldiers from the Irish army in County Cork (Figure 1.1). They were part of the Cork Western Front Association and all had relatives who had served in Irish regiments of the British army during the Great War. Today, Cork is known for the stand it took against the British during the Anglo-Irish War of 1919–21, as well as its ardent republicanism during the civil war of 1922–1923. In the period 1917–23, 747 people were killed for political reasons in Cork city and county in the struggle over self-government.[1]

Yet one of my guides, Adrian Foley, showed me the above photograph which encapsulates a forgotten dimension of the history of a notorious Irish county. The picture is from a cracked glass plate which Adrian found hidden in one of the local museums. It shows the turnout of people at the unveiling of the Cork Great War memorial in March 1925. This was only four years after parts of the city had been burnt to the ground by the British Crown forces in one of the most infamous reprisals to have happened during the Anglo-Irish War[2]; at least four years after the county had earned the nickname of 'rebel Cork' as a tribute to its resistance to British authority during that conflict; and, according to the orthodox histories, long after Irish Catholics had turned their backs on the British war effort and those who had fought for the Allied cause to pursue Irish independence instead.

This image shows ex-soldiers, many of whom had been in the local British infantry regiment, the Royal Munster Fusiliers (RMF), surrounding the war memorial holding their hats in their hands as a mark of respect to comrades who had fallen in action; women and children standing behind them in memory of lost family members; local dignitaries with sashes and wreaths seemingly united in the object of the day; and of course the crowd, packed from one end of the street to the other in a widespread demonstration of mourning and remembrance. More striking perhaps are the flags: the republican tricolour in the foreground symbolizing Ireland's independence from Britain, which republicans and the constitutional nationalists before them fought hard to achieve. Yet behind it lies the Union Flag draped over the war memorial, demonstrating that the flag which many Irish people had recently fought against to gain independence still held some meaning, even if it was not a political attachment, when they remembered Cork's involvement in the Great War.

**Figure 1.1** Unveiling the Great War memorial in Cork, 1925. Courtesy of Adrian Foley.

All classes and creeds turned out in Cork for the unveiling of the memorial.[3] It was an event that would have touched a wide cross-section of people because by the end of 1917, 10,106 men had served in the war from Cork city and county: 5.17 per cent of the total male population.[4] By 1924 the British Legion Society of Ireland estimated that ex-servicemen comprised almost 21 per cent of Cork city's population (i.e. 16,000 men out of a population of 76,673).[5] A total of 3,774 men were killed, including those who had tangible connections to the city and county: more than five times as many as Cork people killed in the struggle for independence.[6] This large figure does not diminish the significance of the lives lost in the political struggles from 1917 to 1923, and it is possible that those who turned out on this day in Cork were also mourning for the Irish who fell in these wars as well given the complications that arose over commemorating the civil war in Ireland, as Anne Dolan has brought to light.[7] However, it puts the losses of the Great War into perspective, as Cork was a largely Catholic county (356,269 Catholics: 35,756 Protestants) and is more remembered in twentieth-century Irish history for its revolutionary past than for its involvement in the Great War.[8]

I became even more intrigued by the photograph when I discovered that such gatherings of ex-servicemen were not unique to Cork but were common across interwar urban Ireland at a time when the new Irish state was attempting to diminish the legacy of British administration. In Louth, at least 2,475 men fought in the war, 816 of whom were killed or died of wounds up to 1925.[9] Of these men 2,173 came from Dundalk and Drogheda – towns whose male populations in 1911 were 6,773 and 6,055 respectively. Some servicemen only had affiliations to Louth and the recruitment figures also included some women, but most of the fallen came from these towns, representing a significant percentage of the population to have taken part in the conflict.[10] Armistice Day commemorations actually flourished in Louth during the 1920s and 1930s which, as Donal Hall has argued, 'is an indication of a society much more at ease with the legacy of World War I than some recent historical studies would have us believe'.[11] Similarly in Kilrush, Co. Clare, a seaport town of 3,666 people (3,533 of whom were Catholic), more than 414 men fought in the war; 36 were killed.[12] The imprint of the conflict on Kilrush was obvious in later years, as some republicans felt that the town 'was not a great Sinn Féin town' and 'did not fall into line' with the republican party's desire to eradicate 'Britishness' in the new Irish state because of, in part, its participation in the war. Eamon de Valera, the Sinn Féin leader and long-serving statesman, reputedly claimed that Kilrush was really 'a little British town'.[13]

Visual evidence of huge crowds commemorating the war in Dublin from 1923 to 1930, as well as in smaller largely Catholic centres such as Longford and Bray, reveals that Cork was not unique in remembering its contribution to the British war effort during the interwar period (Figures 1.2 and 1.3).[14]

These images illuminate the central paradox of the Irish war experience: How could so many people turn out to mourn their war dead in towns and villages across Ireland when Catholics had supposedly turned their backs on the Allied war effort during the conflict itself? And why did Protestants and Catholics often turn out together at remembrance events when the conflict had deepened the domestic political divisions between them?

**Figure 1.2** Mourners surround cross dedicated to the 16th (Irish) Division, College Green, Dublin, Armistice Day, 1924. Courtesy of the National Library of Ireland.

**Figure 1.3** Armistice Day, Market Square, Longford, 1925. Reuters via British Pathé.

The answers to these questions lie partly in the years which followed the Great War and historians have offered different explanations for the large turnouts. In Cork, the unveiling of the memorial took place on the feast of St Patrick's Day, a public celebration, while in Dublin the authorities were keen to make a gesture to 'Protestant capitalism' due to that group's influence on the political and economic life of the city.[15] But these explanations do not sufficiently explain why so many Irish people of both creeds turned out together to commemorate a conflict that the majority of people – the Catholic-nationalist population – allegedly did not support. The large turnouts can only be explained by looking at the war years themselves – the years to which this book is dedicated – to understand what exactly happened in wartime Ireland to have encouraged these demonstrations of inter-communal remembrance. The 'long shadow' of the conflict is still evident today, embodied within organizations such as the Cork Western Front Association.[16] Adrian Foley is one of many members who went to great lengths to trace the war records of relatives that served in the war. He discovered that his great-grandfather, William Foley, a soldier of the RMF and a Catholic who survived the conflict, participated in ex-servicemen's associations until his death in 1960. The organization's determination to reclaim the memory of these British ex-servicemen is a local manifestation of a wider process of reclaiming the memory of the 1914–18 war in Ireland, one which was especially evident in the recent centenary, at which the conflict was put at the centre of Irish political life in both the North and the South.

The subject of this book is thus the war years themselves, 1914 to 1918, and Irish responses to the Great War on the home front in Ireland and other Irish diasporic communities. Undoubtedly the years 1914 to 1918 have been the subject of much research due to the domestic political developments from 1912 to 1923 that set Ireland on a path towards independence, partition and civil war. In the historiography of the war years, many aspects of Irish men's performance at the front and of the revolutionary crisis at home have been examined in great detail by historians, but astonishingly we still lack a systematic analysis of the home front in Ireland and other Irish home fronts in each and every year of the war. How did people feel about and behave towards the conflict? In what ways did they engage with the war effort? Did they support its objectives and why? How did their attitudes and behaviour change over time? How did engagement differ between urban and rural areas? And why have historians – and for a long time, much of the public – believed that Irish Catholics were broadly against the war effort? This book attempts to provide some answers to these questions. It aims to shift the emphasis of Irish involvement away from enlistment and the respective desires of unionism and nationalism onto the war effort itself. Its foremost concern is the Catholic Irish (though Protestants also appear in this study), as it is the commitment to the Allied war effort of this large and diverse group that is most in question, especially from 1916 to 1918 when the character of Irish nationalism changed.

However, let me be clear about some matters that can give rise to misunderstandings. The subject matter of this book is those Catholics who assisted the war effort, not those that did not. Advanced nationalists, the collection of radicals that included members of Sinn Féin, labour activists, suffragists, socialists, pacifists and others, are not the focus of this study. Historians have tended to categorize this group as one that was broadly anti-war and as Chapter 2 discusses, the vocal and demonstrative anti-recruitment activities of many of these radicals have been used as evidence to generalize about anti-war sentiment within Catholic Irish society at large. This book challenges this characterization of Irish society (indeed, it should be noted that there is a lack of scholarly work on the various individuals and groups that comprised Ireland's advanced nationalists and how they felt about the war in each and every year of the conflict's duration. To characterize all radicals as anti-war is thus a generalization which has not been tested). Nonetheless, Irish radicals are excluded from this study. The emphasis here is instead on the individuals who were not on the extremes and who have tended to be excluded from studies of the Irish revolutionary period; the individuals who formed the backbone of the war effort in Ireland.

This book argues that Irish Catholic support for the war effort lasted for longer than is commonly accepted across much of the existing literature. This does not mean that opposition to the war in Ireland was non-existent or that the traditional weighting of the importance of Sinn Féin as a political force is 'wrong'. It may well mean, however, that historians of Ireland will have to recognize that there was a tradition of support and even sympathy for the British war effort which survived 1916 and 1918, support which was rendered in sections of Irish society (other than Protestant) and geographical areas other than Protestant parts of the North. It was this – together with the widespread familial legacies of personal involvement – that may have helped to provide the basis for the dramatic renewal of interest in the conflict in Ireland, and sympathy for those who took part in it, at the end of the twentieth century.

There was a surprising degree of cross-confessional cooperation in the war effort, which has gone virtually unnoticed in existing scholarly accounts and which this book brings to life. This does not mean that the political divisions between unionists and nationalists were insignificant, nor does it mean that a posture of hostility and actual violence played less of a role in preconfiguring the struggle for independence and the Northern Irish 'Troubles' that would disfigure the twentieth century. Rather, this book is about a constituency – and the sources suggest that it was a very sizeable constituency – that cannot be accommodated within the historiography of unionism and nationalism, or the political history of 1916–23.

My book is instead about the people who took part in the phenomena it describes and analyses. It aims to provide a more complex picture of the Irish war effort, illuminating the changing dynamics of Catholic involvement. It is simultaneously a plea for a pluralistic view of twentieth-century Irish identities and attitudes, and, more pertinently, the history of Ireland and the Irish in the world's first total war.

## Irish civil society

How does one assess 'support' for the war effort among Catholics when a society as complex as Ireland did not have a single, uniform reaction to the conflict? As Catriona Pennell has noted, in 1914 the reactions of more than 40 million people across the whole of the UK were complex and ever-changing, and the same is true of the considerably fewer 4.4 million inhabitants of Ireland.[17] However, broad trends and patterns of engagement with the war can still be detected when civil society is put at the centre of analysis.[18] In the present analysis I use the notion of civil society as comprising a range of interacting groups that represent different interests.[19] In wartime Ireland, these groups included elected public bodies (urban, district and rural councils, boards of guardians, corporations and harbour boards), interest groups (cooperatives, farmers' unions, medical associations, political organizations and commercial representatives), faith groups (Catholic and Protestant associations), educational institutions (schools and universities), the press and philanthropic foundations (charitable associations and war-relief societies). Civil society represented the multiple divisions in Irish life including class, religion, age, sex and geography, which distinguished Ireland as a society. It is thus a lens through which one can view patterns and trends regarding Irish people's engagement with the conflict.

To gain a more accurate understanding of the individuals involved in the war effort in Ireland, this book has made extensive use of the 1911 census of Ireland. Census data illuminates important background information on individuals involved in the war effort, including, among other factors, their religion, which in wartime Ireland was essentially a synonym for political persuasion. The long-standing link between religion and politics in Ireland means that it can be assumed that those people who were listed as Catholic in the census were more than likely nationalist in political persuasion, except in the case of senior army and police officers, magistrates and high-ranking civil servants. A large proportion of them must have become more radical in their nationalism as the war went on to have accounted for the victory of Sinn Féin in the 1918 general election. By using the census to discover the religion of the individuals involved in Ireland's war effort, from 1914 to 1918, we can establish whether Irish nationalists supported Britain and the Allies and if that changed as the war went on, particularly in the years 1916 to 1918 when radical nationalism was gaining strength, giving a more empirical way of addressing the assumption that nationalist support was, in general, weak.

Of course, use of this source comes with its own set of challenges. This census was taken some years before the Great War and was the last one to be taken in Ireland under the British administration (the next census would be taken in 1926 under the Free State and after considerable migration of people due to partition, the wars of 1919–23, and emigration).[20] There is no absolute guarantee that the people identified in the 1911 census are the same people that appear in contemporary wartime sources, though every effort has been made to make correct identifications; any assumptions that are made are discussed at length in the relevant notes. Where an individual within a source cannot be identified in the census, a process of deduction allows the range of possible candidates to be narrowed; often these candidates shared the same faith, which permits the observation that a Catholic was involved in a war-related activity, even if the specific individual cannot be identified. As such, the risks involved when using this source can be minimized and are massively outweighed by the granularity of detail it provides on assessing who was involved in Ireland's war effort.

This book is largely a study of the 'Home Front': the people involved in orchestrating and implementing Ireland's war effort on the ground. The bulk of participants that emerged from this research include solicitors; physicians; farmers; clergymen; students; professors; businessmen; politicians; justices of the peace (JP) and of course the wives, sisters and daughters of the men who filled these roles – groups similar to those studied by Pennell with reference to 1914.[21] Many of these belonged to, or aspired to join, the professional middle classes, which had 'a locus of extensive social and political power' in early twentieth-century Ireland.[22] In 1911, close to 20 per cent of the managerial classes were Protestants. They accounted for almost half the lawyers, over a third of doctors and nearly three quarters of bankers in Ireland.[23] The remainder, however, about 80 per cent of this middle class, were Catholic, forming a confident and ambitious group of socially mobile men and women that emerged during the late nineteenth century as a result of 'British interventionist policy in Ireland and a long campaign to force successive governments to improve educational facilities for Catholics'.[24] It is this group that appears most frequently in the sources, and it is this group on whom the study largely concentrates.

However, the middle classes were not the only group that assisted the war effort, and this book illuminates how a wider spectrum of people felt about the war, including the upper classes, who were largely Anglo-Irish and members of the Church of Ireland in 'Southern' Ireland (the twenty-six-county entity created under partition and the 1920 Government of Ireland Act, later known as the Irish Free State). Members of this group often had access to significant leisure time and were by and large financially secure, which enabled upper-class men and women to become patrons of war-related associations and to host fetes in aid of charitable causes, in addition to donating considerable sums of money to war-relief. While this group appears often in the sources, it is not this study's focus, as most Catholics, with whom this study is concerned, were from the middle and working classes.

Indeed, a concerted effort has been made to elucidate the attitudes and behaviour of the broadly termed working classes towards the war effort. This has been difficult, as much source material (as discussed below) tends to privilege the middle and upper classes, skewing the emphasis of this work. However, insight into members of the working class can be deduced from the occasional written source but it can be more easily determined from their behaviour, particularly crowd behaviour, which reveals 'the non-institutional political activity of ordinary people below the level of the social and political elites'.[25] As Pennell has argued, popular collective behaviour 'is a blessing to the researcher of "history from below", and in particular the researcher of popular opinion'. It helps reveal working-class attitudes towards the war, though 'the task of identifying the "faces" of historical crowds is problematic'.[26] Still, popular collective behaviour can be dissected to understand why a particular gathering happened, who or what inspired it, and its relative popularity or absence at critical moments. When used in conjunction with written source material – as is done often in this book – further light can be shed on working-class attitudes and responses towards the conflict.

Geographically, the book concentrates on urban Southern Ireland, as the bulk of Irish recruits came from urban areas and most war-related activity was concentrated in urban centres. Defining the term 'urban' is difficult, however. Between 1851 and 1911, Ireland was becoming relatively urbanized, though outside of the north-east this was the result of rural decline rather than urban growth. In this period, the proportion of Irish living in towns of 2,000 or more people rose from 17 per cent to 33.5 per cent, the greatest increase occurring after 1891.[27] Yet a significant number of towns and villages that appear in this book had populations under 2,000 people and above 1,000. Defining them as urban is debatable but this work includes them in its rather capacious understanding of 'urban Ireland'. Case studies of urban Ulster are included alongside Southern Ireland to illuminate the commonalities in war experience across the country, though differences are highlighted when appropriate.

The primary focus of this study is thus on the Catholic middle classes from urban centres in 'Southern' Ireland, though as outlined above, this study also illuminates the experiences of a wider range of social groups in both rural and urban Ireland across both the North and the South. It also goes beyond the island of Ireland to include groups within the diaspora. In 1911, more than two million Irish-born people lived outside Ireland at a time when the population of the island was 4,390,219.[28] Almost one-third of Irish-born people did not live in Ireland when war commenced in 1914. Emigration had been institutionalized in the Irish psyche since the early nineteenth century and from 1856 to 1921, Ireland lost between 4.1 and 4.5 million people in a country that had a population of 8.5 million before the Great Famine in 1845. The majority of these emigrants were Catholics. Perhaps 3.5 million of the 4.5 million emigrants lived in North America, mainly in the United States, and more Irish men and women were living in the United States than in Ireland itself in 1900.[29] Yet, despite these large Irish concentrations, wartime Ireland appears to have had a stronger connection to the British Dominions. To take Cork as an example, during the Great War, only thirty-six men from Cork were killed while serving in the American forces.[30] This may reflect the fact that America entered the conflict relatively late, officially in April 1917, with the bulk of its troops arriving in 1918, though it incurred upwards of 320,000 casualties.[31] However, until the 31 August 1921, at least 3,738 men from Cork (most of whom were Catholics) were killed while serving in the British and Dominion forces.[32] A significant part of Ireland's wartime history thus lies outside the national territory, and this study concentrates on case studies of the settler-Irish who lived within the former British Empire.

Since the 1700s, Irish Catholics had established settler communities throughout the British Empire and historians have demonstrated their political, social and ecclesiastical reach during the nineteenth and twentieth centuries.[33] But who exactly constituted an Irish settler and whether Irish-born should be a criterion for studying the Irish is a matter of debate.[34] Mark McGowan has argued that place of birth is only one of many factors that should be considered when analysing the settler-Irish and it is 'a limited one at that'.[35] First and second generations often felt as 'Irish' as their Irish-born parents and grandparents despite not having a locational connection to Ireland, and for Australian-born Irish persons 'the balance of their allegiance was decidedly Australian, but that did not mean it ceased to be Irish'.[36] Irish-born and first-generation settlers are therefore included when examining the settler-Irish, as well as those from the second generation who also considered themselves part-Irish. Thus a broad and eclectic approach, which straddles localities, regions and countries, and which takes into account the attitudes and behaviour of a wide spectrum of people, is adopted when exploring Irish Catholic support.

The changing dynamics of the war itself are also considered. The Great War of 1914 bore little resemblance to the conflict of 1918, whether that was through the revolution in military tactics and technologies, or Westminster's response. Reactions and attitudes to the war of attrition – one in which machine power replaced the human and animal muscle used in the early months of the conflict, and which required the complete subordination of societies to serve the needs of the war effort – differed greatly from responses to the 'business as usual' attitude of the government following its outbreak, and this book aims to show how opinion evolved as the conflict dragged on.

In his monumental study of how Europe went to war in 1914, Christopher Clark emphasized that his book would be 'saturated with agency'. By giving priority to the sequence of interactions that materialized in the run-up to war over remote and categorical explanations of why the conflict broke out, he opened up the history of the July crisis to an 'element of contingency'.[37] This book follows Clark by giving agency to the men and women who assisted the British and Allied war efforts rather than those who did not, for it is their agency which has been squeezed out of the historical record by 'grand narratives'. To this end, a vast range of evidence has been consulted encompassing written, statistical and visual sources. These reveal what individuals felt about the war, the ways in which they assisted the war effort, and how they behaved in response to 'an unanticipated and unprecedented crisis'.[38]

## The evidence

The digitization of many newspapers has provided new opportunities for researchers of Britain and Ireland.[39] As Pennell has argued, newspapers 'provide an excellent foundation for establishing popular reactions to the war'. Pitfalls including bias, inaccurate reporting and the difficulty in deciphering whether readers agreed with claims advanced by editors are 'massively outweighed by the benefits of this source'.[40] Newspapers contain multiple forms of public sentiment including both facts and opinion. During the war, they reveal the latest happenings at the front and advertisements for war causes, publishing, for instance, useful subscription lists for war-relief efforts run by humanitarian organizations such as the Red Cross, and these lists include the names of donors whose backgrounds can be checked in the 1911 census. Letters to the editor shed insight into how a more proactive section of readership felt about the war while editorials offer analysis and criticism of contemporary affairs that was designed to both shape and reflect public opinion. As editors relied upon sales, they did not want to be too out-of-tune with their customers' views, though their interpretation of affairs could vary to a considerable degree (though not always in kind) from the ordinary reader.

The most significant value of this source is that it observes and records different types of public behaviour. Newspapers and magazines are windows through which we can explore what people were doing during the war years and their behaviour tells us much about popular feeling towards the conflict. They report local events, such as fundraising in aid of war-relief, often revealing the names of the organizers and the participants, the size and response of the audience that attended, the popular culture exhibited, the amount raised for war-relief and the relative success of the event. They also report on attendance figures and the general mood expressed at war-related activities, shedding insight into feelings and behaviour towards the conflict as expressed by groups other than the middle classes. All of these factors can be cross-checked and compared with similar gatherings in different periods of the war, allowing the historian to test whether popular feeling towards such activities – as expressed by a range of social classes – significantly changed in particular months or years.

Irish newspapers are especially informative as the provincial and national press held certain political affiliations. Before the Easter Rising, most mainstream provincial newspapers supported the constitutional nationalist line (i.e. they generally believed that legal political agitation should be the primary means of repealing the 1801 Act of Union to bring about Home Rule, which, had it come into being, would have granted a measure of self-government to Ireland), though they diverged in the degree to which they supported the main Irish Nationalist Party that championed this cause, the Irish Parliamentary Party (IPP). For this study, a range of these newspapers from across the country are scoured to excavate the activities of war-relief associations, attitudes towards Germany and the Allies, the opinions of influential members of Irish society and behaviour towards aspects of the war.[41] Several independent-nationalist newspapers – whose political affiliations were not necessarily aligned with the IPP – are also explored, the foremost of which is the national newspaper, *The Irish Independent*, which sold 56,462 copies a day in 1913.[42] It was owned by the Catholic businessman and Dublin magnate, William Martin Murphy.[43] In some chapters, or with reference to particular issues, a greater number of provincial newspapers are analysed to assess the impact of a particular event on people throughout the country.[44] The changing nature of 'moderate nationalism', whereby the character of Irish nationalism evolved during 1914 to 1918 from desiring a constitutional settlement within the framework of the UK to a desire for complete independence, is also kept in mind.[45] This change should be embodied in the press, enabling one to assess whether political change affected Catholic attitudes and behaviour towards the war.

Newspapers also illuminate diasporic reactions to the conflict. *The Montreal Gazette*, a conservative organ, offers a window through which Irish-Canadian responses to the war can be explored, while Irish-Australian opinion is investigated using the Sydney-based newspaper, *The Freeman's Journal*, and the Catholic and largely Irish organ, *The Catholic Press*. A wider range of Australian newspapers is surveyed to establish international reactions to events in Ireland and the broad circulation of the Dominion press is useful for assessing the opinion of groups within the settler-Irish populations, shedding light on how multiple social groups experienced and felt about the war.[46]

While mainly concerned with the Catholic majority, I am also interested in illuminating the relationship between Irish Catholics and Protestants during the war years, specifically with regard to their behaviour in, and attitudes towards, war-related activities. Newspapers have provided valuable evidence, and the national newspaper *The Irish Times* is particularly helpful. Those who read it were 'by no means a monolith – not just Anglicans, not just unionists – [but] it is recognized that being Church of Ireland and loyalist are its overwhelmingly dominant characteristics'.[47] *The Church of Ireland Gazette*, the weekly organ of the Church of Ireland, illuminates Anglican opinion towards Catholics when Catholics had supposedly disengaged from the war effort, while the provincial press is examined for information on inter-confessional war-relief associations.

It is possible that newspapers and similar written sources may withhold information about Irish reactions to the war, projecting 'biased' accounts that toed the government line, as wartime censorship was in operation. However, censorship was 'far from draconian' in 1914.[48] It became more severe as the conflict dragged on, but the authorities were most concerned with censoring military matters of strategic significance rather than clamping down on popular discontent, giving the press the freedom to record this type of behaviour.[49] To ensure that press accounts were not 'staged', the censorship reports compiled by Dublin Castle during the war (the seat of the British government's administration in Ireland) were examined; these do not reveal any attempt by authorities to systematically quarantine cases of opposition towards the war.[50] The opinions and events recorded in Irish newspapers were not, therefore, an attempt by Westminster to carve a propagandistic account of everyday life in Ireland, allowing the historian to take seriously the behaviour, opinions and feelings of individuals.

Yet the press is by no means the only source that can illuminate Irish public opinion. Senia Pašeta was one of the first historians to use educational archives in her study of constitutional nationalists, using college magazines, personal papers, memoirs and written evaluations by universities to tap into the opinions of the middle-class Catholic student body.[51] This book follows Pašeta by exploring educational publications, concentrating attention on how the war was institutionalized within Catholic communities through fundraisers, appeals, behaviour towards departing comrades and remembering the fallen.[52] They directly focus attention on a wide spectrum of middle-class Catholics, not just students, as parents, alumni, benefactors, teachers and clerics all coalesced in some capacity through elite educational institutions. Articles produced by these publications had to be in tune with the opinion of this wider cohort, partly because some individuals donated valuable funds which were essential to the running of elite schools and universities.

These sources are supplemented with private papers, personal diaries, war journals and letters to highlight any discrepancies between public and private spheres of correspondence. Some of the major bodies of letters and private papers I explore include those written by predominantly middle-class Catholic Irish women to T. V. Nolan, the provincial superior of the Jesuit Province in Ireland regarding the accommodation of Belgian refugees; letters to Nolan from Jesuit military chaplains who served in Irish, British and Dominion regiments; the private papers of various Irish and British servicemen and the papers of the influential clerics, Archbishop William Walsh of Dublin and the head of the Catholic Church in Ireland, Cardinal Michael Logue. For Australia, a wider range of Irish-Australian sources was consulted including the personal papers of the influential Irish Catholic Australians, John Daniel Fitzgerald, and the Archbishop of Sydney, Michael Kelly; the clerical correspondence of Kelly and some other Irish-Australian bishops, as well as Lenten pastorals. Pamphlets, the minutes of other associations, and artworks are also consulted.

As written sources tend to present the opinions of the more literate classes, particularly the middle and upper classes, much emphasis is placed on visual evidence throughout this book to shed light on the attitudes and behaviour of what might broadly be termed the working classes. Images reveal the horrors of the war, which were important incentives behind self-mobilization when witnessed at the time or when printed in the press. They can demonstrate the popularity of events, such as recruitment meetings, and can be analysed (often in conjunction with written sources) to understand which social groups were present, and whether women and children were in attendance, reflecting their important agency in creating a culture of support or ambivalence towards the war effort.

Though in some respects less immediate in reflecting views and passions, primary sources published after the war, such as memoirs and autobiographical accounts, can bolster or contradict the evidence that emerged during the war years. A limited number of sources have been taken from Irish republicans who gave witness statements recalling their involvement in the struggle for independence, from 1913 to 1921. The BMH started to collect these sources in 1947, and Roy Foster has argued that they are not unproblematic, as the 'idea of accumulating records of supposedly straightforward personal experience, innocent of an interpretive gloss' was not always achieved.[53] Discrepancies between these records and records published during the war are highlighted within the text.

Lastly, official reports and maps have painted pictures of activity at a national level, such as statistical trends within voluntary war-work or submarine attacks off the coast of Ireland. Red Cross reports and documents compiled by the war-relief department of the Royal College of Science reveal how Irish counties responded to the war effort, situating Ireland's war effort within the context of the UK, and permitting comparison between Ireland's contribution and that of the other British nations.

Cumulatively, the range of evidence is designed to show the multifarious ways in which the war impacted upon civil society and how the Irish responded to its demands in each and every year of the war. Though many of the sources reflect the opinions and behaviour of the broadly termed middle classes, these sources, in addition to others, permit the inclusion of a wider range of social groups, allowing some conclusions to be made about a cross-section of Catholic opinion towards the war effort.

### *Chapter outline*

This book broadly adopts a thematic structure while paying close attention to chronology to illuminate how people responded to major aspects of the war effort over the duration of the conflict. When viewed in isolation, each chapter offers a narrow view of the Irish response, but when different aspects of the war effort are investigated together and as a whole in this book, better insight can be gained into the impact of, and people's responses to, the war as a whole, enabling a more holistic understanding of Catholic involvement in the Great War.

The book begins by looking at the field of enquiry today, and Chapter 2 situates this study within the growing historiography of the war years. It highlights disparities that have emerged from the history of revolutionary Ireland and the social and cultural history of Ireland and the Great War, and it illuminates the evolution of Irish memory towards the conflict.

Chapter 3 turns attention to the home front where women played important roles. It demonstrates that much of the war-work across Ireland (including in Ulster, where political divisions were most stark) was in fact inter-confessional, and it tries to assess the extent to which Catholic Irish women participated in war-work when compared to their Protestant and unionist contemporaries. The aim of this chapter is not to arrive at a particular figure of the number of Catholic Irish women involved in Ireland's war effort or to seek a comparison between the Protestant and Catholic contributions; rather, it looks specifically at an array of war-related associations and examines the religious composition of the groups that underpinned them to get a sense of whether Catholic participation was more difficult to find and less visible than that of Protestant women and whether Catholic participation declined as the war dragged on.

Chapter 4 looks at one under-explored dimension of the military campaign, the war at sea, and how it influenced Irish attitudes to the conflict as a whole. It explores the gradual development of German submarine warfare and assesses how Irish (and particularly Catholic Irish) attitudes changed towards Germany, as submarine attacks on Allied shipping became more frequent, more indiscriminate between military and civilian vessels and more dishonourable in light of the contemporary understanding of military codes of conduct. It argues that these attacks played a crucial role in constructing the notion that Germany was an enemy that had to be defeated. Part of the chapter explores rural Ireland's reactions to German submarine warfare. Through a series of case studies, it explores how submarine attacks influenced the perception of who was 'right' and 'wrong' in the conflict, as well as how rural communities responded to renewed German submarine warfare in 1917 and 1918 when radical nationalism was gaining strength.

Chapter 5 shifts the emphasis away from the island of Ireland to concentrate on Irish Catholic diasporic responses to the war. Focusing on Irish-Canadians and Irish-Australians, it provides some historical context to the significant presence of Irish emigrants and their descendants in the wartime British Dominions, and drawing on the work of scholars of specific settler-Irish populations, it adopts a transnational perspective to illuminate Catholic-Irish feeling, behaviour and attitudes towards the war. It brings to light the importance of a sense of loyalty to the British Empire in framing diasporic feeling towards the war, as well as the influence of Nationalist Ireland's commitment to the war effort, which was used by diasporic elites to mobilize settler-Irish populations. The final section combines the international with the national, interweaving members of one settler-Irish population with the Irish in Ireland through the case study of an Irish-Canadian regiment, the Irish-Canadian Rangers, a battalion of which toured Ireland in early 1917.

Chapter 6 explores Irish Catholic attitudes towards the international context of war. It reveals the large-scale support which the Irish had for Britain in the war effort, at least until the Easter Rising; after this point, it explores the complications which arose between the government and Irish nationalists, and how this impacted

Catholic support for the British war effort. Importantly, the chapter demonstrates how nationalists after the Rising began to distinguish between Britain's war effort and that of the other Allies, drawing on the discourse of 'barbarism' and 'Prussianism' (hitherto ascribed to German 'methods' in the war) to describe Britain's actions towards Ireland. It also investigates how changing attitudes towards Britain impacted attitudes towards the other Allies, illuminating important complexities that challenge the orthodox view that Irish Catholic support for the war effort declined precipitously in the last two years of the conflict.

Chapters 7 and 8 discuss the significance of some of the findings in this book and explore the question of what happened once the Armistice of 1918 was declared and veterans began to return home. It looks again at the notion of 'amnesia' in the interwar period, something which other scholars have challenged as of late, and takes a long view in offering some thoughts on the place of the Great War in Ireland's twentieth and twenty-first centuries.

## Chapter 2

## MEMORY, HISTORY AND THE GREAT WAR

### Remembering and writing 1914 to 1918

For decades, Irish Catholic memory of the Great War was essentially a 'closed book'.[1] In 1967, F. X. Martin identified the 'national amnesia' that characterized Irish nationalist perceptions of the conflict, a claim which he explicitly linked to the Easter Rising, observing that in independent Ireland, it was 'difficult to find men and women who will acknowledge that they are children of the men who were serving during 1916 in the British Army'.[2] Recent research has interrogated the alleged 'Great Oblivion' of Irish nationalist memory of the war in the decades following independence. The large turnouts at interwar Armistice Day parades in Dublin,[3] the British and Irish governments' scheme to build houses for ex-servicemen,[4] the involvement of the Irish Free State in the construction of a national war memorial at Islandbridge in Dublin[5] and the relative success of integrating British ex-servicemen into post-war Irish life complicate the narrative that Catholics whitewashed their role in the conflict.[6]

Nevertheless for many nationalists, memory of the conflict eclipsed its history, and this was particularly true for Irish republicans who never considered the conflict to be a part of their past. In 1987, the Irish Republican Army (IRA), a paramilitary organization dedicated to the belief that all of Ireland should be an independent republic, deliberately chose Remembrance Sunday to blow up the Enniskillen War Memorial in Fermanagh, Northern Ireland, killing eleven people. The bombing revealed the extent to which the Great War had been disowned by radical nationalists and associated with British interference in Ireland. Following the country's partition in 1921, commemoration gradually became the preserve of unionists in Northern Ireland, who were (and remain) almost entirely Protestant and support political union with Great Britain, though it is as yet unclear when the character of commemoration changed to embody this largely Protestant and unionist tone. Keith Jeffery has argued that those who controlled Remembrance Day services were 'more inclined to relate the war service of soldiers to the establishment of the new Northern state and the maintenance of the precious unionist link with the rest of the United Kingdom'.[7] This message was enhanced by the grievous losses of the largely Protestant 36th (Ulster) Division, a division of Lord Kitchener's New Army formed of mainly

Protestant volunteers from Ulster, on the first day of the Battle of the Somme. More than 5,000 Ulstermen were killed, wounded and invalided from the Somme in one day alone, on 1 July 1916.[8] During and after the war their sacrifice became bound up with the conviction that Ulster was a territory apart from the rest of Ireland, one that was loyal to the Crown, and this contributed to the republican belief that the conflict was a British war rather than one in which Ireland (and Irish Catholics) also took part.[9]

However, historians were simultaneously challenging the republican and Ulster unionist doctrines that the Great War was an exclusively Protestant (and a Protestant British) enterprise. Irish Catholics had a history in the conflict as well, as a large number of Catholics made up the rank and file of two of the three Irish divisions formed in Ireland during the Great War. The 10th (Irish) Division was the first to be formed and attracted the most enthusiastic young men from across the political spectrum and both religious confessions. Young subalterns were drawn from Trinity College Dublin Officers' Training Corps (OTC); experienced captains came directly from the inspectorship of the Irish police force, the Royal Irish Constabulary (RIC); seasoned colonial officers returned to the colours, while youthful recruits volunteered from middle- and working-class Protestant and Catholic backgrounds.[10] The 16th (Irish) Division was in some ways a mirror image of the 36th since it was largely Catholic, and many servicemen supported the policies of the Irish Nationalist party, the IPP.[11] Further research has revealed the extent to which Catholics participated in the war. David Fitzpatrick has estimated that 210,000 men enlisted in the British war effort from all Ireland (excluding those who enlisted outside of the country). Fifty-seven per cent were Catholics.[12] Neil Richardson has argued that over 145,000 men came from the predominantly Catholic South while 63,000 came from Ulster (including both northern Catholics and Protestants).[13] The war was thus a part of Irish nationalists' history, even if many did not consider it to be.

Renewed interest in the Catholic Irish soldier during the Great War was enhanced by the changing political context in which these histories emerged. The end of the Cold War and the drastic amelioration of geopolitical tensions brought about a broad European desire to understand the 'seminal event in the cycle of violence and ideological extremism that marked the twentieth century'.[14] Ireland was not immune from this wider resurgence of memory, but Irish interest was uniquely stimulated by domestic affairs and the efforts of British, Irish and Northern Irish representatives to end the conflict in Northern Ireland. The 'Troubles', which started at the end of the 1960s, had reached their apogee. In 1998, the Good Friday Agreement was signed. It gradually brought peace to Northern Ireland, and this was followed by the lengthy decommissioning of arms by paramilitaries, a process which was largely completed by 2009. With the implementation of 'peace', devolution restored the Northern Irish parliament to Stormont, though the implementation of power sharing has been a rocky process; most importantly, it removed British soldiers from the region's streets, thus 'allowing the past involvement of Irishmen in Britain's wars to re-emerge less contentiously'.[15]

These changes created a space in which it became legitimate to remember Ireland's involvement in the Great War, and prominent representatives aided the process of making its memory acceptable to the Irish of both creeds. In 1998, the former president of Ireland, Mary McAleese, and Queen Elizabeth II presided at the opening of the Island of Ireland Peace Tower in Mesen/Messines, Belgium, in memory of the collaborative war effort by the 36th (Ulster) and 16th (Irish) Divisions in the Battle of Wijtschate-Messines Ridge, which happened in June 1917.[16] In 2010, McAleese visited Gallipoli, where Catholic and Protestant men – many from the 10th (Irish) Division – suffered more than 3,000 losses during the landings at Suvla Bay and Sedd-el-Bahr in April and August 1915.[17] These losses were comparable to those suffered by the Australians,[18] whose feats at 'ANZAC Cove' enshrined the army designation, Australian and New Zealand Army Corps (ANZAC), into national life as a vehicle to express the Australian national identity.[19] Yet this was the first visit of an official Irish representative to the site where so many Irish men had perished ninety-five years before because the rich commemorative tradition of the Great War that had been generated in Australia lost out in Ireland to 'a commemorative calendar crowded with memories of Easter 1916 and the Anglo-Irish War'.[20]

Remembrance of the war has continued since then and has morphed into a vehicle for reconciliation not only between Catholics and Protestants but also between Ireland and Britain. In 2011, Queen Elizabeth visited the Irish Republic, the first visit of a British monarch to the Irish state, to commemorate the Irish dead who had served Britain in the conflict of 1914–18 as well as those who had fought against the Crown from 1919 to 1921.[21] This was a significant moment of reconciliation between two countries which had been divided for some time. Important diplomatic gestures have continued, as in May 2012 the former IRA leader and then deputy first minister of Northern Ireland, Martin McGuinness, shook Queen Elizabeth's hand in a symbolic act of reconciliation between some republicans and the British state while in April 2014, McGuinness visited Windsor Castle alongside the Irish president, Michael D. Higgins: the first visit of an Irish president (not to mention a former IRA leader) to the royal residence since the formation of the Free State in 1922.[22] More recently, the ambassador of Ireland in Britain laid a memorial wreath on the London cenotaph on Remembrance Sunday in 2014, which appears to have been the first time that a representative of Ireland officially participated in a wreath-laying ceremony in London since the 1920s, while, in November 2017, Leo Varadkar, the Taoiseach (Ireland's prime minister) wore an Irish-themed poppy – a 'Shamrock Poppy' – lapel pin in the Dáil 'to recognize Irish soldiers who fought in World War I': the first time an Irish Taoiseach marked Remembrance Day in Ireland's parliament.[23]

Popular memory of the war has exploded since the 1990s and this has been facilitated by a growing literature on the Irish war experience. In European studies, the resurgence of interest in the home front has been the most striking development, and historians of Ireland have followed their British and European counterparts in recognizing that the conflict was intertwined with societies. Jay Winter, Annette Becker, Jean-Louis Robert and John Horne have been at the forefront of a larger school of thought whose 'bottom up' approach has illuminated larger issues previously neglected in studies of the war, such as class, gender, welfare, psychiatry, entertainment and emotional responses to death and remembrance.[24] Three influential volumes now exist addressing many aspects of the home front on topics including recruitment, the economy, the politics of unionism and nationalism, women's participation and survivors.[25] These works have been part of a renewed interest in studies of the civilian response and many topics have been explored, including the military chaplaincy,[26] religion,[27] specific Irish counties during wartime[28] and self-mobilization in 1914.[29] Historians are now better placed than ever before to revisit some of the conclusions that have been made about Ireland and the Great War, and they can do this because there is a popular willingness to accept fresh perspectives, ideas and facts about the Irish war effort which in previous years had been inflammatory.

One historian who has used this changed context to investigate contemporary Irish attitudes to the war is Catriona Pennell, who investigated popular reactions to the conflict as it developed from August to December 1914. One of Pennell's major findings was that there was little difference between how British or Irish people (both Catholic and Protestant) responded to the conflict. Large sections of both populations took up the war effort wholeheartedly, united in a common desire to defeat Germany.[30] Pennell's study has reopened the question of whether Irish Catholics supported the Allied war effort in later years, particularly after the Easter Rising when radical nationalism came to the fore.

## Politics, apathy, and Irish nationalism

The problem, however, is that it is widely thought that Irish Catholics were not especially committed to the Allied war effort *at any point* during the conflict, especially after Easter 1916 when Ireland's revolution got underway. As Horne has argued, '[t]he terrible sacrifice in the war underwrote the *refusal* of Irish independence by unionist Northern Ireland, whereas the Easter Rising and the path to independence were founded on *rejection* by nationalists of the British war effort [emphasis in original]'.[31] This conclusion largely rests on the changes that occurred within nationalism during the war years and the apparently poor recruitment rates in Ireland. In the general election of December 1918, the IPP, which supported the British war effort, was electorally obliterated and replaced by the radical party, Sinn Féin, whose core comprised an articulate cohort of anti-war activists. The radicals won seventy-three seats, while the IPP won six, eradicating the latter from the political forum.

Examining the histories that have tied Catholic support for the Allies to the changes within nationalism is important, for it illuminates the tension between the political history of nationalism in the period 1914 to 1918 and the sociocultural history of the war effort. These two bodies of research often intertwine making it difficult to completely separate one from the other, and some are more nuanced in their discussion of the war effort than others. However, the distinction generally applies and is more fruitful than not when illuminating the inconsistencies which have emerged between two bodies of scholarship whose research focus includes the war years.

In the political history, various reasons have been put forward to explain the electoral change in 1918. Discontent with the Nationalist party's policies and the pro-imperial affinities of the long-serving IPP leader, John Redmond, have been traced back to earlier periods in Irish life. (Redmond led the party from 1900 until his death in March 1918, having previously chaired the Parnellite faction of the party from the death of 'the uncrowned king' until the party's reunification.[32]) Though these views have come to be challenged,[33] it is widely accepted that the changing fortunes of Home Rule influenced the outcome of the election.

Home Rule was the biggest project in Irish nationalism, dominating much of British domestic politics since the 1880s. In mid-September 1914, Home Rule was placed on the statute book, but its operation was suspended for the period of one year or until the end of the war, whichever was longer, and it was acknowledged that when the time came for it to be enacted, special provision would be made for Ulster.[34] In the months leading up to the outbreak of the Great War, Ireland looked on course for civil war as a result of the bill. Unionists had formed a paramilitary organization, the Ulster Volunteer Force (UVF), to prevent the imposition of Home Rule on Ulster. Nationalists had responded in kind, forming their own paramilitary unit, the Irish Volunteers, to defend self-government once Westminster implemented the measure.[35] The outbreak of the Great War transformed the political situation in Ireland and offered the respective leaders of Irish Nationalism and Unionism the chance to strengthen their case for or against Home Rule with Westminster. Redmond hoped that by assisting the British war effort, Westminster would look more favourably upon the Home Rule situation, as the war would give Ireland an opportunity to take its place as an equal partner within the British Empire. Ironically Sir Edward Carson, the Ulster Unionist leader, believed that Unionist war service would prevent the enactment of Home Rule, and both party leaders set about encouraging their respective Volunteers to enlist en masse.[36]

A major strand of Redmond's war policy was thus the promise of Home Rule and historians have linked Irish Nationalist participation in the conflict to the fate of the bill.[37] Redmond and IPP representatives were tied 'hip and thigh' to the British war effort, unlike the wider nationalist community, which was allegedly deeply ambivalent towards the international conflict.[38] Following Redmond's commitment to active service at Woodenbridge, Co. Wicklow in September 1914 whereby he encouraged nationalists to go 'wherever the firing line extends', the Irish Volunteers split into two groups which disagreed over his declaration. Approximately 9,700 to 11,000 men did not think that Irish men should fight for Britain, and they broke from Redmond under the leadership of Eoin McNeill. They retained the name of the Irish Volunteers, and some initiated the Easter Rising. The majority of members followed Redmond (approximately 150,000 to 170,000 men) in assisting the war effort, taking the name of the Irish National Volunteers (INV).[39] Roughly 32,000 of these Volunteers actually enlisted according to

Fitzpatrick. They comprised one in three Catholic recruits,[40] though Peter Karsten has argued that 'most Volunteers followed Redmond into his National Volunteers, and most of these served in Europe'.[41] Nevertheless, the INV 'disintegrated' in the Irish Midlands by the end of 1914.[42] The reason behind this was because volunteers were supposedly afraid of being 'sucked' into the army (though this did not seem to trouble the INV in Dublin, as in April 1915, 20,000–25,000 INV members participated in an Easter Volunteer Review which attracted massive crowds. The unionist *Irish Times* estimated the size of the crowds to be nearly 200,000 people).[43]

The growing lethargy of the INV in the Irish Midlands and the uncertainty of many of its members towards recruitment appeared to have been reflected more generally in the largely Catholic and agricultural South, which suffered from persistently low recruitment rates throughout the conflict. Michael Wheatley has argued that when recruitment levels from rural Ireland are compared to those in rural England, Scotland and Wales in late 1914, a period which attracted many recruits from both Ireland and Britain, 'the contrast with the middle and west of Ireland was startling'. In November 1914, the percentage of eligible males aged nineteen to thirty-eight who were listed in the 1911 census and who had enlisted in the English counties of Cornwall, Devon and 'Cumberland & Westmorland' was 7.7, 12.7 and 9.2 per cent respectively. The Irish counties of King's (Offaly), Queen's (Laois), Meath, Longford and Westmeath had only yielded 1.9 per cent of their eligible male population while Connaught (Roscommon, Leitrim, Sligo, Mayo and Galway) fielded 1.5 per cent. Wheatley subsequently asked the question, 'How far was provincial nationalist Ireland "behind Mr Redmond" in his advocacy of Ireland's participation in the war? The collapse of the Volunteers, lack of recruiting, and Militia Ballot panic indicated that the somersault of nationalist opinion in England's favour did not extend to whole-hearted participation in the war effort.'[44]

This was certainly the case for advanced nationalists, including the 'anti-war, anti-imperialist members of the Irish labour movement' who made their hostility to the conflict known from the beginning.[45] For the radicals, England, not Germany, was Ireland's enemy, and the concept of assisting the Empire through military service was nothing short of a catastrophe, particularly for socialists such as James Connolly.[46] These radicals expressed their disdain for the war through rhetoric, propaganda and other means, but it was most obviously manifested through a campaign against recruitment, an historic method of protesting against Westminster, though its impact is hard to measure.[47]

Yet a degree of uncertainty about enlistment also existed within Redmond's party itself, lending support to the notion that Catholic Ireland was lukewarm about the war effort. Some IPP representatives were 'from the very outset of the conflict, deeply uneasy about the Party's war policy'.[48] Following Redmond's speech in which he encouraged Irish men to join the British forces, the ex-Fenian, John Phillips MP, whose constituency was South Longford, left the party for Sinn Féin.[49] Another former Fenian, the chairman of Sligo County Council, was 'rather more guarded' in his subsequent speeches on the IPP's behalf as was the local priest, Brian Crehan, because they thought that Ireland should only send men to the front when the country had its own distinct army.[50]

Home Rule MPs did not respond to the war with the same level of personal commitment as their British parliamentary counterparts. In summer and winter 1917, approximately 160 MPs across the UK were serving in the war, 'though many of these enjoyed desk jobs in Britain and appeared not infrequently in the House'.[51] Only six were IPP representatives, though at least ten MPs had relatives that enlisted (and at least seven lost family members). However, the difference is less stark than it first appears, as approximately 100 of the British members were reservists who were recalled to the colours following the outbreak of war.[52] The IPP never had strong links to the British military, unlike their Conservative and Unionist counterparts in Westminster, many of whom had familial ties to the Armed Forces; therefore few of its representatives were reservists in 1914. The relatively small number of British Liberals who joined up in comparison to Unionists further illustrates the importance of the familial military connection. Circa 125 of the 270 Unionist MPs were 'absent in the Armed Forces from time to time while only 32 of the 260 Liberal MPs 'were thus engaged, in addition to a small handful of Irish [Nationalists] and one or two Labour Members'.[53]

The generational profile of the IPP also precluded many men from joining up, as by 1914 the party had the 'largest proportion of men over military age within parliament'. Though this seems a good reason to have prevented MPs from enlisting, James McConnel has suggested that it wasn't good enough, contending that the problem of age might have been mitigated if the War Office had been more willing to compromise with the Nationalists, as it had done for the MPs, Willie Redmond and Stephen Gwynn.[54] However, these are hardly good examples. The former at the time of joining up was fifty-three years old. He was almost unfit for service and was allowed to fight only for political reasons at his own insistence (he was promptly killed in action).[55] The latter (at the time of joining up, was fifty-one years old) was on active service for approximately ten months in total (including training, travelling and one month spent in hospital recovering from influenza) and was regularly deployed back in Ireland where he campaigned to encourage recruitment.[56]

The War Office certainly did not help drive nationalists into the forces. From almost as soon as war was declared, Edward Carson, the Ulster Unionist leader, and Redmond 'attempted to extract every ounce of political advantage from the new situation created by war'. Both 'jockeyed for position' with the government with regard to the war service of their respective paramilitaries, hoping that they would be recognized as integral units of the British Army.[57] Carson was more successful, as he secured advantages for the 36th (Ulster) Division including a specific regional designation, political emblems and insignia that Redmond was unable to extract for his beloved 'Irish brigade', the 16th (Irish) Division, which he saw as a successor to the famous Irish brigade that assisted the French forces during the seventeenth-century wars against the Williamites. Redmond appeared to lose out to Carson again when he rejected a position in the coalition government, formed in May 1915. Carson, on the other hand, accepted, becoming attorney general for England and Wales, and in December 1916, First Lord of the Admiralty. This gave the IPP little political leverage when the government executed sixteen rebels involved in the Easter Rising, leaving the fate of nationalists open to Tory hardliners in the government (the prime minister, Herbert Asquith, was politically vulnerable at this time, which encouraged him to allow the more uncompromising members of the coalition to dictate Westminster's response to the Rising).[58]

London's lukewarm attitude to Nationalist recruitment and the barriers to enlistment which prevented Nationalist MPs from joining up probably hindered the recruitment drive, but McConnel has gone further, suggesting that MPs were even more reluctant to back Redmond's support for the war. MPs could have indirectly assisted the recruitment campaign, thus showing their commitment to the war effort in other ways, yet 'the great majority ... did not encourage enlistment after Redmond's Woodenbridge speech'.[59] Such 'cold feet' may have reflected fears that military conscription would be introduced, as there was reticence among MPs to appear too supportive of the Allied war effort lest compulsion became a proposal.[60] However, the great bulk of Nationalist MPs were simply reluctant to become 'recruiting sergeants for John Bull' at any point throughout the conflict, ignoring the question of recruiting entirely in their public pronouncements or dealing with it 'en passant'. McConnel has therefore concluded that MPs came to adopt the 'mental neutrality' which Charles Townshend has claimed to have characterized Catholic Irish opinion towards the war.[61]

Committed to a policy of active participation in the war effort, but with little inclination among party members to assist the recruitment drive (not to mention London's unwillingness to compromise over Nationalist concerns), the extent to which the IPP actually supported the war effort is questionable. That support is thought to have further diminished following the failure of Home Rule to come into operation. When the question of self-government reappeared in political circles following the Rising, Redmond's war aim was thrown into stark relief, as the government recommended that Home Rule be implemented immediately with the exclusion of Ulster. The threat of partition, which had entered the Home Rule debates in 1912, was therefore made real, and it became clear that the bill which had been passed in 1914 was no longer going to be implemented in the un-partitioned form in which it had been placed on the statute book (Redmond had in fact agreed to the temporary exclusion of Ulster following his negotiations with David Lloyd George, the Minister for Munitions and later prime minister, who spearheaded the talks between the government and Irish parties in May and July 1916. When it became apparent that Lloyd George had actually promised Carson permanent exclusion, the IPP rejected the proposal but the damage to the party had already been done[62]). Support for the bill waned in the years that followed and ran out of steam by December 1918, when Sinn Féin won the general election. For those who had enlisted to secure Home Rule for Ireland or who had lent their support to the Allies for this reason, the waning fortunes of Home Rule meant that they had less of an incentive to lend support to the British war effort in the final two years of war.

For the IPP, the reasons to champion the war effort seemed even weaker. The general reluctance among party members to support recruitment, the loss of the IPP's main champion for the war effort (Redmond was effectively removed from the political scene in early 1918 due to ill-health and died in March) and the growth in support for radical nationalism meant that the party faced other challenges after Easter 1916, as 'the war eclipsed the Home Rule project and provided the context for the destruction of the Irish Party'.[63]

The IPP's perceived lack of action on the Allies' behalf, and growing support for Sinn Féin, which had a cohort of anti-war activists, has become a crucible through which the attitude of the wider Catholic population has been considered. Even though their attitudes have never been put at the centre of analysis in the political history of nationalism, generalizations have been made, and people were thought to have exhibited the 'mental neutrality' towards the war that was displayed by their elected representatives.[64] Apathy towards the war, which allegedly turned to hostility and 'war-weariness', has been blamed for the downfall of the Redmondites and the rise in support for Sinn Féin.[65] In the final year of war, people were noticeably more hostile to recruitment meetings than they had been in previous years which, at a time when the IPP's fortunes were declining, appeared to demonstrate a link between the electorate's growing hostility to the conflict and declining support for the party.[66] The reinvigorated political question following the Rising also reignited the bitterness which had existed between nationalists and unionists prior to the war, further dividing both groups by bringing domestic politics back into the foreground, and the war itself helped to accentuate those divisions.[67]

The single greatest factor thought to have underlined Catholic uncertainty towards the war effort was the pervasive fear of compulsion, which had worried nationalists since the outbreak of war in 1914.[68] It has been argued that Westminster's plans for the imposition of enforced military service 'would end Ireland's support for the war' and fear of conscription since the early months of conflict made nationalists 'wary of supporting the Allied cause'.[69] Foster has argued that 'even before Irish opinion had turned conclusively against the war effort, compulsory drafting of Irish civilians had been deemed unacceptable'.[70] When Ireland was threatened with conscription in the spring of 1918, there was a tremendous protest against the bill by all shades of nationalists, which has been seen as evidence that Catholics had turned against the Allied campaign. One of the major forces behind the protest was the Catholic Church. Townshend has argued that 'the [Catholic] Hierarchy opposed compulsory military service not just on universal principle, but specifically for Ireland – on the basis that the Irish had not given their consent to the war'[71] (obviously the former claim is not accurate: the Catholic Church never opposed conscription in any of the Catholic countries in continental Europe, including Italy, France, Belgium and Austria-Hungary).

The view that Irish Catholic support for the war effort was limited from the outset and that it was tied to the changes within nationalism after Easter 1916 has had a long history and is cited most often in studies exploring Ireland's route to independence. However, the anti-war picture of Catholic Ireland that emerges from these accounts is not accurate. The social and cultural history of wartime Ireland, which does not reduce Ireland's war effort to the relative strength of constitutional nationalism, contains contradictions and anomalies which do not fit the political narrative. These must be placed front and centre to illuminate the inconsistencies between the political history of wartime Ireland and the social history of Ireland and the Great War.

## Reappraising the war

While the political situation between Ireland and Westminster was certainly of consequence in shaping attitudes towards recruitment, some elements of this relationship had less of an impact on enlistment than the political history suggests. In the first instance, historians have been too concerned with the problem of nationalist and unionist insignia as a factor behind recruitment levels. When the concessions granted to the 36th (Ulster) Division are compared with those given to the 38th (Welsh) Division, which enjoyed Lloyd George's patronage, they were comparatively minor. It is therefore hard to claim that they were a major concession to Ulster unionists in the face of antipathy towards nationalists.[72] The notion that nationalist 'needs' (such as extracting from London a specific regional designation, political emblems and insignia for the 10th and 16th (Irish) Divisions) were not harnessed to the British war machine deserves scrutiny as well. In the vast majority of cases, nationalist recruits chose to join a range of military units, many of which had no Irish identification whatsoever. To briefly illustrate the point, when one searches the Commonwealth War Graves Commission (CWGC) website for men who died from three Irish towns selected at random, only a minority of men that died who were affiliated to that town and who are listed on the site joined specifically Irish units.[73] Though the CWGC database does not list every Irish man that was killed, it does help to demystify the notion that the Catholic Irish mainly served in units with a national identification to Ireland and that the War Office's unwillingness to compromise over nationalist insignia significantly impacted recruitment to the Irish regiments.

For the men that did join Irish regiments, the latter, it must be remembered, already had distinctively Irish symbols and regional affiliations, including harps, shamrocks, the mythological symbol of *Ériu* (the goddess of Ireland), mottos and slogans. Many had their headquarters in Irish towns and had been a part of local life since the second half of the nineteenth century, though Irish soldiers serving under the government had been common on Irish streets since the 1600s.[74] The Irish regiments also had long histories of military service, which inspired much pride among nationalists of all shades. Even during the Boer War, in which almost 30,000 Irish soldiers fought for the British at a time when constitutional and advanced nationalists were firmly against the Empire's war effort, some IPP members (including Redmond) praised the gallantry and martial prowess of Irish soldiers in the Empire's service – even though they were strongly opposed to the war – because they were proud of Irish militarism.[75] Militarism 'transcended political divisions' throughout the Boer War (1899–1902) and the Anglo-Irish settlement of 1921–2 because 'soldiery was an ideal to be extolled rather than a menace to be confronted'.[76]

Though it may have been the case that the demise of the IPP was related to its official support for the British war effort, it is more difficult to draw a direct link between Catholic enlistment and the fortunes of the Irish Party. Most Irish recruits were not in fact members of the INV, nor were the bulk of unionist recruits members of the UVF. For example, from 15 December 1914 to 15 December 1915, a period which claimed roughly one-quarter of recruits from Ireland, 51,000 Irish men enlisted. Of these, 10,794 were INV members, 8,203 were from the UVF while 32,144 belonged to neither group. Historians have demonstrated the wide range of reasons that accounted for why individuals joined up and these were generally unrelated to (though perhaps influenced by) the politics of unionism or nationalism.

Recruits were propelled by a mix of 'high' and 'low' causes. The First World War was, in terms of the rhetoric voiced at the time, a war for 'big words' such as democracy, civilization, liberty, freedom, king and country. These words were essential to the rhetoric of wartime political leaders but 'there is evidence that concepts of national duty and high moral motivation had real meaning among those crowds of volunteers pressing to get into the recruiting offices' in summer/ autumn 1914.[77] In Britain, there was widely accepted moral justification for going to war against Germany.[78] In parliamentary rhetoric, the war was conceived of as one for the 'freedom of small nations' and this cause resonated with nationalists, most notably the pro-European Nationalist MP, Tom Kettle, who was in Belgium when the Germans invaded and whose internationalist ideals formed a major reason why he believed the war was one for liberty.[79] For many nationalists, the freedom of Belgium and Serbia was considered that of Ireland as well. Thus when Belgium was invaded by Germany (the larger military aggressor which had a considerable Protestant population), Catholic outrage in Ireland was palpable; it was expressed throughout the Catholic Church, the press, and in party circles, and there was much sympathy for the country's plight.[80]

'Low' causes were equally important in determining responses towards the conflict. Some 18,000 reservists from Ireland were mobilized at the start of the war. Though, as reservists, they had no option but to return to the colours when called up, their original motivation for enlisting was often economic. Catholics comprised no less than 68 per cent of reservists mobilized in August 1914, and they were just as likely to come from Munster and Connaught as they were from Ulster. Many of these men, and their Protestant counterparts, were members of the INV or the UVF.[81] Economic incentives were also important at an individual level. For example, Jim Donaghy, a working-class mill worker from Derry who was laid off during the first week of war, enlisted for financial reasons.[82] Similarly in Wexford, James English found that when he combined a soldier's wage with the amount given to his family through separation allowances, he and his family were 154 per cent better off once he joined the army.[83] Grayson's detailed study of wartime Belfast reveals a similar pattern. Linen production was a major source of employment in the area and the loss of some continental markets following the outbreak of war had an immediate hit on the industry. On 7 August, members of the Power Loom Manufacturers' Association cut working hours to 28 hours per week while on 11 August, Combe Barbour's Fall Foundry closed, leading to the layoff of 1,800 workers. Mackie's Albert Foundry had closed most of its departments some days earlier. 'Even though many workers were taken back within a month, the layoffs had already boosted recruitment.'[84]

However, economic reasons were not significant in propelling skilled workers, clerks and professionals who came from stable and relatively secure workforces.[85] For them, one of the most important reasons for joining up was loyalty to friends and families; hence, 'so many recruits had belonged to paramilitary organizations, fraternities, sporting clubs, schools or universities, where each member felt under strong psychological pressure to conform to group expectations'.[86] Men as a whole were more likely to enlist in Ulster than elsewhere and previous service in the Ulster or Irish Volunteers tended to dispose men towards joining up.[87] Excitement, friendship, adventure and mate-ship must all be taken seriously when exploring motivations behind enlistment.[88]

The war itself also provided serious incentives to enlist. The bulk of British recruits that enlisted in 1914 did not join up in the first few days of August in a rush of 'war fever' and 'few were swept up by the alleged "war hysteria" of August 1914'.[89] Most recruits actually joined in the last week of August and in the first two weeks of September, periods which coincided with news of the retreat from Mons and the Battle of the Marne in which the regular Irish regiments of the British Army suffered heavy losses. Most British recruits in this year enlisted in September 1914 as well, which was 'the month with the strongest recruitment (462,901 men) not just in 1914 but for the whole war, representing 9 per cent of the overall enlistment in the army'.[90] However, the majority of Irish recruits actually joined in 1915 when the war was much more serious and 'the dreadful human cost and uncertain outcome of the war were universally understood'.[91] This was long after the INV became inactive, the Home Rule bill had passed, and Redmond's party had lost the support of its Midland nationalists.

The bulk of recruits came from urban areas. When compared with urban Britain, Ireland's contribution appears more favourable, as the rural–urban divide played an important part in a man's decision to enlist regardless of religion, political persuasion or nationality. By 4 November 1914, industrial areas in Ulster, Dublin, Wicklow and Kildare had produced 127 recruits per 10,000 people, a number just under the contribution of industrial areas in Yorkshire, Northumberland and Durham (150 recruits per 10,000 people). Recruitment figures for urban Ireland were actually better than the contribution of western England (88 recruits per 10,000 people) and East Anglia (80 recruits per 10,000 people). In rural Britain, low recruitment rates were not a demonstration of people's apathy towards the war, as 'their loyalty was better expressed through increased agricultural output than by enlistment to the army'.[92] Rural Ireland's support for the war effort may have resembled that of rural Britain, especially as farmers were given 'a solid economic stake' in the conflict and 'a reason to avoid [military] participation' when the naval war interrupted food imports, stimulating markets at home.[93] Overall, Ireland's military contribution was not insignificant. According to the 1911 census, Jeffery argues that there were approximately 700,000 men aged between fifteen and thirty-five in Ireland (the age range that attracted most recruits). Roughly between a quarter and a third of all available young men in Ireland served in the conflict, which was 'a strikingly high proportion in the absence of conscription'.[94]

However, Irish recruitment steeply declined from 1915 onwards, which has contributed to the belief that Catholic Ireland did not back the Allies. In fact, Jeffery has argued that recruitment declined in rough proportion to the rest of the UK, which can be seen in Table 2.1, as recruitment declined roughly by half in the six-month period between January and August 1915 in comparison to the previous six months. Urban Ireland was not so 'dramatically out of kilter' with the British war effort at least until early 1916, after which point comparisons become unfeasible due to the introduction of conscription in Britain (excluding Ireland).[95] It is often forgotten that recruitment actually declined in all of the British Dominions after early 1915, which resulted in the passage of Military Service Acts in Britain in January 1916 (in May 1916 the bill was extended to include married men; in April 1918, the upper age of men compelled to enlist was raised to fifty, with provision to raise the age to fifty-six if the need arose), New Zealand in August 1916, Canada in August 1917, and two failed attempts to introduce the measure in Australia in October 1916 and December 1917.[96] Irish recruitment actually rose during the last three and a half months of wartime 1918, five months after all shades of nationalists had protested in their hundreds of thousands against the imposition of conscription (Ireland was included in the new Military Service Bill of 1918 but its application was delayed),[97] the Irish Party had lost significant support, the Home Rule bill was in tatters, and the costs of joining up were well known.[98] Historians

**Table 2.1** Recruits raised in Ireland and across Britain per six-month period

| Period | Ireland | Britain |
|---|---|---|
| 4 August 1914–February 1915 | 50,107 | 1,342,647 |
| February 1915–August 1915 | 25,235 | 666,245 |
| August 1915–February 1916 | 19,801 | 523,792 |
| February 1916–August 1916 | 9,323 | 705,397 |
| August 1916–February 1917 | 8,178 | 494,382 |
| February 1917–August 1917 | 5,609 | 555,387 |
| August 1917–February 1918 | 6,550 | 214,135 |
| February 1918–August 1918 | 5,812 | 374,546 |
| August 1918–11 November 1918 | 9,845 | 76,236 |
| Total | 140,460 | 4,952,767 |

*Source*: Callan, cited in Jeffery, *Ireland*; The Army Council, *General annual reports*. Jeffery, *Ireland*, p. 7. This figure differs from Fitzpatrick's, who suggests that approximately 144,000 recruits were raised in Ireland during the war. The balance of the remaining men was made of regulars, reservists and several thousand officers not otherwise included in these statistics, Fitzpatrick, 'Militarism', pp. 386, 388. British figures are taken from The Army Council, *General annual reports on the British army (including the territorial force from the date of embodiment) for the period from 1st October, 1913, to 30th September, 1919* (London, 1921), p. 60.

have been unable to explain this increase because it does not support the narrative that the Catholic Irish became progressively disenchanted with the international conflict as radical nationalism grew in strength. Colin Cousins has argued that 'there is no definitive explanation for the increasing numbers of Irish recruits during summer and autumn of 1918'.[99] Colin Reid has suggested that it may have borne some relation to a voluntary recruiting initiative that was underway in mid-1918 and it was thus 'a wonder' that recruiters 'managed to boost Irish enlistment figures at all'.[100]

The rise in Irish recruitment in the latter part of 1918 suggests that there was not 'an unequivocally direct correlation between recruitment and political opinion'.[101] This conclusion is further supported by the multiple other ways in which Irish society engaged in the war effort. After all, men of recruitment age were only a small segment of Irish society, an extremely important point that is often forgotten, as the military effort simply could not have taken place had it not been for the support rendered by those who did not fight at the front. Women, men outside the military age for enlistment (as well as those who did not meet the initially strict criteria set by the War Office, which eased as the war went on) and children assisted the war effort, and their activity must be given due consideration if Ireland's war effort is to be understood in its proper context.[102]

Though relatively unexplored in comparison to the history of Ireland's military effort, a wider sphere of support for the Allied campaign existed on the home front. Eileen Reilly has shown that Irish women of both creeds participated in war-relief associations across Ireland during 1914 and 1915, and in at least one of these, women from both confessional backgrounds collaborated together until at least Easter 1916, after which point Reilly speculates that such 'unity' came to an end.[103] Throughout the war, victims of the naval campaign were cared for by Irish coastal communities because of the proximity of German submarine warfare to the Irish coast.[104] Even during the period of nationalist radicalization, supposedly anomalous instances of solidarity with the Allies can be found which cannot be explained in light of the orthodoxy that nationalist Ireland turned its back on the war. Jérôme aan de Wiel found that Irish Catholics donated significant funds to relieve Poland in 1917 'at a time when Ireland was in a political turmoil and when the war had become very unpopular in the country'.[105]

The disparities that have emerged between the political history of wartime Irish nationalism and sociocultural histories of the war effort are good reasons for re-examining Catholic Irish support for the Allies. While the changes within nationalism cannot be ignored, nor can the reasons that have led to the conclusion that Catholics turned their backs on the Allies, there are enough anomalies, contradictions and outliers to warrant a fresh examination of how civil society – both Protestants and Catholics – were affected by, and responded to, the world's first total war.

## Chapter 3

## IRISH WOMEN AND WAR-RELIEF ON THE HOME FRONT

No country would have been able to fight the First World War without the support of the home front, where women played important roles. An integral dimension of the military effort was the production of armaments, food and clothing, but it was equally important for soldiers to have the moral and humanitarian support of the societies from which they came to sustain them throughout the conflict. While historians have opened up important avenues into exploring the home front in wartime, much work remains to be done, and the scale of the humanitarian effort has still not been realized.[1] Irish women often took the lead in organizing and carrying out Ireland's response, but their services have been understated, treated as an addendum to the military effort rather than a serious indicator of voluntary engagement with, and commitment to, the British and Allied war efforts. From knitting socks and running support homes to fundraising and caring for wounded servicemen, Irish women engaged in a host of activities to support the war effort, and both Catholics and Protestants took part, often collaborating in voluntary associations throughout the duration of the conflict. All manner of women helped to make war-work a success and in some instances, helped to make Ireland's response stand out internationally and even throughout the Empire itself, but this chapter concentrates predominantly on the middle classes, whose involvement emerges most clearly from the sources.

### War-relief across Ireland

The British Red Cross Society (BRCS), the national branch of the International Committee of the Red Cross, which rendered humanitarian relief during times of war, was formally constituted in 1905 following the Boer War and was granted its royal charter in 1908 by King Edward VII and Queen Alexandra, who became its first president. Following the outbreak of the Great War it merged with the Order of St John of Jerusalem, a charity which administered first aid, to form the Joint War Committee, and both organizations administered relief-work under the authority of the Red Cross emblem and name. Members were arranged into Voluntary Aid Detachments (VADs) – the label stood for individual volunteers as well as groups of workers – and they were trained to offer civil, auxiliary and some medical assistance in wartime. VADs had county branches in Scotland, England,

Wales and Ireland, and while they comprised both men and women, one source has estimated that two-thirds of the 74,000 VADs in 1914 Britain were female.[2] In Ireland, all units came under the Joint VAD Committee for Ireland, and members were trained, examined and awarded first aid certificates that were recognized by the War Office.

One of the most zealous organizers of this work in Ireland was Lady Aberdeen, a philanthropist and wife of the Viceroy (the king's representative in Dublin) who became the president of the City of Dublin BRCS. Lady Aberdeen was well known for her social and philanthropic work in Ireland, particularly in her desire to tackle tuberculosis through the Women's National Health Association (WNHA).[3] In wartime, she initiated the instruction of nursing skills and ambulance driving, which were financially and administratively supported by the Department of Agriculture and Technical Instruction (DATI): a cooperative association founded by the moderate Protestant unionist, Horace Plunkett.[4] By 1914, DATI had an extensive network throughout Ireland, consisting of more than 1,000 affiliated societies and almost 90,000 members.[5] It thus provided a nationwide structure through which Red Cross work was disseminated.

Eileen Reilly has argued that those involved in administrating war-work were generally the upper and middle echelons of Irish society: 'The titled ladies of the landed gentry, and the wives and daughters of senior officials, politicians, businessmen, clergymen and professionals.'[6] For those women organizing and managing operations dedicated to relief-work, projects required the investment of significant amounts of time, which only women with independent means could spare, and this partly explains why most of the patrons and founders of charitable associations were Protestants because this group represented the majority of the affluent classes. For example, the Catholic Countess of Fingall remembered the wartime activity of her upper-class friends, most of whom were Anglican: May Limerick 'was running a Canteen for soldiers on their way to the Front'. Mary Greer and Ethel Mulock 'were running Sir Ernest Cassel's convalescent home on the coast' while Olive Guthrie and Lady Fitzgerald established a soldiers' club in Dublin.[7] Wealthy Protestants made their homes or parts of their premises available to BRCS associations. The landlords of Dunamon Castle in Roscommon and Castle Taylor in Galway turned their properties into convalescent homes for incapacitated men, as did Richard Cherry, the Chief Justice of Ireland.[8] Others, such as the wife of Richard Kellett, a colonel in the Royal Irish Regiment, organized comforts' appeals for servicemen and lobbied on behalf of the first and second battalions of the regiment from her home in Clonmel, Co. Tipperary.[9]

However, the middle classes were extensively involved in war-relief as well, and this was true of Catholics as well as Protestants. On 10 August 1914, the first wartime meeting of the BRCS was held at the Leinster House, Dublin, to inaugurate war-work in Ireland and there was a large turnout of groups from this section of society, regardless of denominational differences. Lady Aberdeen recalled that

> on arrival we found the big hall packed from floor to roof. It was a wonderful representative assembly, including the St John's Ambulance Association, the

St Patrick's Ambulance Association, the Department of Technical Instruction, the Irish Volunteers Voluntary Aid Association, the Dublin branch of the Ulster Volunteers, individual members of the Cumann-na-Mban, though not in a representative capacity, the Women's National Health Association, the United Irishwomen, and, in addition, the leading members of the medical and nursing professions.[10]

Humanitarian work appeared attractive to a large swathe of urban middle-class opinion early on in the war, and prominent individuals attended the meeting to support the establishment of Red Cross work in Ireland. These included medics such as the Protestant doctor and founder of the St John's Ambulance Association, John Lumsden, and the Catholic president of the St Patrick's Ambulance Association, Thomas O'Shaughnessy.[11] Other well-known persons included Sir Lambert Ormsby, the Protestant New Zealander who became colonel and honorary consulting surgeon of the New Zealand Expeditionary Force (he founded the Dublin Red Cross Order of Nursing Sisters); Sir Andrew Horne, a Catholic and former president of the Royal College of Physicians; and Sir Conway Dwyer, a Catholic, surgeon and president of the Royal College of Surgeons.[12] Support for humanitarian work also existed outside of the medical community, as Irish peers were well represented at the Leinster House gathering, many of whom became patrons of war-relief associations. These included Viscountess Sybil Powerscourt, the wife of the Protestant landowner, and Lady Winifred Weldon, wife of Sir Anthony Arthur Weldon, a major with the 4th Battalion Leinster Regiment who had been Vice-Chamberlain and Steward to the Viceroy.[13] Businessmen also backed the endeavour, such as the Catholic civil engineer, Edgar Anderson, and the prominent Catholic business magnate and proprietor of *The Irish Independent*, William Martin Murphy.[14] Even religious groups gave tacit support to the objective, as the auxiliary Catholic bishop of Dublin, Nicholas Donnelly, and the vice-president of the Methodist Church in Ireland both attended the meeting.[15] The only major group not present was labour, yet working-class representatives participated in a similar event in Cork some days later, revealing that a wide cross-section of urban Irish civil society was willing to back the humanitarian endeavour in August 1914.[16]

The cross-sectional attendance was important in light of the speeches that were made. Instead of using the war to support the respective political agendas of unionism and nationalism, speakers emphasized solidarity in a pending crisis. Henry Harrison, a Protestant nationalist and former MP for mid-Tipperary who represented the predominantly Catholic Irish Volunteers' Voluntary Aid Association, declared that all classes and creeds should stand together 'with an absolutely united front'.[17] This sentiment was shared by the Dublin Unionist Volunteers' representative, Mary Bolton. The members of her organization 'were anxious to work with the Dublin women, and give any assistance they could in this matter'.[18] Even more radical women's groups were present at the meeting, as Lady Aberdeen noted that followers of the staunchly nationalist association, Cumann na mBan, attended, though they did so as individuals rather than as political representatives (the organization was initially divided over its decision whether to support the war effort, though most members came to support Redmond's stand by the end of 1914. Only a minority refused to render assistance. In August, the organization was especially interested in what Lady Aberdeen had to offer because its members realized that they could get First Aid training for free[19]). Though Ulster Unionist women – many of whom were part of the staunchly Unionist Ulster Women's Unionist Council (UWUC) – volunteered their services to Lady Aberdeen, they chose to pursue their own war-work agenda, reinforcing the distinctiveness of Ulster, hoping that the Great War would further cement its political position as a 'territory apart' from the rest of Ireland (in addition, Ulster Unionist women had already set up hundreds of nursing units prior to the outbreak of the Great War in the event of civil war with nationalist Ireland over the Home Rule Bill).[20] Nevertheless, their willingness to assist the war effort was applauded by the Leinster House audience. In early August 1914, rendering humanitarian assistance to Irish men at the front was an action supported by a wide cross-section of Irish society.

Importantly, influential representatives of the Catholic Church also backed the humanitarian appeal, lending an important example to the Catholic laity. Nicholas Donnelly 'proposed a resolution calling upon the women of Ireland and men who were not serving with the Army or Volunteers, to qualify themselves for Red Cross work by forming classes for first aid and nursing on the lines laid down by the Department'.[21] Donnelly's superior was the influential prelate, Archbishop William Walsh, whose anti-recruitment stance and general hostility towards the conflict became well known during the war years.[22] Republican sources compiled after the war claimed that Walsh's anti-war attitude even extended to humanitarian work. His right-hand assistant, Monsignor Curran, wrote in 1952 that Walsh 'went so far as to discountenance war hospital and Red Cross collections' because he believed that they were a 'ruse for recruitment'.[23] However, Donnelly's endorsement of the Red Cross was not completely out-of-tune with Walsh's opinion, as the influential archbishop can be found to have rendered humanitarian assistance to the war effort on other occasions (see, for example, pp. 72, 89), suggesting that he must have approved of Donnelly's actions in early 1914 as well.[24]

Yet, it was precisely when the war became serious that voluntary work intensified in Ireland. For five days beginning the 25 August 1914, the German army retaliated in response to a Belgian surge and destroyed the Belgian city of Louvain. Louvain was effectively burned to the ground and looted. Its university and library of ancient manuscripts were destroyed and its citizenry was subject to mass shootings. The attack was a turning point in British public opinion, as it provided the first opportunity to record German criminal behaviour in-depth. The town was briefly recaptured by the Allies following the siege giving a rare opportunity to verify the devastation.[25]

In Ireland, news about the destruction of Louvain generated negative reactions towards Germany, particularly among Irish Catholics whose long-standing links with Catholic Belgium were well known. The invasion, the resulting atrocities and, in particular, the burning of cathedrals, churches and the destruction of the library of the Catholic University of Louvain as well as the church of St Pierre 'enraged Catholic Irish opinion and rallied support for "little Catholic Belgium".[26] Sympathy for stricken Belgians was widespread and the invasion prompted the Catholic Church in Ireland to raise a staggering £28,352 in four months for Belgian refugees from collections from Catholic parishioners.[27] As for the British, Louvain was the first significant event that gave the Irish reason to believe that Germany was in the wrong, and Pennell has noted that support for victimized Belgium was a significant motivating factor for men to enlist.[28]

Little is known about how the Irish of both creeds mobilized to support victims of German aggression, particularly the refugees who began to arrive in Ireland later that year. While it is difficult to discover the exact number of refugees that arrived in Ireland in late 1914, by the end of October, two nationalist sources estimated that 2,000 Belgians had sought refuge there.[29] The first batch arrived in Inniscarra, Co. Cork on 17 and 27 September, yet despite the early hour of arrival, 'the wharf was thronged ... cheers were again and again renewed as the Lord Bishop of Cork, Most Rev. Dr. O'Callaghan, appeared on the scene'. A further sixty-eight refugees arrived on 16 October.[30]

These enthusiastic greetings were widespread across Ireland. That the Belgians were welcomed is in itself striking, for early twentieth-century Ireland was hardly a warm place for refugees, and as late as 1956, Catholic, anti-Communist Hungarian refugees were given a difficult time in the Republic.[31] On 21 October, approximately eighty to hundred refugees arrived in Dublin. 'Notwithstanding the early hour, hundreds of people awaited their arrival ... and gave a hearty and encouraging cheer as the refugees drove off in motor char-a-bancs and cabs to the homes prepared for them in the city and neighbourhood.'[32] The refugees were brought to provincial locations, allowing the victims of Germany's invasion to be seen by people across the country. In Kildare, the local newspaper reported that there was a 'festive air about the normally rather sluggish little village of Celbridge' (1,158 of the 1,485 people who lived there were Catholics) in preparation for the refugees' arrival while in Limerick, 'enthusiastic scenes on the part of the citizens' was noted (39,031 of the 42,808 people who lived in urban Limerick were Catholics).[33] This was the same in Sligo, where the Catholic Bishop of Elphin met the refugees who 'received an enthusiastic welcome by a large crowd assembled at the railway station' (9,408 of the 11,163 people who lived in Sligo Urban were Catholics).[34] The refugees were a mix of men, women and children from different backgrounds, and pictures of them were printed in the unionist and nationalist provincial and national press (Figure 3.1).[35]

While it is difficult to determine what people felt when they saw such images, the extent to which individuals and groups mobilized to succour these victims of war suggests that helping them was considered the right thing to do. At least twelve counties in Ireland established voluntary associations in aid of Belgian relief once refugees began to land on Irish shores. These included Cork, Galway, Wicklow, Kildare, Limerick, Clare, Dublin, Tipperary, Waterford, Down, Antrim and Meath.[36] Large numbers of middle-class Catholic women volunteered to accommodate them, especially in the months of September and October 1914,

**Figure 3.1** The Catholic Lord Mayor, Henry O'Shea, meets Belgian refugees in Cork, 27 September 1914. Courtesy of *Irish Examiner* archive. White and O'Shea, *Great Sacrifice*, pp. 52–3 (image originally printed in *CE*).

writing to the Irish Jesuit Provincial, Thomas. V. Nolan, who helped coordinate Ireland's response to the refugee crisis. Annie Dooley, a fifty-one-year-old shopkeeper in Carrick-on-Suir, Tipperary, offered to accommodate two Belgian nuns, a gesture which may have been made easier by the fact that Dooley spoke some French. Mrs Maggie Mallan, a Catholic schoolteacher in Wicklow, wrote that she could accommodate one Belgian refugee.[37] These women often stipulated what class of person they were willing to accommodate, maintaining the social divisions of pre-war life. In Dublin county, the Ballybrack and Killiney refugee committee wrote to Nolan and requested 'women and children of the shopkeeper class'. They also made clear who they would not like to accommodate: 'Our committee would not like to take Jews or agricultural labourers.'[38] May Dooley from Carrick-on-Suir wrote to Nolan on 'behalf of a Belgian nobleman's family' (Monsieur le Baron du Bois de Chantraine) to see if 'there might be a gentleman's family who would receive them, and accept payment at the conclusion of the war'.[39] Francis Mulligan, a farmer in Castleblayney, Co. Monaghan, offered to 'give a comfortable home and fair wages to a Belgian who knows something about farming and [who] is willing to work'.[40] Other generous offers can be found.[41] The willingness of these individuals to assist the refugees was further incentivized by what was happening in the war at this time, as Irish soldiers had begun to fall in costly battles in Belgium and France. When John Bernard Hamill, a twenty-year-old law student from Dundalk, Co. Louth, wrote to Nolan on behalf of his mother who wished to adopt a Belgian girl, he did so because of the seriousness of the conflict, stating that they 'may prove a help to some orphan who has suffered by this cruel war'.[42]

In Britain, the refugees' arrival made the British 'unequivocally aware that this was a war in which civilians suffered as well as soldiers'.[43] Most wars throughout the nineteenth century had imposed some form of segregation between societies and battlegrounds, but the Great War was so new because it made civilians legitimate targets, and the Irish witnessed this first-hand. Though they were not suffering like their French or Belgian counterparts, the Belgians' arrival in Ireland in late 1914 was the start of an unfolding humanitarian crisis that Irish people would have to face for more than four years, and the voluntary efforts of both men and women continued to be demanded following the arrival of thousands of wounded servicemen.

## War-work in Southern Ireland

One visible part of the conflict was soldiers and sailors on convalescence, and from late 1914 a constant stream of wounded service personnel began to arrive in Ireland to be taken care of by Irish medical staff and volunteers. This was particularly evident in Dublin. In October, injured soldiers and sailors landed at Kingstown (today Dún Laoghaire) and the North Wall (east of the city centre), prompting the owners of Corrig Castle in Kingstown and Temple Hill House in Blackrock to donate their homes to be used as hospitals and convalescent homes for the BRCS. The Catholic Sisters of Charity also received wounded men at Linden, Blackrock.[44] As at the Leinster House meeting in August, creed was no barrier to engaging in the humanitarian effort in 1914 to help wounded British servicemen.

A Red Cross report published in 1921 and other sources suggest that at least twenty-two hospitals operated in Dublin during the war years which rendered assistance to wounded service personnel.[45] This surpassed the care rendered in other parts of the UK, such as in Scotland, where eleven hospitals rendered care in Edinburgh while fifteen operated in Glasgow.[46] Perhaps the most famous of these was Dublin Castle, the seat of British administration in Ireland, which was converted into a Red Cross hospital following the efforts of Lady Aberdeen, who sought and received the approval of the presidents of the Royal College of Physicians (the Anglican, Ephraim MacDowell Cosgrave) and the Royal College of Surgeons (the Catholic, Sir Conway Dwyer) to turn Dublin Castle into a hospital.[47] Thereafter, Dublin's medical community agreed to cooperate in the endeavour, as did the Lord Mayor, the Catholic Lorcan Sherlock, and as Lady Aberdeen recalled, 'right nobly did they carry out their self-imposed duties during the whole of the war'.[48] Early on in the conflict, an appeal for £5,000 was issued for equipment and 'donations from all parts of Ireland, and from all classes, poured in, and it appeared that, for the first time in its life, the Castle was actually going to be popular'.[49] The Castle, as a symbol of British rule in Ireland, was politically contentious to nationalists, and it was no surprise when a campaign against its use as a sanitary facility soon erupted, denting the enthusiasm that had initially surrounded it.[50] Nevertheless, the disagreement was not significant enough to prevent the hospital from being opened, which it did initially with beds for 250 patients. This soon increased to 300 beds, 19 of which were for officers. The financial appeal was of immediate success as well, as on the day the Castle opened on 27 January 1915, £4,813 had been raised.[51] Both Catholic and Protestant volunteers were involved in the project. In January 1915, the hospital officially opened, and the elite magazine, *Irish Life*, reported that 'some thousands of people availed themselves of the opportunity of visiting the Hospital, which has been most beautifully arranged'.[52] Speeches were made, and some of the speakers included Lady Aberdeen, Ephraim Cosgrave, the solicitor William Fry JP and William Martin Murphy (Murphy was still the hospital's chairman of finance and sat on its General Purposes committee in January 1918[53]).

Entertainment was an important aspect of nursing injured servicemen back to health and Lady Aberdeen remembered that every Thursday during the four years of its existence, Alderman James Moran, a nationalist and hotelier from Clontarf East, who was a member of the Dublin Recruitment Committee for the British forces, and C. M. Jones, a Protestant and director of the Tivoli theatre, 'brought a company of artistes from different theatres and music halls to give an entertainment, on which occasions the soldiers in other hospitals in Dublin who could attend were invited'.[54] The Abbey Theatre, of which W. B. Yeats was a founder, also held at least one concert to raise funds for beds.[55]

Donors were entitled to name a bed in a ward if they donated £20 or more and groups within the middle and upper-middle classes fundraised with this end in mind. In 1915, the Licensed Grocers' and Vintners' Protection Association forewent its annual banquet and donated fifty guineas to the Castle Hospital Fund (the equivalent of £52.50). The assistant secretary of the association in 1915 was the Catholic nationalist, Martin O'Byrne, who corresponded with Redmond.[56] In Enniscorthy, Co. Wexford, the local BRCS branch raised funds to establish 'The Enniscorthy Bed'. The branch president was the Catholic Lady Talbot Power and the vice-president was the Catholic, Mrs Thomas Esmonde (her husband was a Nationalist MP).[57] The Catholic author, Katharine Tynan, appealed for the hospital in various London papers and Selfridges gave up advertising space for that purpose.[58] Tynan recalled that 'the appeal brought me several donations of ten pounds to found a bed. I had made up with a couple of friends another ten pounds'.[59] Sales of Tynan's war poem, *Flower of Youth*, were also donated to the hospital fund and in her memoirs it is clear that Tynan's efforts on behalf of the hospital were perceived to have been great by her friends and admirers.[60]

While it is difficult to establish how many wounded personnel were stationed in Dublin hospitals during the conflict, Red Cross reports published after the war state that 800 male VADs transported 17,510 wounded servicemen in the City of Dublin alone, excluding any of the work done by the Royal Army Medical Corps (RAMC).[61] It is hard to say whether this figure represented the total number of wounded men who passed through the city during wartime who received some assistance from VADs, or only those that were incapacitated and required special assistance. Nonetheless, the commendable efforts of the volunteers were remembered by Lady Aberdeen, who recalled that VADs unloaded hospital ships, transferred the sick and wounded to ambulances and trains, and carried casualties to hospitals and convalescent homes.[62] They were assisted by the gentlemen's motoring association, the Royal Irish Automobile Club, which transported wounded men to recuperative centres.[63]

The presence of thousands of wounded soldiers in Ireland brought the destructive consequences of the military campaign home to the urban Irish, blurring the segregation between the front and home front (at least for those who did not join up), as they could witness the violence of the conflict, both in the city's hospitals and on its streets. In April 1915, Tynan was with Patrick Butler, a captain in the Royal Irish Regiment and the son of Lieutenant General Sir William Francis Butler, when they met wounded soldiers on an unnamed Dublin street who had been cared for at St Vincent's Hospital. One had been blinded at Ypres and Butler remarked to them, "'You did very well at wipers, splendidly." "We did our best, sir," said the blinded man humbly.'[64]

Irish women cared for these wounded personnel. Professional nursing emerged in Britain in the latter half of the nineteenth century, becoming an acceptable occupation for women by the early 1900s. It fitted the perception of life-giver and was suitably feminine.[65] Nursing provided a major route through which women could 'support their country in its time of need', and the medical services were a vehicle through which they could express their patriotism in a manner that was acceptable within the restrictive patriarchal environment that they were forced to negotiate.[66] At least eighteen nursing divisions were operating in Dublin in January 1916.[67] These varied in size. Two hundred students qualified as nurses in Kingstown following the outbreak of war: an eight-fold increase on the thirty members which comprised the unit before the conflict.[68] In January 1916, fifty-eight members comprised the St Stephen's Green division. Harcourt Street and south Dublin's nursing divisions sent nurses on active service. As there were 3,214 nurses in the capital in 1911, 2,079 of whom were Catholic, Catholic nurses must have rendered assistance to wounded personnel.[69] Indeed, as Figure 3.2 shows, some well-known Catholics volunteered, though it is unclear whether they served as professional nurses or as VADs. These women were pictured again by *Irish Life* on 9 June 1916 working in war hospitals in Gallipoli and France.

The capital was not the only centre to assist wounded men, as in Cork at least seven hospitals cared for Allied personnel in the city itself, excluding hospitals in the county, though the number of men treated is unknown. Red Cross and auxiliary hospitals also rendered assistance to incapacitated servicemen in the counties of Louth, Kildare, Kilkenny, Meath, Westmeath, Wicklow, Wexford, Waterford, Queen's County, Limerick, Longford and Kerry.[70] Many of these were equipped and maintained by 'voluntary contributions, at a total cost of £100,000, exclusive of grants from the Joint War Committee'. Catholics comprised the bulk of nurses in these counties so must have played an important role in the recuperation of wounded servicemen.[71]

Provincial Ireland was heavily involved in other types of relief-work as well, as BRCS branches, VADs and St John's Ambulance Association units sprung up across the urban South. In early 1916, voluntary associations comprised predominantly of female civilians operated in, for example, the counties of Cork, Clare, Tipperary,

**Figure 3.2** Great grand-daughters of Daniel O'Connell serving in a nursing capacity, *IL*, 20 June 1915. Courtesy of the National Library of Ireland. These women were also suffragists. I am grateful to Senia Pašeta for this information.

Galway, Queen's County, Wicklow, Kilkenny, Carlow, Sligo, Leitrim, Limerick, Meath, Mayo, Kerry and Roscommon.[72] Southern Protestants participated in these organizations and in some cases maintained confessional exclusivity, such as in Dublin City, where the local VAD was only comprised of Protestants.[73]

However, many war-relief associations contained Protestant as well as Catholic war-workers. This is significant given the well-known political differences that had been fostered in the predominantly Catholic South over the Home Rule crisis. For example, in November 1914 in Kildare, the Protestant Countess of Mayo and Lady Weldon attended a religiously mixed meeting in aid of finding accommodation for Belgian refugees, which was presided over by a Catholic, M. J. Minch.[74] The task of accommodating stricken Belgians across Ireland during 1914 and 1915 was taken up by two Catholics, Fr Nolan and Philippa Lawless, who coordinated the administration of the national Belgian Refugees' Committee from their headquarters alongside the London-born Anglican governess, Georgina Fowle.[75] Similarly in Clonmel, Co. Tipperary, Protestant and Catholic war-workers cooperated in aid of the war effort. Catholics made up different sections of the organization, as the executive officer of the association was the physician, Patrick James Byrne, whose wife served as a VAD.[76] The organizing committee included Ella and Ellanine de le Poer, as well as the Anglican, Kathleen Cleeve.[77] The cross-community nature of the committee was reflected in the composition of the VADs, as Catholics, Misses Annie and Mary Cooney, whose mother was a shopkeeper, worked alongside Anglicans, Mrs Emily Clibborn and Mrs W. H. Smith.[78]

However, the Easter Rising and the executions of the rebel leaders reinvigorated the political debate in Ireland which affected a process of divergence between unionists and nationalists that would continue until the end of the century.[79]

Chapter 6 discusses how this new situation impacted nationalist perceptions surrounding recruitment, particularly after the conscription crisis of 1918, but it is unclear how the revival of debates surrounding self-government impacted the war effort itself, particularly the voluntary effort on the home front. Reilly has claimed that 'the shift in nationalist political priorities in the aftermath of the 1916 rebellion and the rise in Sinn Féin in 1917 certainly impacted upon women's support for the war effort and an investigation into how this change registered itself on a local and national scale needs to be carried out'. However, as Reilly's study finishes in 1915, the premise that Catholic women withdrew their support has not been investigated.[80] One source produced long after the war suggests that Reilly's assumption is correct. Desmond Martin, the brother of the Catholic VAD worker, Marie Martin, recalled many years after the conflict that the Rising had changed the opinion of Dublin Catholics towards war-relief. When Marie returned to Ireland in 1917 having served in casualty hospitals in Malta, Desmond alleged that 'war-work was not as popular as it had been: helpers had withdrawn' and 'one had to be careful in conversation'. This did not appear to affect Marie's decision to continue assisting the war effort however, as she resumed war-work in a hospital in Leeds in March 1918.[81]

However, a significant change towards war-work among the middle classes cannot be detected in sources printed at the time. *Irish Life*, whose readers spanned the confessional divide, remained committed to reporting local activities undertaken to support the war effort for the duration of the conflict and it does not suggest that VADs which had been formed before the Rising and which comprised Catholics were disbanded in its aftermath. By extension, when the religious backgrounds of war-workers reported after May 1916 are searched in the 1911 census, war-relief associations continued to be cross-confessional in their membership.

One example of such an association was the Arklow and Avoca War Hospital Supply Depot, pictured in Figure 3.3. In September 1916, Lady Beatrix Francis Petty-Fitzmaurice, the Marchioness of Waterford, who coordinated the establishment of war hospital supplies across Ireland, visited the depot to assess its activities (she was the president of the Irish War Hospital Supply Depot at Merrion Square in Dublin and in Bray, Co. Wicklow during 1916. Her father was the wealthy landlord, Lord Lansdowne, a prominent Unionist and former leader of the Conservatives and Liberal Unionists in the House of Lords.[82]) Its members included the Protestants, Miss E. Kearon, Miss Page and Mrs Annie Philpot, and the Catholics, Miss Linehan, Miss M'Govern and Mrs O'Reilly.[83] The Marchioness was also part of a cross-confessional civilian committee which, in February 1916, met in the Viceregal Lodge under the auspices of Lady Wimborne (wife of the new lord lieutenant) with the objective of extending 'the activities of the women of Ireland in the task of ameliorating the conditions brought about by the war on the wives and families of our soldiers and sailors'. Prominent Catholics attended this meeting including Helen Butterfield (her husband became Lord Mayor of Cork in 1916), Elizabeth Burke-Plunkett (the Countess of Fingall) and James and Annie Gallagher (the Lord Mayor and mayoress of Dublin), as did leading

Photograph        RECENTLY INSPECTED BY THE MARCHIONESS OF WATERFORD.        R. Power.
   **Top row (left to right)**—Miss Glover, Miss Brigge, Miss A. Kearon, Miss Broad, Mrs. Whitehouse, Miss Fry, Miss Rowe, Miss Collins, Miss Barrett, Miss Roscoe, Miss Harrington, Mrs. Rowe, Miss Walsh, Mrs. Pierce, Miss E. Kearon, Mrs. Philpot, Miss Page.
   **2nd row**—Miss Deane Olliver, Miss ——, Deane Olliver, Miss Ellis, Miss McGillivray, Mrs. Crosbie, Mrs. Strong, Miss Kearon, Miss Green, Miss McCullagh, Miss Kearon, Mrs. Coleman, Mrs. Kearon, Miss D'Arcy, Miss Hore, Miss Crosbie, Miss M'Govern, Mrs. O'Reilly.
   **3rd row**—Miss Menzies, Miss Wynne, Miss K. Bayly, the Countess of Wicklow (President), the Marchioness of Waterford, Miss Hamilton, Miss Wylie, Miss Linehan, Mrs. Hadow.
   **4th row (seated on grass)**—Miss Deane Olliver, Mrs. Harrington, Miss McCullagh, Mrs. Sheridan, Miss Kearon, Miss O'Reilly, Miss Kearon, Miss Murphy, Miss Mulligan, Miss Hogue, Mrs. Gorman.

**Figure 3.3** The Arklow and Avoca War Hospital Supply Depot, *IL*, 1 September 1916. Courtesy of the National Library of Ireland.

representatives of women workers including the WNHA, the Central Committee of Women's Employment of which the Countess was the president, and the Ulster Ladies' Association.[84]

Other cross-confessional associations can also be found. In August 1917, one such organization in Cashel, Co. Tipperary, was pictured in *Irish Life*.[85] The women photographed included the Catholics, Mrs Charles E. Doran, Mrs Corby and Miss Moloney, and the Anglicans, Mrs Mary McKinley, Miss Trayer and Miss Butler Lowe. These war-workers cooperated to produce medical supplies for hospitals which aided the recuperation of wounded men.[86]

Figure 3.4 shows 'a flourishing Red Cross detachment in the kingdom of Kerry', as reported by *Irish Life* in October 1917.[87] The VAD was inaugurated in November 1916 and contained approximately thirty-five members, some of whom were Catholic. The commandant was a Catholic, Mrs R. Fitzgerald. Other Catholic VADs included Miss M. Whelan and Miss Quill.[88] The man pictured was the physician, Abraham Hargrave, an Anglican. He set examinations for the VADs.[89] Writing about the organization, he declared that its results had been 'very excellent' suggesting that its female war-workers were still committed to their work. At the time of publication, some members were nursing in Red Cross hospitals and engaged in other relief schemes but the VAD was 'very much alive, and, we understand, most anxious for an opportunity of proving their efficiency'.[90]

The commitment of middle-class Catholics to war-work and the endurance of cross-community associations can be found in later periods as well. In May 1918, at the height of the conscription crisis in Ireland, *Irish Life* was enthusiastic about a

Photograph                    KERRY 4 V.A.D., AUGUST, 1917.                    Healy, Tralee.
Top row (standing).—Miss Mathews, Miss Kelly, Miss Stack, Miss Shorten, Miss Raymond, A. H. Hargrave, Esq.,
        M.D.; Miss Quill, Mrs. Revington, Miss Quinnell, Miss Baily, Mrs. Frazer, Mrs. Hifle.
Middle row (sitting).—Miss Henderson, Miss Johnston, Miss Rowan, Lady Superintendent; Mrs. FitzGerald,
        Commandant; Mrs. Chute, Quartermaster; Mrs. Hargrave, Miss M. Rowan, Mrs. R. E. McCowen.
Bottom row.—Miss M. Vine, Miss Shriner, Mrs. Hampson, Miss D. Hilliard, Miss M. Whelan.

**Figure 3.4** Kerry No. 4 VAD, *IL*, 12 October 1917. Courtesy of the National Library of Ireland.

sporting competition held by VADs, and it published a photograph of the winners. They included the Catholic VAD, Miss Sheelah Plunkett, the Anglican worker, Vivienne Caldecott, and the commandant of the detachment, Aileen O'Kelly, a Catholic who is pictured holding the winner's cup.[91] O'Kelly's family was the definition of the socially mobile Catholic middle class which emerged in Ireland in the late nineteenth century. O'Kelly's father was a land commissioner, while her mother, Norah, described herself as a 'Barrister in Law not in practice' (she had received her Bachelor's degree at University College Dublin, but as women were not allowed to practise law until 1919, it is interesting that Norah still chose to call herself a barrister when the census was taken in 1911.) Aileen's two brothers worked as a solicitor's assistant and stock exchange clerk respectively, while her sister was an art teacher.[92] Notably, the prize-giver for the competition was the Dublin Unionist, Lady Arnott, who fundraised for the Royal Dublin Fusiliers (RDF) in wartime.[93]

These examples suggest that neither religious nor political differences were a barrier to all inter-communal war-work in Southern Ireland, nor did the radicalization in Irish politics precipitate a noticeable change in the cross-community character of much BRCS work engaged in across the country. Indeed, when the number of voluntary nursing detachments inaugurated to support the war effort in the predominantly Catholic South are compared with the largely Protestant North, there was not much of a difference between them, which is surprising in light of the well-known contribution of 'loyal' Ulster and the supposedly uncertain commitment of the Catholic South. In a report published after the war by the Joint War Committee of the Red Cross, the society noted that Cork city and county raised the first VAD in southern Ireland, and at least four detachments operated in the area throughout the war; one more than the predominantly Protestant county of Antrim (including Belfast), despite the fact that Cork had fewer people and was predominantly Catholic (Cork city and county had 356,269 Catholics: 35,756 Protestants. Antrim – including Antrim county and the city of Belfast – had 132,994 Catholics: 415,659 Protestants.[94]) Cork also had 400 VAD members: double that of Belfast and 151 members more than all of Co. Antrim, which had a membership of 249.[95] There were twenty-two hospitals in Dublin that assisted wounded servicemen during the conflict while only eight hospitals can be found in Belfast and at least seven can be found in Cork city (Cork county also had hospitals).[96] This is not surprising given the strategic location of both Cork and Dublin (Dublin was also the capital of Ireland), but their contributions to the voluntary effort on the home front have been understated.

One explanation as to why the capital and many Catholic Irish women across the country felt obliged to continue assisting the war effort was because of the humanitarian crisis created by the conflict. Wounded men continued to demand the care and support of nurses and volunteers, who laboured to render support. In Tipperary, a depot for disabled men was established in 1916 because 'some Tipperary gentlemen were struck with the helplessness of the soldiers discharged from the Army by reason of the effect of wounds or illness'. It specifically cared for men who served in Kitchener's New Army Irish infantry regiments and had a capacity of 4,000, though approximately 2,000 men were in residence at the time the report was made. Male and female voluntary workers were charged with nursing the soldiers back to health so as 'to "fit" as many men as possible to return to the front in the shortest possible space of time' and to prepare them for re-entry into civilian life after the war.[97]

The depot had the approval of the military authorities, who were consulted about the scheme in January 1916 by a cross-confessional civilian committee, which subsequently inaugurated a fundraising appeal to establish the recuperative centre. The committee chairman was Monsignor Arthur Ryan, the parish priest of Tipperary and a sincere nationalist, who declared at the committee's inaugural meeting that 'surely it is incumbent upon all Irish men, and Irish women, to do what they can towards improving the future prospects of those soldiers who have deserved so well of their country'.[98] Ryan rendered support to Irish soldiers throughout the war, as in December 1916, he visited the 16th (Irish) Division at the front accompanied by the brother of the nationalist leader, Willie Redmond. There, he was 'loudly cheered' by the Irish men he spoke to, declaring that he had come 'to thank them for their sacrifices and to express the admiration of Ireland for their deeds'.[99] Ryan's patriotism was shared and praised by Christopher Fox, a private with the RDF and a working-class Catholic from Dublin who had volunteered to join up (he was formerly employed as a 'grocer's porter') He wrote to Monica Roberts, an Anglican war-worker in Dublin, to say that 'we have Monsignor Ryan out here on a visit to us I suppose you know him he is Parish Priest of Tipperary a great Irish man'.[100] Other Catholics were involved in setting up the Tipperary depot as well. These included Daniel Kelly, the chairman of Tipperary Urban District Council,[101] and J. Heffernan.[102] They sat on a cross-confessional civilian committee which included Reverend Chastel de Boinville from the Rectory in Tipperary and George Townsend, a land agent and the committee's honorary secretary.[103] At the inaugural meeting in January 1916, at which the cross-confessional committee was formalized, 'it was unanimously decided to grant every possible facility to the military in the matter'.[104]

Wounded servicemen were cared for elsewhere in Ireland throughout the duration of the conflict, notably at the Dublin Castle Red Cross hospital and at Lucan hospital, which, like many of the Red Cross auxiliary hospitals across Ireland, cared for men well into 1919 (Figure 3.5). Some of the nurses, VADs and auxiliary helpers who worked there had family members at the front, such as Kathleen O'Brien, a nurse at Lucan hospital and daughter of an international cricketer. She had a brother that had been killed at the Somme in 1916 (Timothy O'Brien, a lieutenant in the Royal Field Artillery).[105] When the Catholics Marie and Ethel Martin respectively qualified as VADs in 1914 and 1916, their two brothers, Tommy and Charlie, joined the Connaught Rangers and the RDF as officers, while another sister, Violet, joined the St John's Ambulance Association.[106] Jay Winter has argued that during the conflict organizations such as the Red Cross became a lifeline for people whose relatives had gone missing in action.[107] This was the case for the Martin family when Charlie Martin was reported missing at the Dardanelles on 27 December 1915. Marie was serving in a hospital in Malta when she heard the news. She tried to find out more information about Charlie by enquiring at different hospitals and arranging a phone call (a new form of communication) to Salonika, while her family in Dublin attempted to contact someone in the higher echelons of the War Office and Red Cross for information. Her mother 'had the family rosary offered every night for Charlie and religious communities were asked to help with their prayers'. To ease her anxiety, Marie's mother began a diary which took the form of a daily letter to her missing son. In this, she told Charlie all about the Rising and the events which transpired

**Figure 3.5** Wounded men at the Dublin Castle Red Cross Hospital, *IL*, 5 January 1917. Courtesy of the National Library of Ireland.

in Dublin, and when twenty British soldiers commandeered farm carts from the Martin's house to set up a barricade outside their premises, it was probably the fact that Mrs Martin had sons in the army and daughters in casualty clearing hospitals that prompted her to write that 'I felt sorry for them and sent out lemonade, stewed rhubarb and a big jug of tea to them'.[108]

In June 1916, her worst fears were confirmed. She received a telegram from the War Office which announced that Charlie, who had been wounded on 8 December 1915 and subsequently captured by the Bulgarians, had died of wounds two days later. Thus, for six months, the Martin family had lived with the uncertainty of whether Charlie was alive or dead. This perhaps explains Marie's decision to stay in Ireland for much of 1917, yet her commitment to VAD work had not been dented as in March 1918 she resumed war service at a hospital for wounded officers in Leeds.[109] Nor was the Martin family unique in its reliance on the Red Cross. Some 51,000 written communications were sent out each and every year of the war by the Enquiry Bureau for 'Wounded and Missing Soldiers and Prisoners of War' which had opened in Dublin in February 1915.[110] 'Hospital Searchers' interviewed all wounded Expeditionary men who arrived and responded to queries such as those from the Martins. These figures represent the tip of the iceberg, as an unknown number of letters and other types of correspondence were sent through channels other than the Dublin Bureau. For instance, on 23 December 1917, Elizabeth Meaney from Cork wrote to the chaplain of the RMF, Fr Francis Gleeson, regarding her son who had been serving in the 1st Battalion. He had gone missing that month, and Elizabeth had corresponded with Gleeson in the hope that he might be able to locate him. On 10 December, she received a letter about her son and wrote to Gleeson that

> I am most happy to be able to inform you that he is a prisoner in Germany. ...
> I have gone through untold agonies since I received the information he was missing but went at once to the Font of All Consolation and power who sent me within the space of a few days a letter from Geneva from the Red Cross Agency there giving me an entry from an official list sent on from Berlin stating he was taken at Ypres unwounded and set direct to Dülmen Camp.[111]

Fear, worry and panic awakened Meaney's religious sensitivity, and news from the Red Cross assumed a spiritual-like quality as she waited to hear if her son had been found. Meaney wrote that her son was 'all I have in the world and the best and kindest creature God ever gave to any one'. Her gratefulness to the Red Cross was clear, revealing its integral significance for many Irish women and their families who found themselves in a similar position, whose correspondence may have comprised some of the 204,000 enquiries received by the Red Cross bureau in Dublin over the course of the war.[112]

Urban Southern Ireland was heavily bound up in the war effort, as many middle-class Catholic and Protestant war-workers, as well as the Anglo-Irish gentry, laboured to assist the thousands of wounded men recuperating in the country. That they often worked beside one another and continued to do so despite their political differences, which were brought back into the foreground after the Rising, suggests that the voluntary war effort overshadowed these differences and could continue despite the changing nature of Irish nationalism. This was also the case in parts of Ulster.

## War-work in Ulster

From the outset, several committees dedicated to war-work were formed in Ulster that attracted Irish women of both creeds. In the religiously mixed town of Newry, Co. Down (8,924 Catholics: 3,039 Protestants), 'it was unanimously decided to form a Guild, and a Committee representative of all the religious denominations in Newry was appointed'.[113] The guild was in aid of the sick and wounded and its members included middle and upper-middle class women, such as the Catholics, Bella McCann (the wife of a 'Master Baker'), Mrs Mullan, Emily Gartlan and Miss Murray.[114] Protestants included the Misses Swanzy, Mrs Lucy Slipper (a minister's wife and captain of the Salvation Army) and Mrs Marion Wade (a civil engineer's wife).[115] This united response to the war may have been in line with the phenomenon of unity which manifested itself across Ireland during the early weeks of August.[116] However, it endured well beyond this month, prompting acts of voluntarism from both Catholics and Protestants, who often collaborated in aid of the war effort.

In December 1914 in Newtownstewart, Co. Tyrone (577 Catholics: 736 Protestants), *The Derry Standard*, a unionist organ, described a concert which 'was the first held for a long time, in which all creeds and parties united, and consequently it turned out to be a great success'.[117] A cross-community endeavour was particularly noticeable following the influx of Belgian refugees and relief committees sprung up in Ulster as they had done in the South. This was significant because of the historic relationship between Catholic Ireland and Belgium, which arguably offered reasonable grounds for deterring Protestants from assisting 'little Catholic Belgium'. In Rostrevor, Co. Down, one association counted among its membership the Anglican Reverend T. W. E. Drury, Catholic Reverend Edward MacRory and Presbyterian Reverend J. L. Rentoul. In December 1914, these clerics appeared on the same platform 'at a large and influential meeting of the general public [with regard to] making arrangements for the reception of Belgian refugees'.[118] One of the most visible signs of the war in Armagh was the arrival of the Belgians and 'initially, at least, religious tensions faded, as both Protestant and Catholic groups and institutions proved eager to provide homes for the stricken Belgians and to assist in educating their children'. In Lurgan, the Sisters of Mercy Convent provided Belgian girls with education and boarding while teachers at the Protestant-run Portadown Technical School, James Edwards and the Catholic Joseph Getz (who himself was born in Belgium) were praised for their efforts to educate Belgian children.[119]

Of course, the religious dimension of assisting the Catholic Belgians was not lost in Ulster, where Catholics and Protestants had a long history of sectarian tensions that often centred on the religious question. These came to the fore in Armagh. Colin Cousins has noted that Ulster Protestants could not renounce the fact that Germany was the 'birthplace of the Reformation and the homeland of Martin Luther', and some unionist organs cultivated the notion that Germany was not really a Protestant country but was actually aligned with the Catholic Church.[120] In Belfast, the Catholics F. W. Cotter and J. O'Neill wrote to Fr Nolan as representatives of the Down and Connor Belgian Refugees' Committee, declaring that 'our committee was formed for the express purpose of preventing the proselytism of Belgian refugees'. This concern was widespread and when three Catholic Belgian families that had been placed in Protestant homes in Armagh converted to Protestantism in 1916, the episode prompted strong condemnation by Cardinal Michael Logue, the head of the Catholic Church in Ireland.[121] Religious prejudices were not confined to Ulster however, as in Dublin, Philippa Lawless wrote to Fr Nolan regarding a proposed art exhibition to raise funds for the refugees:

> The treasurer of Mrs Fowle's committee not being a Catholic, I would not consent to give him the profits from this proposed exhibition. ... My sisters do not approve of mixed committees nor do I, but if this money was given into your hands it would be alright. I shall not be mixed up with any committee again.[122]

Yet prejudices and suspicions were not immutable, even in Ireland's most sectarian city. Cotter and O'Neill had been impressed by Nolan's cross-community committee in Dublin but did not feel that a mixed committee could be established in Belfast: 'Living as you do in a City where you can call upon broad-minded Protestants to help you in a work of this kind ... that they will act in an honourable manner it is difficult to realise the state of affairs in a City such as this when the whole atmosphere is anti-Catholic.'[123] However, Nolan must have encouraged them to pursue a cross-community endeavour since Cotter and O'Neill met with the Presbyterian Lord Mayor of Belfast, Crawford McCullagh, who 'received us in a very friendly manner. ... The protestants therefore have determined to act honourably. ... We are leaving matters largely to [the] Lord Mayor and that we would not insist on the majority being catholics seeing the excellent temper of the protestants themselves.'[124]

Nor was this the only example of cross-confessional integration in Belfast, though further investigation would need to be done to establish how widespread this was. In January 1915, a children's 'paper carnival' was held in the Ulster Hall to raise war funds at which some Catholics and many Protestants from the upper and middle classes attended. A total of 150 children took part in the competition for which they had to design paper costumes and approximately 700 people attended.[125] The judges included several Protestant ladies, such as Margaret Lady Pirrie (wife of the chairman of Harland and Wolff shipbuilders), Lady Dill (wife of Sir Samuel Dill, Professor of Greek at Queen's University Belfast), Mrs Thomas Hamilton (Hamilton was a minister, president and vice chancellor of Queen's University Belfast) and Mrs Robert Meyer (her husband was the town clerk of Belfast).[126] While there were many more Protestants than there were Catholics, which might have been expected to have influenced the competition's results, the winner was the eight-year-old Maureen McKeown, a Catholic whose father was a wine and spirit merchant.[127] The other winners included ten-year-old Vivienne Stuart, whose father was a cashier at the Bank of Ireland, as well as the twelve- and thirteen-year-olds, Vera and Muriel McMeekin (their father was a master flax spinner).[128] Cross-confessional collaboration in Belfast was also seen at the front, as Richard Grayson has shown that working-class nationalists and unionists from the west of the city often enlisted alongside one another, fighting together in battles such as the Somme.[129] Such integration was remarkably new in the north, as class, religious and political differences meant that these groups had rarely had much opportunity to mix in the decades leading up to the conflict, particularly in Belfast where divisions were most stark.[130]

In rural Ulster, it is also possible to find examples of cross-confessional integration in aid of the war effort. In Cavan, for example, a predominantly Catholic county (74,271 of the 91,173 persons in County Cavan were Catholic in 1911), the County Cavan Women's Patriotic Committee (CCWPC) was formed in early September 1914 to 'assist in alleviating the distress that must inevitably follow the outbreak of war'.[131] Reilly has argued that from its inception, the CCWPC 'aimed to be representative "of all sections of the community", and counted amongst its members women from unionist and nationalist backgrounds'.[132] Mrs E. H. Lough – wife of the Lord Lieutenant of Cavan and Liberal MP, Thomas Lough, a staunch home ruler and proponent of the cooperative movement – served as the committee president.[133] Other members included Cecilia Beatrice Kennedy (her husband was a Nationalist MP); Aileen, Lady Farnham, wife of the 3rd Baron, served as patron of the County Cavan BRCS branch and fundraised on the CCWPC's behalf (she was also president of the county Soldiers' and Sailors' Families Association.) T. J. Burrowes and Fane Vernon, the wives and daughters of unionist county deputy lieutenants, were also part of the CCWPC, while middle-class women from the rural areas and towns made up the remaining members.[134]

Though religiously mixed, the CCWPC was supported by members of Cavan's Catholic community. In October 1914, days after John Redmond encouraged nationalists to join the British forces, the Roman Catholic Bishop of Kilmore, Patrick Finegan, wrote to the local press to support the CCWPC.[135] For the rest of the year, the organization worked with the Catholic and Anglican churches to raise funds for stricken Belgians while entertainments in many of the CCWPC members' homes were held as a means of fundraising. Reilly has noted that cross-community collaboration on the CCWPC's behalf was 'warmly expressed' and the first collection in aid of Belgian relief raised £840. By February 1915, the CCWPC had netted a further £450 and had made 3,500 garments for wounded soldiers. More than 200 women were thanked for their contributions. Local schools were also involved in supporting the CCWPC. The pupils of Ballymachugh raised money to purchase tobacco for Irish servicemen while those of Killashandra and the Catholic school, Aghakee, formed knitting groups in order to send socks, mufflers and mittens to their locally recruited unit, the 2nd Battalion Royal Irish Fusiliers.[136]

One of the CCWPC's most prominent forms of war-work was its contribution to the National Egg Collection scheme. Mrs Lucy Blackley, an Anglican and wife of a land agent, was the CCWPC's secretary and a prominent administrator of Cavan's egg collection initiative.[137] She appealed to teachers and pupils for eggs in May 1915 and in June, the provincial unionist newspaper, *The Irish Post and Weekly Telegraph for Cavan and the Midlands* [hereafter *Irish Post*] listed the schools which had taken up her appeal: 'Convent School, Cavan, 14 dozen; Farnham School, 12 dozen; Stradone School, 9 dozen'.[138] At least one of these schools was Catholic (Convent School) suggesting that a wider sphere of support for the objective existed in Cavan in mid-1915, an assumption which historians have doubted in other counties for the same period.[139] Catholic support continued beyond 1915 since in February 1916, the CCWPC published its third list of subscriptions and Aghakee primary school had contributed.[140]

Importantly, no significant difference can be found in contributions to the CCWPC after the Rising. Four months after the execution of the rebel leaders, the annual meeting of the CCWPC revealed that its committee remained the same. Mrs Thomas Lough presided as she had done in 1915. The meeting was attended by the Catholic Mrs Kennedy, as well as a host of Protestant middle-class women from different denominations including the Anglicans, Lucy Blackley, Mrs Mathilda Hallowes (wife of a medical doctor) and Miss Harriet Berry, the daughter of an auctioneer.[141] Reports from the various CCWPC branches were 'considered very satisfactory' by the members, suggesting that support for war-work, which had existed in 1914 and 1915, had not significantly changed. Towns and villages which had contributed to the CCWPC and which were discussed in the September 1916 meeting included Belturbet (956 Catholics/1,371 people), Virginia (2,473 Catholics/2,722), Cootehill (1,200 Catholics/1,550), Killashandra (1,216 Catholics/1,624) and Ballyconnell (905 Catholics/1,245).[142] However, a slight dip in voluntary contributions occurred that year. From September 1915 to September 1916, £636 17s 10d was raised and more than 4,000 garments were sent to the front while from September 1914 to September 1915, £679 7s 7d had been collected and 6,000 garments (including large quantities of cigarettes, tobacco and other articles) had been dispatched.[143]

Could this decline have reflected a weakening in support for the CCWPC? Further investigation suggests not, as 3,500 garments were collected during the five-month period, September 1914 to February 1915 (approximately 700 garments per month) while in the following seven months, only 2,500 were collected (approximately 357 garments per month). Since this was more than a year before the Rising, other reasons must have been behind the decline. Significantly, this figure is comparable to the estimated 333 garments produced on average per month in the year ending September 1916 when the noticeable decline should have appeared but did not.

Other cross-confessional war-work committees and associations continued to thrive during 1916 and beyond, such as the Belgian Refugees' Committee. In August 1916, a meeting was held in the local courthouse presided over by the Catholic medical doctor, John Clarke.[144] Attendees included William Finlay, a carpenter, and the merchant and clerk, Peter Levins (Levins was Catholic).[145] Protestants also attended including the solicitor's wife, Amelia Fegan and one Miss Vance.[146] A letter was read from the Belgian chaplain, Fr Golyverest, who 'thanked the committee and people of Cavan for their great kindness to the refugees, whom he was sorry to hear were about to leave'. Two clergymen of different faiths also sat on the committee and when their time as members came to an end, the committee was 'unanimous' in appointing one Catholic and one Protestant clergymen to replace them.[147]

Other activities held in aid of the war effort can be found in Cavan after the Rising, attracting people of both creeds. In December 1916, a gift sale in aid of war-relief was held in the local town hall which raised £246 4s 3d. The organizers included the Catholics, Mrs Vincent Kennedy (her husband was a Nationalist MP), Sarah McCarren (the wife of a local merchant and farmer) and J. P. Gannon, secretary of the local branch of DATI.[148] In January 1917 in the diocese of Kilmore, where most of Cavan was located, another fundraiser was held to support the BRCS. *The Irish Post* recorded that 'the parishioners of Kilmore of all creeds and classes threw themselves heartily into the project, and, with the visitors from neighbouring parishes, attended in such large numbers that the hall was crowded throughout the afternoon and evening'. It declared that £119 was raised, much of which came from sales of livestock donated by local farmers. Expenses amounted to only 13 shillings 'as nearly all the work which usually incurs expenditure in connection with such efforts was done voluntarily'.[149]

The CCWPC continued to send eggs to the National Egg Collection depot until the end of the conflict, and though collections varied by month, no obvious decline can be detected in the number of eggs donated until September 1918, after which point returns can no longer be found.[150] The CCWPC continued to publish the results of its work in the local press until the end of the war, including in nationalist organs such as *The Anglo-Celt*, suggesting that its readers were still interested in what the CCWPC had to say. When the committee met for its annual meeting in October 1918, its membership appeared to be unchanged, as Mrs Thomas Lough continued to act as president, and Mrs Blackley continued to act as secretary. The organization was supported by some largely Catholic parts of Cavan as well as villages that had significant Protestant minorities, as the villages of Bawnboy (967 Catholics: 1,111 people), Blacklion (84 Catholics: 127 people), Derrylane (9 Catholics: 37 people) 'and other districts are all helping, and many garments have been sent away during the year, and a large number of eggs, etc'.[151] Cavan town raised £40 17s 6d, produced 186 articles, and collected 5,118 eggs for the war effort in addition to other sums raised as gift sales and concerts (a War Hospital Depot was also established there in 1917). Belturbet raised £391 7s 5d and produced 296 garments; Killashandra raised £109 6s 11d, dispatched 334 garments, 5,000 bandages and dressings and collected 312 eggs; Ballyconnell raised £20 10s 11d, forwarded many dozens of socks and collected 1,092 eggs; Cootehill raised £96 and sent 72 parcels to soldiers abroad while Virginia sent many parcels to local men at the front and made 146 pairs of socks.[152] Large sums of money were also reported to have been raised. Since its formation, the committee raised more than

£4,000 and sent approximately 20,000 garments to Cavan sailors and soldiers.[153] When it is realized that the city of Dublin BRCS sent 50,000 garments over the course of the conflict, Cavan's contribution was far from insignificant given the obvious geographical, demographic and economic differences between the two places.[154]

Pleas to assist the Red Cross in Cavan did not cease after the 1918 Armistice and nor did the public response. On 23 November 1918, a Red Cross sale was advertised which appealed to the farmers of Castlepollard, Co. Westmeath and district, close to the Cavan town of Virginia.[155] A public meeting regarding the sale was scheduled to take place on the 27 November in the local courthouse and the advert hoped that farmers 'will come to the front, as usual, and support this excellent project, as a token of their appreciation of having been saved the horrors of war by the noble heroism and self-sacrifice of our gallant Irish men and women'. This advert was placed by Fr Patrick Daly, a priest who spoke Irish and English, who was the chairman of another inter-communal committee.[156]

War-relief was thus taken up across Ulster and, in many cases, was both managed and executed by the cross-confessional middle classes who collaborated to make the war effort a success. The case study of Cavan reveals that different groups of Catholics – including politicians, schoolteachers, farmers, clerics, carpenters and doctors – participated in war-work, and while this was definitely the case in 1914 and 1915, there is little available evidence to suggest that voluntary organizations were any less successful in subsequent years. No changes were made in the cross-confessional membership of the CCWPC after the Dublin rebellion, and its collections continued throughout most of the war, even increasing during 1917 and 1918 despite the political change within nationalism. Other types of war-work continued to take place in the county during 1917 and 1918, attracting both Catholics and Protestants. That Cavan was not unique in its cross-confessional endeavours suggests a broader picture of humanitarian engagement with the conflict across the country.

### An all-Irish endeavour?

One measurable form of war-work was *sphagnum* moss production. In November 1915, the Royal College of Science (RCS) established a Central Sphagnum Moss Depot which acted as a department of the Irish War Hospital Supply Depot.[157] Cotton wool, traditionally used on dressings, became scarce soon after the conflict began and the peat-moss, *sphagnum*, formed an excellent substitute. Plentiful, cheaper and more absorbent than cotton wool, scientists realized that Ireland was well-adapted to meet the great demand for dressings, and they consequently worked in conjunction with the medical department of the War Office to facilitate the collection of moss as dressings. T. Johnson, a professor of botany at the RCS, recorded that 'the bogs of Ireland, with *Sphagnum* as their basis, cover one-seventh of its surface, there being one square mile of bog to every 1,000 people in the island'.[158] These favourable conditions led to the establishment of 44 sub-depots across Ireland, which gathered and treated the moss, in addition to 200 collecting stations in 25 counties.[159]

One of the leading figures in *sphagnum* moss production was the London-born Elsie Henry, the daughter of a successful physician. She had Anglo-Irish connections to the Stopford family, one of whom was the nationalist historian, Alice Stopford Green, her mother's sister.[160] Henry's husband, Augustine, was a professor of forestry at the RCS.[161] Like many women of her class, Henry's family was heavily involved in the war effort. Her elder brother had joined a Canadian regiment while her younger brother, Edward, joined the RAMC (he was killed on 8 October 1917). Her male cousins also joined up. Henry volunteered to assist the war effort in one of the few means open to females. Living in Dublin, she attended a First Aid class and subsequently joined a VAD attached to the RCS. In late 1915 however, she became Quartermaster of the RCS Sphagnum Department, which became the Central Sphagnum Depot for Ireland, and her commitment to the war effort was so great that in 1918 she was awarded an OBE.[162]

The physical exertion involved in moss-picking and the different levels of production required to turn it into a dressing gives some indication of the effort involved in this form of war-work:

> No one who has not gathered moss on a bog can realise how arduous is this part of the work. Even under ideal summer conditions the moss can only be reached over wet boggy ground, and when to this is added continuous rain and cold in autumn and winter, which involves wading to obtain it, it can be imagined that the collector's task is not an easy one.[163]

Once picked, moss samples were sent to local collecting stations; from there, they were sent to the central Dublin depot. Volunteers in the depot treated and separated the moss according to its features. The thickest and most absorbent was set aside for surgical dressings; thinner varieties were used for dysentery pads while the thinnest were used for 'stretcher pillows'. All were torn into pieces of various sizes before being given to machinists who stitched muslin bags into which the moss was placed. Male carpenters, who volunteered to help, sourced timber to make cases to transport the moss to hospitals in Ireland and at the front (Figure 3.6).[164]

A report from the organization recorded that from November 1917 to November 1918, at least 109 workers volunteered in RCS central depot and 242 collectors across Ireland supplied them with samples. The spread of counties and the approximate number of regular collectors within them included Armagh (1), Carlow (4), Cavan (3), Clare (5), Cork (6), Donegal (2), Down (1), Dublin (21), Fermanagh (4), Galway (15), Kerry (13), Kildare (6), King's County (29), Leitrim (1), Limerick (4), Longford (3), Mayo (22), Meath (10), Monaghan (2), Queen's County (4), Tipperary (7), Tyrone (1), Westmeath (29), Wexford (2) and Wicklow (3).[165] This type of war-work is noteworthy since it was part of an all-Ireland effort that incorporated Ulster counties. As in the example of the National Egg Collection scheme, some aspects of Ulster's war effort were national in scale rather than concentrated within the province.

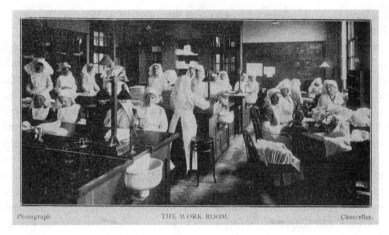

Photograph                      THE WORK ROOM.                      Chancellor.

**Figure 3.6** Treating the moss at the RCS Central Depot, Dublin, *IL*, 26 July 1918. Courtesy of the National Library of Ireland.

In this year, the two largest contributions came from Co. Kerry (Kenmare: 70,286 dressings and Kilgarvan: 57,880 dressings). This was in spite of the fact that Ulster had contributed as well, since the Armagh depot submitted 22,725 dressings and the Rostrevor Depot in Co. Down submitted 33,209 dressings. Londonderry city only contributed 2,767 dressings, suggesting that this type of war-work was more popular in the predominantly Catholic and Anglican South than in the Protestant North.[166] While this almost certainly had much to do with the geography of Ireland, it is significant given the political hostility towards Westminster brewing within rural southern Ireland during this period. Henry witnessed this first-hand when she visited the depots in Kenmare and Kilgarvan in April 1917. Some local people, who were presumably working-class Catholics, were hostile to the moss-pickers. She recalled that 'the collecting has been difficult, as the Kilgarvan people have boycotted the workers, and also at first tried to prevent the collection of moss. They attacked the moss gatherers one day, men and women, and one woman scratched Miss Constable's face so badly that blood poisoning resulted.'

These serious accusations cannot be discounted, and though it is unclear why exactly the local community was hostile to the war-workers, it is not improbable to speculate that hostility towards Westminster's actions in Ireland in the months following the Rising was conflated with assisting the British war effort. The seriousness of these attacks reflected the politicization of the war effort in Ireland, a subject interrogated in greater detail in Chapter 6. However, it is the sustained effort of other Catholics engaged in moss-picking in Kerry which suggests that the Kilgarvan example was not wholly representative of attitudes to moss-picking more generally in the county, at least in April 1917. Henry recalled that

the workers are all poor, mostly farmers' daughters, whose mothers do all their share of the home work in their absence; one post-office girl, two or three old

Biddies; one of them Peggy Shea, comes down 5 miles from the mountains on foot, at 10 a.m.; does all the carbolizing [*sic*]; gets into her uniform and works away at moss and returns 5 miles in the evening. After she carries a sack of moss down from the mountains on her back.[167]

There were forty-four farmers in Kilgarvan, forty-one of whom were Catholic, as were eight of the nine farmers who lived in Ardtully where the depot was located.[168] It is likely that the female war-workers were Catholic, as Henry comments that they were from financially deprived situations. In fact, all women named Margaret Shea (the abbreviated version was 'Peggy') who lived in Kerry in 1911 were Catholic, and it is possible that the Constable family she refers to were Catholics as well.[169]

Henry also suggests that Kilgarvan's hostility to war-work was not paralleled in Kenmare (172 persons: 118 Catholics), though resentment towards 'Englishness' – which itself was likely bound up with hostility towards Westminster – was manifest: 'There is a strange and active bitterness which does not exist around Kenmare itself. The feeling is all anti-English, but the Kenmare depot itself has not encountered any active resistance.'[170] Catholic volunteers engaged in moss-picking elsewhere in rural Ireland. They included Miss O'Donovan from Skibbereen, Co. Cork, Miss E. Halloran from Inagh, Co. Clare, Miss Annie Smith from Co. Cavan and Mary Anne McMenamin, a Gaelic speaker from the Irish-speaking district of Glenties, Donegal.[171] Catholics from urban centres also took part in the scheme, such as Margaret Carberry, a nurse who worked in the central depot, though class differences existed between women who worked in the central depot and the moss-pickers themselves (another committee member included Henrietta Fletcher, an Episcopalian and the wife of DATI assistant, George Fletcher, who served as the honorary president. Their son, George, was killed in the war.[172]) The management committee at the central depot comprised mainly Protestant members of the medical profession including Harriet Reed, a nurse, William Winter, a physician, and Mrs Grenville Cole, wife of a geology professor at the RCS.[173]

Catholic and Protestant Irish women's diligence in picking moss for the humanitarian effort was reflected in the organization's success. On 23 February 1916, Henry wrote in her diary that the War Office had put *sphagnum* moss on its official list of dressings and by the end of 1918, the depot recorded that almost one million *sphagnum* dressings had been handpicked and processed in Ireland.[174] The dressings had been dispatched to sixty-one hospitals in Ireland, England, France, Italy, Egypt, Salonika, Mesopotamia and India.[175] The endeavour was so successful that Canada and America followed Ireland's lead by making *sphagnum* moss production a central part of their own war efforts.[176]

Table 3.1 shows the total number of dressings collected by the RCS in the three southern provinces from November 1915 to November 1918.[177] Dressings more than doubled from 1916 to 1918, and the biggest increase occurred in the twelve-month period, November 1916 to November 1917. This increase is impressive given the difficulties faced by the organization in 1917 and 1918, as 'the ranks of voluntary workers were necessarily depleted by the needs of the Army services, prices of all materials rose, the collection of funds became harder, and in the case

**Table 3.1** Number of *sphagnum* moss dressings collected by the RCS excluding Ulster

| Period | Number of *Sphagnum* dressings |
| --- | --- |
| November 1915–November 1916 | 183,620 |
| November 1916–November 1917 | 323,130 |
| November 1917–November 1918 | 398,889 |

of moss collectors, locomotion to and from distant bogs became an ever greater problem'.[178] Significantly, there was no decline in the number of dressings produced after April and May 1916, or even after April 1918, when a decline might have been expected had Catholic attitudes towards the war effort significantly changed. Moss production (which we have seen, attracted both Catholic and Protestant volunteers) actually increased in this period. Additional moss collecting depots, increased efficiency in production and perhaps even more collectors are all plausible explanations for the increase, but the growth is so great that one might ponder if a larger reason prompted the surge. Henry's diary does not shed light on this, and there is a gap in her records from April to November 1917. Her last entry, dated the 4–12 April 1917, affirmed the ongoing commitment of the Dublin depot, which was engaged in 'a very large output of work and all of the highest standard'.[179] The demand created for dressings by the military campaign may explain the surge, as the largest increase happened between November 1916 and November 1917, a period that coincided with the end of the Battle of Verdun (February–December 1916), the entire Battle of the Somme (July–November 1916) and the third battle of Ypres (July–November 1917), all of which would have necessitated the production of dressings long after the battles had formally ceased.

Indeed, the serious nature of the war in the final years of the conflict demanded a proportionate humanitarian response, and many Irish people offered their assistance. From 1915, the BRCS selected a day in October to be marked as 'Our Day', the aim of which was to elicit financial donations to the Red Cross. In Ireland, contributions to 'Our Day' could take place over several days and would be added together as representative of particular regions. Proceeds from the three southern provinces were amalgamated while Ulster arranged its own 'Our Day' event. Pageants, concerts and auctions were some of the activities held to encourage donations while pins, flags, badges and other objects, which depicted the Allied colours, were sold at the price of a penny (the proceeds were donated to the Red Cross). If Catholics had turned their backs on the Allies after the Rising or conscription crisis of 1918, or had significantly disengaged from the humanitarian effort, one would expect a decline in financial contributions, as the total amount raised would reflect the fact that fewer people had donated funds.

A Red Cross report issued in 1921 documented the contribution made by the three southern provinces during the Our Day events of October 1917 and October 1918, as well as proceeds raised for the same events in England and Wales.

In 1917, the total sum raised by England and Wales amounted to £341,631. The report noted that the combined population of England and Wales was 36,070,492 persons. In 1911, the population of the three southern Irish provinces was 2,808,500 (approximately one fifteenth of that of England and Wales). However, demographic differences between the Irish, English and Welsh would have influenced monies raised in Ireland. Ireland's history of emigration meant that a large share of its residents were aged under twenty or over sixty, a problem which had not affected England or Wales. Similarly, the relative wealth of England and Wales compared to that of Ireland was much greater. The report claimed that it was 'at least twenty-five times that of Ireland'. These factors should have made Ireland's financial contribution to the Our Day fund significantly less than that of England and Wales, not to mention the volatile political situation which, in some quarters, provided an environment not conducive to assisting the war effort. The report recognized these uniquely Irish challenges:

> It is common knowledge that the number of persons enjoying large incomes from commerce alone in Ireland, is, by comparison, very small. The result clearly demonstrates that Ireland's contribution to the War is *astonishingly great*. When it is recognized that a proportion of the population stood aloof, and offered no help, it will be obvious that the discrepancy is handsomely made up by the remainder.

Taking these factors into account, the report recorded that Ireland's proportionate offering should have been £13,665. 'It actually amounted to £62,600, or more than four and a half times as much.' Contributions actually increased in 1918 as the Our Day Collection

> amounted to almost £70,000 and showed excellent promise of reaching £100,000 when the Armistice was proclaimed on November 11. This naturally caused a suspension of effort. These excellent results were doubtless in large measure due to the thoroughness and efficiency with which Ireland was organized. No possible source of revenue was left untapped. Moreover, the giving by the people was on a most generous scale.[180]

Evidence from across the country supports the BRCS findings, as it reveals sustained activity to assist the Red Cross in predominantly Catholic areas during 1917 and 1918. In Clones, Co. Monaghan (1,517 Catholics/2,401 people), the October 1917 Our Day fund raised £314 8s 7d: over three times more than that raised in 1915 (a sum which 'realised over £100').[181] In Carrick-on-Shannon (1,902 Catholics/2,061 people) and Drumsna (1,150 Catholics/1,218 people), Co. Leitrim, local people raised £199 9s 7d for the October 1917 Our Day fund, which was not dissimilar to the £121 raised by the former district from November 1915 to January 1916.[182] In Drogheda, Co. Louth (11,604 Catholics/12,501 people), the comparatively large sum of £528 was generated for the Our Day fund in November 1917.[183] In Limerick (34,865 Catholics/38,518 people), over £2,000 was generated

for Our Day in September 1918: £1,000 more than a major BRCS gift sale which
took place there in January 1916.[184]

Southern Ireland's contribution was perceived by the BRCS to have been
comparable to that of Britain and the Dominions:

> Taking all the circumstances into account … there is no room for doubt that
> the total sum contributed by the three [southern Irish] provinces, in money and
> in kind, considerably exceeded half a million, a sum which would correspond
> with a contribution by Great Britain of about fourteen millions. … Aggregating
> the entire effort of the three Provinces in financial value, and by way of personal
> service, it is doubtful if any other part of His Majesty's Dominions contributed
> more generously.[185]

Other examples demonstrating an increase in support for the voluntary war effort
during the period when nationalist Ireland allegedly turned its back on the Allies
further suggest that there was a sustained and ongoing commitment to the war
effort at the same time as a political shift to Sinn Féin was happening. In Galway
during the period March 1915 to March 1916, the local War Fund generated £1,691
11s 9d for prisoners of war (POWs) from the Connaught Rangers, while from June
1917 to June 1918, approximately £1,200–1,300 was raised for the regiment.[186] This
latter subscription was in addition to the £1,523 9s 1d raised by Galway for *The
Irish Times* Red Cross appeal in December 1917 (*The Irish Times* Red Cross Fund
raised almost £63,000 from May 1917 to May 1918. From May 1918 to May 1919, it
raised £69,472.[187]) From December 1915 to June 1917, three flag days were held in
Cork city and county for war-related causes. The first raised £160 for wounded and
captured RMF soldiers, the second raised £150 for Irish soldiers (excluding the
county contribution) and the third raised £219 11s 2d for the French Red Cross.[188]

Were the contributors to these funds solely generous southern Protestants? The
evidence presented above suggests not, as Catholics can be found across Ireland in
committees that orchestrated the war effort and as donors to the cause. The BRCS
certainly did not think so, since it declared that

> contributions from Ireland represent all social grades of the people, and all
> religious denominations, Catholic and Protestant, Nationalist and Unionist,
> rich and poor, have shown in the most practical manner their loyalty to the Red
> Cross, and to War Funds subscribed to help the fighting forces of the Empire. …
> these outstanding facts are of supreme importance, especially in an atmosphere
> highly charged with political electricity.[189]

While its conclusions mask the class, religious, political and regional differences
between the Southern Irish, the BRCS believed that war-work in Ireland was
participated in by much of civil society. This chapter has demonstrated examples
of engagement from the Catholic middle classes, whether that was through VAD
work, the nursing services, the National Egg Collection scheme, sorting out moss for
bandages, hosting fundraisers or by accommodating Belgian refugees (activities in

which the upper classes also played a role), but some working-class Catholics also contributed to the forms of war-relief examined here, whether that was through the arduous work of picking moss or contributing money to the Our Day appeal. Many of these activities were cross-confessional; some were an inter-class effort; most appeared to endure throughout the duration of the war. The reinvigoration of the political question must have posed some challenges to assisting the war effort, as the example of moss-pickers in Kilgarvan might suggest, yet its consequences are hard to discern in the sustained commitment of middle-class war-workers and supporters of the humanitarian effort, who made Southern Ireland's contribution stand out within both the UK and, at times, the British Dominions. Though these examples are not sufficient to make general conclusions about Catholic feeling towards war-work across the entire period of the war, there are enough indicators to suggest greater engagement with, and consistency in, responses towards the war over the conflict's duration, despite the changing domestic political climate. One major reason behind this support was because of the conflict itself which, many people of all backgrounds feared, had come very close to home.

# Chapter 4

## THE WAR AT SEA: ENCOUNTERING THE GERMAN 'ENEMY'

Over the course of the Great War, German U-Boats sent 'over eleven million tonnes of Allied shipping to the bottom of the sea as well as inflicting damage to another seven million tonnes'. It brought Britain to the brink of a food crisis in 1917 and was a major reason why America entered the conflict on the side of the Allies in April.[1] However, not much is known about how the naval campaign impacted civilians in Ireland and the ways in which its impact was felt.[2] The little that has been written suggests that Irish farmers benefited from the war at sea, as the value of agricultural produce increased, and when German submarine activity disrupted Britain's trade with her traditional food suppliers overseas, Ireland's 'entire rural economy prospered in the course of satiating British appetites'.[3] By contrast, this chapter reveals a widespread, popular and engaged response to the effects of the naval campaign that went far beyond financial gain, as both rural and urban communities mobilized to render support for the Allies. In 1917 and 1918, rural Ireland mobilized to safeguard Ireland itself, when the country appeared to be under imminent threat by the German U-Boat. From helping Allied victims of war and demonstrating solidarity with the bereaved, to increasing production of agricultural goods and donating funds for victims of German submarine warfare, Irish communities were highly engaged with the war at sea over the conflict's duration, and from mid-1915, a wide range of individuals and groups came to believe that Germany was an enemy that had to be defeated.

### Bringing Ireland within the war zone

From almost as soon as the conflict began, rumours about a possible German invasion circulated in Ireland, though it was not clear to people in the early months of war exactly how the Germans proposed to invade. For a time, the British military authorities feared that German nationals had already infiltrated the UK, as 60 per cent of arrests of foreign suspects under the 1911 Official Secrets Act occurred in August 1914 while the remainder were made in October and November.[4] The authorities encouraged people to beware of the 'enemy within' and provincial newspapers echoed these claims. The unionist *Cork Constitution* warned readers about possible German agents in Cork disguised as 'spies acting as musicians'.[5] In

January 1915, Dublin and Cork Corporations withdrew the honour of freedom of the city from Dr Kuno Meyer, a German scholar of literature and Celtic philology, because he made a pro-German speech in New York.[6] In May, the agricultural newspaper, *The Clare Journal*, did not protest when the German-born subjects, Mr Josef Fehrenbach, a Catholic watchmaker and repairer in Ennistymon, and Francis Augustus Esch, the Catholic manager of the 'Golf Links Hotel' in Lahinch, were arrested alongside the Austrian-born businessman, Franx Bittar, simply commenting that they were 'removed by train to Old Castle, Westmeath, to be interned'.[7] Long-term residency in Ireland, eminence in local social life or even being Catholics were not enough to allay suspicions that those of German and Austrian extraction were 'enemies' of the Irish people – an attitude held against immigrants that was displayed across wartime Europe, as 'spy fever transformed many of these foreigners into citizens of enemy nationality'.[8]

Total war had opened up different avenues from which the Germans could invade, and this generated uncertainty. In January 1915, the republican, Liam de Roiste, wrote in his diary that 'the country people of ... the whole south coast of Cork are very much perturbed since yesterday. The police have intimated to them, in case of a German invasion, the military orders are, they must, at an hour's notice, move with all their portable possessions, to Mallow and destroy hay etc'.[9] Even republicans were uncertain what to do if Germany were to invade, though some publicly cultivated the notion that Germany was Ireland's friend in the advanced nationalist press. Seán T. O'Kelly, honorary secretary of Sinn Féin, recalled that at a meeting of the Irish Republican Brotherhood in September 1914, Arthur Griffith, founder of Sinn Féin, and the other men present, 'decided to accept an offer of German help if it was forthcoming but to fight German troops if they landed without invitation'.[10]

In 1914 and early 1915, there was concern regarding whether Germany might invade from the sky. The independent-nationalist *Irish Independent* printed several articles about the modern airship, the German Zeppelin. On 11 September 1914, it published the comments of a German-American correspondent who claimed that the Germans had engaged thousands of workmen to build Zeppelins at Krupps, the prestigious German armaments manufacturer, with the aim of occupying Calais to carry out 'a zeppelin invasion of England'. The *Independent* was so affected by this prospect that it printed the story three times in a single issue![11] Speculation became worry when Irish newspapers debated whether the ship had the functional capabilities to reach Ireland, and there is some evidence to suggest that local communities believed that it could, such as in February 1916, when 'several residents rushed into the street' in the largely Catholic town of Askeaton, Co. Limerick because they had heard 'loud noises'.[12] The nationalist *Limerick Leader* reported that they were 'alarmed and much frightened, and they [thought] a Zepelin [sic] or some other hostile threat was paying a visit to the town'.[13]

However, most of the discussion regarding Zeppelins revolved around Germany's plan to invade England, and when German bombs were dropped on English towns in 1915 and 1916, anger against Germany was provoked in some quarters.[14] Following the loss of life in the January 1916 bombardment of the

English Midlands, the nationalist *Connacht Tribune* condemned it as evidence of 'Prussian Methods'.[15] It implied that the attacks were evidence of the aggressive form of militarism which, in the eighteenth century, had underlined the expansion of Prussian state and society but by the time of the Great War had been equated with a lust for power allegedly desired by all Germans.[16] This perceived aggression was what the Allies had (supposedly) mobilized to 'defend' the world against and such attacks gave legitimacy to the notion of German 'barbarism'.

However, the real threat of German invasion came from the sea. Liam and John Nolan have argued that Queenstown, Co. Cork (renamed Cobh following independence), played an important part in the conflict that has gone unacknowledged in the histories of the war. This was reflected in an editorial by the London *Times*, which on 17 June 1919, declared that 'the part that Queenstown played during the Great War is not generally known, by reason of the very necessary veil of secrecy that was drawn over its work'.[17] *The Times* was referring to the plans drawn up by Winston Churchill, First Lord of the Admiralty, who in early 1915 requisitioned 'an assortment of tramp-steamers, fishing trawlers and sailing ships' which were to act as decoys to German submarines following the loss of British shipping in 1914.[18] These vessels aimed to draw submarines closer to them and contained a hidden team of gunners which would fire upon the submarines when in range. The vessels were designated 'Q' ships because they were stationed at Queenstown.[19]

In February 1915, most of the waterways surrounding Ireland were open to German attack.[20] German submarines initially headed for Ireland via the Dover Straits, but when this was cut off by the British, marauding U-Boats had to take the northern route around Scotland and down the Irish west coast. Submarine commanders found the waters between Fastnet, a small islet at the southernmost point of Cork, and Waterford in the southeast, 'to be especially rich in targets in their devastating campaign to cut off Britain's supplies and starve her into submission'.[21] The Germans actually nicknamed this stretch of water 'Torpedo Alley' due to its success in bringing about British losses.[22]

An analysis of the Galway-based nationalist newspaper, the *Connacht Tribune*, illuminates the growing concern among coastal residents about the proximity of German submarines to Ireland. This concern began to develop in February 1915 when the newspaper printed a large article entitled 'Submarines in the Irish Sea. War Coming Near Our Shores'. It reported that a German U-Boat had sunk trawlers off the Antrim coast of Larne but commended the 'considerate' actions of the German commander who gave the crews ten minutes to escape before firing upon the vessels.[23] This was in accordance with the rules of the sea, as the Germans had followed the principle that attacking vessels must make provision for the enemy's civilian crew before they fired upon it.[24]

However, when the Germans realized that 'Q' ships contained weapons, the rules of the sea changed and submarines 'began a policy of shooting first and asking questions later'.[25] The *Tribune*'s attitude changed accordingly. Commendation became condemnation when submarine attacks killed 112 people on the British steamers, the *SS Falaba* and *SS Aguila*, which were torpedoed in April 1915. The *Tribune* called it 'deliberate murder' and remarked on the Germans' 'frightfulness'.[26]

By early May, the newspaper had aligned itself against Germany and when the *Fulgent* was torpedoed near Co. Kerry killing two people, it wrote of 'the murder policy of the modern Hun'.[27]

Events were simultaneously happening on the Western Front which were lending credence to the notion of German 'barbarity'. This discourse had some currency in Ireland ever since the sacking of Louvain in August 1914 and was revived again in April and May 1915 in light of renewed German attacks. When the Germans first used poisonous gas against the French and Canadians in April 1915, newspapers of both political persuasions called it 'brutal' and 'barbaric'.[28] The *Independent* described the use of gas as 'a method of warfare up to now never employed by nations sufficiently civilized to consider themselves bound by international agreements'.[29] Germany was perceived to have sealed its reputation as a breaker of international treaties, firstly, through its violation of Belgian neutrality, which the German Chancellor, Theobald von Bethmann-Hollweg, had famously and controversially described as a 'scrap of paper', and, secondly, through its use of poisonous gas, which, though it was not specifically outlawed at the time, was perceived to have been contrary to the 1899 and 1907 Hague Conventions.[30]

Germany's desecration of international treaties was further confirmed by the manner in which it was perceived to have violated the rules of the sea, and though Britain had also dishonoured these rules, the popular notion was sealed that only Germany was waging war against innocent civilians rather than fighting in a righteous and 'legal' manner in line with accepted methods of warfare. The 'turning point' – insofar as it deepened and confirmed the prejudices whipped up in wartime 1914 – in Irish opinion against Germany was on the 7 May 1915, when the U-20 torpedoed the New York-Liverpool bound passenger liner, the *RMS Lusitania*, off the coast of Cork. Out of the 2,000 people aboard 1,198 passengers were killed, a number of whom were children. This death toll was comparable to the approximately 1,500 people who died on the *Titanic* in 1912. The latter was a tragedy which reverberated for the next hundred years and haunted the modern imagination; the former was indeed exploited by the media at the time but was forgotten at some stage in the post-war years. In mid-1915 however, it was perceived to have been more horrific than the *Titanic* disaster because it was the result of a deliberate attack on civilians rather than an accident – the equivalent, at the time, of mass murder. It came just days after the use of poisonous gas on the Western Front and the day before German submarines sunk two steamers near Waterford, the *SS Centurion* and the *SS Candidate*.[31]

However, there has been no systematic exploration of how Irish Catholics responded to the sinking of the *Lusitania*, and a number of major scholarly works on the war and Ireland have neglected to discuss the tragedy at all.[32] When the event has been recorded, it has been in the context of advanced nationalist reactions to the propaganda generated by the British government in the aftermath of the ship's demise. When the question was asked as to whether Irish nationalists believed the advanced nationalist version of events, which assumed British culpability, or the British accounts, which identified Germany as the aggressor, Irish radicals were thought to have been more successful, since they 'drew on a deep folk tradition [which reinforced the notion of English oppression to Ireland] to produce images that already had achieved the status of icons'.[33] The radicals' interpretation of events won the hearts and minds of the people because they had 'facts' about England's hostility towards Ireland whereas the British did not have a litany of German abuses towards the Irish to substantiate their claims regarding the *Lusitania*.

However, when popular reactions to the ship's demise are explored, it is clear that many people at the time believed that Germany was at fault. Nearly all of the provincial nationalist newspapers devoted prominent space to the tragedy in their columns.[34] The *Cork Examiner*, which toed the Redmondite line, was stringent in its condemnation: 'Huns Awful Crime Lusitania Torpedoed Off Cork Harbour'.[35] The unionist *Irish Times* printed a large sketch of the ship with the caption, 'Lusitania Torpedoed. Great Liner Sinks in Eight Minutes. Feared Loss of Over 1,300 Lives. 600 Survivors Landed At Queenstown'.[36] Yet it was the response of the *Independent* that is the most striking. Its headline was similar since it called the attack upon 'hundreds of non-combatants … murderous'.[37] However, it was this organ that produced an artist's impression of the sinking ship which became the centrepiece for British propagandists. As Figure 4.1 reveals, the newspaper's artist sketched a Union Jack on the *Lusitania*'s stern.

The illustration has been discussed in at least one historical work, which has concluded that the flag 'was perhaps a slight error of judgement on an Irish poster' because the author believed that the artist was British.[38] That the designer was actually a member of the *Irish Independent* staff reveals that the choice of flag was deliberate, reinforcing to Catholic readers the righteousness of Britain's cause in mid-1915. Throughout Ireland, editorials discussed the calamity and the discourse

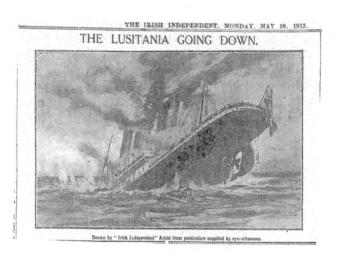

THE IRISH INDEPENDENT, MONDAY, MAY 10, 1915.

THE LUSITANIA GOING DOWN.

Drawn by "Irish Independent" Artist from particulars supplied by eye-witnesses.

**Figure 4.1** *Irish Independent* artist's impression of the sinking *Lusitania*. The Union Jack is visible. Courtesy of the Irish Newspaper Archives.

of German barbarity was widespread. *The Irish Times* exclaimed that 'Germany's crowning act of piracy has been accompanied by murder on a large scale and of the most cowardly kind'.[39] The *Limerick Leader* compared 'Germany's appalling crime' to the *Titanic* and could not believe that Germany 'would be found diabolical and inhuman enough to commit a tragedy even more horrible than that terrible accident'. It blamed the act upon German '*Kultur*', which was allegedly a specific form of German culture intent upon achieving imperial dominance.[40] The *Clare Journal*, which tended to report on agricultural affairs, wrote of 'the latest German horror ... acts of the Nation of Kultur'. It used medieval inferences to find Germany's 'Teuton character' at fault.[41] The *Connacht Tribune* found its fullest expression of anger to date. It drew upon the discourse of anti-Semitism, which had currency in nationalist thought since at least the Limerick boycott of 1904, to proclaim that 'Germany today stands as the Ismaelite amongst all civilized nations'. It evoked a comparison with the most despised aspects of Irish history, stating that 'the reign of Cromwell in Ireland, bad as it was, and in an age of greater savagery and license, scarcely supplies a parallel for the horrors that Belgium has been made to bear at the hands of the Huns'.[42]

Did these editorials reflect the opinion of local populations? The evidence suggests that they did, particularly as the catastrophe was the first time that innocents had been killed so close to Ireland on such a large scale. The following day, the Catholic coroner, Thomas Butterfield, who later became the Lord Mayor, held an inquest at Kinsale courthouse and the jury was 'made up of local fishermen and shopkeepers'.[43] No list of the members of the jury has survived, but the composition of the relevant groups in Cork suggests that it must have comprised several Catholics. For there were 1,923 fishermen in Cork in 1911 (1,850 Catholics: 73 Protestants) and 831 shopkeepers (763 Catholics: 68 Protestants), thus suggesting that the jury comprised Protestant and Catholic representatives.[44] Upon examining five bodies and having questioned Captain Turner, who commanded the fated vessel, John Horgan, the coroner and a prominent Nationalist, announced the jury's verdict. He 'charged the emperor of Germany, the German government, and the officers of the submarine with wilful murder'.[45] This judgement inspired renewed anger and both the Redmondite and independent-nationalist press found Germany irredeemable.[46]

One reason why the Kinsale verdict was reached was because several of the fated civilians were Irish. One victim was the national icon, Hugh Lane, a Protestant who was an art collector and director of the National Gallery of Ireland, a nephew of the well-known Irish dramatist, Lady Gregory.[47] Both the *Independent* and *Irish Times* dedicated obituaries to him and his loss was felt among Southern Protestants, who wrote letters of sympathy to *The Irish Times*.[48] The Catholic Countess of Fingall recalled the last time she saw him 'before he went down in the Lusitania', demonstrating that the trauma was still with her when she published her memoirs in 1937.[49] Less prominent persons were also victims. The *Connacht Tribune* reported at least fourteen missing locals.[50] The Midlands nationalist newspaper, *The Anglo-Celt*, reported three missing persons, while the nationalist *Ulster Herald* claimed that in Limavady, Co. Derry, a mother and daughter had been aboard and while the daughter had been saved, the mother was still missing.[51]

The local impact of the *Lusitania* tragedy upon Irish communities was heightened by the survivors' stories which flooded the press in subsequent days. Headlines such as 'A Dublin Doctor's Story', 'Saved from Lusitania. Cavan Passengers' Experience', 'Exiled Kerry Couple Returning Home Lose All But Are Safe' and 'A Donegal Survivor' showed its impact on families across Ireland.[52] Horrific stories were recounted in full and did not shy away from gruesome details, though an element of sensationalism characterized some accounts. For instance, one Catholic farmer from Sligo and native Irish speaker, James Battle, told the *Independent* that 'nobody could know the horror of that time. ... A man was clinging to my legs with one hand, his other hand and arm from above the elbow was hanging off.'[53] Many victims were emigrants returning to Ireland from the United States. Their loss added further moral and national pathos to the calamity, tied up as these victims were in the lamentable history of Irish emigration. An American doctor told *The Kerryman* that he had been chatting to Patrick O'Carroll from Dundalk, a bricklayer in Chicago who had been 'going home to see his father in Dundalk after an absence of 30 years'. O'Carroll was missing.[54]

One reason behind the intensity and vividness of Irish anger was the visual evidence of destruction. Hundreds of bodies were brought to Queenstown in the aftermath of the event and the importance of this shock factor for cultivating bitterness against Germany has gone unacknowledged. 'Queenstown became the town of the dead as the temporary morgues filled with bodies.'[55] Three mass graves were dug for over a hundred victims in a Queenstown cemetery. Sixty-eight of the gravediggers were members of the 4th (Extra Reserve) Battalion Royal Irish Regiment, which had been formed of volunteers in Kilkenny during August 1914. Figure 4.2 shows them digging the graves. Irish civilians that had enlisted, not regular soldiers, were thus given their first taste of German atrocities in Ireland rather than in France or Belgium. Images of the mass graves were printed in the national press, bringing visual evidence of the tragedy to readers across the country. The local press was similarly preoccupied as on the 12 May, the *Cork Examiner* published a photograph entitled 'The Murdered Innocents' which showed three rows of clothed bodies on the floor of a morgue in Cork.[56]

The press was not the only medium through which the *Lusitania* tragedy was conveyed. Though difficult to capture retrospectively, eyewitness accounts and rumours would have been powerful mobilizers of public opinion expressed at the time. Cork civilians would have disseminated both word of the German attack and depictions of the *Lusitania* dead. Diary entries hint at the shock which permeated Cork society, as the Protestant businessman, John Bennett, recorded in his diary that the tragedy 'caused great sensation. Many bodies landed at Queenstown.'[57] Charles Brett, a Belfast Episcopalian who had already enlisted, was in Cork at the time. He recalled that 'farm carts came up from the harbour to the Military hospital each piled high with corpses, many of them women in light dresses, it was a horrible thing to see, and made a deep impression on me, giving me a bitter dislike for all Germans and a desire to kill as many as possible'.[58] Many locals were able to see the deceased first-hand and 'a morbid fascination drew people to the

**Figure 4.2**  Members of the Royal Irish Regiment dig graves in Queenstown. Also published in *II*, 10 May 1915. Courtesy of the National Library of Ireland.

morgues to witness the grim trophies of war [as] nude and semi-nude corpses lay in rows all around'.[59] A harrowing sight was the rows of infants who awaited identification. *The Cork Examiner* printed images of a local morgue in which the remains of a boy aged perhaps eleven to thirteen years were clearly visible (Figure 4.3).[60] Images such as Figures 4.4 and 4.5 shocked the eyewitnesses that visited the morgue. This striking evidence of what the Germans had done to innocent women and children – evidence that was reported in both the press and spread via word of mouth by the people who saw the *Lusitania* dead – lent substance to the pre-existing gendered discourse which claimed that Germany was deliberately targeting women and children – a discourse which had already been depicted in British recruiting posters as a propagandistic incentive for men to enlist.[61]

Irish civil society's response was therefore significant. Charles E. Lauriat, an American survivor, recalled that 'I found the people [of Queenstown] furious through the act itself'. This recollection corresponds with the contemporary newspaper evidence, as does Lauriat's description of local people's willingness to support victims and survivors. He noted, 'When we went up the street in Queenstown it was filled with people willing to help and do anything in their power to relieve our sufferings. I have heard stories of Scottish hospitality, but I never saw anything more spontaneous or genuine or more freely given that the Irish hospitality of Queenstown.'[62]

Mourning was one way to demonstrate solidarity with the victims, and sympathy was both sincere and widespread. Resolutions of condolences to the American consul were recorded in the minutes of most public bodies.[63] On the day of the

**Figure 4.3** The Catholic cemetery at Queenstown. The Bishop of Cloyne, Robert Browne, is the prelate in white. Hutton Archive, Getty Images. Versions of this photograph also appeared in the *II* and *CE*, 11 May 1915.

**Figure 4.4** Children lay 'doll-like' in morgues. O'Sullivan, *Lusitania*, p. 81. I spoke with Patrick O'Sullivan, who originally published Figures 4.4 and 4.5, to find out if these pictures could have been doctored in any way. He categorically said that they were not. Reproduced with the kind permission of The Collins Press.

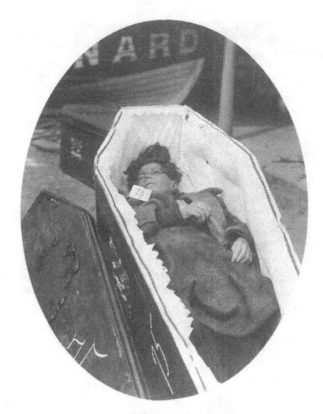

**Figure 4.5** Unknown woman awaiting identification. O'Sullivan, *Lusitania*, p. 81. The Collins Press.

mass burials, 'a very large congregation including many friends of the victims and survivors attended St Colman's Catholic Church' and an 'impressive memorial service' was held in the Protestant Church, followed by a 'huge funeral' which was a 'most imposing and impressive function … all the shops were closed and blinds drawn while the cortege passed through the streets'.[64] The funeral cortege was reported to have been at least two miles in length. Soldiers stood to attention on both sides of the road while local people stood on the ditches listening to a band of the Royal Irish Regiment play Chopin's *Funeral March*.[65] The spectators appeared to have worn their best outfits, most obvious in the number of women's hats and smartly dressed men, as people expressed solidarity with the victims and families of the *Lusitania* dead. The coffins of American victims were draped in the national flag while those of the British victims displayed the Union Flag (see Figure 4.6). These national symbols reinforced the virtue of the Allied cause to the mourners. Military and naval troops lined the streets for the cortege while Catholic and Protestant clergymen read services at the gravesides together. Cork INV offered its condolences to the American ambassador, who 'expressed his most intense appreciation of the spirit which had animated the people of the south of Ireland'.[66]

**Figure 4.6** The extensive line of mourners. The Union Flag covers the coffin on the first hearse. Hutton Archive, Getty Images.

Sympathy for the *Lusitania* victims was expressed elsewhere in Ireland, demonstrating that the tragedy was also felt outside of Cork and among different sections of people. Many public bodies passed resolutions of sympathy including members of the United Irish League (UIL) in Mayo, a movement that underpinned the IPP which supported additional land reform in Ireland; urban councils in Louth and Tralee; working and middle-class employees' unions including the Dublin Railway Clerks' Association, the city of Dublin's Public Libraries Committee, Kiltimagh Teachers' Association in Mayo, Kildare Working Men's Association and Clare Committee of Agriculture; Tralee Harbour Commissioners in Co. Kerry and boards of guardians in north Dublin, Limerick, Ennis and Kilrush.[67] A wide cross section of society, including administrators of the Poor Law (the system of poverty relief that had been in place since the Irish Poor Law Act of 1838), thus demonstrated their solidarity with the victims. Most described the act as 'barbaric' and some individuals called for vengeance, such as the resolution proposed by Cornelius Quilligan, a Catholic on the Limerick board of guardians and a tea, wine and spirit merchant, which was unanimously endorsed:

Such an inhuman outrage, and such reckless disregard of the laws of civilized warfare will only nerve us to greater determination to continue the war until we shall, in association with our gallant Allies, have not only vindicated the rights of human liberty, but shall also have avenged the hideous crimes committed by our enemies on the soil of France and Belgians, and on the waters of the ocean.[68]

Similarly, P. E. Kenneally, the Catholic chairman of Ennis Urban Council who later joined the British forces, condemned the act 'in the strongest possible manner' and stated that 'it was the duty of everyone to do all that they could, to put a stop as soon as possible to the terrible warfare; and it was the duty of every Irishman, he did not care what his creed or politics might be, to do all they could to put a stop to such things'.[69] The *Connacht Tribune*, which only three months earlier had been moderate in its appraisal of the Germans, now turned the inquest's verdict of 'wilful and wholesale murder' into a policy which should be conducted against Germany: 'The day will yet come when that verdict will have to be met, and those who lend their help to the Allies will hasten that day'.[70] The *Irish Times* expressed a similar desire, as the editor declared that 'so far as this country is concerned, it will be sternly and infallibly avenged. If Germany thought to frighten us by this outrage, she has made a fatal mistake'.[71]

A national relief fund was set up for victims' families which raised £462 3s 10d by 17 June 1915, a relatively small sum when compared with, for example, the £5,636 raised in Ireland between 27 May 1916 and 8 July 1916 for the Irish National Aid Association and Volunteer Dependants' Fund (INAVDF), a fund inaugurated to help the dependants of the Easter Rising rebels.[72] However, unlike the latter subscription, the victims of the *Lusitania* were largely English and American nationals. Many individuals felt moved to donate funds to citizens of other nationalities and subscribers straddled all classes, creeds and ages, including Sir Lambert Ormsby, a Protestant New Zealander and surgeon in Meath Hospital, the Protestant Countess of Mayo, the Catholic Mother General of Loreto Abbey in Rathfarnham and 'A Poor Irish Girl'.[73] Archbishop William Walsh of Dublin even gave £10 10s and called the tragedy 'that horrid massacre'.[74]

While doubt exists regarding how effective British *Lusitania* propaganda was in motivating Irish men to fight,[75] it is clear that the tragedy itself was a crucial stimulus. Martin Staunton has argued that it was one of many motivations which prompted men to join the largely Catholic RMF.[76] Similarly on the west coast, the *Connacht Tribune* reported that 'the atrocity of the Lusitania's fate ... had a magnetic effect in drawing men into the army'. At the Whitehall recruiting office in Galway 'there was a steady stream of men in or about 30 years of age from foundries and shops eagerly joining the army, and even men up to 55 years of age'.[77] Even in the Irish Midlands, the *Anglo-Celt* noted that 'the sinking of the Lusitania has given a great spurt to recruiting'.[78] The tragedy was also important for motivating some men who had already joined up, such as the northern Protestant, Brett, who was given 'a definite incentive' to fight when he witnessed the *Lusitania* dead.[79]

The shock factor of the *Lusitania* persisted long after the event, partly because victims continued to wash up on Irish shores for days and weeks on end. Rosamond Stephen, a London-born Irish Anglican who lived in Belfast, recorded in her diary on 21 July 1915 that 'three bodies were washed up in Kerry, two at Castlegregory near Tralee, and one at Glenbeigh'. Two more bodies washed up the following day. Her comments regarding the reactions of Kerry people, most of whom would have been Catholics from the working and lower-middle classes, further suggest that many Catholics from different backgrounds believed that Germany was at fault: 'The country people look at it that all that is the Kaiser's own work, and I am not sure that they are wrong.'[80] This attitude also existed in the west of Ireland, as the Mayo conservative newspaper, *The Connaught Telegraph*, cultivated the notion that it was now essential to stop Germany from invading Ireland: 'Those who tell us that this is England's war are liars. The whole future of our country is at stake. ... We have seen enough of the war to know what will happen if the Huns gain a foothold in Ireland.'[81] Remembrance of the tragedy in Dublin reinforced the notion of 'German culpability'. On 5 April 1916, a raft from the ship was borne on a float through the city centre, which was accompanied by reserve cavalry and Trinity College Dublin OTC. The *Limerick Leader* declared that 'thousands of spectators' watched the procession. A prominent streamer floating above the raft declared: 'A Souvenir of Germany's Brutality. The raft to which defenceless men and women clung.'[82]

From early 1915, the war at sea thus brought the Irish firmly within the war zone, making the possibility of a German invasion more real. The torpedoing of the *RMS Lusitania* occurred at a time when the discourse of German barbarism had been revived in Ireland and the deaths of so many innocents, some of whom were Irish, hardened a range of people from both Catholic and Protestant backgrounds against Germany, which individuals and sections of civil society considered an 'enemy' that had to be defeated. Anger and contempt were expressed by the middle and working classes in urban Ireland but the war at sea also impacted largely Catholic rural Ireland, encouraging a cross section of people to believe in German wrongdoing because of a perceived threat to Irish life.

## Rural Ireland and 'Black '47'

Irish farmers may have chosen to assist the British war effort because of the financial return on food production,[83] but an inducement much closer to home was a crucial factor as well. From December 1916 to April 1917, a period that encompassed the resumption of German unrestricted submarine warfare, the Irish were seriously concerned that Germany would stop imports and precipitate a food shortage in Ireland. While the British also had this concern, the Irish had a traumatic history which made this possibility even more frightening.

The death of one million people during the Great Famine – the series of successive potato failures during the 1840s that killed almost one-eighth of the entire Irish population – was still within living memory, and the horror of this tragedy was magnified by nationalist accounts passed on to later generations.[84] The fear of a second Great Famine, this being a widely acknowledged possibility, caused rural Ireland to mobilize to an unprecedented scale, and the magnificent response of farmers (large and small), landholders and labourers to the pending food crisis reveals that these groups were prepared to prevent the country from starvation.

Powerful interests in Irish civil society took up the task of encouraging rural Ireland to cultivate more food, including the Catholic Church, and leading clerics used their influential positions to bring home the reality of the crisis to rural Irish men and women. This was evident in speeches and in the Lenten pastorals of 1917, when almost *all* of the higher clergy urged farmers to produce more tillage, including Cardinal Michael Logue, and the following bishops and archbishops: Denis Kelly (the Bishop of Ross); Thomas O'Dea (the Bishop of Galway, Kilmacduagh and Kilfenora); Joseph Hoare (the Bishop of Ardagh and Clonmacnoise); Jacob Naughton (the Bishop of Killala); James Browne (the Bishop of Ferns); Michael Fogarty (the Bishop of Killaloe); Robert Browne (the Bishop of Cloyne); Patrick McKenna (the Bishop of Clogher); Patrick Foley (the Bishop of Kildare and Leighlin); Patrick O'Donnell (the Bishop of Raphoe) and Patrick Finegan (the Bishop of Kilmore).[85] Bishop Browne of Cloyne urged 'farmers, cottage-holders, and labourers' in Queenstown to grow more 'food in Ireland to stave off a threatened famine in the near future'.[86] Bishop Finegan warned a large attendance of Cavan farmers that 'if this [tillage] be not attended to what happened in 1847 may happen again'.[87] Cardinal Logue stated that 'if talk does not quickly give place to very energetic action, we may be prepared for something little short of famine'.[88] The *Independent* discussed their pastorals under the headline: 'Bishops and Food Peril. Urgent Need of More Tillage. The Lesson of "Black '47"'.[89] The significance of the food crisis was revealed when only four bishops used their pastorals to discuss the fall-out among nationalists as a result of the Rising, a situation which had been created by the growing prominence of Sinn Féin as a challenge to the IPP. These included Patrick Morrisroe of Achonry, Jacob Naughton of Killala, John Harty (the Archbishop of Cashel) and Thomas Gilmartin of Clonfert. However, *ten bishops* discussed the tillage scheme, suggesting that it was the more immediate concern of the higher clergy in February 1917.[90]

Outside of the Catholic Church, famine was a widespread concern, and groups and individuals evoked memories of 1847. Jas Higgins, a representative of the Evicted Tenants' Association, spoke at a meeting of Blackrock Urban Council in Dublin where he stressed that it was 'most urgent that there should be a return to the land if the famine days were not to be repeated'.[91] The chairman of the Co. Louth Farmers' Association called a meeting to discuss how best farmers might increase tillage and the question of the hour was 'were they to have famine'.[92] Editorials and letters in nationalist newspapers reflected this fear in titles such as 'The Potato Famine Discussed ... Ireland to protect her food supply and not starve as in 1847'; 'Towards Famine'; 'Food or Famine in 1917' and 'The First Echoes of the Famine'.[93] Southern Protestants were not immune to the potential food crisis. J. F. Williamson, a land agent from Mallow in Co. Cork, wrote to *The Irish Times* that 'the food problem of Ireland may easily prove to be a matter of life or death to the country' and that Ireland's chief agricultural instrument, the spade, was 'absolutely useless for the deep subselling [sic] required [and was] far too antique in this terrible emergency'.[94]

The Bishop of Ross whose diocese was centred around Cork, which had experienced the *Lusitania* tragedy and thus had direct experience of German submarine attacks, urged parishioners to cultivate more food, positioning the war at sea as a threat to Irish life:

> You live along the southern seaboard of Ireland. You are aware of your own knowledge that the ships carrying food for man and beast are being sunk. Many of you have seen with your own eyes the destructive operations, the wreckage and dead bodies washed ashore; and also, happily, living members of the rescued crews.
> ... It is no longer a question of money-making, it is now a question of living.[95]

The *Independent* blamed Germany for the crisis. It declared in its editorial that if the war were to become 'a starvation match' between Germany and her enemies, 'the submarine might place Germany in a position to dictate terms'. It concluded that 'nothing should now be left undone which would help to avert the danger of famine'.[96]

Fears of a food shortage were acute as crop failures were not uncommon in wartime. At a meeting of Oughterard Guardians in Co. Galway, the committee discussed the potato crop failure in Connemara in 1916 with one representative stating that 'in her district there would be scarcely any potatoes about the 1st January [1917]'.[97] Shortages were discussed with regularity and headlines read 'Essential Foods. Serious Shortage in Ireland'; 'Food Shortage in Achill' and 'Milk Supply in Danger'.[98] Food supply problems were severe in remote areas such as Donegal.[99] The unpredictability of Irish weather troubled the stability of crop yields, such as when a tremendous rainstorm in summer 1917 worried the inhabitants of Athlone, Dublin and elsewhere that 'the main crop potato for miles is submerged'.[100] Concern for the urban poor was widespread, especially the impact of milk shortages upon pregnant mothers.[101] While these concerns also troubled the Irish before and after the war, the difference was that in wartime, imports could no longer be relied upon to compensate for crop failures and nutritional deficiencies. This was highlighted in editorials, as the *Independent* demanded that 'people must pay serious heed to the submarine warfare and its effects on shipping and on our food and other supplies', while the *Connacht Tribune* warned readers that due to the German 'submarine danger ... we can depend very little on imports from abroad, as there is a very big shortage in the stocks available in foreign and Colonial countries'.[102]

Many groups of people mobilized to safeguard their local food supplies, and meetings were held across urban and rural Ireland to address the looming crisis. Some of the bodies which discussed tactics to prevent famine included the urban councils of Dungannon (Tyrone), Enniskillen (Fermanagh), Athy (Kildare), Rathmines (Dublin), Blackrock (Dublin) and Pembroke (Dublin); Limerick County Council; Belfast and Drogheda corporations; the rural councils of Dunshaughlin (Meath), Carrick-on-Shannon No. 1 (Leitrim) and Derry No. 2, as well as representatives of Cork and Tipperary boards of guardians.[103]

At a time when many nationalists were still rankled by the government's handling of the Dublin rebellion, it is interesting to find that in several of these meetings, some Catholics reconciled their rancour with asking the government for help. In

January 1917, Athy Urban Council asked the government 'to compel landowners to till 10 p.c. [per cent] of their holdings and 20 p.c. [per cent] of their grass lands'. One member said that 'defaulters should be brought up under the Realm Act, and sent to jail'. Drogheda Harbour Board called upon its local MPs and the prime minister to take steps to increase Irish food production. Carrick-on-Shannon No. 1 Rural Council 'unanimously asked the government to commandeer non-residential holdings and large ranches for those who did not own land in order to amass food supplies'.[104] Farmers from Louth, Dublin and Westmeath called for the government to fix food prices.[105] In Louth, they also wished to know if they could temporarily hire soldiers for farm labour.[106] Drogheda Corporation went even further in its call for government intervention. Michael McGowan, the president of the Trades Council and later Mayor of Drogheda, moved a resolution 'that the police and military be empowered to seize all stocks of potatoes withheld from market'.[107] This he later amended, but his point was made. Strong government interference was deemed necessary to prevent a national food shortage. Other sections of Catholic civil society also advocated government assistance. In his Lenten pastoral of 1917, Bishop Foley urged 'cooperation with the authorities in the efforts to provide food for the people'.[108]

Some prominent Catholics, who tried to prevent a possible food shortage, believed that the UIL would provide an effective way to organize rural Irish opinion, and branches were mobilized to promote tillage schemes in, for example, Limerick, Galway, Cavan and Longford.[109] Bishop Finegan attended a public meeting of Cavan UIL and stated that 'there is an organization at hand through which the people can speak and act – the United Irish League'. He urged farmers to flock into it to 'ensure that their representatives in Parliament and the leaders of the organization would devise a policy' to press on the government.[110] The IPP played an important role in the tillage campaign since it organized a Food Control Committee which took forward a resolution to the government calling for compulsory tillage, which some bodies, such as Rathkeale Board of Guardians in Limerick, had advocated.[111] At a time when any hint of the word 'compulsion' triggered fears about enforced military service,[112] it is notable that the Irish adopted the word themselves to mobilize support for extra tillage through the threat of state involvement.

Talk soon turned into action. By 6 January 1917, the government had introduced compulsory tillage, which required labourers to till an extra 10 per cent of their holdings.[113] The penalty for disobeying the order was state requisitioning of the land, which would then be shared among compliant farmers and labourers until additional tillage was no longer necessary, a penalty which, one would think, would have been harshly criticized if applied in provincial nationalist Ireland, where the struggle for land ownership had generated a revolution in proprietorship from 1879 to 1903, yet this policy had been specifically requested by some members of Catholic civil society.[114] Likewise, as Irish farmers had demanded, prices were fixed for wheat, oats and potatoes. Some Southern Protestants feared that Ireland may not be able to meet the government's demands due to the number of Irish labourers, many of whom were Catholic, serving at the front. An Anglican land agent from Cork, Robert Sanders, wrote to the *Irish Independent* that 'the best men in Munster of the farm-labouring class have joined the army'.[115]

Despite these fears, individuals of both creeds encouraged their rural counterparts to adhere to the scheme and prominent individuals cultivated the notion that in doing so, they were undertaking a national obligation. DATI, which played a prominent role in the campaign and whose membership included both Protestants and Catholics, published advertisements which framed the tillage scheme as a 'national duty'. These propagandistic announcements concluded that 'there need be no scarcity of food if the Irish farmers do their duty and they will'.[116] Different sections of civil society believed that increased food production was a national obligation. Newspapers, such as the Redmondite *Limerick Leader*, declared that cultivating additional tillage was 'the duty of the hour'.[117] The *Independent* believed that increased food production reflected 'a desire to be doing something useful as a contribution to the required national effort'.[118] Prelates, such as Bishop Finegan, described the production of more tillage 'as a duty of patriotism and prudence'. Bishop Foley adopted metaphors used to attract Irish men to Kitchener's New Armies, declaring that 'it remains for every citizen to respond to the call in the great crisis' and that every man should do his 'duty of helping his country and God grant there would be no shirkers'.[119] Rural interest groups interpreted the scheme in terms of patriotism and loyalty as well. The County Galway Farmers' Association passed a resolution stating that more tillage was 'a duty they owed to the nation'.[120] At a similar meeting in Mullingar, Co. Westmeath, where Catholics including James J. Coen (a brewers' agent and chairman of Westmeath County Council), Robert Downes (a farmer and the former council chairman) and Protestants including A. E. Gray and John David Fetherstonhaugh (a retired army colonel) attended, both groups agreed upon a resolution which had been written by the Bishop of Meath, Laurence Gaughran.[121] It 'earnestly calls upon the owners and occupiers of land to take immediate measures to meet by increased tillage, this great national food demand so as to preserve our people from the danger of want'.[122] Like Catholics, rural Southern Protestants conceived of the scheme as a 'national' duty to Ireland, and this was made clear in articles produced by *The Irish Times* as well as in letters to the editor, such as that of the land agent, Henry Powell Bridge from Roscrea, Tipperary, who declared that 'in a national crisis farmers should do all in their power to help the country'.[123] For both Southern Protestants and Catholics in rural Ireland, extra tillage was required to save Ireland from potential famine.

Naming and shaming counties which were not considered to have fulfilled their national duty was a useful tactic to pressurize less willing participants to cultivate more land. T. W. Russell, the secretary of DATI and long-serving land reform Liberal MP for South Tyrone, declared that five counties had 'shirked' their responsibility.[124] This triggered a response by farmers in these counties. In Kildare, Frederick Devere, a Catholic journalist and secretary to the local Farmers' Union, protested over the 'suggestion that the occupiers of land of the 5 counties referred to are less patriotic, and less anxious to respond to the national call for increased food production than those of the rest of Ireland'. He countered Russell's implication by stating that 'I doubt if there is a county in Ireland in which the [government] order has been received in a better spirit'.[125] Even for 'shirkers', the campaign was important enough to ensure that they were not perceived to have shirked their 'national duty'.

The degree to which rural Ireland mobilized was consequently remarkable. Landholders, farmers and labourers took up the appeal with gusto. On 15 January 1917, the *Independent* felt confident to write that 'there are signs innumerable on every side that the country is wakening up to the necessity of hearkening to the government's call for increased tillage'.[126] Countrywide reports reveal a committed Irish farming population which adhered to the policy of compulsory tillage. 'Strenuous efforts' were being reported by local farmers in Tipperary in March 1917. Cork workers stated that there was 'increased tillage on many holdings' with west Cork having 'tillage operations in full progress everywhere'. Wexford representatives reported that 'as many as 6 teams are to be seen working in one field' while in Cavan, 'ploughing [was] in full swing across the county' as it was in Kerry and Clare. In Waterford, the 'countryside [was] dotted with ploughed fields. ... Everywhere teams are at work'.[127] A 'hastily improvised' Food Supply Committee was also set up in Navan and within weeks, the large sum of £3,800 had been collected, most of which had been guaranteed by local businessmen and farmers.[128] These newspaper reports were substantiated in personal diaries, as on 20 March 1917, the London-born Elsie Henry, Quartermaster of the RCS *Sphagnum Moss* depot in Dublin, wrote,

> Mr [George] Fletcher came to tea at the [Sphagnum Moss] Depot and says the Tillage scheme is going grandly, a success far beyond their wildest dreams. The lady gardener, who paddles around the environs of Dublin says there has never been such activity and that it is grand to see the Citizens after office hours hurrying to their plots instead of to their pint at the pub. There is a grand new Something coming in the near Future – possibly a Prepared Pasture where the lion and the lamb may lay down together (without any inconvenience to either).[129]

Though it is unclear what Henry meant in her last sentence, her assessment of Irish civilian participation in the scheme concurs with the newspaper evidence and the findings of DATI. By 17 May 1917, Russell claimed that 700,000 acres had been brought under the plough in the space of five months, a result which was 'better than England and Scotland combined'.[130] 'The increase in tillage all over Ireland was perfectly astounding. ... It was beyond doubt now that the tillage movement was a phenomenal success.'[131] A total of 4,500 applications had been made to the department for exemption from the scheme, only 720 of which had been granted, and 248 interventions were made to retake the land by compulsion. Ireland's massive voluntary effort prompted commendation from several quarters. The Earl of Desart, a moderate Conservative Irish peer, stated in the House of Lords that 'the greatest credit was due to the farming interest in Ireland for the effort made to meet the tillage orders'.[132] Those further on the Right, such as the Earl of Crawford, an associate of Andrew Bonar Law and Arthur Balfour, declared that 'the patriotism of Irish landowners and farmers had been so remarkable'.[133] Newspapers praised their local farmers and the *Independent* accredited the Irish for responding to an 'emergency arising out of the submarine menace [that] demanded the largest possible addition to the supply of home-grown food'.[134]

The evidence suggests that Irish farmers adhered to the government's tillage policy despite the growing influence of Sinn Féin (the party had secured two by-election victories in February and May 1917). When a new tillage order was announced in November 1917 compelling Irish farmers to till an extra 5 per cent of land in addition to the 10 per cent that they were already cultivating, the *Independent* noted that the plan was enthusiastically adopted.[135] This was after further by-election victories for Sinn Féin in July and in August. Why did Irish farmers adhere to a Westminster policy when Sinn Féin, which was gaining electoral support, sought to sever those ties?

One reason was because the war took precedence over political aspirations when Irish life was at immediate risk due to German submarine warfare. In fact, when the word 'submarine' is searched as a keyword in the digitized versions of the national press and compared with terms related to Irish self-government, it is clear that the war at sea preoccupied nationalists and unionists to an astonishing degree. These figures do not represent specifically Irish feeling, as they include reports about other countries and submarine warfare elsewhere.[136] However, they are a useful indicator of the frequency with which high politics and the war at sea were discussed in the national press before and during the war years.

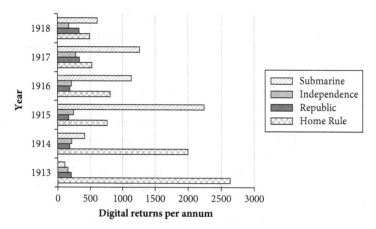

**Chart 4.1** Terms related to self-government and 'submarine' as reported in *The Irish Times*, 1913–18. Search queries used on *The Irish Times* digital database from 1 January 1913 to 31 December 1918.

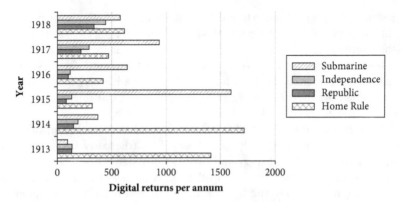

**Chart 4.2** Terms related to self-government and 'submarine' as reported in *The Irish Independent*, 1913–18. Search queries used on *The Irish Independent* digital database from 1 January 1913 to 31 December 1918. Accessed via the Irish Newspaper Archives.

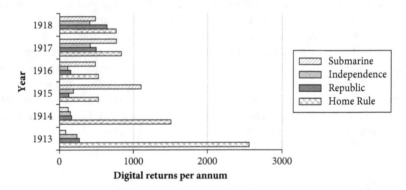

**Chart 4.3** Terms related to self-government and 'submarine' as reported in *The Freeman's Journal*, 1913–18. Search queries used on *The Freeman's Journal* digital database from 1 January 1913 to 31 December 1918. Accessed via the Irish Newspaper Archives.

Submarine warfare dominated the political discussion in both *The Irish Times* and *Independent* during 1915–17. Home Rule was reported more often than submarine activity in 1916–17 by *The Freeman's Journal*, which reflected the Redmondites' attempt to stop the seepage of electoral votes to Sinn Féin. It is of note that in two of the papers during the war years, discussion of high politics did not reach the same level of intensity as they had done in 1913, even though the years 1916 to 1918 have assumed greater significance in the historiography of the Irish Revolution.

When the terms 'republic' and 'independence' are combined and compared to 'submarine' in both the radical-leaning *Irish Independent* and unionist *Irish Times* during 1915–18 – terms which were of immediate significance to Sinn Féin, particularly towards the end of the war – at no point did they outstrip reporting of the war at sea. Only in *The Freeman's Journal* did they achieve a slight advantage, suggesting that this paper was more immediately concerned with domestic high politics during the period of nationalist radicalization than the others, which had the war at sea as their central focus. The reason behind their concern about submarines is revealed in Map 4.1 which shows the number of successful German submarine attacks upon Allied vessels around Ireland during the period when the tillage scheme was initiated.

The map shows a concentration of German submarine activity around the south-east and south-west coasts of Ireland. While more vessels were sunk by the Germans in the English Channel, the Irish comparison is important because several successful German attacks occurred there as well. The map does not show unsuccessful assaults upon Allied shipping, and this reminds us that the number of attacks around southern Ireland was even greater than the image reveals. It explains why Irish farmers, landholders and labourers genuinely felt that Ireland was at risk of starvation, even to the extent of asking Westminster for help, because Ireland was firmly within the war zone of naval operations.

The efforts of rural Ireland to cultivate more tillage in early 1917 were an important means by which those who lived in agricultural areas responded to the demands of war. Pennell has argued that British farmers and labourers expressed their loyalty to Britain in wartime through increased agricultural output rather

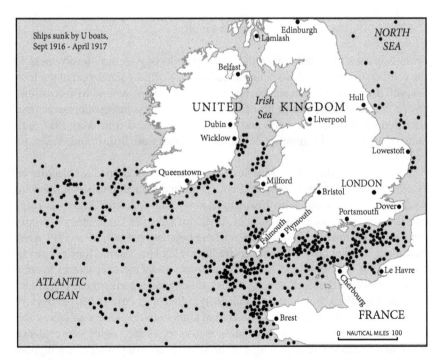

**Map 4.1** Ships sunk by German U-Boats from September 1916–April 1917, Stokes, *Death*, p. 9.

than military enlistment.[137] Those who produced more food for Ireland at a time when the country needed it the most were, like those who joined up to defend Ireland against a potential German invasion, considered by many individuals to have been undertaking a national duty. They revealed their commitment to Ireland by saving the country from another 'Black '47'.

It is therefore important that both Southern Protestants and Catholics believed that the cultivation of more food was a national obligation, for it suggests that this national interest was non-sectional and non-partisan: it was instead an emergency created by the war for Ireland as a whole. This was a qualitatively different conception of self to the political definitions of nationhood projected within the politics of Unionism or Nationalism. The sense of 'national being', which had been generated in response to the German threat, was premised upon defending the land of Ireland and the people who lived on it from a perceived German 'aggressor', suggesting that when Irish life was directly threatened by a foreign 'other', both groups shared a common allegiance to Ireland and some common definition of Irish peoplehood. Ireland remained within the war zone until the end of the conflict because of intensified Allied activity in the Atlantic, and Southern Protestants and Catholics were affected by naval operations. Both groups thus had good reason to retain a common allegiance to Ireland even when the domestic political question forcefully raised its head.

## Ireland's 'enemy'

From February 1917 and during the initial months of America's involvement in the conflict, German U-Boats consolidated in the North Channel, part of the Irish Sea, and the south-western approaches, harassing shipping around Irish coastlines with a corresponding loss in life. Map 4.2 shows how German submarines had encircled particularly the south and north-east of Ireland from May 1917 until January 1918 and the number of successful attacks on British and American vessels.

By 5 July 1917, thirty-four American destroyers were stationed at Queenstown as well as two destroyer tenders (tenders provided maintenance support to destroyers).[138] Liam and John Nolan have noted that following America's entry into the war, 'there were thousands of American sailors in Cork', many of whom were in Queenstown, which, for a town whose population was 8,209 in 1911, must have made it rather busy.[139] The sailors frequently left Queenstown for Cork city in the pursuit of recreation and 'American uniforms and American accents became commonplace in the Cork streets, shops, restaurants, entertainment places and public houses'. For a time, businesses allegedly pulled in an extra £4,000 per week.[140]

However, some serious fights occurred in Cork between American sailors and local men, and there has been speculation as to whether these fights were evidence of increased anti-war activity in light of the assumption that Catholics lost support for the Allied war effort. In his recollections of the conflict, the American admiral, William Sims, declared that Cork Sinn Féiners were openly hostile to British

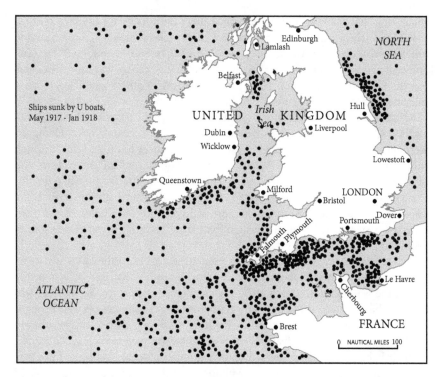

**Map 4.2** Ships sunk by German U-Boats, May 1917–January 1918, Stokes, *Death*, p. 9.

and American sailors, so much so that he imposed a ban on these servicemen from going within three miles of the city.[141] Yet Sinn Féiners were not the only group hostile to the American sailors, which complicates the notion that fights reflected anti-war feeling. The English Captain, G. W. Nightingale, with the 1st Battalion RMF, wrote to his mother in June 1917 that 'it is very nice being back in Cork again. ... The whole place is full of American sailors, who don't get on at all with our fellows – neither officers nor men.'[142] Nightingale revealed that even Irish soldiers in the British forces who were both Catholics and Protestants, and other English officers like him, did not get along with the Americans, suggesting that Irish hostility towards the US servicemen had grounds on non-political motivations. This claim appears more likely as other people welcomed the Americans. Josephus Daniels, the secretary of the American navy, wrote in his memoirs that the Cork malcontents were 'an exception' as the wider population welcomed the sailors.[143] Similarly, Sims declared that Queenstown people 'received our men with genuine cordiality'.[144] Moreover, the close links which many Irish families shared with the US due to Ireland's history of emigration must have meant that many US servicemen had an Irish ancestry which would have strengthened relations between the Irish and the Americans.

These Americans' memories of how Cork people treated the US servicemen are important because the city was bound up with the conflict until its conclusion, suggesting that the sailors were welcomed there until its very end. Sims recalled that 'Queenstown was the one place where [he] could intimately see and hear and touch the realities of the war that at times seemed so remote in London'.[145] For him, Queenstown was within the war zone while the British capital was more detached. For the 6,976 Irish Catholics, 1,203 Protestants and 30 others who lived there, it must have been as well.[146]

Other parts of Cork continued to experience German 'aggression' in late 1917 and 1918, as at least four ships belonging to the Cork Steam Packet Company were sunk in 1917 with many local deaths. Dermot Lucey has found that 'through subscriptions, concerts and a bazaar, money was collected for the widows and orphans of the men, and in September 1918 the Committee responsible for this Fund reported 96 lives lost and over £7,280 collected'.[147] These attacks struck at the population's moral core. Resolutions expressed sympathy with relatives and often reflected a sustained belief in German 'barbarity' because 'it wasn't possible to avoid indignation at the Huns'.[148]

Other Irish towns were haunted by submarine attacks in the latter two years of the war, which helped to sustain a nationwide feeling that Ireland was firmly within the war zone. In March 1917, the auxiliary British ship, *The Werner*, was sunk off the coast of Galway, and sixty-nine surviving crew members were brought to the city. Local support was great as 'the men, who were only scantily clad were cordially received upon arrival and every attention was paid to them. A collection on their behalf was at once opened up by a number of local people, and the War Fund Committee provided the men with food and clothing'.[149]

That Irish people had suffered at Germany's hands prompted some individuals to think that Germany was intent on attacking the Irish, particularly innocent civilians. In June 1917, the *Connacht Tribune* reported that submarines had destroyed Irish fishing boats from Kenmare on the north Atlantic to Howth on the Irish Sea. The newspaper believed that German brutality was specifically directed at innocent Irish fishermen and its editorial cultivated this notion. As only seven of the eighty boats in the fishing fleet had been sunk, it demonstrated its support for the Royal Navy in the comment: 'Were it not for the appearance of a British patrol boat, which caused the U-Boat to submerge, it is probable that the whole fleet would have been sunk'.[150] Similarly, on 31 May 1918 when the Connemara fishing boat, *The Pretty Polly*, was sunk killing seven Connemara fishermen, the *Tribune* called it 'a German necessity to terrorize Irish fishermen from off the seas'.[151] On one occasion it claimed that the Germans wanted to have 'every Irish fishing boat sunk in a month' and 'intended shelling the villages shortly'.[152] Apparently this claim was not conjecture, as the log book of Captain Freiherr Degenhart von Loë of UB-100 suggested that after shelling the English town of Scarborough he had considered shelling parts of Ireland as well. After he sunk the *Adela* near Holyhead on 27 December 1917, he wrote 'I take to the South of Ireland, hoping to be able to fire during the night at the South coast'.[153]

The presence of mines around Ireland's western seaboard, which were laid by the Germans and Allied forces to sink enemy vessels, often resulted in the tragic loss of Irish life. On 23 June 1917, nine Connemara fishermen were reportedly 'blown to atoms' due to 'the explosion of a German mine which they had fished ashore'. A representative attendance of townspeople, including the Galway peer, Lord Killanin and Fr T. Heaney, turned out to comfort bereaved relatives, and all of the dead men were Catholics.[154] The townspeople had no evidence to suggest that the mine was German in origin yet this was the contemporary belief. Similarly, when a comparable tragedy occurred in December 1917 with the loss of four Irish men, 'suggestions of a British mine [were] disproved'. The *Tribune* believed that Germany was at fault and made this clear in its headline: 'Another German mine disaster'. The victims included a father and son.[155]

These attacks ripped apart Irish families and communities, and this inspired venom against Germany until the end of the war. The seven victims of *The Pretty Polly* came from the Gaelic-speaking hamlet of Carna on the west coast of Galway, which only had a population of 175 people in 1911, all of whom were Catholic.[156] One family lost 'all its male members'. The local priest, Fr McHugh, wrote to the *Connacht Tribune* that the Germans were 'cruel butchers' and evoked the memory of the *Lusitania*, demonstrating that the sinking of the passenger liner horrified even the most rural parts of western Ireland and that he conceived of the *Polly* disaster in a similar vein. He declared that 'one old man was so overcome by the sad news that he fell off his chair dead, and several others are so prostrate that I have been called to their bedsides to administer the last Rites of the Church'.[157] Fr M. Donnellan, the parish priest of the nearby fishing community of Roundstone, 'denounced German brutality in sinking an unprotected fishing boat'.[158] He evoked a comparison with the book of Genesis, calling the German attack 'the crime of Cain' in light of what was thought to have been humanity's first murder, and he asked the government to protect Irish fishing fleets.[159] McHugh established a relief fund for the victims' families, which by 31 August totalled over £1000. Some donations came from Keady (Co. Armagh), Dublin, Belfast, Limerick and Tullamore (King's County), revealing a nationwide response to the tragedy. Catholics were well represented among subscribers, especially local Galway residents, but Protestants did not feel excluded from the appeal even though the victims were Irish-speaking Catholics and peasants. Two donors, for example, were Dr Plunket, the Protestant Bishop of Tuam, Killala and Achonry and the Anglican Reverend R. M. Guirn from TCD.[160]

The war in the Atlantic continued to trouble the Irish in the south and west, and cities such as Cork remained within the war zone until the end of the conflict. It was a significant base for Allied shipping and forty-seven of the eighty US destroyers which were sent to Europe between 1917 and the end of 1918 were based at Queenstown.[161] However, U-Boat attacks generally shifted to the east in 1918, and Map 4.3 illuminates the growing concentration of submarines in the Irish Sea.

Since 1915, the east of Ireland had become an integral part of the British war effort, and from 1917, of the American one as well. Kingstown (Dún Laoghaire), situated to the south of Dublin city, became a functioning naval base, and in October 1918, one light cruiser, eleven British and seven US destroyers, as well as submarine chasers, operated from there to Holyhead.[162] The mail-boat, the *RMS Leinster*, was used to transport officers and troops between the two locations,

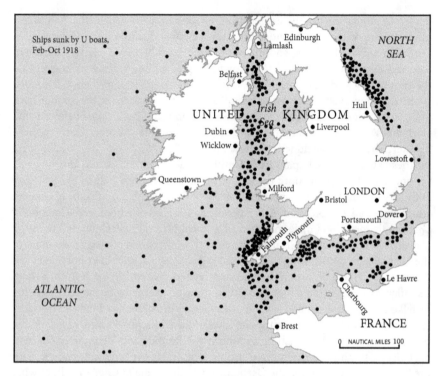

Ships sunk by U boats,
Feb–Oct 1918

NORTH
SEA

Edinburgh
Lamlash

Belfast

UNITED *Irish* KINGDOM          Hull

*Sea*

Dubin ●                   ● Liverpool

Wicklow ●

Lowestoft

Queenstown

Milford                    LONDON

● Bristol

Dover
Portsmouth

Falmouth   Plymouth

Le Havre

ATLANTIC
OCEAN

Cherbourg

● Brest       FRANCE

0   NAUTICAL MILES 100

**Map 4.3** Ships sunk by German U-Boats in the Irish Sea, February–October 1918, Stokes, *Death*, p. 9.

and it did not escape German attention. While the Anglo-American alliance had reduced German submarine attacks on Allied shipping by April 1918 (Germany had sunk one ship for every two days spent on patrol in spring 1917 and this rate had fallen to one ship per 14 days by summer 1918), Germany was aware of the strategic importance of the Irish Sea and thus redoubled its efforts in this stretch.[163] The Catholic Countess of Fingall recalled that 'the Irish Sea [was] full of submarines' and on one journey to Holyhead when she stood on the bridge of the *Leinster* with the ship captain, he 'showed me, not very far off, a little dark object in the sea. "That is a periscope," he said'.[164]

On 10 October 1918, U-Boat 123 fired torpedoes at the *Leinster* as it travelled from Kingstown to Holyhead which resulted in the ship sinking. Accounts of the number of passengers onboard vary from 771 to 811 persons including military members and crew. At least 500 people were killed though figures varied at the time.[165] Little is known about the tragedy's impact on public opinion, but an analysis of newspaper reports which followed reveals that the *Leinster* disaster evoked a comparable degree of outrage to that expressed following the sinking of the *Lusitania*. Though the shock factor that had accompanied the earlier tragedy was no longer as great due to more than three years of attacks on Allied shipping, references to the earlier tragedy were immediate. In some ways, the attack seemed even more profound as the *RMS Leinster* was owned by the City of Dublin Steam Packet Company and had been carrying many Irish people.

*The Freeman's Journal* called it 'Ireland's Lusitania', no doubt in an effort to whip up the emotions expressed following the earlier tragedy.[166] Provincial nationalist newspapers, some of whose political allegiances may have been more radical in the aftermath of the conscription crisis, evoked the tragedy in their reports, with the *Connacht Tribune* calling it 'the brand of Cain'.[167] For the *Independent*, which had been sufficiently radicalized and was now sympathetic to advanced nationalism, it was 'a diabolical crime … barbarous methods of warfare … [and] outside the pale of civilization'.[168] Thus for a spectrum of the nationalist press, the horrors of the earlier tragedy, which had cemented the notion of German barbarism, were reinvigorated following the *Leinster* calamity. *The Irish Times* was just as angry, as the editor declared that 'Germany has committed one of her foulest crimes against humanity' and prayed that the *Leinster* 'will be among the last'.[169] A significant minority of Protestants lived in Kingstown (11,961 Catholics: 5,258 Protestants), and they experienced the *Leinster* tragedy directly.[170]

It is possible that censorship played a role in press accounts of the attack, creating an impression that the disaster was more keenly felt than was true. It is therefore significant that republicans remembered the tragedy in their recollections of Ireland's revolution, most of whom recalled their experiences in the 1950s. While they did not discuss the calamity with reference to their allegiances in the international conflict (though one republican, a Mr Lane from Co. Cork, protested at a meeting that discussed the *Leinster* that 'they [republicans] were not pro-German'[171]), their remembrance of the ship's demise so many years after it occurred demonstrates that the shock was real at the time.[172]

The *Leinster* had many Irish passengers aboard when it was sunk and it 'remains to this day the greatest disaster to befall Irish citizens travelling in Irish waters'.[173] For Dubliners, it brought the 'horror of war to their doors'.[174] The *Independent* had a grim column entitled 'The Identified' under which read many Irish names and *The Irish Times* also printed several Irish fatalities.[175] The event was catastrophic for Irish postal workers. Out of twenty-one members aboard, *The Irish Times* noted 'all lost but one'.[176] As in the earlier tragedy, survivors' stories were common.[177] Well-known persons were reported missing, such as Thomas Foley of Dublin Corporation and his wife. Their personal stories augmented the tragic nature of the affair, as it was reported that 'Mrs Foley was on a journey to England to visit her brother, who is lying wounded in a military hospital'.[178]

The sinking of the *Leinster* thus forced the people of Dublin, particularly the more affluent Catholic and Protestant sections of Kingstown, to experience mass death in Ireland just as the people of Cork had experienced in May 1915. By 11 October, 149 bodies were recovered prompting a local coffin shortage.[179] 'Anxious relatives of the missing and hundreds of Kingstown residents remained on the Marine Road overlooking Victoria Wharf all night'.[180] The City of Dublin Steampacket Company was 'besieged by callers enquiring after relatives and friends', while the Dublin and South Eastern Railway dispatched special trains to Kingstown where hundreds of people assembled awaiting news of their relatives' fate.[181] St Michael's Hospital was 'crowded out' with worried relatives and had scenes of the 'most heart-rending character'.[182] Victims were laid out in the morgue as they had been after the *Lusitania* disaster.[183] Newspapers did not shy away from reporting the brutal inflictions on the victims' bodies, with reports of 'bashed brains', 'lost eyes' and severed limbs adding to its general gruesomeness. The locus of suffering was at times gendered: the *Independent* reported that 'twenty dead were laid out in rows in the mortuary, the majority terribly disfigured, the women particularly'. It suggested that the victims had not died peacefully: 'On the faces of all there was a look of pain and anguish telling of the terrible nature of their struggle before the end came.'[184]

For a week after the tragedy, mugshots of the missing and dead occupied spaces in the Irish press usually reserved to acknowledge Irish servicemen killed in action.[185] Funerals for the victims occurred across Ireland in subsequent days and sympathy for bereaved relatives was felt nationally. The son of the late Anglican archbishop, W. Alexander, was buried in Derry's Protestant Cathedral.[186] The deceased trade union leader and Alderman for Derry Corporation, James McCarron, was 'escorted to Derry by the chairman and officials of Dublin Trades Union Council'.[187] 'Touching scenes' were noted at a Catholic graveyard in Tralee where Miss Nora Galvin, Miss Lizzie Healy and Miss Chrissie Murphy were interred.[188] 'Huge crowds attended their funerals.' In Cahir, Tipperary, the Catholic Miss Margaret Cooke was buried, 'the cortege being extremely large'.[189] In Galway, Captain Edward Ramsay Milne, who had previously won the Distinguished Conduct Medal with the Canadian Infantry, was buried in the Catholic Pro-Cathedral with Clare McNally, the daughter of a late Connaught Rangers major. Bishop O'Dea presided and 'practically the whole city was in mourning during the funerals'. The Rangers and Surrey Yeomanry saluted the dead at the graveside.[190]

Many public bodies expressed sympathetic resolutions for the victims as well as anger towards the Germans.[191] Galway Board of Guardians called the Germans 'savages'.[192] Cork Harbour Commissioners expressed 'intense indignation' at the act since they had friends aboard.[193] So had Blackrock UIL in Co. Dublin, and its members called it 'murderous outrage'.[194] J. S. Young JP, a representative of Galway Harbour Commissioners, stated that 'the Germans, as they were in the beginning of the war, were still murderers'.[195] This sentiment cut across creed, since the Catholic chairman, T. C. McDonogh JP, called it 'the most cruel and murderous thing that occurred since the sinking of the Lusitania. There was no reason for it'.[196] The prelates were palpably angry, including the two most prominent representatives of the hierarchy. At a meeting of the Catholic Truth Society, in which 'gloom was cast over the proceedings' because of the 'torpedoing of the Leinster, with its terrible results', Cardinal Logue claimed that 'he believed the present catastrophe was even worse than the sinking of the Lusitania, and from every country on earth a cry of execration has been raised against the perpetrators'.[197] Archbishop William Walsh made a rare appearance into the public forum. He wrote to nationalist newspapers informing clerics to offer up their masses for the souls of the 'fallen victims perpetrated yesterday by hostile arms in the Irish Sea'.[198] Nationalist MPs condemned the crime, including Captain Stephen Gwynn, who 'was well received' at a meeting in Clontarf town.[199] In Belfast, a nationalist convention presided over by Joseph Devlin MP, an IPP representative in Belfast West who was very influential in the northern nationalist community and who survived as MP in the 1918 general election, passed a resolution of 'intense abhorrence and profound indignation ... regarding the piratical and murderous action of the German High Naval Command', especially since it had consigned to the sea 'men, women, and children belonging to our own race and country'.[200] The last sentence arguably summed up why the disaster had touched the Irish of both creeds to the extent that it did.

On 16 October 1918, a relief fund was set up for victims and their dependants by the Lord Mayor of Dublin. *The Freeman's Journal* called it 'Dublin's Practical Support for Dependents'.[201] However, the *Independent* and *Irish Times* framed it in terms of the nation, respectively calling it 'Ireland's Sacred Task' and the 'National Fund', as in the tillage crisis, it was the 'national duty' of Irish people of all backgrounds to assist their countrymen and women who had been bereaved by the Germans.[202]

After more than four long years of war in which individuals of all backgrounds had regularly dipped into their pockets for war-relief schemes – not to mention donations to the families of the executed Easter Rising rebels, or the large subscription that amounted to at least £250,000 for the Irish National Defence Fund to protest against conscription in 1918 – one might expect the fund to have had limited success.[203] Yet this was not the case. At the inaugural meeting of the *RMS Leinster* fund, a 'large attendance' of the Dublin elite was present including the Primate of All Ireland and Lord Archbishop of Armagh, John Baptist Crozier, numerous Catholic clergy and Denis Coffey, president of University College Dublin. Archbishop Walsh sent a cheque of '£100 in aid of the good work which you are about to inaugurate', a sum nearly ten times his contribution to the *Lusitania* disaster fund and the same amount as Sir John French, the lord lieutenant.[204] Within 17 days, £5,095 13s had been raised with contributions from Ireland, England and beyond. This was *more than double* the amount raised, compared per day, than in the first six weeks of the INAVDF (its first appeal for funds had been issued on 27 May 1916 and it had raised £5,636 by 8 July 1916).[205] Some donors contributed to the INAVDF as well as to the *Leinster* fund, such as Archbishop Walsh, who offered logistical assistance to Irish-American Catholics when they sent funds to the INAVDF, yet he morally and financially contributed to the *Leinster* appeal.[206] Political reasons may have been the primary motivation behind those who contributed to the INAVDF,[207] but humanitarianism was another important incentive in light of Walsh's contribution to both funds, assisting victims of both British and German 'aggression'.

The Lord Mayor of Dublin framed the subscription in terms of 'Christian charity', calling upon donors to part with their funds for charitable reasons.[208] This was certainly a major reason why individuals gave money to assist those bereaved by the *Leinster* disaster, but a desire for vengeance was another motivation, though how strong a motivation is difficult to tell. The *Irish Independent* urged readers to remember 'the meaning of this war', a statement that reminded readers exactly why the Allies had to defeat Germany. Just as *The Irish Times* had called for enlistments in the aftermath of the *Lusitania*, the *Independent* nailed its colours to the mast: 'Indignation at the enemy's inhumanity should powerfully stimulate voluntary recruiting throughout the country.'[209] At a meeting of Kingstown Urban Council, the chairman, J. J. Kennedy, stated that 'this outrage demanded retribution, and the Kaiser would surely get his deserts.'[210] When one member, the Catholic Christopher Rochford, who worked in the slate industry and whose wife was a maternity nurse, drew a distinction between a German and 'German methods', his fellow Catholic, Mr O'Brien, 'jumped from his seat, rushed across the Council Chamber, and ... eventually struck him [Rochford] a blow on the side of the head'.[211] In Croom, Co. Limerick, John Coleman, a Catholic JP and member of the district council and board of guardians, stated that 'the Irish people should give a hand in punishing the savages who sank it, and if he were a young man he would have no hesitation in being a party to punish these infernal murderers'.[212]

Thus the war at sea helped sustain the notion that Germany was a 'menace' that had to be defeated, and this belief was held by many individuals and groups until the end of the war. Since April and May 1915, Germany was perceived to have deliberately targeted innocent civilians through submarine attacks off Irish shores and was blamed for mine explosions that killed Irish fishermen, even when there was little actual evidence upon which to base this claim. The torpedoing of the *RMS Leinster* and the severe loss of Irish life renewed the horror which had been felt in Ireland after the sinking of the *RMS Lusitania*, a major event that cemented Germany's 'enemy' status. Germany was perceived to pose an even greater threat because its submarine activity directly threatened Ireland's food supply, prompting opinion shapers to remind the Irish population of the horrors of the Great Famine, which was itself a stimulus for intensifying agricultural production.

Nationalist radicalization may have been underway, but the war at sea loomed large in the history of 1915 to 1918 Ireland, yet it has been excluded from virtually every scholarly account of the period. Increased agricultural production may have been a means to preserve and defend Ireland – an incentive that was more about Ireland than it was about helping the Allies to achieve victory – but Germany's persistent and 'criminal' attacks on Allied vessels made the Irish response intimately connected to international events and helped to propel both Catholics and Protestants to lend ideological and humanitarian support to the Allies – and, as we have seen, even instances of military support. They had further reason to support the Allied cause, as the next chapter shows, because Irish diasporic Catholics were supporting the Allies in Britain and throughout the British Empire.

# Chapter 5

## GREATER IRELAND AND CATHOLIC LOYALISM

Since the 1700s, emigration was a major part of Irish life and one popular destination for Irish Catholics seeking opportunities outside of Ireland was that contentious entity, the British Empire. Debate exists regarding Ireland's 'colonial' status, but over the course of the nineteenth century, Irish Catholics increasingly contributed to the functioning of the Empire and many persons had a vested interest in its success.[1] During the Great War, a significant number of Irish settlers joined Dominion regiments, fighting in every theatre of the war, and both women and men supported formidable war efforts on the home fronts of the Dominions. Yet historians have not considered their contributions a part of Ireland's war effort even though the Irish did at the time, as the multi-volume series, *Ireland's Memorial Records*, published in 1923, embraced those Irish who had served in imperial units, unlike the histories of the Irish in the Great War which emerged at the end of the twentieth century.[2]

This chapter transcends the nation state and situates the Catholic Irish war experience within its proper international and transnational context. Irish settlers were intimately connected to Ireland. They were often staunch Irish nationalists, lobbying and generating funds to support the achievement of Irish self-government, but they were also deeply concerned about the British Empire, mixing their allegiances to Ireland and Empire in their support for the imperial war effort. The Irish in Ireland also had ties to the Empire, and when a battalion of an Irish-Canadian regiment visited the 'mother' country eight months after the execution of the Dublin rebels, the extensive cross-confessional response to the visit was an important indicator of attitudes towards the conflict at a time when Irish politics was driving Unionists and Nationalists apart.

### *Moderate nationalism and the war*[3]

Ireland and Irishness were an integral part of the British Empire and by the time of the Great War, significant concentrations of Irish Catholic settlers lived in Canada and Australia. By the 1870s, almost 850,000 Irish-born persons lived in Canada as a result of emigration before and after the Great Famine, making them the second largest ethnic group after the French and roughly one-quarter of the Canadian population. By 1911, there were almost 1,100,000 persons of Irish ethnicity living in Newfoundland and Canada.[4] About 60 per cent of the emigrants were Protestant who clustered in Ontario and the western provinces as well as in New Brunswick, Prince Edward Island and Nova Scotia. The remainder were Catholic. In the Maritime Provinces, both groups were equally distributed. Catholics had a significant presence in the eastern province of Quebec and in the separate Dominion of Newfoundland, where almost half of Newfoundland's population had Irish origins and most people were of Irish Catholic descent.[5]

Australia had a significant Irish population as well. In 1911, 141,331 Irish-born persons lived there (3.2 per cent of the Australian population), though 229,156 had lived there in 1891.[6] Patrick O'Farrell has found that these immigrants were mainly post-Famine, attracted by the gold rushes of 1851–60 (101,000 Irish immigrants came to Australia during this decade).[7] The settler-Irish concentrated along the east coast (though Perth was also noted for its Irish character) and in 1871, one in four people living in Victoria was born in Ireland.[8] While immigration had declined by 1900, particularly among Irish Catholics, Catholics still comprised 71.3 per cent of the Irish-born population living in Australia in 1911, most of them being migrants from the 1880s or earlier.[9] As Jeff Kildea has argued, before the Great War Catholics in Australia were 'mostly Irish by birth or descent, the Irish were mostly Catholics, and Irish Catholics were mostly on the lowest rungs of the socio-economic ladder'.[10]

These numerically significant groups of Irish Catholic immigrants were even greater when the later generations are considered, though it is impossible to quantify the size of the settler communities. Mark McGowan has claimed that by 1911 most of the English-speaking Catholics in Toronto were the children, grandchildren and perhaps the great-grandchildren of Irish and Scottish immigrants, who had arrived in the city before Canadian Confederation (the unification of the Canadian colonies into the Dominion of Canada in 1867), while Donald Akenson has estimated that 24.3 per cent of Ontario's population was of Irish ethnicity (approximately 614,502 persons).[11] In 1911, 103,720 persons of Irish ethnicity lived in Quebec (roughly 5.2 per cent of the provincial population and the second largest group after the Francophone population), and Montreal had districts which had an Irish Catholic character, such as the borough of St Ann's, which had 8,000 Irish-born residents out of a population of 50,000 in 1921.[12] While the Irish presence was 'more symbolic than real', the only candidates returned in the borough during the 1917 general election were of Irish descent, preserving its Irish character electorally despite the fact that fewer than one-fifth of persons in residence were from Ireland.[13] Similarly, O'Farrell has noted that the states of New South Wales (NSW) and Victoria had a close association with Ireland, particularly the city of Melbourne where Irishness was strong.[14]

First- and second-generation descendants also held allegiances to Australia and Canada where they were born. These affiliations may have been greater than their loyalty to Ireland, which was based on an inherited familial nationality rather than a locational connection.[15] Yet Ireland and Irishness were still important strands of identification to these settlers at the turn of the twentieth century because they had been sustained in civic life for many years before the Great War through religion, journalism, associational activities and, particularly during the 1910s, through Irish nationalism.

Irish immigrants tended to cluster when they settled in sufficient numbers and the Catholic Church often became the centre of settler-Irish Catholic life.[16] The prominent position accorded to the church was related to the 'Cullenization of Irish society' when the influential prelate, Cardinal Paul Cullen, who led the Catholic Church in Ireland from 1850 to 1878, implanted a rigorous form of Roman Catholicism within Irish religious institutions. As the nineteenth century progressed, several of Cullen's students were appointed to ecclesiastical positions in Australia, New Zealand, Canada and the United States, and they disseminated his religious doctrine within the settler communities of the New World, often making the church the focal point of diasporic life.[17]

Journalism played an important role in keeping Irishness alive. In Australia and Canada, some newspapers had a distinctly Irish tone such as the Melbourne *Advocate*, the Queensland *Australian*, *The Catholic Register* (an Irish Catholic weekly in Toronto), *The Freeman's Journal* (Sydney) and the Saint John's *New Freeman*, which was independent of clerical control and was fervently nationalist (the name of the latter two newspapers was copied from Dublin's nationalist newspaper, *The Freeman's Journal*). These organs 'gave the local Irish a voice and a sense of commonality, linking them with people of like mind and culture, and bringing them much closer to Ireland itself'.[18] At least two major Canadian newspapers reported Irish affairs, and these included the Toronto-based newspaper, *The Globe*, and *The Montreal Gazette*.[19] In Canada and Australia, the Catholic press had close links with Irish clerics and Irish society, and many of its articles were reprinted from nationalist newspapers in Ireland.[20]

The international circulation of newspapers that reported on Irish affairs and their interest in Irish nationalism suggests that constitutional nationalism was in some ways an intercontinental movement. Though historians have recognized that the IPP had overseas supporters, most studies of the party have been at the level of high politics and have explored the IPP within its UK framework as a party which operated through Westminster.[21] Yet the party had a significant structural basis outside of Ireland and had popular support in Irish diasporic communities, both in Britain and in the New World. In Britain, many of the 500,000 Irish-born men and women who lived there prior to the Great War were members of the United Irish League of Great Britain (UILGB) and Nationalism was strong in Liverpool where the IPP representative, T. P. O'Connor, was consistently elected at by-elections even after 1918, though he effectively stood as an independent after this date.[22] The UIL's reach was even greater in the 1910s, as it had branches in Australia (Melbourne, Victoria, Sydney, Adelaide, Perth, Brisbane), Canada (Montreal, Toronto, Ottawa), New Zealand (Wellington) and South Africa (Pretoria, Benoni), though it is unclear how many members these branches had or what their contribution was to the Nationalist movement.[23] The Ancient Order of Hibernians (AOH), the Catholic fraternal association that Joseph Devlin MP helped to make an organizational arm of the IPP, also had an international network.[24] In 1917, its Saskatoon branch in central-southern Canada comprised the social and political elite of the city, including Emmett Hall, future Chief Justice of Saskatchewan; Joseph Foley, a former mayor of North Battleford; Walter O'Regan, a lawyer and member of Saskatoon city council; and Thomas Molloy, future Deputy Minister of Labour in Saskatchewan and president of the Regina Trades and Labour Congress. These elites were predominantly first-generation Irish, some of whom, like John Joseph Leddy, the president of the AOH and the Canadian Knights of Columbus, became the leader of local Catholic opinion. His parents had left Ireland during the Famine period, establishing themselves in the agricultural heartland of Ontario by the 1870s.[25]

While it is true that the IPP voiced nationalist concerns through Westminster, the parliaments of some of the other British Dominions also encouraged London to pass Home Rule for Ireland. Irish self-government was an international concern, and some of its most forceful advocates were settlers of Irish descent, such as Charles Murphy in Canada, secretary of state in Wilfrid Laurier's Liberal government throughout much of the 1910s and a regular correspondent of T. P. O'Connor's.[26] He urged Laurier to pass motions in favour of Irish Home Rule in the Canadian parliament, which Laurier did in 1904 and 1907.[27] On at least one occasion, both Houses unanimously passed a resolution in favour of Home Rule for Ireland.[28] Historians have found that Irish immigrants and their descendants were deeply interested in the achievement of Irish self-government in this period.[29] Representatives such as Murphy may have been responding as much to grassroots pressure from their own settler-Irish communities to support Irish Home Rule as they were demonstrating their solidarity with the IPP.

Nationalism, in addition to Catholicism and journalism, thus helped to sustain an Irish Catholic and moderate nationalist identity outside of Ireland in the years preceding the Great War. Though settlers could maintain their Irishness within the Dominions in which they lived, these communities were connected with one another through what John Redmond called the 'mother country' of Ireland, a concept that appealed to him as an advocate for the positive virtues of Empire. In 1902, Redmond declared in a speech that 'there is a form of Imperialism – the Imperialism of the murderer and the robber, which no doubt is a disgrace and a source of weakness … there is another Imperialism which I can quite understand Englishmen being wedded to … the idea of having the Empire … united … to what they call the mother country'.[30] Redmond's desire was in many ways already active, connecting Ireland to its Irish world, as IPP representatives often visited Australia and Canada to generate funds and moral support for the Home Rule movement. In these tours, Irish MPs were assisted by Irish-born and first-generation settlers.[31] From 1865 until 1931, Irish Jesuits in Dublin contributed to the running of elite Catholic schools throughout Australia and New Zealand, and decisions were often delayed in these institutions until approval had been received from Dublin.[32] Emigrants and their descendants wrote letters to family members and friends in Ireland, as did Irish Catholic clerics and politicians.[33] Transnational networks of families and communities (both religious and political) were the reality of Irish life in the nineteenth and early twentieth centuries, and 'mother Ireland' was at the heart of these networks.

When war broke out in 1914, the response of nationalists in Ireland was therefore one of many factors that influenced the diaspora. When Redmond spoke in the House of Commons on 3 August 1914 declaring that Nationalists would support the government in the event of war, his declaration was referred to by the leaders of Irish-Canadian and Irish-Australian Catholic opinion. John Meagher, a Home Ruler from Co. Clare who was the proprietor of a successful chain of drapery stores in NSW and who had helped to organize the reception for the Redmond brothers when they toured there in the 1910s, sent a telegram to Redmond on behalf of the Catholic Federation of Bathurst:

> On behalf of the bishop and Catholics of the Bathurst diocese, whom I am commissioned to represent in the cause of Home Rule, as well as on my own behalf I congratulate you on your wise and prudent act in offering for the protection of Ireland the services of the National Volunteers to join in the patriotic act with the Orange Ulster Volunteers to make common cause in the protection of Ireland from the invasion of a foreign foe.[34]

Similarly in Brisbane, the Queensland Home Rule Association held a meeting in which the war was discussed and 'warm approval was expressed of Mr John Redmond's announcement. ... It was considered that his action would substantially aid in the realization of Ireland's national aspirations.'[35] £1,000 had been raised for the Home Rule cause and members of the association included P. J. McDermott (an Irish-born emigrant who became under-secretary to the Premier, and president of the Queensland Irish Association), the Limerick-born Archbishop of Brisbane, James Duhig, Peter Murphy (a Leitrim-born businessman who was involved in the brewery, financial, hotel and electricity trades) and the Roscommon businessman and confidante of Archbishop Duhig, T. C. Beirne.[36]

Redmond's pronouncement was also warmly received in Irish-Canada, when Fr Gerald McShane, the parish priest of St Patrick's Church in Montreal, the primary place of worship for Irish Catholic Montrealers, endorsed the Nationalist leader's position in a sermon on the first Sunday after the declaration of hostilities.[37] Around a similar time, Charles Murphy wrote to T. P. O'Connor to back Redmond's declaration and Murphy published O'Connor's response in the Canadian press, informing readers of Irish descent of the IPP's stance on the war. Murphy, who was soon engaged in mobilizing Canadians to assist the Empire, believed Irish Canadians should know that Nationalist Ireland was behind the war effort.[38] Prelates such as Bishop Fallon of London, Ontario, a first-generation Irish man, also approved of Redmond's stance. He printed his approval in the *Catholic Record* for the Catholic Irish of Ontario to read (the province was comprised of 34.5 per cent Irish-born and first-generation Irish Catholics in 1871).[39]

Redmond's actions also had an impact closer to home, such as in Scotland, where his speech was warmly received by nationalists. It was referred to on 5 August at a meeting of the Irish National Foresters (INF) in Edinburgh who declared that 'if help was required from the Irishmen in Scotland it would not be wanting'.[40] Similarly in Dunfermline, Thomas J. Kenny, an auctioneer and rifle enthusiast, wrote to Redmond and sent him his rifle. He believed that Redmond's actions had made civil war in Ireland impossible, declaring that 'I trust you may not require to use it for the original purpose for which it was intended, and indeed now I do not think it will ever be required since your historic and patriotic pronouncement in the House of Commons. ... I may tell you it has raised our status in this country 100% on what it used to be.'[41]

Redmond's speech on 3 August committing Protestant and Catholic troops to the defence of Ireland was welcomed by diasporic nationalists in Britain, Canada and Australia. It may have even resulted in some enlistments as in Montreal, Fr McShane met with twelve Irish Canadians to discuss how best to form an Irish regiment that would be strictly for home defence.[42] This policy reflected Redmond's strategy and was different from the rationale that underwrote the formation of other Canadian regiments so early in the war. The 90th Winnipeg Rifles, for instance, was formed in August 1914 and immediately raised troops for active service with the 8th Battalion Canadian Expeditionary Force (CEF).[43] In Scotland, Redmond's support for the British 'was widely interpreted as a call for Volunteer recruits and in this respect its impact was immediate'. In Motherwell, UILGB members formed a Volunteer corps in response to Redmond's declaration with 200 on-the-spot enrolments. In Glasgow, seventy-five recruits enrolled at a similar meeting. It was not only men that responded in this manner as in Edinburgh, Irish Catholic women affiliated to the 'Division Twelve' AOH 'rushed to form an ambulance corps for field service'.[44]

Of course, considerations other than Irish nationalism propelled the settler-Irish to assist the war effort. The enthusiasm of the Canadian and Australian populations to rally to the Empire's defence has been documented and the Irish would have been drawn in by the mass mobilization of the societies in which they lived.[45] Friendship and fraternal loyalties were important motivators for many groups of men to enlist in Ireland and England, taking shape, for example, in the numerous 'Pals battalions' formed throughout the UK, and they probably were for Irish Catholic male settlers in Australia and Canada as well.[46] Irish women, like those of other nationalities, had a direct obligation to assist male family members that enlisted. Women served in the war effort for a wide range of reasons, including, not least, patriotism, and a belief that serving was the 'right' thing to do.[47] Many supported the war effort through producing comforts for the troops, joining the medical services, or through fundraising.[48]

However, the important point is that Nationalist Ireland's decision to support the British war effort helped to influence the response of Irish settlers because the diaspora was concerned about Ireland, most recently because of the struggle for self-government. Thus when the Home Rule bill was passed on 18 September 1914, it was an additional blessing for settlers who were taking up the war effort in their respective Dominions. IPP members received congratulatory telegrams, resolutions of praise and letters from the settler-Irish, particularly UIL branches (these included branches in Cape Town, Fremantle and the national UIL branch of Australia) as well as from prominent individuals, such as Thomas Shaughnessy, the chairman of the Canadian Pacific Railway.[49] In Toronto, leading Irish nationalists were reported to have met 'to commemorate the final signing by His Majesty of the Home Rule measure. They also sent a cable to Redmond, warmly endorsing his appeal to the Irish people to answer Lord Kitchener's call for men to fight the Empire's battles.'[50]

Though the bill was put on the statute book in September 1914, Ronan Fanning has argued that it was unlikely to have been put into operation because British politicians had not solved the question of Ulster.[51] Popular responses to the bill's passage have consequently not received sufficient attention because Home Rule, as conceived in 1914, never came into operation. Yet people did not know that the bill would not be enacted in the form in which it had been passed. There is evidence to suggest that settlers entered the war in the belief that the Irish question was once and for all resolved, acting as members of a self-governing Ireland when they took up arms on the Empire's behalf.

In Australia, six days after the bill's passage, the editorial of *The Freeman's Journal* (Sydney) read 'Home Rule' and claimed that 'the long struggle of a hundred and fourteen years has ended'. Prematurely, the newspaper declared that 'there can be no going back on that unless the whole fabric of British constitutional government were to be turned topsy turvy'.[52] This was not only the opinion of the editor, as Irish Catholic settlers in Sydney also seemed to believe that the Irish question was solved. At a large gathering of Sydney Hibernians to celebrate its silver jubilee (the Hibernian Society was 'the largest flourishing "Irish" organization in Australia'),[53] one member, Sister O'Sullivan, 'proposed what she considered the most important toast on the list, "Ireland a Nation"'. She enthused about the bill and 'the toast was drunk with the singing of "God Save Ireland" followed by "God Save the King"'.[54] Elsewhere in Sydney, a 'Home Rule' fair was held in Surry Hills to erect a new Catholic church, which the Lord Mayor and mayoress attended alongside a large turnout of Irish Catholics. In a speech, Fr Collender declared that 'he would like it to be known that though the fair was denominated Home Rule, the proceeds would not go into a Home Rule fund: there was, indeed, no further need of a fund in the interests of Home Rule, which was now an accomplished fact'. The names of the stalls manned by Irish women were distinctly Irish and referenced both nationalism and British Liberalism. They included the 'Young Ireland Stall' and the 'Robert Emmett Stall', symbols of Ireland's revolutionary tradition that were also part of the heritage of constitutional nationalism. A 'Parnell Stall' and 'Redmond Stall' reflected allegiances to the IPP, while debt to the Liberals was marked by 'the Asquith Stall' and 'the Gladstone Stall'. Most suggestive of all was the one entitled 'College Green Stall' where the new Home Rule parliament would be located in Dublin.[55]

Though it is difficult to establish the extent to which the bill's passage impacted upon recruitment, it did not appear to impede it. Following Redmond's commitment to home defence following the United Kingdom's entry into war on 4 August, the manufacturer, A. Maguire, wrote to Redmond from Liverpool and volunteered to organize the local INV for the war effort: 'I cannot let the passing of the Home Rule Bill go by without congratulating you most heartily on this great step in the cause to which you have given your life.'[56] When Redmond extended his policy of home defence to active service with the British forces three days after Home Rule was placed on the statute book, many diasporic nationalists commended the IPP's achievement and Redmond's decision to support the British. In Newcastle, England, an Irish battalion of 1,100 men was formed in two weeks following T. P. O'Connor's meeting in the city in October 1914 at which reference to Home Rule was made.[57] At St Andrew's Hall in Glasgow, 'the most enthusiastic demonstration ever held in Scotland in the forty years' history of the Home Rule struggle [took place]'. It had been organized by the UILGB to express confidence in Redmond and his policy to support 'the just war of the Allies against Prussian militarism' and more than 400 representatives of Irish organizations in Scotland attended, including magistrates, MPs, Liberals, Labour town councillors, soldiers and Belgian refugees. Local reports suggest that 6,000 nationalists turned out. A pledge was made 'to every Irishman, whether by unity, loyalty and patriotism at home' to join the forces 'so that old traditions shall be maintained and new lustre be added to Irish arms in this great Continental war'. Support for Britain and the Allies was demonstrated through singing their national anthems and O'Connor was authorized to 'forward telegrams pledging support of the cause of the Allies to King George, King Albert, President Poincaré, and the Irish leader'. At the end of the proceedings, the audience sang the constitutional nationalist song, 'A Nation Once Again', which probably had greater relevance in light of the fact that Home Rule was on the statute book.[58]

Many diasporic nationalists in Britain and Australia were enthused by the notion that nationalist Ireland had backed the British war effort. Their enthusiasm was made more apparent when the Home Rule bill was passed and Redmond announced his support for active service. Alongside the wider mobilization for war within the societies in which Irish settlers lived, the diaspora had many reasons to throw their lot in with the Allies, one of which was a deep sense of loyalty to the British Empire.

### Irish Catholic loyalism

As the nineteenth century progressed, Irish Catholic settlers increasingly assimilated within the imperial system and most people came to believe that their adopted societies were good ones.[59] Growing social mobility had encouraged this process, as was evident in cities such as Toronto, where Irish Catholics started to identify more and more with Canadian life and values over the period 1887 to 1922 – 'a consequence of the rise of new Canadian-born generations of Catholics, better integration of Catholics into Toronto's socio-economic structures, indigenized Catholic leadership, and a greater willingness among Catholics to participate in civic life'.[60] This was also the case in NSW and Victoria, where notable Irish feast days, such as St Patrick's Day, took on more significance from 1880, as statesmen of Irish descent became prominent organizers in the annual celebrations.[61]

Many influential Irish Catholic settlers were committed nationalists who held allegiances to both Ireland and their Dominion. During the war, they were some of the Empire's most ardent defenders, and one influential group which held these allegiances were Catholic clergymen, such as the Newfoundland-born Archbishop, Michael Francis Howley. Howley was first-generation Irish, spoke Gaelic, and was a member of the Dublin Royal Society of Antiquaries. During the 1880s he visited Ireland and was interviewed by *The Freeman's Journal*, declaring that he supported Irish self-government and that Home Rule would restore power to the Irish, protecting them from bungling British governance; a state of affairs he compared with how Newfoundland Catholics were treated by the Newfoundland House of Assembly. Howley also played an integral role in developing a Newfoundland national consciousness in the 1900s. When war broke out in 1914, he supported the enlistment of Newfoundland Catholics because 'it was the first time the colony had the opportunity to offer military support in an Imperial conflict'. It was also 'the first true test of whether the ideals the Church had preached to the Catholic community', which linked Catholicism with patriotism, were instilled within the populace.[62]

Bishop Michael Fallon of London, Ontario was another 'avid supporter' of Home Rule and during the war years his papers 'reveal a consistent interest in the "Irish Question"'. Following the Easter Rising, he 'remained convinced that dominion status for Ireland would strengthen the Imperial war effort'. In spring 1917, he wrote to the prominent Irish Canadians, Charles Doherty (minister of justice in Robert Borden's Conservative government, the son of emigrants from Derry and Cork, and one of the signatories for Canada in the Treaty of Versailles) and Charles Murphy (shadow secretary of state in Wilfrid Laurier's Liberal Party, as mentioned above), suggesting that prominent Irish Canadians in non-political roles sign a petition in support of dominion status for Ireland (Doherty shared Fallon's 'patriotic anxiety'[63]). Fallon was also deeply committed to Canada, and he encouraged recruitment in his sermons, believing that it was 'an opportunity for Catholics to establish a public identity as patriotic and loyal Canadians'.[64]

Some clerics made their allegiances to Ireland and their Dominion of residence explicit when they supported the war effort, such as Fr McShane of Montreal. He helped to form the Irish-Canadian regiment, the Irish-Canadian Rangers, in September 1914, and when the regiment deposited its colours in St Patrick's Catholic Church in June 1916, McShane spoke to a crowded congregation of soldiers and onlookers and stated, 'Remember the shamrock on your uniform and emblazoned on your banner, and never do anything to bring disgrace to that emblem.' The elderly priest, Fr Donnelly, also spoke at the event and declared that if he had been a younger man, 'I would certainly go to the front, and I would go, not as a priest, but as a soldier and a man, and count it the happiest hour of my life that I could fight in such a cause. As a priest of God and a good Irishman I feel that it is your duty to do this.'[65]

The commitment of Irish-Catholic Australian clerics to both the Empire and war effort seems less certain however, primarily because of the rhetoric expressed by the Cork-born anti-conscriptionist and Archbishop of Melbourne, Daniel Mannix. Mannix became a forceful advocate for Irish independence and played an integral role in the defeat of the Australian conscription referenda in October

1916 and December 1917.[66] To mobilize Catholic opposition against the bills, he followed the line of the Catholic press in Australia, which criticized the British government for the execution of the Dublin rebels following the Easter Rising. On two occasions, Mannix declared that with regard to the war, 'Australia had done enough', implying that whatever support Irish-Australian Catholics had for Australia's involvement in the conflict had ended.[67] His forceful rhetoric and actions have been considered indicative of Irish Catholic feeling throughout Australia (both clerical and lay), leading one historian to conclude that two distinct Australian identities were being forged in wartime Australia: 'One that wished to break off with the Empire and that was backed by Mannix and Catholics, and another one that wanted to remain closely involved with Britain and that was supported by [prime minister] Hughes and Protestants.'[68]

This analysis does not hold up, however, as in 1920 in the middle of the Anglo-Irish war, Mannix took part in a St Patrick's Day parade in Melbourne in which his car was preceded by fourteen Australian Victoria Cross (VC) winners on mounted grey horses (see Figure 5.1), all of whom had served in the Australian Imperial Force (AIF). Archivists at the Australian War Memorial have established that ten of the VCs were Catholics while four were Protestants (all had Irish connections). During the parade, Mannix took part in a presentation in which he gave one of the VCs, the Catholic, John Patrick Hamilton, the collage shown in Figure 5.2. It was presented on behalf of Mannix and the Irish citizens of Victoria, and depicted photographs of the Irish-Australian VC winners – the Protestants as well as the Catholics. Notably, Mannix's image was centred along with that of the event organizer, John Wren, the son of working-class Irish immigrants.[69] This collage (and its presentation to Hamilton on St Patrick's Day) was intimately symbolic. Mannix clearly wished to demonstrate his support for Ireland, Australia

**Figure 5.1** Archbishop Mannix accompanied by fourteen Irish-Australian VC winners, 17 March 1920. National Library of Australia, *Professor Patrick O'Farrell Photograph Collection*, PIC P2215/10 LOC BAY 44 3/4.

**Figure 5.2** Composite photograph of fourteen Irish-Australian VC winners, presented to Lieutenant John Hamilton VC by Archbishop Mannix on 17 March 1920, Australian War Memorial (hereafter AWM), P01383.017.

and Irish-Australians of both creeds (particularly the Catholics) who had fought on Australia's behalf in the Great War, and he chose to do this on the feast day of Ireland's national saint.

Mannix's notoriety has been overstated by historians, however, as he was not as important as other members of the Australian Catholic hierarchy in the

mobilization to defeat the conscription referenda.[70] During the Great War, *all* of
the Australian archbishops were born in Ireland without exception and almost all
of the bishops were Irish or of Irish descent. These included archbishops Michael
Kelly of Sydney (born 1850, Co. Waterford), Patrick Clune of Perth (born 1864,
Co. Clare), Patrick Delany of Hobart (born 1853, Co. Galway), John O'Reily (also
spelt O'Reilly) of Adelaide (born 1846, Co. Kilkenny) and his successor, Robert
William Spence (born 1860, Co. Cork), James Duhig of Brisbane (born 1871, Co.
Limerick), Thomas Carr of Melbourne (born 1839, Co. Galway) and his successor,
Daniel Mannix (born 1864, Co. Cork). The bishops included John Dunne of
Bathurst (born 1845, Co. Cork), the brothers, Patrick Vincent Dwyer of Maitland
and Joseph Wilfrid Dwyer of Wagga Wagga (born to Irish parents from Kilkenny
in 1858 and 1869), Matthew Gibney of Perth (born 1835, Co. Cavan), Joseph
Higgins of Rockhampton (born 1838, Co. Westmeath) and Patrick Phelan of Sale
(born 1856, Co. Kilkenny).[71] The Catholic hierarchy in Australia was thus virtually
all-Irish and intrinsically connected to the 'mother country' during the main years
of forging the Australian national identity. Some of these prelates played a major
role in the Dominion's war effort, such as the Archbishop of Perth, Patrick Clune.
He became senior Catholic chaplain of the AIF, putting him at the head of military,
civil and clerical relations of Australian Catholics in wartime. His brother, Francis,
served as chaplain with the ANZAC forces and was awarded the military medal.[72]
In October 1916, Archbishop Clune visited the House of Commons where he met
with John Redmond, and he expressed a wish to visit Clare where his brother was
recovering from wounds received at the front.[73] Clune's ties to Ireland were also
later demonstrated in 1920, when he tried to promote peace between the British
government and Sinn Féin during the middle of the Anglo-Irish war (he was not
successful[74]).

The Archbishop of Sydney, Michael Kelly, also supported the Australian war
effort. In early August 1914, he declared his support for the Sydney Lord Mayor's
fund which was established to aid wartime distress.[75] His sermons reinforced
support for the Australian Catholic troops and cultivated dislike for the Germans.
In December 1914, he told parishioners to 'remember the Belgian nuns and
widows and orphans who have been treated by military tyrants as the Holy Family
were once treated by Herod', while in a 1916 Lenten pastoral, he declared that 'our
cause, indeed, is that of Public Right; but nations of prodigious power are arrayed
against us, and, so far, we are hard set in withstanding their aggression. Let us pray
for our army, for the fallen, for the suffering, and for Victory.'[76]

Kelly continued to promote constitutional nationalism after the Rising.
Following the death of Major Willie Redmond, the brother of the Nationalist
leader, at Messines Ridge in June 1917, Kelly held a memorial service in St Mary's
Cathedral in Sydney 'in view of the great sacrifice which the departed soldier
made on behalf of his native land'. *The Catholic Press* devoted an entire page to the
service, and the cathedral was 'completely filled'.[77] At least thirty-three priests and
prominent Australian Catholic representatives with Irish connections attended,
including the Lord Mayor of Sydney, Alderman Richard Denis Meagher (the first
Labour Lord Mayor of the district and son of an Irish policeman), the editors

and managers of *The Catholic Press* and *The Freeman's Journal*, the Australian Knights of Columbus and the Jesuit school, St Ignatius College, which had links to the Dublin province.[78] Irish associations were in abundance, including the Irish Executive Association, the INF and the Hibernian ACB Society, of which 'the whole of the city and suburban branches were well represented by their quota of members'. Kelly's sermon dwelt on nationalist Ireland's response to the conflict and made clear that the 'mother country' had influenced Irish Australia's response: 'John Redmond recruited. John Redmond went down to Wexford and said "We are with the Allies in this war; we are for the Empire in this war, for the war of the Empire is against injustice."'[79]

Germany was perceived to be the unjust party. This was a different sense of injustice than that held by the Irish in Ireland, for whom the war at sea and the feared consequences of food shortages were an important part of creating a discourse which associated wrongdoing with Germany. Rather, Kelly believed that Germany had threatened the political, religious and economic 'freedoms' which Catholics had secured within the Empire. In a pastoral letter in October 1916, he told parishioners that 'our sacrifice even of life and limb is demanded. Otherwise we may be victims of the more powerful enemy, who will take away our liberties and despoil our possessions.'[80] Kelly believed that the Empire had bestowed liberty and freedom on Irish Catholics in Australia, an attitude that was reflected more generally throughout the Irish Catholic world, as in Ontario, Bishop Fallon encouraged his parishioners to respond to Canada's war call, calling it their 'imperial duty'.[81] For Fallon, the conflict was a case of 'victory or the disappearance of the British Empire with its liberty and tradition. ... We are one, because we know Britain's cause is just.'[82] Sir Charles Fitzpatrick, Chief Justice of the Supreme Court of Canada and the grandson of Irish Famine immigrants to Quebec, echoed these sentiments at a recruiting meeting for the Irish-Canadian Rangers in July 1916. He referred to the advantageous economic and social positions Catholics had secured in Canada, which he felt were worth defending: 'We Irish have not done badly here. ... Who is the head of the greatest railway in the world? Who is the Minister of Justice in Canada? And what am I?'[83]

This positive vision of the Empire was qualitatively different from the negative perception held by advanced nationalists in Ireland, who trumpeted the Empire's wrongdoings and shortcomings. Memory of this less savoury Empire was not forgotten by Irish Catholics in Australia either, who made a clear distinction between the Empire of an earlier age and the Empire of freedom and liberalism, which clerics including Kelly believed he was part of during the Great War. In his speech at Willie Redmond's memorial, Kelly referred to the Empire of the nineteenth century as a 'corrupt' entity, yet urged parishioners to continue lending support to the contemporary Empire, which was fighting to defend its 'liberty' in 1917.[84] His conception of the earlier Empire was bound up with Irish nationalism, as both the Empire and England had, in nationalist accounts, historically oppressed Irish Catholics, giving them a distinct sense of nationality. This view was more widely held within Irish clerical circles throughout the Irish Catholic world, as Bishop Fallon was 'the first to admit English wrongdoings against Ireland' and

'consistently underlined his support for Irish Home Rule' because his parents had
been forced to leave Ireland when they were evicted by landlords. Yet his Irish
identity, forged as it was against English oppression, was reconciled with the
Empire by the time of the Great War because he believed that the imperial system
had given Irish Catholics prosperity and freedom.[85] Charles Fitzpatrick shared
this view, and in April 1916 he used the Irish nationalist memory of English and
imperial oppression to encourage Catholic Montrealers to fight for the Empire
he admired. He referred to historic dates when England had oppressed Ireland,
claiming that the England of 1917 had transformed Anglo-Irish relations because
of Liberal and Conservative policies:

> Ireland is no longer the Ireland of '96, '98 '48 or even of 1860. A new order of
> things has arisen (hear hear). The land laws are altered. Home rule practically
> conceded, and it now remains for Irishmen to show that as they know how to
> resent wrong and injustice, they also know how to appreciate fair and honest
> treatment ... the old dream that 'England's difficulty is Ireland's opportunity'
> was never so true as today, but it was an opportunity to help in the prosecution
> of the Empire.[86]

The Easter Rising and the execution of the Dublin rebels threatened to puncture
the new Empire narrative, reviving the Empire of past wrongs at a time when
Irish Catholic elites across the new world were trying to appeal for more Irish
recruits. Settlers were very concerned.[87] In Canada, readers of the *Montreal
Gazette* learnt of the rebellion in its entirety, and there was no attempt by Canadian
authorities to censor news emanating from Dublin.[88] Headlines read, 'Executions
must cease. Even loyal nationalists would revolt at continuance.' The newspaper
called for Dublin Castle to be overhauled: 'Ireland must have [a] radical change
in rule.'[89] At the end of May Irish events still dominated the front page. Readers
learnt of Roger Casement's attempt to form an alliance with Germany through
encouraging Irish POWs to form a brigade in Germany's service (in this Casement
was unsuccessful).[90] They also learnt of Casement's subsequent execution by the
British, the imposition of martial law in Ireland and the hostility of Irish-American
organizations to the government's actions.[91]

Support for the IPP in both Canada and Australia began to diminish after the
rebellion.[92] Robert McLaughlin has argued that Irish Catholic Canadians switched
their allegiances to Sinn Féin by supporting the party's claim to 'independence'.
Some Irish Catholic Montrealers were sympathetic to radical-leaning associations,
writing to Archbishop William Walsh of Dublin to propose raising a collection for
those who had suffered in the rebellion, especially the families of the executed.[93]
This collection became the INAVDF.[94] Following a request by Walsh, Irish-
Australian bishops also contributed to the fund to demonstrate sympathy at the
lives lost and destruction wrought in the rebellion's suppression.[95]

However, diminishing support for the IPP and increased sympathy for
the INAVDF were not signs of increasing Irish-Australian support for Irish
republicanism, as radical nationalist organizations remained 'thin on the ground'.

Many Catholics believed that the rebels had betrayed Redmond's chances of achieving Home Rule, which they felt was the type of government most suited to Ireland's development, putting Ireland on a par with Irish Australia. O'Farrell has argued that support for the IPP in Australia actually waned because many Irish-Australians felt that the party should have done more to have influenced the government's handling of the rebellion and executions. Moreover, when rumours emerged that the party had agreed to the permanent partition of Ireland, it was discredited in Irish Australia's eyes, even though the rumours were not true.[96]

Despite these challenges, *at no point* did Irish Catholic settlers lose their belief in the value of the British Empire, one that they were willing to mobilize for and defend. This was the case in Australia, where 'Irish Australia joined in the great surge of loyalty ... the leading Home Rule families were unquestionably pro-British, to the degree of giving their sons. ... The Irish Catholic community was as heavily committed to the war as any other sector of Australia.'[97] In Canada, McLaughlin has argued that 'to publicly express support for Irish independence had always been sharply restrained by virtue of the continued imperial connection'.[98] In Montreal, recruitment remained unaffected by Irish affairs. On 12 June 1916, the *Gazette* stated that 'the recruiting work of the Rangers had been maintained without interruption, and with good results in Montreal, and in districts of the eastern townships covered by the campaign'.[99] When recruitment fell towards the end of the year, the decline was paralleled with every other military district in Canada over the same period.[100] This was probably due to the disastrous consequences of the Somme, at which Canadians had suffered heavily (the Canadian infantry suffered more than 24,000 casualties from September to November 1916, excluding the Newfoundland battalion's losses on 1 July 1916), as well as the realization that the war was far from over, especially when large-scale offensives had not substantially moved the trenches in the Allies' favour.[101] Robin Burns has argued that the Rising appeared to have had no impact on the commitment of Irish Catholic Montrealers to the Canadian war effort: 'The only evidence to be found of Irish disaffection in Montreal during the Great War was the pro-German statements made by a solitary Irishman. These were made shortly after the Easter rebellion while the executions were being carried out.'[102]

Why did the Dublin rebellion fail to influence Irish Catholic settlers' loyalty to the Empire and support for the war effort even though they were evidently concerned about Ireland? The sources suggest that over the course of the nineteenth and early twentieth centuries, Irish Catholics had increasingly come to consider themselves as co-owners of the British Empire. 'Greater Ireland', the Irish world that cohered within the Empire, had been built by emigration and Catholic mobility within the imperial system. By the time of the war, Irish Catholics had come to hold some of the most influential positions within the Dominions, motivating settlers to rally to the Empire's defence.

As Sinn Féin began to gain electoral ground in Ireland, advanced nationalists in the 'mother country' promoted a different form of Irishness that sought to break the connection with England and sever Ireland's imperial ties. Irish Catholic imperial settlers could endorse (with enthusiasm) severing the English connection, as they firmly believed in Irish self-government and the right to govern themselves, which explains why Irish Canadians could lend support to Sinn Féin. However, settlers could not sanction the party's willingness to break from the Empire because this was anathema to their conception of self. For some time, the Irish Catholic settler nationality had been reconciled with the imperial system and while settlers supported Irish 'independence', they could only ever support the Irish republican movement in a limited way.

This may explain why the settler-Irish became less intrinsically connected to the politics of the 'mother country' once Sinn Féin took power and sought to sever the British and imperial connection, as settlers could not endorse the anti-imperial elements of Sinn Féin's nationalism. This in itself is worth considering, for it suggests that elements of constitutional nationalism reigned strong in settler-Irish communities even when support for the IPP had waned. In his landmark study of Irish Home Rule, Alvin Jackson has argued that Home Rule was 'always more than Redmondism and the Irish Party; and when these each faded into oblivion, other aspects of this great national alliance lived on'. A parallel can be drawn for the settler-Irish, for whom the ideological basis of Home Rule reflected their own attachment to the Empire. Catholic loyalism was 'greater than loyalty to any single political party or leader'; it had deeper roots that 'outlived the lifespan of the Home Rule programme', and when the IPP lost the support of its voters in Ireland and the sympathies of the Irish abroad, major aspects of the Home Rule programme 'lived on' within the settler-Irish communities of the New World.[103]

If the Rising had no discernible effect on the diasporic commitment to the war effort, what about the proposed imposition of conscription? It is well known that Irish Catholics played a leading role in protesting against the military service bills proposed in Australia and that Archbishop Mannix linked affairs in Ireland to his stand against enforced military service.[104] However, O'Farrell has argued that Mannix's hostility to compulsion actually had little to do with Ireland or the prosecution of the war. Irish Catholic Australians 'and a massive section of the whole population' were hostile to the bills because they held a deep conviction that the Tory British Australian government was intent on oppressing them and conscription was 'the enslaving program of the ascendancy party'.[105] Though this does not seem a sufficient explanation to account for the vehemence against adopting conscription in Australia, Catholic Irish-Australian hostility was further compounded when details of the bills emerged, as the ruling governments threatened to conscript ministers of religion. This had been done in New Zealand and Irish Catholic clergymen in Australia were intent on making sure that the Australian government did not do the same to them. They therefore used their influential positions to whip up hostility against conscription, directing their flocks to defeat the bills because compulsion threatened their lives as well.[106]

Conversely in Newfoundland and Canada, Irish Catholics were forceful advocates of enforced military service. The significant Irish Catholic population of St John's in Newfoundland supported conscription which the Protestant minority rejected.[107] Similarly in Canada, Catholics of Irish descent helped to enforce compulsion, though there were domestic political divisions between those who supported the Union Government and those who supported the Liberals. In the general election of 1917 in which conscription was made a core issue, Union representatives that supported the bill, including Charles Doherty, won over 6,000 votes from the predominantly Irish Catholic riding of St Ann's, which was more than the combined votes cast for his opposing candidates (approximately 4,323 votes).[108] Furthermore, the Canadian clergy were exempt from compulsory military service, which probably explains why the Church did not take a stand against the proposals as it had done in Australia.[109]

Catholic loyalism was thus a major factor that prompted Irish settlers, particularly those who had benefited from social mobility within the Dominions, to rally to the Empire's defence. Loyalists were often staunch Irish nationalists, and while some may have lost support for the IPP after the Rising, the rebellion had no significant impact upon their commitment to the Empire's war effort because Irish Catholic settlers – largely elites, educated and in prominent positions – believed that they owned the imperial system; it was worth defending from foreign attack. This imperial conception of the Irish Catholic nationality was sealed when the diaspora fought at the front.

### 'Ireland's half million'

In a welcome letter issued to the Irish-Canadian Rangers who were touring Ireland in early 1917, John Redmond claimed that he was proud of the 500,000 men of the 'Irish race' who had voluntarily joined the colours. Since Redmond had no accurate figures for Irish diasporic enlistments, his claim was hyperbole, though it was widely cited throughout the Empire.[110] Even today, the wider Irish military contribution is impossible to accurately state, partly because of a lack of research. An unpublished document from the Canadian Department of National Defence has suggested that at least 20,000 Irish-born soldiers served in the CEF excluding those who crossed over the border from the United States.[111] Kildea has estimated that approximately 6,600 Irish-born men served in the AIF (1.58 per cent of total AIF enlistments, that is, 417,000 men), about 60 per cent of whom were Catholics. The Australian Irish, both Protestant and Catholic, enlisted in proportion to the overall population.[112]

Another impediment to estimating the number of Irish men within the Dominion forces was the British habit of recording the ethnicity of Irish Catholic enlistees as 'British'. Scholars have attempted to circumvent this problem by analysing the religion of men who joined up because so many Catholic settlers had Irish origins. In Canada, McGowan has argued that up to June 1917, Irish Catholics volunteered in the CEF in proportion to their numbers if not more heavily. Excluding the French-Canadian population, which accounted for 30 per cent of Canada's volunteers yet the majority of Roman Catholics, 36,512 English-speaking and 'ethnic' Catholics enlisted; that is, circa 4.87 per cent of the total non-francophone Catholic population and roughly 10.29 per cent of all recruits regardless of denomination. In Nova Scotia, where the majority of Catholic residents were Irish or Irish-born, Catholics accounted for 47 per cent of recruits by 1916 while comprising only 28 per cent of the province's population.[113] Similarly in Newfoundland, Irish-Catholic Newfoundlanders volunteered in great numbers, encouraged by their almost wholly Irish clergy.[114]

The Catholic Irish also comprised a significant number of British recruits. A report from the UIL in Scotland issued on 14 December 1914 claimed that 15,559 Irish nationalists had enlisted with large contributions from Glasgow (7,056), Edinburgh (1,648) and Dundee (1,500). The organization declared that 'we possess the names of all the nationalists in these returns'.[115] By the same date, Liverpool had purportedly raised 12,000 Irish men and Manchester 9,000. John Dillon, speaking in April 1915, drew on UILGB statistics to declare that 27,511 Irish men or their sons had joined the colours in Scotland, in addition to the 10,000 who had previously been in the forces. While these statistics were open to exaggeration, Elaine McFarland has argued that they provide a useful indicator of Irish-born and later generation Irish Catholic enlistment in British cities in the opening two years of war. St Joseph's Parish (North Woodside, Glasgow), St Peter's (Partick, Glasgow), St Luke's (Govan, Glasgow), St Andrew's (Dumfries) and the Catholic Young Men's Society (Sterling) are some of the parishes and organizations where the local rolls of honour exhibited Irish Catholic sacrifice.[116]

These figures suggest a substantial Irish diasporic military contribution which was made through non-Irish regiments. Other units which had significant numbers of first- and second-generation Irish men for which we have no figures include the Canadian Irish Fusiliers, the Irish Regiment of Canada, the New Zealand Expeditionary Force, the South African Irish Regiment, the 5th Battalion South African Infantry Regiment, the United States Army, the Liverpool Irish, the London Irish Rifles, the Tyneside Irish Brigade, the Northumberland Fusiliers and the Black Watch. This is implied in the sources, as on 4 December 1914, the chaplain, Henry Gill SJ, wrote to his superior that 'I wish it were possible to obtain details of the immense numbers of Irishmen who were in the British army in units other than Irish'.[117] Some of these men included William Keogh, a Catholic from Wicklow who had worked as a policeman in Liverpool, NSW, before he enlisted in the AIF in November 1914.[118] James McDowell had been a policeman in London for four years before he was called up as a reserve with the Grenadier Guards.[119] Patrick Butler, a Catholic from Croom, Co. Limerick, left Ireland for New Zealand in 1909 to work with his uncle. He joined the New Zealand Expeditionary Force.[120] Frank Kenny, an alumnus of Mungret, the Jesuit school in Limerick, had worked on an Indian rubber plantation before moving to Canada. He enlisted in the CEF and later transferred to the Connaught Rangers as a lieutenant.[121] Irish Catholic chaplains were particularly visible in the Empire's war effort. Six Irish Jesuits served with the AIF, while forty-three Irish Jesuits from the Irish and English Provinces served in Irish, British and Canadian detachments. Six were killed, and two died from illness.[122] While a separate study is needed, the 'Irish' character of the United States' armed forces was also apparent, as on 27 March 1917, one Father McCann wrote to his superior that 'I have been chaplain to two American vessels here for some time. Most of the RC are of Irish descent[.] Two were born in Ireland'.[123]

Most emigrants and their descendants had families, friends and former colleagues in Ireland, linking the Irish in Ireland to the fortunes of the diaspora. Jack Timony, a sergeant with the CEF, had a brother in Galway who was the organist at Loughrea Cathedral.[124] James O'Callaghan, a Catholic from Enniscorthy, enlisted in the 13th Battalion Cheshire regiment. One of his uncles, M. J. O'Connor, was a solicitor in Wexford while the other was a military chaplain.[125] William and Catherine Doyle, a shopkeeper and dressmaker in Kilkenny, were the parents of Matthew Doyle who enlisted in the Australian Army Medical Corps.[126] Their other children (Mary, Brigid, James and Patrick) were respectively employed in Kilkenny as a schoolteacher, seamstress, scholar and carpenter's apprentice.[127] Patrick Kiely, a Catholic from Blackpool, Co. Cork, emigrated to Australia sometime after 1911 to follow his brother, Robert. Both enlisted in the AIF in 1914, leaving behind twelve family members who owned a flour and meal store on York Street.[128]

Ireland thus had a physical presence within the Empire's war effort, and a Redmondite conception of Irishness was visually and verbally inscribed within diasporic armies, such as in the Irish-Canadian Rangers. Its allegiances to Ireland and Canada were symbolically displayed in the regiment's cap badge, which featured a crowned shamrock above a maple leaf. The shamrock was the biggest symbol and its central position foregrounded the Irish identity within the Empire's service. Redmondite Irishness was further depicted in the Irish harp that was stitched onto the collars of men's uniforms and the regiment's motto was *Quis Separabit* ('Who Shall Separate Us'), which was a similar motto to that of five other Irish regiments.[129] The Tyneside Irish cap badge reflected these allegiances, as it displayed a large harp topped with a smaller crown.[130]

Ireland featured in the propaganda used to entice potential recruits. Figure 5.3 shows a prominent recruiting poster issued in Canada in July 1916, which encouraged Irish settlers to join the 199th Battalion Irish-Canadian Rangers, which recruited for active service. Burns has argued that if recruitment could have had a theme, 'it was Irish unity, the unity that had been achieved by Irishmen in Canada'.[131] One of the poster's architects was Sam Hughes, a Protestant, member of the sectarian Protestant fraternal association, the Orange Order, and the Minister of Militia and Defence in Robert Borden's Conservative government.[132] Hughes claimed that men of Irish descent should join the Rangers 'so that the Orange of Ontario could don the Khaki and fight shoulder-to-shoulder with the Green of Quebec'.[133]

His appeal for 'unity' through common war service was disseminated in the largely Catholic province of Quebec as well as the largely Protestant province of Ontario, and it resembled the notion of unity championed by John Redmond (Redmond hoped that common war service by Irish Protestants and Catholics would transform unionist-nationalist relations and, more fundamentally, allow Protestants to accept the imposition of Home Rule.[134]) As in Ireland, the war was viewed in Irish-Canada as an opportunity to rid cities such as Toronto of their sectarian divisions. This was the popular conception in Australia, and 'for a time this goal seemed attainable with Catholics and Protestants joining together to support the war effort'.[135] 'Unity' between divided groups was actually a common

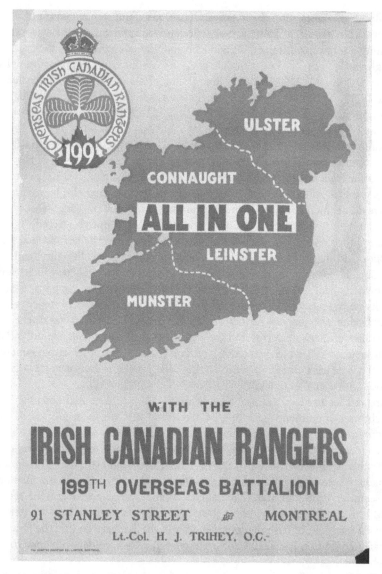

**Figure 5.3** Recruitment and 'unity' in Irish-Canada. © IWM (Art. IWM PST 12459).

theme championed by many leaders in wartime, at least until the cracks which had divided these societies before the war re-emerged when the ideal of political unity had crumbled away.[136]

Nonetheless, many Irish Catholic settlers went to war in the belief that Ireland had backed the Allies and 'Redmondite' Irishness, which intertwined allegiances to Ireland and the Empire, featured heavily in the Dominions' military efforts.

Groups of Irish men often enlisted together, prompting the Irish-born chaplain with the AIF, Patrick Tighe, to comment that 'the Queenslanders are the most Catholic and most generous people in Australia – plenty of Irish blood and Irish faith manifest'.[137] Irishness was also expressed through popular culture. Songs evoked a nostalgic attachment to Ireland and the Dominion from which settlers had come, and on 10 March 1916, the Catholic sergeant, J. J. Makin with the 21st Battalion AIF, described a concert his troops attended at Fremantle, Western Australia, in which Irish and other songs were sung. It had 'all the popular songs, including "The sands of the desert", "Mother Machree" and "my little grey home in the west"'.[138]

St Patrick's Day was an important occasion for the diasporic Irish even though they were serving in non-Irish regiments. Celebration of the feast had increased in Australia since the mid-1890s when leading clerics began to promote it, especially as the Home Rule crisis had given Irish Catholic Australians a purpose to celebrate their Irish roots.[139] At the front, St Patrick's Day afforded soldiers a chance to identify with something familiar when stationed in war-torn regions, but it also physically linked the Irish in Ireland to the imperial diaspora through the gift-giving of shamrock. Francis Browne, a chaplain with the Irish Guards and nephew of the Bishop of Cloyne, thanked the Irish Jesuit Provincial, Fr Nolan, for the shamrock he received from him on the 15 March 1916.[140] That year, Major T. D. McCarthy with the same regiment recorded in his diary that he received shamrock, and that 'a long fine concert took place in the evening singing jigs etc'.[141] Ever since the Second Boer War, the Irish Guards has been allowed to wear sprigs of shamrock (an honour bestowed on them by Queen Alexandra for their war service), but the Guards was not the only regiment that maintained the tradition during the Great War.[142] John Bannon, the son of a solicitor's clerk in Dublin, had emigrated to Australia with his brother, Nicholas, both of whom enlisted as gunners in the 2nd Field Artillery AIF.[143] In March 1915, John wrote in his diary that 'mother sent us a few boxes of shamrock, and we shared it with about 2 dozen of the lads, and we all went on parade as proud as punch'. For John, the episode evoked memories of Ireland: 'I am sure the pubs are doing a good business in Ireland to-day.' The importance of the symbol to Nicholas was clear when an officer told him to 'take that flower out of his cap, but Nick would not'. When the officer was told that it was St Patrick's Day, he changed his attitude: 'He said he was sorry, "Shure", he said, "I should have a piece up myself for I'm Irish", and we saw him half an hour after with a great piece in his own cap.'[144]

St Patrick's Day was also celebrated within Irish regiments, and the day was marked by men of both creeds. In March 1915, the Dublin Presbyterian, Noel Drury, recalled 'a great evening' spent with the officers and men of the religiously mixed 6th Battalion RDF who held a concert: 'Stuffner Byrne came on the stage dressed like a stage Irishman gone mad. He had on a pair of white hunting breeches which were so tight that it seemed as if he had been melted and poured into them, a green tail-coat and a large check waistcoat and shilleleagh [sic] completed his rig.'[145] In March 1918, the remaining Irish men in the 10th (Irish) Division (the division had been effectively destroyed at Gallipoli, Serbia and Palestine), compiled an itinerary of activities to celebrate the day and the celebration was cross-confessional, including the Ulster Presbyterian, F. P. Crozier, the Cork Anglican, Henry Gerald Livingstone and the Catholic officer, T. S. P. Martin.[146]

Neither politics nor religion appeared to have prevented the Irish in Ireland from sending shamrock to their troops of both creeds. In Co. Armagh, Delmege Trimble, the proprietor of the unionist newspaper, *The Armagh Guardian*, and the organizer of an Armagh-based war-relief association, sent 'shamrock galore' to the locally recruited and religiously mixed regiment, the Royal Irish Fusiliers, in 1915 and 1916.[147] Similarly in 1915, the 2nd Battalion RMF received 'two enormous boxes of shamrock' from the Irish Quaker, Mrs Blennerhasset, and the Anglican landlord, Lord Dunraven. The Cork Anglican, Major Victor Rickard, an officer in the Munsters whose father-in-law was the rector of Mitchelstown, remarked that

> the shamrock was brought up in an ammunition cart and placed on the steps of the altar. It was blessed by Father [Francis] Gleeson, and the men came up one by one and received a spray.[148] All the time we could hear the guns firing away quite near. I am sure the men will never forget it. ... The men made wreaths of shamrock and put them on the graves of all the men killed in the district, and a wreath and cross on Major Ryan's grave – the only officer buried there.[149]

The gift-giving of shamrock and celebration of St Patrick's Day linked the Irish in Ireland, Australia, Canada and elsewhere (as well as the Irish at the front) to an 'imagined community' of Irish people that assumed intercontinental dimensions.[150] David Feldman has argued that a shared Jewish ethnicity was held by men who served in the war that were from different countries within the Empire, linking them to a religious community that straddled national borders.[151] A parallel can be drawn for the Irish, for whom men of different political and religious backgrounds shared a common Irish nationality that had transnational dimensions. Though it masked the differences that divided settlers and the Irish in Ireland – factors relating to politics, religion, economics and class that were dependent upon the nature of the societies in which they lived – Irishness was a capacious enough identity to subsume these differences at a transnational level. In all cases, it is likely that celebrating St Patrick's Day brought the celebrants closer to Ireland, if only in their imagination, reinforcing the 'mother country's' importance to them while fighting on the Allies' behalf.

But the war also brought some settlers physically closer to Ireland due to its proximity to the front and some visited the 'mother country' when on leave. Daniel Joseph Scanlon, a Catholic sergeant with the 49th Battalion AIF, was born in Fraser's Hill, Brisbane. In late 1916, he was stationed in England and took the opportunity to visit cousins in Lissycasey, a village in rural Co. Clare (700 people, all of whom were Catholics) where he met his extended family for the first time.[152] On 27 December 1916, his cousin remarked in a letter:

> He came to visit us unexpected which came to a great surprised [sic] to us to see him. ... When he came in we did not know him & he said I am Dan Scanlan.

So we had hearty welcome for him & recived [*sic*] him with the greatest of kindness. We were more than rejoiced to him he had not a long stay … . We felt awfully bad when he was leaving. All the neighbours & friends came to see him (could not tell you how we felt for him he was such a nice person & a grand looking man).[153]

The visit of an Irish-Australian sergeant in khaki generated much enthusiasm in Lissycasey, despite being eight months after the Rising when hostility to Westminster was growing. It gave Scanlon's relatives a reason to monitor Australia's fortunes in the war and pay attention to his whereabouts, as in January 1917, Scanlon remarked to his nephew that 'my cousins in Ireland write to me regularly asking me to come over again'.[154] He evidently felt welcome in Clare, since he wrote to his niece that 'You may be sure I had a warm welcome – when I get my full leave I intend to see my mother's people & visit Ennis again'.[155]

Many Irish Catholic settlers and the Irish in Ireland were thus tied to the Empire's war effort. This was evident in the sheer number of Irish men who enlisted in the Dominion forces; the visual and verbal insignia of the diasporic New Army regiments, and through familial connections to Irish men serving in the Empire's forces. Irishness was an important marker of identity for Irish men at the front, and on occasions such as St Patrick's Day, it linked them with the Irish in Ireland and the Irish in the Dominions to an imagined global community, one that subsumed cross-confessional and other differences. This community was also broad enough to subsume different views on the British Empire, as revealed when a battalion of an Irish-Canadian regiment visited Ireland in early 1917.

### *Meeting Irish-Canada*

In late 1916, the British Conservative politician, Andrew Bonar Law (who had himself Canadian and Ulster origins) corresponded with the Canadian prime minister, Robert Borden, about the Montreal-based regiment, the Irish-Canadian Rangers, which was to embark on active service with the CEF.[156] Bonar Law wanted part of the regiment to tour Ireland before travelling to the front to stimulate interest in Irish recruitment, which had declined since 1915[157]: a symptom, it has been suggested, of a growing aversion to the Allied war effort.[158]

　By 1917 something new was afoot in Ireland. The advanced nationalist party, Sinn Féin, had grown in size and support, benefitting from the government's response to the Rising (though the initial beneficiary was, as Robert Kee has pointed out, the Home Rule party itself).[159] By early 1917, however, the IPP was in trouble. Its leadership was in crisis because of Westminster's handling of the executions, and the future of the Home Rule bill itself was now in doubt.[160] Debate about Irish self-government had been reinvigorated after the Easter Rising, putting an end to the political truce which had existed between Unionists and Nationalists during the war. In June 1916, when Lloyd George proposed to introduce immediate Home Rule for Ireland, he put forward the recommendation with the exclusion of Ulster, which effectively invalidated the bill that had been passed in September 1914.[161] Political discontent appeared to be growing, evident in the February 1917 by-election victory of the advanced nationalist candidate, Count Plunkett, the father of the executed rebel, Joseph Plunkett, which was the first electoral demonstration that all was not well with Redmond's party. Plunkett won almost twice as many votes as Redmond's candidate, though he 'stood on no very clear policy at all'. His single most important claim on the electorate was 'as the father of his dead boy and his two sons who were suffering penal servitude'.[162]

In the middle of these political developments a battalion of the Irish-Canadian Rangers visited Ireland. How the public responded to these Irish Catholic loyalists, whose commitment to the Empire was great, was a test of public feeling towards the war effort, Ireland's contribution to the Empire, as well as political feeling within Ireland itself, for ample opportunities for dissent and protest were created by visit. The battalion visited Dublin, Armagh, Belfast, Limerick and Cork, towns and cities that were different enough from one another to illuminate a cross-section of opinion. Limerick, for example, was a largely agricultural town and well known for its production of bacon, while Belfast, Dublin and Cork were more industrial.[163] Armagh occupied a middle-ground, since it was the administrative centre for rural south Armagh as well as the industrial north. Industry had stagnated there since the mid-nineteenth century, though its surrounding areas were still important centres for linen production.[164] It was also the ecclesiastical capital of Ireland, where the seats of both the heads of the Catholic Church and Church of Ireland were located.[165]

The level of interconnectedness these places had with the Empire also varied. Cork, Belfast and Dublin were thriving imperial ports and trading centres.[166] The British military also had regimental headquarters in Armagh, Belfast and Dublin, which were the respective headquarters of the Royal Irish Fusiliers, the Royal Irish Rifles and the RDF (though the latter was located outside of Dublin in Naas). Cork also had a large military barracks and 'the sight and sound of English, Welsh and Scottish soldiers around the streets of Cork not only brought benefits to the local service industry; it was also a direct reminder of the interconnectedness of the Empire and the union with Britain'.[167] Limerick did not have a military barracks but was one of the counties that provided recruits to the RMF, which also recruited from Cork.[168]

These centres were religiously mixed and had militarized to some extent during the Third Home Rule crisis. Sectarianism existed in different degrees, notably in Belfast, where the 1886 riots had resulted in approximately thirty deaths, while it was in Armagh that the sectarian Orange Order had its genesis in the north of the county.[169] Limerick had also demonstrated religious prejudices against its Jewish minority in 1904 when Catholics had instigated a boycott against its resident Jewish population.[170]

All of these places had contributed men to the war effort, but police inspector reports for early 1917 state that they were suffering from low recruitment.[171] Was this a reflection of growing hostility or apathy towards the war effort? One source suggests that it was. In 1952, Monsignor M. Curran, secretary to Archbishop Walsh from 1906 to 1919, issued a testimony for the BMH in which he recalled how the battalion was treated in Dublin. Noting that the archbishop had declined an invitation to meet the men, Curran declared that

> this visit of the Irish-Canadians was purely a recruiting device. It was a fiasco and made no appeal to the popular point of view. Between the icy winds and the growth of Sinn Féin, there was no popular demonstration though the press and official world did their utmost to promote its object ... the bishop of Cork did not attend the Cork reception.[172]

The press did its best to promote the tour, as nationalist and unionist organs advertised the trip in their columns.[173] These reports were far from hostile. The *Limerick Leader* reported that 'there is no doubt that Limerick, like the other cities to be visited, will give them a reception worthy of the best traditions of Irish hospitality'.[174] The *Cork Examiner* looked forward to the tour and declared that the Rangers were fighting for liberty: 'What Irishmen at home have striven for, and no one doubts that on the field of battle the Irish-Canadians will do honour to both Ireland and Canada.'[175] The *Irish Independent*, which became more critical of the IPP after the Rising, devoted an editorial to the trip and claimed that the Rangers 'naturally wish to visit the land of their forefathers, which many of them will see for the first time'.[176] The *Irish Times* also dwelt upon emigration, echoing the comments of the Catholic Lord Mayor of Dublin in the phrase: 'Every part of Ireland, and every school of thought and opinion here, can claim some members of the regiment as specially its own.'[177] The staunchly northern unionist newspaper, *The Northern Whig*, declared that 'considerable interest' was being aroused in light of the Rangers' pending visit, and noted that some of its officers had ties to Ireland. The adjutant of the battalion, Captain F. Shaughnessy, was the 'only surviving son and heir of lord Shaughnessy of Ashford County Limerick' while Major Campbell Stuart was a member of 'the well-known Omagh family'. The Protestant chaplain of the Rangers was Major Reverend James Smyth, formerly the Methodist pastor of Ormeau Road church in Belfast, and the newspaper announced that the battalion was under the command of 'a prominent Irish Roman Catholic lawyer of Montreal [Lieutenant-Colonel H. J. Trihey]'. The all-Irish experience of emigration was brought into the foreground in the press discussions of the Irish Canadians, who were 'coming to see the land of their forefathers and will number about 1000'.[178]

As Curran recalled, the 'official world' worked hard to promote the tour, endorsed as it was by city and town mayors.[179] Thomas Butterfield, the Catholic Lord Mayor of Cork, stated in a meeting of Cork citizens that the visit 'has neither military nor political significance (hear hear). They are coming as visitors'.[180] At a similar gathering in Limerick, Mayor Stephen Quin, a Catholic, claimed that 'the visit of this gallant regiment had nothing to do with recruiting or politics'.[181] Neither mayor used the visit to further a domestic political agenda, nor did the Lord Mayor of Dublin, the Catholic James Gallagher. This was also the case for the Protestant and Unionist Lord Mayor of Belfast, James Johnston, who spoke at a 'representative meeting' and claimed that the regiment would be welcomed by all groups, as the Canadians 'were nearly all descendants of Irish parents'.[182]

Catholic and Protestant elites encouraged local people to support the trip through financial donations. A subscription fund was established (the names of individual donors and subscribers were published in the press) and a significant contribution was made by the middle classes including centres of commerce, the professions and officials. In Cork, companies which subscribed at least £10 each to the fund included the Cork Steamship Company, the brewers, Beamish and Crawford, and the Catholic-owned brewing and distilling company, J. J. Murphy and Co. Irish bankers contributed the same, if not more, and subscriptions were received from the Bank of Ireland, the Munster and Leinster Bank, and the Hibernian Bank.[183] Affluent persons donated money, including Protestant and Catholic solicitors (e.g. the Anglican Francis Levis, and the Catholic Nationalist, J. J. Horgan), shop owners, such as Mr Keating from Cork Furniture Stores, professors such as Sir Bertram Windle from University College Cork and several justices of the peace (including the Catholic Denis Buckley and Jewish Simon Spiro).[184]

However, Curran's account appears less reliable in its recollection of popular responses to the visit, as a wealth of evidence shows that the battalion was enthusiastically welcomed by many groups of people. On 25 January 1917, the troops disembarked at Dublin's North Wall to be met by crowds who had gathered in the city from an early hour. A band of the Royal Irish Fusiliers was present and played the songs 'The Maple Leaf' and 'The Irish Emigrant' to welcome the Irish Canadians and reinforce the ties between Ireland and its settler population. This crowd was not a hostile one as the Rangers were met with 'frequent bursts of applause and cries of "Well done Canada", and "Bravo, Ireland", from the spectators'.[185] In January 1917 it was bitterly cold in Dublin.[186] Yet the weather did not prevent Dubliners from turning out in large numbers, as 'crowds of spectators lined the pavements and gave the Irish-Canadians a rousing reception'. Their excitement got out of hand when spectators 'in their demonstration of enthusiasm burst through the cordon of police and crowded out the Lord Mayor and the Right Hon. the Recorder'. At Phoenix Park, where the battalion had lined up for the lord lieutenant, the Union Flag was flown and the bands played 'God Save the King' without any associated protests.[187] This was not a reflection of nationalist acquiescence with British rule, as the authorities were soon grappling with republican flags that were hoisted in Limerick, Galway and elsewhere, but in January 1917, political discontent had not yet boiled over in this part of Dublin to result in outward hostility to British symbolism.[188] The press reports were confirmed in private sources, as Private Christopher Fox of the Royal Dublin Fusiliers wrote to the war-worker, Monica Roberts, that 'I think I was reading about the Canadian Rangers been in Dublin. ... They got a great Reception. ... I expect we will have them out here shortly'.[189]

The imperial press reported the Rangers' visit to Dublin and commended its cross-community nature, dwelling upon Ireland's contribution to the war with headlines such as 'Dublin gives greeting to Canadian Rangers. Press of all

shades of politics Warmly Welcome Visitors'; 'Canadian Rangers' Visit. "This
Ireland's War"'; 'Ireland and the Empire'; and "'Irish Race and the War": 500,00
Voluntarily Fighting.'[190] Following the Viceroy's inspection, the Rangers wer
treated to lunch at the Mansion House where a number of moderate nationalist
and unionists were present, some of whom would later take part in the much feted
Irish Convention (the series of meetings which took place during 1917 and 1918
to address the 'Irish Question' and other constitutional problems relating to the
enactment of self-government).[191] They included the Anglican, Dr James Ashe, a
former unionist-turned-Home Ruler who lobbied the government to convene a
meeting of representative Irish men (the meeting became the Convention). Ashe
also published a pamphlet, the subtitle of which read 'A Final Plea for Lasting
Conciliation', encouraging unionists and nationalists to work together in a Home
Rule Ireland within the Empire.[192] Some other attendees who later took part in
or contributed to the Convention included the Protestant unionist, Sir Horace
Plunkett, who formed Ireland's first cooperative, and his Catholic colleague,
T. P. Gill, the secretary of DATI.[193]

Some of the Mansion House attendees had direct experience of the conflict
and had mixed with people of different creeds via the war effort. A sense of unity
had emerged from their common endeavour which they were keen to promote
through their actions and rhetoric. Bryan Mahon, for example, had commanded
the 10th (Irish) Division in Gallipoli, though at the time of the Rangers' visit,
was commanding the British forces in Ireland. A Protestant and unionist, he
contributed to writing the history of the division and, in this work, was described
as an 'Irishman without politics' (though Charles Townshend has argued that 'this
meant he was a Protestant and an unthinking not to say pig-headed conservative'
because Mahon had led the flying column that relieved Mafeking during the Boer
War).[194] Nevertheless, the non-sectional nature of the division was stressed in its
divisional history, and this was partly due to the actions of two of the division's
clerics.[195] The Anglican, Canon McClean from Limerick, was at the Rangers'
reception. He had served as chaplain with the RDF alongside the Catholic priest,
Fr Murphy, and in Gallipoli both clerics became good friends and held their
church services in the trenches together.[196] Another attendee who believed that
the war had fostered a sense of unity between the Irish was Alex Fisher, a solicitor
from Warrenpoint, Co. Down. A Presbyterian and former unionist, Fisher had
signed the Ulster Solemn League and Covenant to protest against Home Rule in
1912.[197] In wartime, however, Fisher had been active in several cross-community
associations around the northern town of Newry including the Red Cross, the
National Federation of Discharged and Demobilized Sailors and Soldiers, and
recruitment meetings, where Catholic and Protestant clergy had spoken on the
same platform.[198] By the time of the 1918 general election, Fisher chose to run as
an independent candidate for South Down on a platform of Irish unity, where he
received 436 votes.[199] At one election meeting, he told a crowded room of listeners
that 'he would do all that he could to lead to that day that was fast approaching,
when all Irishmen and Irish women would unite together, regardless of creed or
class, and work only for the good of their own country: Ireland. (Applause)'.[200]

en, many of whom were political moderates, believed that something
bot in Ireland as a result of the war. This was not the divisive politics
n or Nationalism but was premised on a sense of common endeavour
ough the shared experience of conflict. No doubt this feeling was
by the number of cross-confessional associations in Ireland which
b assist the war effort, and the Rangers' visit inspired a similar cross-
al response. In Armagh, Protestants and Catholics united to form
n committee to greet the men after a meeting of Armagh citizens
under the presidency of Thomas M'Laughlin JP, the chairman of
:ity council. The staunchly unionist *Northern Whig* reported that
ers included the Catholic curate, Joseph Brady, and the Catholics,
/Neill JP, William Gallagher (a solicitor) and Edward Cowan (a pub-
¹ Armagh Protestants on the committee included the Archdeacon of
, the farmer, James Wilkins JP, and Hans Leeman, a merchant.[202] 'A
:rable sum' of money was handed in by local people of both creeds, who
enerally from the middle classes.[203] Even the *Northern Whig* commended
oss-community response: 'A reception committee, representative of both
ous denominations, was formed and the generous support accorded to the
/ement by all sections of the inhabitants enabled the committee to prepare
ull and comprehensive programme for the entertainment of the men on a
yal scale.'[204]

The cross-sectional response to the Rangers reflected the composition of
ne regiment itself, as Protestant and Catholic Montrealers of Irish descent had
contributed to its formation. The Rangers' headquarters was located in the Stanley
Presbyterian Church in Montreal despite one of the main committee members
being the Catholic priest, Fr McShane. Most but not all of the officers were of Irish-
Catholic descent, the remainder being descendants of Irish Protestants.[205] When
stationed in Montreal, the regiment marched to church services on Sundays,
splitting into two groups with the Catholics proceeding to 'St. Patrick's Church for
Low Mass, and the Protestant party to the Church of St. John the Evangelist'.[206] The
wider Montreal Irish reflected the Rangers' cross-sectional nature, made up as it was
by settlers of both creeds. In February 1916, the St Patrick's Society, a recreational
centre for Irish Catholics in Montreal, and the Irish Protestant Benevolent Society,
which had fractured from the former organization in the 1850s over diverging
political interests, jointly held a 'monster meeting' at Montreal's Windsor Hall,
in aid of giving 'moral support' to the religiously mixed regiment, at which the
presidents of both societies presided.[207]

Many sources thus referred to the Rangers as the 'Orange and Green' regiment
and its mixed nature was advertised as such across Ireland, Britain and the
Empire.[208] Most of these articles were descriptive but some commented on the
regiment's composition and expressed positive sentiments: 'A blending of colors
in a holy cause – good luck to them'[209]; 'a capital idea and an excellent example'[210];
'More power to the boys who are putting the call of Empire before bigotry and are
ready to fight for the Empire side by side with those from whom they differ on
other matters.'[211]

His Eminence Cardinal Logue, with Officers of the Irish Canadians.

**Figure 5.4** His Eminence Cardinal Logue with Officers of the Irish Canadians. Drysdale, *Canada*, p. 11.

When the men arrived in Armagh, they carried on in the tradition which had been established in Montreal as they split into two groups along religious lines, one of which proceeded to the Protestant cathedral for a service with the Lord Primate of All Ireland and Lord Archbishop of Armagh, John Baptist Crozier, while the other went to the Catholic cathedral for High Mass with Cardinal Michael Logue.[212] Crozier, a staunch unionist, offered the men 'a right royal welcome, "*Cead mile failte*".[213] Crozier's use of the well-known Gaelic greeting demonstrated that he considered the language part of his cultural heritage – something which had been challenged since the late nineteenth century when the Irish language had become increasingly intertwined with Catholicism and later, advanced nationalism.[214] He used the expression in a patriotic moment when loyal defenders of the Empire had visited Armagh and in tandem with his loyalty to the Crown, as the sermon concluded with the singing of 'God Save the King'.[215]

At the Catholic cathedral, Cardinal Logue welcomed the men (pictured in Figure 5.4 with the officers). His sermon was important because it was made in front of the international press at a time when there was growing political uncertainty within nationalist circles, yet it was distinctly imperial in tone:

> The Rangers had a distinct Irish existence. They were the first outside of the divisions raised in Ireland to establish a real, genuine Irish regiment, and to come forth to maintain the credit, honour and glory which their countrymen, scattered through the other troops of the dominions, had already won. Reading over the lists of honours, they knew that a large number of them were Irishmen from the dominions who knew how to maintain, and even to add to the fame

which Ireland ever possessed for bravery in the field of battle. ... They in Ireland had preserved the faith in spite of persecution, and they had carried it to distant Canada, Australia, and America and wherever the British flag flew the Irish Catholic was a missioner, and contributed to the grand, old, unfailing Irish Faith in all these countries.[216]

Though one historian has concluded that Logue made this speech to caution nationalists against radicalism, thereby reinforcing the underlying conservatism of the Catholic Church,[217] it seems likely that Logue was actually dwelling on the religious dimension of Ireland's relationship with the Empire. As Colin Barr has argued, Irish Catholic clerics had increasingly staffed the British Empire since the mid-nineteenth century and they were proud of that contribution.[218] Logue's speech reflected the sense of ownership which many Irish Catholic clerics felt for the Empire because they had helped to make the Church a formidable international institution.

Yet Logue's speech was just as related to the war and what the Irish-Canadian troops were perceived to have been defending from German attack. The Rangers drew many people onto the streets to welcome the men as Figure 5.5 reveals, and press reports suggest that these crowds were enthusiastic, as Protestants and Catholics turned out to greet the regiment together. The *Irish Independent* reported that 'all classes and creeds united in a cordial welcome. The streets were bedecked with flags and bunting and a large crowd accompanied the visitors to the Cathedrals. Orange and green favours were sported by many of the spectators.'[219]

THE MARCH TO THE CATHOLIC CATHEDRAL AT ARMAGH.

**Figure 5.5** The Catholic Irish Canadians arriving at Armagh Cathedral, 10 February 1917. Drysdale, *Canada*, p. 160.

*The Irish Times* reported that 'orange and green never blended more happily … bunting was profusely displayed, and the Union Jack was especially prominent'.[220] Contemporary police reports verify these claims, as the Armagh county inspector informed his superior that 'the Duchess of Connaught's Own (Irish) Canadian Rangers visited Armagh on 28 January and were cordially received by all parties and was entertained. They were much pleased with their reception'.[221] The imperial press made much of the trip as *The Toronto World* printed a large article entitled 'Orange and Green Join in Honoring Canadians. Visit of Canadian Rangers to Armagh Results in Blending of Emblems For First Time Since Battle of Boyne'.[222]

The Rangers' next stop was Belfast and more than forty people of Protestant and Catholic backgrounds arranged the trip. The organizing committee comprised the Catholics, Patrick Tiernan JP (a tobacconist) and Patrick Dempsey (a city councillor, spirit merchant, and senator at Queen's University), as well as the liberal Unionist ex-Lord Mayor of Belfast, Sir Crawford McCullagh – who in 1914 had welcomed the notion of a cross-confessional committee in Belfast formed to help Belgian refugees – and the Protestant chairman of the Harbour and Water Commissioners, Robert Thompson, and Robert Wilson.[223] Almost every county, rural and district council in Ulster issued a message of greeting to the men, as did prominent individuals including John Redmond, Sir Edward Carson, Cardinal Logue, the Catholic Bishop of Down and Connor, the Methodist vice-president, and the mayors of Dublin and Limerick.[224]

The well-known patriotism which Belfast Protestants had for the war effort was reflected in the enthusiasm displayed for the Irish Canadians, and the historical connections between Ulster and the Empire were much emphasized. The *Northern Whig* dwelt upon this history, remarking that Ulstermen had come from 'St John's to Vancouver and from [the] American line to [the] arctic'. It declared that 'we in Ulster are glad of the opportunity of testifying to our colonial brethren that our hearts beat in unison with theirs. Their love of Empire, of freedom, of justice, and of right can be no stronger than ours'.[225] Belfast's loyalty, which curiously resembled that of Irish Catholic settlers in the New World, was referred to with pride by the staunchly unionist organ, *The Belfast Telegraph*. Its editor used the city's loyalty to differentiate between Ulster's response to the war and that of the three southern provinces, as one editorial declared that Belfast had provided more recruits 'than all of Ireland put together'. It hinted that that contribution had been an Ulster Protestant one, since '30,000 of the Canadian soldiers were Ulstermen following Sam Hughes'.[226]

Yet the unionist press did not focus exclusively on the Protestant and unionist contribution, as the *Northern Whig* stated that 'whether they are Protestants or Roman Catholics, sympathizers with us who are unionists or with those who are home rulers, does not concern us in the least'. The most important factor was loyalty that had 'prompted so many of the Irish-Canadian Rangers to give up lucrative situations at home in order to fight for the Empire and for civilization in France'.[227] *The Belfast Telegraph* also declared that 'we welcome as Irish, irrespective of creed or politics, those who have come to strike a blow for the Empire which is nowhere loved more than in Ulster'.[228] The *Whig* could not resist a jibe at Redmond, however, reflecting on the poor recruiting situation in Ireland which it implicitly blamed on nationalists. It criticized Redmond's claim that 'Irishmen at home have set an example to Irishmen abroad'.[229]

These goodwill gestures went beyond the press, as the Unionist attorney-general for Ireland, Sir James Campbell, commended Catholic war service and declared that 'orange and green would carry the day'.[230] Some unionist organs criticized his speech, such as the *Belfast Evening Telegraph*, though it was commended by Ulster nationalist papers, such as *The Irish News* and the Newry-based newspaper, *The Frontier Town*, which hoped that his comments would 'have a very considerable bearing on the amelioration of the political condition of our country'.[231] While prejudices and political differences may have been the reality in Ulster, the Irish Canadians were considered the property of all sections, which helps explain why people of all backgrounds turned out to welcome the men as shown in Figure 5.6.

The *Independent* enthused that 'Nationalist and Orange districts, the residents of which, probably for the first time in recent years, join[ed] equally in the demonstration of welcome. Union Jacks and Irish flags were displayed on many sides'.[232] This report was confirmed by a Belfast police inspector, who wrote to his superior that 'the Canadian Rangers ... received a hearty and loyal reception from all parties, and were publicly entertained by the Lord Mayor and citizens'.[233]

BELFAST'S WELCOME TO THE IRISH-CANADIAN RANGERS : THE LORD MAYOR ADDRESSING THE REGIMENT OUTSIDE THE CITY HALL.

**Figure 5.6** The Irish Canadians in Belfast, *The Illustrated London News*, 10 February 1917.

The representative response was reported throughout the Empire, particularly in Australia, where the Melbourne-based *Argus* declared that 'the streets were packed with cheering people, who pinned orange and green ribbons and sprigs of shamrock on the men's tunics'.[234]

Was the Catholic turnout in Ulster simply a turnout of IPP supporters, given the party's electoral victories in the province in the 1918 general election? It would appear not, as in Cork, where the IPP was electorally eradicated, a cross-community committee was formed to meet the men following a public meeting in Cork council chambers on 12 January 1917.[235] It was presided over by James Bernard, the Protestant Earl of Bandon who had held several roles in British governance in Ireland.[236] Committee members included the Protestants, Richard Tilson JP, a merchant in the water industry, and the Protestant nationalist, A. F. Sharman-Crawford JP, as well as the Catholics, Thomas Butterfield (the Lord Mayor), James McNamara (a businessman), James Crosbie (a journalist) and John Horgan (a solicitor and leading Nationalist), alongside twenty-four other men of mixed confessional backgrounds.[237] When the Rangers arrived, they were welcomed by several hundred Cork people, many of whom were wearing working men's flat caps, demonstrating a strong turnout among the working classes (Figure 5.7).

The local police inspector wrote that 'the visit of the Irish Canadian bn [battalion] as reported in the Press was an unqualified success'.[238] The *Irish Independent* declared 'Stirring Cork Welcome' while *The Irish Times* championed 'Cork's great welcome'.[239] A reception committee 'comprising representative citizens of all classes' awaited the men and soldiers from the Royal Dublin Fusiliers, Leinster Regiment and Royal Irish Fusiliers 'played Canadian airs'.

MARCHING TO THE CITY HALL, CORK.

**Figure 5.7** The Irish Canadians in Cork. Drysdale, *Canada*, pp. 19–20.

The *Montreal Gazette* reported that Cork women also turned out, 'all of them wearing orange and green, the colours of the battalion'.[240] The *Quebec Telegraph* told Canadian readers that Ireland's welcome appeared warmer to its journalists every day and 'at every cottage and city tenement near the railway line there is the same reception'.[241] As the Irish Canadians marched to Victoria barracks, they were forced to make their way 'through crowds of spectators, who heartily greeted the visitors. Flags were displayed from many houses'.[242] A film was taken of the visit which confirms these reports.[243] No dissent was associated with the visit to Cork, and Dublin Castle censorship reports do not reveal any instances of censored protests, further confirming that the enthusiastic responses and warm welcomes were real (Figure 5.8).[244]

If Cork people were not hostile to the Irish Canadians as Monsignor Curran had claimed, why did 'the bishop of Cork ... not attend the Cork reception'?[245] The inspector general of the RIC suggested that it was not hostility to the war effort that had promoted Bishop Cohalan to stay at home. He wrote to the authorities that 'at Cork too, unionists and nationalists, Catholics and Protestants, joined in the reception; the Roman Catholic Bishop, however, though a member of the [organizing] Committee stayed away from the functions giving as his reason that he would thus have more influence over the Sinn Feiners'.[246] The bishop's absence was because of the growing influence of advanced nationalism in Cork, which he wanted to control. That he was a member of the organizing committee for the Rangers yet did not turn out to greet them suggests that he was playing both sides, upholding his influence with the establishment as well as with those who were

FORMED UP IN FRONT OF THE CITY HALL.

**Figure 5.8** Large crowds welcome the Irish Canadians outside Cork City Hall. Drysdale, *Canada*, pp. 19–20.

against it, though this had little to do with the Irish Canadians themselves, who he supported by arranging their trip to Cork.

The Rangers' last stop was the largely Catholic city of Limerick (34,865 Catholics: 38,518 persons).[247] It was the seat of the radical Bishop O'Dwyer, who heavily influenced the Catholic population. His hostility to the government was well known.[248] In May 1916, he sent an inflammatory letter to General Maxwell, the commander who had authorized the executions of the Easter Rising rebels, which was printed in the press, calling Maxwell the 'military dictator of Ireland' and declaring that his 'regime has been one of the worst and blackest chapters in the history of the Government of this country'.[249] The letter was widely published to great acclaim from nationalists, demonstrating the hostility which many felt towards the military regime in Ireland.[250] O'Dwyer was also a pacifist and, since the outbreak of war, had highlighted the inconsistencies within the Allied discourse as well as the Allies' 'barbaric' war tactics, in an attempt to imply that the Allied strategy was no different from that of the Central Powers. He subsequently encouraged Catholics to look impartially at the war and in his Lenten pastoral of 1917, told parishioners that 'the people read nothing but war, war; hatred of the Germans, the certainty of victory, but never a word of human responsibilities'.[251]

Yet Limerick people also turned out in large numbers to greet the Irish Canadians. Following 'a large and representative public meeting in the Town Hall', a cross-community committee was formed including the Catholics, Fr Fenton, James Quin JP (a merchant in the tea and wine industry), Stephen Quin (the mayor in 1916 and 1917) and Francis Edgar Kearney (a solicitor), as well as the Protestants, William Kidd (a grocer), Raymond Orpen (the Bishop of Limerick, Ardfert and Aghadoe) and Lord Dunraven (a landlord).[252] Dunraven contributed fifty guineas to the arrangements but subscriptions to the amount of £200 were donated from the predominantly Catholic city.[253]

Upon their arrival, musical bands with nationalist affiliations accompanied the Irish Canadians as they marched into the town centre. The bands included the St Mary's Fife and Drum band, the Sarsfield Fife and Drum Band (a reference to Patrick Sarsfield, the Jacobite, who had defeated William of Orange at the Siege of Limerick in 1690) and the Boherbuoy Brass and Reed Band, which, in October 1910, had played at the head of a crowd of Catholic men when they seized a delivery of English Sunday newspapers that Bishop O'Dwyer and the Catholic laity had marked as 'seditious'. The newspapers were promptly burned while the band played the nationalist tune 'Garryowen na Gloire' ('Limerick is Beautiful').[254] Some of the band members were on active service at the time of the Rangers' arrival.[255] Figure 5.9 shows the substantial crowd that welcomed the men. *The Irish Times* reported that 'thousands of people crowded the streets, to such an extent that it was extremely difficult for the men to get through. ... Flags were displayed from most of the houses in the main thoroughfares, and cheers were frequently raised on the way to the City Hall'.[256] The inspector general of the RIC wrote that 'the Irish-Canadian Rangers made a brief tour in Ireland. From Dublin they visited Armagh, Belfast, Limerick and Cork and at each of these towns they received a cordial reception and were hospitably entertained'.[257]

THE IRISH CANADIANS MARCHING THROUGH LIMERICK.

**Figure 5.9** Large crowds observe the Irish Canadians in Limerick. Drysdale, *Canada*, p. 1.

One reason behind the enthusiasm was because the Irish of both creeds had a shared history of emigration, and this was made clear when 'one woman when she saw her son in the ranks ran and embraced him. The hardy young soldier could not restrain his tears at the sight of his mother.'[258] For the majority of Catholics, support for the Irish-Canadian troops in a war which a large proportion of the Catholic Irish in Ireland still supported was *not* contradictory to their growing support for a political programme that proclaimed the abuses of British governance and reminded nationalists of the oppressive Empire of the nineteenth century to rally support for self-government. The political hostility which many nationalists felt towards the Empire when it was perceived to have quashed the rights of minorities, such as during the Boer War, was a different conception of the Empire than the ties which bound Catholics in Ireland to the achievements of their imperial brethren. Historians have hinted at the notion that some Home Rulers were proud of the successes of their imperial counterparts before the Great War.[259] This pride did not dissipate during the conflict, as the warm response of Catholics in Ireland to the Catholic and Protestant Irish-Canadian soldiers reflected enduring admiration for those Irish who had come to hold the most significant positions in the imperial system.

Even for the minority of Catholics who were against the war for humanitarian reasons, such as Bishop O'Dwyer, his pacifism and estrangement from the government did not prevent him from greeting the men. It has been suggested that O'Dwyer 'was at loggerheads with the Cardinal [because of the visit]', but this conclusion is hard to substantiate, particularly as the bishop invited two officers of the Rangers to his home.[260] For O'Dwyer, there was fundamentally nothing wrong with welcoming Irish Catholic settlers to the 'mother country' even if he did not agree with the war.

Ample opportunities for protest and dissent were created during the Rangers' visit and if Catholic dissent towards the troops existed, it should have been channelled through the radical press. It is therefore surprising that republican and labour organs made no reference to the visit at any stage before or throughout the tour.[261] Was the absence of reporting a form of protest against the trip? Perhaps, though silence would not have helped advanced nationalists to shape political opinion at a time when the North Roscommon by-election loomed large (the election was held in February 1917 and was won by Sinn Féin, the first electoral evidence of discontent with the IPP and popular political realignment after the Rising), so this explanation does not suffice.

Did radicals fear censorship, given that they were under the eye of the authorities? This is one possibility given their reliance upon the 'mosquito press' – an alternative to the mainstream press which expressed anti-establishment activist journalism – in disseminating politically extreme messages, which the authorities had begun to suppress.[262] However, given that republicans, and other radicals, had admonished the war effort on other occasions, there was no reason for them to avoid doing so on this instance, and Dublin Castle censorship reports do not record any instances of dissent. It can thus be averred that Irish radicals who were against Irish participation in the war were uncertain that protesting against the visit would be effective. Their silence tends to suggest that they were not sure whether readers shared their anti-war convictions, or even their mixed opinions towards Irish Catholic soldiers in the British and imperial armies. In five major urban centres, there appeared to be much support among a cross-section of Catholics for the Irish-Canadian troops, even though recruitment levels were low. Irish radicals therefore let the event pass by in the knowledge that there was little they could do to stop it.

The popularity of the advanced nationalist cause in early 1917 must also be examined in light of the Irish Canadians' visit. In his study of Bristol during the period 1790–1835, Mark Harrison has argued that crowds assembled because they responded to elite behaviour. To attract 'the masses', elites published dates, times and useful information about an event's whereabouts to attract the largest number of spectators. 'The majority of crowds did not consist, therefore, of large numbers of people who poured spontaneously on to the streets, but rather of an assembly of working people brought by a process of publicity to one place at one time.'[263] A considerable number of people responded to the appeals of officialdom to welcome the Irish Canadians as they passed through Ireland in the wintry conditions of January 1917. The Irish Canadians' visit was heavily advertised in the press, as were the names of the organizing committees, the identities and sums contributed by those who supported the trip, and the mixed confessional basis of the regiment was also widely published. Political radicalization may have been underway but the old order still had much influence across Ireland for it to have attracted such crowds.

The theme of Irish unity was ever present throughout the visit, expressed as it was by the Irish Canadians themselves, the civilian committees that organized the trip, in the funds raised for the tour to take place, in the actions of clerics, and by the enthusiastic public that turned out to greet them. This message was reiterated by elites, as the Catholic Lord Mayor of Dublin, James Gallagher declared that the Irish Canadians 'will, after all, merely confirm the message that has been sent to us repeatedly from the trenches by the men of opposite parties who went from Ireland itself to find in a common pursuit the bond of friendship'.[264] In Cork, the Catholic Lord Mayor, Thomas Butterfield, exclaimed, 'Can we not see the significance of what is illustrated for us today or are we so blinded by our prejudices and distrust of one another that we, who profess to love our country, must continue to hug our discontent?' He concluded hoping that a lesson of collaboration would be learnt from the visit and 'taken to heart by everyone of us'.[265]

That Irish Catholic elites supported Redmond's desire for improved unionist-nationalist relations through common war service with Protestants is unsurprising, but *The Irish Times* voiced these sentiments as well, as the editor wrote that the Irish Canadians 'have been the means of making us prove to ourselves how superficial are our differences of creed and politics when the heart of the nation is truly touched'. It subsequently hoped that 'the lessons which we may all learn from this visit are lessons of unity, not of division', and when the regiment left Ireland in early February the newspaper reflected on the visit, hoping that its truly national character – supported as it was by Catholics and Protestants across Ireland – could in some way be harnessed for the future:[266]

> The Irish-Canadians made a visible impression on the barriers which divide our small island into strict and self-satisfied compartments. They brought together all sorts and conditions of men. They inspired leaders of Irish thought and policy with sentiments which were not only hopeful and patriotic, but had the rare merit of unanimity. They helped us to discover that Dublin, Belfast, Cork, and Limerick are all inhabited by decent and generous Irishmen. In a word, they

charmed us into a realization of the fact that, if Ireland chooses to be a united and, therefore, progressive country, she can get anything that she wants in the world and can give new glory to the Empire.[267]

The visit of the Irish-Canadian Rangers to Ireland in early 1917 was an unqualified success because many Irish Catholics and Protestants in the 'mother country' supported their emigrant brethren, and the diaspora felt a connection to their 'homeland' as well. Though nationalist radicalization was underway, it had not stopped a wide cross section of Irish Catholics from obeying the establishment, and many people of different backgrounds turned out in their droves to welcome diasporic Catholics, whose conception of the Irish nationality was intrinsically bound up with the Empire. The reinvigorated political tensions between Unionists and Nationalists did not stop Protestants and Catholics from joining ranks in a demonstration of solidarity for the imperial diaspora because both groups had a history of emigration and were proud when their 'brethren' came home before they went to fight a very real German enemy. These transnational ties helped to bring many Catholics and Protestants in Ireland into the Allied war effort, as did important international connections with the other Allies, though some of these became complicated when Irish politics exploded into the foreground.

# Chapter 6

## IRISH CATHOLICS, BRITAIN AND THE ALLIES

The Great War relied upon international military alliances and Ireland situated itself in this global context as soon as the conflict began. As part of the United Kingdom, the Irish had little choice regarding which side they would officially take, joining the Allied war effort on 4 August, but it remains unclear how committed Irish Catholics were to this Alliance. Historians have questioned the extent to which nationalists were behind the IPP's decision to back the British war effort,[1] and it is well known that some dissident nationalists allied themselves with Germany.[2] This chapter argues that within civil society, people from all social backgrounds, were strongly committed to the Allied war effort from the outset and supported this Alliance until the conflict had ended. Individuals and groups expressed solidarity with Britain and the Allies in a variety of ways, from 1914 to 1918, but their support for the British war effort changed and was complicated by London's treatment of nationalist Ireland in the last two years of the war, particularly after April 1918 when the conscription crisis and Home Rule controversy came to the fore. The explosion of public opinion in this period has been traditionally aligned with anti-war activism, but other explanations present themselves which had in fact little to do with the Allied war effort, which many Irish Catholics continued to support until the end of the war.

### The 'death of innocence', 1914–15

Most people had settled into the war by December 1914.[3] This was surprising because of the contentious political situation, which as late as 31 July 1914, preoccupied the Irish more than continental affairs.[4] Attention turned to Europe over the bank holiday weekend (1-3 August) and when British reservists left Ireland for the front, people of both creeds gave their troops a good send-off and 'cheering crowds were common'.[5] A temporary sense of 'unity' prevailed as integration occurred between Protestants and Catholics in their response to the outbreak of hostilities. Some Unionist peers joined the Irish Volunteers in the defence of Ireland following Redmond's speech in the Commons on 3 August, whereby he encouraged nationalists and unionists to unite if the government found it necessary to enter the European conflict.[6]

In early August 1914, the war actually inspired much association between creeds, as people gathered to support their troops. This even happened in Ulster. In Newtownards, Co. Down, the *Newry Reporter* reported the mobilization of the 4th Battalion Royal Irish Rifles. It declared that 'a week ago such a display of cordiality amongst the people of Ireland … would have been impossible'. The local UVF and Irish Volunteers marched to the train station together and 'platforms were packed to suffocation'.[7] Similarly in Armagh, the St Malachy's Nationalist Band cheered the local UVF and reservists as they departed for the railway station on route to the front.[8] In Enniskillen, Co. Fermanagh, Unionist and Irish Volunteers formed an escort for the Royal Inniskilling Fusiliers while in Omagh and Cookstown Co. Tyrone, both groups accompanied reservists to the train station together.[9]

Such gatherings, whereby people of different backgrounds temporarily joined to support their departing troops, were a typical reaction to the outbreak of war in Britain, Germany and elsewhere.[10] However, with regard to Ireland, doubt exists over whether nationalists retained their enthusiasm for the war effort after August 1914. Martin has argued that nationalists lost interest in the conflict after this date.[11] Fitzpatrick has made a similar claim in his analysis of *The Clare Champion*, arguing that 'the *Champion's* waning enthusiasm for the war effort, to which the Irish Party leaders were irrevocably committed, accurately reflected the mood of the country'.[12]

However, popular reactions to departing troops appeared enthusiastic throughout 1914 and 1915. On 14 November 1914, *The Freeman's Journal* reported that over 100 men from Castlebar were 'given an enthusiastic send-off' in Co. Mayo, most of whom were Congested District Board (CDB) officials (forty-three of the fifty-one CDB members in Mayo were Catholics).[13] Similarly on 16 January 1915 in the largely Catholic town of Athenry (1,524 Catholics: 67 Protestants), Co. Galway, the *Connacht Tribune* reported that seven men joined the largely Catholic regiment, the Irish Guards, and 'the recruits were accorded a hearty send-off … by a number of their friends'.[14] This occurred again in January 1916 when a 'great crowd' accompanied twelve soldiers and sailors to the train station who were departing for the front. The well-wishers 'made a determined rush and forced the entrance to the platform'.[15]

Familial and fraternal support was often strong for those who enlisted. As families were large at the turn of the twentieth century, a wide spectrum of Catholics would have had a personal interest in the war, and, to take Cork as an example, one family out of every seven or eight was estimated to have had a member who had volunteered by the end of 1914, a proportion which increases when the regular army and reservists are considered.[16] The impact of these losses from local communities was noted in Derry, as the *Irish Independent* reported on 6 August 1914 that 'in the working-class districts almost every house has been called on to give up a man; in some cases two or three left the one house'.[17]

Groups and individuals within Catholic civil society publicly supported the men that enlisted, illustrating a wider sphere of support for the Allies among many Catholics who stayed at home. In May 1915, Augustus Hickey wrote to Kilrush Board of Guardians in Co. Clare declaring that he had been accepted as an army medic.[18] One elected representative, the Catholic coroner, Thomas Lillis JP, proposed a resolution 'congratulating the young medical gentleman on his spirit and courage in the cause of humanity'.[19] Another Catholic, Mr Doherty, suggested that he [Hickey] should be allowed half of his salary in wartime, and both proposals were unanimously supported.[20] When a second medical officer joined the army in March 1916, similar resolutions were proposed by the board and were 'unanimously passed'.[21]

Support for Catholic servicemen can be found within fee-paying schools and universities. Such institutions were at the heart of middle-class Catholic society, as parents, alumni, benefactors, teachers, clerics and students interacted in some capacity through educational establishments, though, as Charlotte Bennett has shown, opinions could differ between these groups, both in substance and in kind.[22] Prestigious schools such as Clongowes Wood and Belvedere College published regular accounts of school members in the forces through college magazines, as readers wanted to be informed about their actions.[23] Pašeta has found that several elite Catholic institutions were constitutional Nationalist in their political persuasion in the years preceding the war, and Redmond's commitment to active service was one of the many reasons behind the enlistment of some students.[24] To this end, Denis J. Coffey, the Catholic president of University College Dublin, wrote to Redmond about establishing an OTC in April 1915. He believed that 500 students would enlist and declared that Faculty deans, the registrar and 'some professors' were ready to take an active part in it if it were established.[25] His request was granted by the War Office in June.[26] The Roll of Honour for UCD states that almost 500 members of the predominantly Catholic university enlisted.[27]

UCD's participation was not unique as 352 students from University College Cork (UCC) served in the war.[28] In February 1915, four students were commissioned as officers in the Royal Engineers. They included the Catholics, Vincent McNamara (a solicitor's son) and John Francis Linehan (his father was an estate commissioner, magistrate and a farmer, and his elder brother was a medic).[29] The student journal, *The Quarryman*, declared that 'the day they left Cork for Chatham, about 200 students marched to the Station bearing the College flag, and gave a rousing send off to two College men of whom their fellows will always be proud'.[30] Support for volunteers was sustained in later periods as well. In April 1915, *The Quarryman* considered its wartime contribution relative to that of the other Irish universities and concluded that 'we are glad to be able to say that UCC has not lagged behind her sister Colleges, but has done her part, and that well'.[31] In winter term 1915, a 'UCC War Work Guild' was established by professors and their wives. The president was Lady Windle, the wife of the British-born professor, Bertram Windle.[32] In February 1916, *The Quarryman* remarked that the Guild had sent a 'huge parcel' to serving members, stating that the contributions from the university community had been 'generous'. It encouraged subscriptions, suggesting that '*everyone*, if possible, should help, and by giving a very small sum weekly – even one penny – wonders could be done'.[33] Its support was, in large part, due to the number of students at the front, as in March 1916, *The Quarryman* reported that between 60 and 70 per cent of medics who had qualified in the last three years had joined the RAMC and Royal Navy.[34]

Though the Nationalist MP, Stephen Gwynn, thought that University College Galway (UCG) was a 'hotbed of Sinn Feinism', this did not stop some members from assisting the war effort.[35] Staff members enlisted, such as the Catholic Professor of Medicine, Ralph Bodkin Mahon, who joined the RAMC in May 1915.[36] One hundred and thirty-six members of the university actually served in the conflict, and the majority worked in the medical services.[37] Its Presbyterian president, Alexander Anderson, a physicist, lent his support to recruitment meetings, inspired no doubt by his son who had joined an artillery regiment in October 1914.[38] At a recruitment drive for the western province of Connaught in January 1916, at which representatives from the University's governing body participated, Anderson made clear that UCG supported its serving members: 'Many of its past and present students have obeyed the call to active service in the war, and two have given up their lives as a contribution to the heavy toll which the country is now paying in defence of human liberty.'[39] His support was reflected more generally, as in April 1916 a 'Support Committee' was established to send comforts to UCG servicemen and a book appeal was inaugurated for donors to send books to the college, 'where they would be consolidated and prepared for shipment to the Connaught Rangers'.[40]

However, Catholic attitudes towards the conflict generally began to change as the war dragged on, as the seriousness of the war began to filter home, diminishing some of the innocence which had characterized attitudes in late 1914 and early 1915. 1915 was, as Lyn MacDonald aptly describes, the 'death of innocence' in British society. The enthusiasm of 1914 and early 1915, which had sent British men flocking to the colours, subsided as casualties increased. Hope for a quick victory was extinguished following the costly battles at Neuve Chapelle, Ypres, Loos and Gallipoli.[41]

Irish attitudes towards the war began to change in 1915 during and after the month of May because a number of different tragedies happened together, which brought home the seriousness of the conflict. In this month, newspapers expressed horror that the German army had used poisonous gas on Canadian and French units, which it had done in April (the first time such methods of warfare had been used in the conflict) and, as Chapter 4 has shown, the war at sea had begun to affect Irish life. Just days after outrage was unleashed in Ireland following the sinking of the *RMS Lusitania*, newspapers received word of Irish casualties at the Dardanelles. These occurred among the regular army units, the bulk of which comprised working-class Protestant and Catholic Irish men.[42] Irish deaths were numerous and concentrated, as they had been in battles such as Etreux in 1914, and the attritional nature of the war meant that Irish losses were adding up.[43]

By the 17 and 18 May, heavy casualties from the Gallipoli Campaign – an ambitious and ultimately disastrous campaign devised by Winston Churchill, First Lord of the Admiralty, to control the Dardanelles Straits and open supply routes to Britain's ally, Russia – were being reported.[44] These included men from the Royal Irish Rifles, the Royal Irish Regiment and the RDF – approximately 96 per cent of the 1st Battalion RDF officers and 63 per cent other ranks were killed, wounded or reported missing after their attempted landing at 'V' beach on 25 April 1915.[45] Soldiers wrote home giving horrific descriptions.[46] Denis Joseph Moriarty, an Irish-Catholic sergeant with the RMF, wrote in his diary that 'you could only recognize our dead by their Identity Discs. ... You should have heard what our men said about the Turks and what they would have liked to do to them.'[47] The *Independent* printed the comments of an officer from the RDF, which described how the Turks had shelled the boats of Irish soldiers for the mile and a half journey to the shoreline where they were met by machine guns 'not ten yards from them':

> Before I knew where I was I was covered with dead men. Not knowing they were dead, I was roaring at them to let me up, for I was drowning. ... I was simply saturated all over with blood, and I could feel the hot blood all over me all the way across. When they pulled these poor fellows off me they were all dead and the poor fellow under me was dead. The boat was awful to look at, full of blood and water.[48]

Today his description appears reminiscent of the D-Day landings, which shocked British people at the time, and though it is difficult to establish how such accounts were received in wartime Ireland, it is likely that the Irish were similarly shocked when they read of the horror experienced by their relatives, friends and compatriots in 1915. Captain G. W. Nightingale, an English officer with the Munsters, wrote to his mother when he was invalided to a convalescent ship in which he recalled the horror of the episode: 'We can't even hear the heavy guns from here, and I am just beginning to feel again that life really is worth living when you once get away from nasty things like bullets and stray limbs and decomposed corpses.'[49]

The loss of these soldiers was felt in Dublin – the first instance of mass death to hit the capital:

> Private intimation is now coming through as to the casualties to the men, and this was dismally apparent in many parts of Dublin yesterday, when a walk through the city revealed numerous black bordered envelopes hanging to the doors on which were inserted names followed by 'killed in action'.[50]

Mass death occurred for Dubliners again in August 1915 when Irish men from the 10th (Irish) Division were killed in the disastrous landings at Suvla Bay (a stretch of land in the Ottoman Empire on the Aegean coast of the Gallipoli peninsula). However, unlike the earlier tragedy, which had resulted in numerous deaths among the regular army (the rank and file was predominantly recruited from the working classes), the 10th (Irish) Division was comprised of volunteers. It was the first Irish New Army division to be formed and Philip Orr has argued that it attracted the most enthusiastic young men, many of whom were Protestants and Catholics from the professional middle classes, though the working classes also comprised a large proportion of the unit.[51]

This second instance of mass death in the Gallipoli campaign forced the more affluent classes to experience the grief, sorrow and anger that the working classes had experienced in May and continued to experience in August. One of the severely hit units was the 7th Battalion RDF. 'D' Company of the unit was known as 'The Pals', which had an element of celebrity status, as many members were prominent rugby players drawn from both unionist and nationalist backgrounds.[52] Pals units were established throughout the United Kingdom in wartime, attracting groups of men bound to one another by friendship, sporting and fraternal affiliations.[53] D Company exhibited these characteristics, though Fitzpatrick has suggested that it was 'remarkable for [its] diversity', as members comprised Protestants and Catholics (that this was 'remarkable' is not strictly true, as the sources indicate that it was not uncommon for Irish Protestants and Catholics to find themselves in the same military units where they had to live and work closely with one another, and strong social bonds were often formed between them).[54]

When 'the Pals' left Dublin for Basingstoke at the end of April 1915, the enthusiasm expressed at their departure reveals the high regard in which they were held by Dublin society. *The Irish Times* declared that 'the scenes of enthusiasm that were witnessed yesterday proved that the city pulsates with ardent enthusiasm for the cause of the Allies ... crowds lined the route yesterday, and the departure of the troops was accompanied by continuous cheering by dense lines of spectators'.[55] One officer, Henry Hanna, who compiled a record of the unit's experiences, remembered the 'frequent outburst of enthusiasm' from the large crowds who saw them.[56] The *Independent* also referred to 'the cheering crowds' and declared that 'the scene was quite unique in the annals of Dublin, persons of all ranks and classes taking part in the farewell given to the "Pals" Battalion, which has been largely recruited from the city'.[57]

The Pals, as part of the 10th (Irish) Division, were part of the wave of landings that took place on 7 August 1915, and when Mediterranean Expeditionary Force (MEF) casualties emerged in the press, they were substantial. On 16 August, it was reported that 184 officers and 2,063 men had been killed and 'these include a number of officers of the 7th Munsters and the 5th Royal Irish Fusiliers'.[58] When the *Independent* reported the death of one officer from the Division, it declared that it had no idea that the 10th had even arrived at the front.[59] Wartime censorship had restricted details regarding the whereabouts of troops, intensifying the shock when the casualties turned out to be Kitchener's Irish volunteers. On 28 August, the newspaper printed photographs of the officers. These had been taken before the Division had embarked on active service, and it now identified those who had been killed and wounded, and those who were missing in action. Irish losses were reported well into September, sustaining the grief, anxiety and concern of families who had relatives in the 10th.[60] The RDF had some of the greatest casualties. Captain Nightingale wrote in his diary, 'We saw the Dublins wiped out pretty well to a man – 21 officers and 550 men in 20 minutes were done for!'[61] Neither the 6th nor 7th Battalions, which took part in the campaign, had received any relevant training for amphibious landings, which no doubt contributed to the heavy causalities.[62] Within a week of arriving on the Gallipoli peninsula, 131 of D Company's 220 soldiers were dead or wounded.[63]

These losses affected Catholics and Protestants alike. In December 1915, the former TCD student, Captain David Campbell, recalled that 'it was said that after the landings at Gallipoli, black crepe hung from every door in Coombe' (1,612 persons, 1404 Catholics).[64] In 1919, the Catholic author, Katharine Tynan, described the impact of the landings in Dublin:

> So many of our friends had gone out in the 10th Division to perish at Suvla. … Dublin was full of mourning, and on the faces one met there was a hard brightness of pain as though the people's hearts burnt in the fire and were not consumed. … One met the mourners everywhere.[65]

The trauma of Gallipoli even stretched into the interwar period, as in 1937 the Countess of Fingall, a Catholic well-connected to the Anglican upper and middle classes, remembered how 'the 10th division emptied Dublin of young men and was cut to pieces on the grim rocks of Suvla Bay in 1915'. This was the only episode of mass death in the war that she recalled; its trauma, rather than later instances of mass death at battles such as the Somme, had stayed with her.[66] This was also the case for David Campbell, who continued to mourn his friend, Levis, at every Armistice Day in the decades after the war: 'I remember him every Armistice Day, and mourn his loss afresh.' The trauma of Gallipoli was still with Campbell when he compiled his memoirs in the 1970s, noting that when he drove past Phoenix Park one day, the place where the 7th Battalion RDF had done much training, 'the memories were acutely painful. I could have wept.'[67]

These losses were commemorated at the time in Dublin. Croke Park, the sporting arena owned by the Gaelic Athletic Association (GAA), which took a firm anti-recruiting stance during the War, has a famous mound known today as 'Hill 16' (a reference to the Easter Rising and the freedom which republicans felt that the rebellion had been for). Some of the leading instigators behind the Irish Volunteers' split in September 1914, following Redmond's commitment to active service, and the Rising, held prominent positions within the GAA and the Gaelic League (an organization formed in 1893 to revive the Irish language and culture).[68] However, until at least September 1931 this mound was called 'Hill 60' in memory of the hill which the Dublins were tasked with capturing at Gallipoli.[69] The 'freedom' which Irish men had enlisted to defend and which had resulted in their mass sacrifice at Suvla Bay was recognized by nationalists of all persuasions for many years after the war.

The impact of the landings was so great because it was the first instance in which Irish civilians, who had joined up as volunteers, were killed in large numbers at once. An estimated 2,017 men in the 10th were killed in the Dardanelles campaign and within two months it had sustained 9,000 casualties, including those who were killed, wounded, diseased or who had gone missing (more than half of its fighting strength). Over the course of the Gallipoli Campaign, Tom Johnstone has calculated that 3,411 Irish men were killed in action or died of wounds.[70] This figure was comparable to the losses suffered by the Australians.

How did the Gallipoli landings affect Irish Catholic feeling towards the Allied war effort? Certainly there is evidence to suggest that some of the innocence and enthusiasm which had characterized earlier attitudes towards the conflict waned in both Catholic and Protestant circles after the campaign. Stuart Ward has argued that the British authorities failed to recognize the achievements of the 10th, which incited much disdain from those at home.[71] Sources reflect this contempt. Tynan recalled that 'for the first time came bitterness, for we felt that their lives had been thrown away and that their heroism had gone unrecognized ....'[72] The Catholic Earl of Granard, Bernard Forbes, and the chaplain, Fr Murphy, both of whom were at Gallipoli, chastised Sir Ian Hamilton, the commander of the MEF, who they blamed for the losses.[73]

In the 1916 Lenten pastorals of the Catholic bishops, influential prelates appealed for peace. The Archbishop of Dublin, William Walsh, whose anti-recruitment stance was well known, appealed 'for fervent prayer at this most critical time for the restoration of peace', as did the pacifist Bishop of Limerick, Edward Thomas O'Dwyer, who opposed 'this senseless slaughter'. He criticized the Allies' war policy, claiming that they were using the discourse of 'small nations' as a propagandistic incentive to gain more power.[74] Cardinal Michael Logue, the head of the Catholic Church in Ireland, lamented that the prospect of peace had evaporated, and when *The Freeman's Journal* reported their pastorals it did so under the bold heading: 'the scourge of war'.[75]

However, Protestants were also angry at the authorities for not commending the 10th, as *The Irish Times* ran a series of bitter editorials against the official censors for having attempted to 'suppress the whole story of Suvla Bay'.[76] In his letter to T. P. Gill, the Earl of Granard claimed that he had spoken to the Dublin unionist, Bryan Mahon, the Division's commander, who also blamed Ian Hamilton for Irish losses.[77] Horror at the bloodshed was felt in Protestant circles. When the Dublin Protestant rugby club, the Wanderers, lost five members in the campaign, it did not dwell upon the glorious nature of the conflict but reflected instead upon its costliness, wishing its remaining members 'safe return from the dangers and horrors of war'.[78]

However, rather than weakening support for the men that joined up, the Dardanelles campaign appeared to strengthen the patriotism which many people had for Ireland's soldiers because so many of Ireland's 'best' had fallen. Ward has argued that published accounts, such as those of the nationalists, Michael MacDonagh and Stuart Parnell Kerr, and the Unionist, Bryan Cooper, heralded the Division's sacrifice as the 'mark of a coming nation'.[79] The *Independent* called the victims 'Irish heroes' and declared that 'honour is reflected on their native land by their ungrudging sacrifice'.[80] *The Irish Times* claimed that 'more than once it has been possible to regard the Army of Gallipoli as an Irish Army'.[81] For both the nationalist and unionist press, the sacrifices of the 10th were perceived to be truly national, as the losses cut across class, creed and political persuasion.

Some of the most formative opinion shapers in the country expressed patriotism for those who had died at Gallipoli as well as the Irish men who had died in other battles. Contrary to the claims of Bishop O'Dwyer, who had flagged up the inconsistencies in the Allied discourse, several of the 1916 Lenten pastorals used terms which encapsulated the higher values for which Irish men were perceived to have died, such as heroism, bravery and valour: terms which were at the heart of the cause for which the Allies were supposedly fighting. Bishop Patrick O'Donnell of Raphoe prayed for 'our brave soldiers' while Bishop Robert Browne of Cloyne claimed that Ireland was 'indebted to our Irish heroes at the front'. Other members of the hierarchy made similar comments including Cardinal Logue, John Healy (the Archbishop of Tuam) and the bishops, Joseph MacRory (Down and Connor), Patrick McKenna (Clogher), Patrick Foley (Kildare and Leighlin) and Thomas Gilmartin (Clonfert).[82]

This was not the only element of wartime discourse that the Catholic hierarchy chose to promote, as some prelates simultaneously whipped up hostility towards Germany and, on occasion, the Central Powers. The Bishop of Derry declared that 'Prussian militarism is the very antithesis of what the Catholic Church tells us is required by the law of God'. For the Bishop of Clonfert, the war 'was a just defence against unwarranted aggression'.[83] Speaking in March 1916, Cardinal Logue dwelt upon the Armenian genocide, stating that the massacre 'shocks humanity', marking the Ottomans out as the inhuman architects of the crime. The Archbishop of Tuam made his pastoral a recruiting speech, encouraging largely agricultural parishioners to till more land and to defend it:

> Especially against the Germans … We till the land that bore us, and we mean to hold it at any cost, and Irishmen are able to fight … I hope you will rally to the flag. … The man who strikes a blow against the Prussian strikes a blow for justice, freedom and right.[84]

Fear of a German invasion underlined the Bishop of Cloyne's pastoral, inspired, no doubt, by the proximity of the war at sea:

> Ireland has shown, by the voluntary presence in the armies of the Allied nations of 150,000 dauntless soldiers from this sparsely populated little island, and by as many more of her scattered sons from abroad, that she is determined to protect herself against such a fate as has overtaken Belgium. We, who continue to live in peace at home, are indebted to our Irish heroes at the front.[85]

Other Catholics expressed support for their 'Irish heroes'. Letters sent to the parents of Catholic soldiers who had fallen were at times patriotic, such as that sent by the Limerick chaplain, Raphael McAuliffe. He wrote to the parents of James Barlow from Limerick expressing 'how bravely he [had] died … gloriously leading his men to the charge [at Gallipoli]'.[86] Comments such as these from Irish military chaplains were more rare than those that simply dwelt on the religious dimensions of the sacrifice however, but other groups within civil society demonstrated an enhanced interest in the war following the Gallipoli campaign.[87] Schools such as Clongowes Wood wished to find out how many present and past Clongownians were at the front and the military distinctions they had accrued, suggesting that they were proud of their servicemen's exploits.[88] When UCC students heard that

Vincent McNamara had been killed at Gallipoli, his engineering professor, the Presbyterian, Conel Alexander, wrote part of a large obituary in *The Quarryman*, claiming that 'when the call came for men for King and Country, Vincent McNamara felt it his duty to offer himself'.[89] Alexander would not have written these comments had they been completely out-of-tune with the largely Catholic student body. He concluded with the epitaph: 'For your fellow College men, the name of Vincent McNamara will remain the standard of all that is lovely, honourable and good in those fields and halls that will know your physical presence no more.'[90]

Though it is difficult to establish the extent to which the Gallipoli campaign impacted public opinion more generally towards the war, it is clear that for some Catholics, their commitment to the war effort deepened in mid-1915 because this group became emotionally attached to its cause. No doubt, the tragedy of the *Lusitania* and the increasing mechanistic nature of the war, as discussed in Chapter 4, also helped to shape general attitudes towards the conflict, which were evolving as a result of contingent events and as the conflict dragged on. By mid-1915 the war effort was no longer a 'British' or even a 'British and Irish' war effort but a wider cause involving the Allies as a political entity defined by values which the Irish – both nationalists and unionists – accepted. Solidarity with the Allies was central to the Irish Catholic understanding of the war and Britain was considered by many middle-class Catholics to have epitomized what the Allies were fighting for before May 1916.

## Home Rule, recruitment and Britain, 1914–16

On 18 September 1914, Home Rule was given Royal Assent and placed on the statute book, though its operation was postponed for a one-year period or until the end of the war, whichever lasted longer, and it had an amending clause for Ulster. Home Rule was *the* biggest project in Irish nationalism, one which Pašeta has shown to have reoriented the expectations and whole political culture of the Irish Catholic middle class, who expected that the 'greening' of Dublin Castle would soon be followed by them taking over the administration of the country.[91] Yet there has been little investigation into popular responses towards the bill's passage and in those analyses that do exist, the Irish nationalist public was supposedly unenthusiastic when the bill finally passed. In the Irish Midlands, for example, Wheatley has claimed that 'it was against a background of mounting disaffection that Home Rule became law', generating 'only patchy manifestations of popular support'.[92]

To the contrary, widespread rejoicing took place across Ireland, particularly in urban centres. The bill's passage was considered a tremendous victory by a cross-section of nationalist society. The constitutional nationalist press waxed lyrical on the achievement of a lifetime as the *Irish Independent* proclaimed 'The Day is Won'; 'Ireland's Day'; 'A Nation again'.[93] The *Cork Examiner* recorded that 'joy was manifested in the national triumph'.[94] For these newspapers, the Irish question appeared to have been solved as the struggle for self-government had effectively ended – an opinion which was also aired among some Irish Catholics in Sydney (see pp. 97–8). This was not only the view of the newspaper editors, however, as illustrated by the many popular demonstrations that occurred across Ireland, in counties including Cork. In Midleton, 'almost the entire population of the town and district took part in the procession ... which was gaily illuminated'. Political opponents within nationalism, the Redmondites and O'Brienites, joined together in Millstreet 'for the first time' to rejoice. The All-for-Ireland band and a battalion of 850 Volunteers paraded the streets.[95] Celebrations also took place in Kanturk.[96] In Dungarvan, Co. Waterford, 'huge bonfires and immense crowds in the streets marked the celebration'. In Skerries and Raheny, Co. Dublin, 'practically all the Raheny residents joined in a torchlight procession'. In Kilkenny, flags floated from many houses and the main streets were decorated for the occasion. In Drogheda and Dundalk, Co. Louth, 'the nationalist bands, followed by large concourses of people, paraded the streets. Most of the houses were illuminated and displayed flags'. In Sligo, 'tar barrels blazed at many of the street corners and many of the houses were brightly lit up'. Similar celebrations happened elsewhere in Ireland, including in Mayo (Ballintubber), Roscommon (Castlerea), Galway (Loughrea), Wexford (Enniscorthy) and Tyrone (Dungannon).[97]

These enthusiastic responses were matched by the numerous congratulatory telegrams sent to Redmond and IPP members by elected representatives of nationalist opinion including county (Dublin, Cork, Louth) and urban councils (Pembroke, Blackrock, Midleton, Lismore, Athlone, Westport, Galway, Keady and Longford).[98] Castlerea District Council in Roscommon 'passed a resolution of lasting gratitude to Mr Redmond and the Irish Party'.[99] Parts of rural Ireland enthused over the bill's passage, as Castleknock, Tubbery, Breffni and Ballinasloe Rural District Councils thanked the party.[100] So did boards of guardians in Rathdown, Killala, Trim, Sligo, Loughrea and Rathkeale, reflecting the opinions of those who administered the Poor Law.[101] UIL branches in Belfast, Armagh, Dublin, Cork, Tipperary, Athlone and Longford praised the party,[102] as did AOH branches in Cork, Galway, Roscommon and Mayo.[103] Other Catholic-nationalist organizations followed their example, including at least one group of advanced nationalists: the Glin branch of the radical women's association, Cumann na mBan.[104]

It has been argued that there was no endorsement of the Home Rule bill of 1912 by the higher clergy and no approbation received for it by the archbishops of Armagh and Dublin.[105] Nonetheless, the lower and higher clergy appeared overjoyed when the Home Rule bill actually passed. Lower clerics commended the measure, such as the prominent nationalist Monsignor A. Ryan, Canon M'Fadden (Glenties, Donegal), Fr Brennan (affiliated to the Derry INV), Fr Falconer, Canon O'Neill (Gorey, Wexford) and Fr Nolan (a member of East Limerick Executive).[106] In Banteer, Co. Cork, 'stirring speeches' were delivered by Fathers O'Connor, O'Sullivan and Walsh to an enthusiastic crowd.[107] In Clifden, Co. Galway, 'a public meeting of rejoicing' was addressed by Monsignor M'Alpine, Fr O'Flynn (whose diocese was in Tasmania) and P. J. Waldron CC.[108]

At least seven members of the higher clergy sent congratulatory letters to Redmond, including Archbishop John Harty of Cashel, and the bishops, Patrick

O'Donnell of Raphoe, John Mangan of Kerry, Robert Browne of Cloyne, Thomas Gilmartin of Clonfert, Michael Fogarty of Killaloe and Patrick Foley of Kildare and Leighlin.[109] In Thurles, Co. Tipperary, Archbishop Harty 'walked at the head of the great procession' in a celebratory parade accompanied by Fr Ryan.[110] Bishop Foley sent a telegram to Redmond, which read 'warmest congratulations to Irish Party and incomparable leader'.[111] He clearly believed that Redmond had achieved what former Nationalist leaders had not.

These responses suggest that support for the IPP was strong in September 1914. Moreover, the air of finality which characterized much of the rhetoric surrounding the bill's passage implies that the Irish question was considered by many nationalists to have been solved. As in Australia, many nationalists in Ireland appeared to have entered the war in the belief that Home Rule would come into operation. The expectation that self-government was inevitable was thus part of a mindset that framed nationalist attitudes and behaviour towards the war.

Yet it has been argued that the IPP's support for the British war effort was ultimately what resulted in its downfall, an assertion based on poor recruitment rates and a reticence among middle-class Catholics to become army recruiters, which supposedly revealed the 'mental neutrality' which characterized Catholic public opinion towards the war.[112] Chapter 2 has discussed the issue of recruitment in Ireland, offering reasons why it should not be considered the only determinant of support for the war effort, but the subject deserves further consideration, as behaviour towards joining up evolved over the course of the war.

From the outset, public opinion towards recruitment was highly complex. Individuals simultaneously held multiple viewpoints on the merits of joining up, and it was not uncommon for one individual to hold opinions that were in fact contradictory. These attitudes were exposed after the formation of the Central Council for the Organization of Recruitment in Ireland (CCORI) in early 1915, which soon after issued a circular to elected representatives to see if they would promote recruitment in their localities. Some bodies ignored the request, such as Dunshaughlin Council and Oldcastle Rural District Council in Meath, as well as Ennis District Council and Kilkee Town Commissioners in Clare. Others debated the matter, such as Trim Urban Council, whose chairman, Francis O'Reilly, 'declared himself personally in favour' while the other council members took 'no action on the communication' (conversely Trim Rural Council promised to 'give every assistance' but stated that 'we see no necessity for such a campaign').[113] The members of Killala District Council in Mayo raised multiple views on the pros and cons of promoting recruitment including fear of death at the front, pride for those who wanted to enlist, and hostility towards England (one member was against recruitment because he blamed England for Ireland's history of emigration. He believed that war service was emigration in another form). In the end after some discussion, the Council decided not to nominate a member to the recruiting council.[114]

Many representatives were wary of supporting the CCORI because they feared conscription and felt that it underpinned the recruiting agenda. When Oldcastle rejected the circular, they did so warning against 'any likelihood of conscription or compulsion being enforced'.[115] Kildare County Council held contradictory viewpoints towards joining up, but these viewpoints were not perceived as contradictory by the councilmen. The Council declared that they were 'opposed to coercion in any form' yet 'were willing to do anything they could to encourage recruiting', supporting the 800 men from Kildare that had already enlisted.[116] This contradiction was expressed again in the Irish Midlands, though in this case, the Council decided to support the CCORI. Edward Kelly JP, the Catholic chairman of Carrickmacross Board of Guardians and Monaghan Rural District Council, accepted the CCORI invitation to become a recruiter, yet he also signed an anti-conscription pledge, thus revealing that he was willing to encourage enlistment as long as it remained voluntary.[117]

However, other councils welcomed the CCORI and were happy to help promote recruitment. Navan Rural Council resolved that 'the whole council would form itself into a recruiting committee for the area under their jurisdiction'. Catholic officials promoted the scheme, and they included Charles Lacy, a council clerk and secretary, a chemist, John Timmon, who formed a similar committee for Navan town alongside council chairman, John Spicer, a miller and baker.[118] Galway Urban Council also agreed, forming the Galway Recruiting Committee in June 1915. Its chairman was the Catholic entrepreneur, Martin McDonagh, a leading figure in Galway and chairman of the Employers' Federation and Harbour Board.[119] The council actually encouraged local authorities in Loughrea, Ballinasloe, Moylough, Mountbellew, Tuam, Clifden, Oughterard and Moycullen to form sub-recruiting committees, and in some of these its appeal was successful.[120] Mayo Urban Council (the chairman was the Catholic, M. Hogan) and Edenderry Town Commissioners in King's County (the chairman was the Catholic farmer, Denis Fay) also agreed to promote the scheme.[121]

Though Ireland's recruitment rates declined after early 1915 – a phenomenon which was particularly true of rural Ireland but which was also true of Britain – recruitment meetings attracted much interest in urban Ireland, even if they did not always result in enlistments. In Cork, for example, an estimated 5,000 people attended a recruitment meeting in the city in March 1915, one month before the CCORI was established.[122] *Irish Life*, a magazine for the middle and upper classes, reported that the bands of the RDF and the RMF played in the Grand Parade and afterwards marched through the adjoining streets, where 'an immense crowd of people gathered'.[123] Speeches were made and recruiters included the Catholics, Hyacinth A. Pelly (a bank manager from Galway), David Barry (a professor of physiology) and the Donegal Presbyterian and engineering professor, Conel Alexander (both professors were employed at UCC).[124] The educated sections of the populace were not the only people attracted to the event however, as the prevalence of men wearing flat caps strongly implies that this recruitment meeting attracted working-class men as well. Cork people's interest in recruitment meetings had not diminished by October 1915 as Figure 6.1 reveals, even though the 'innocence' of the war had somewhat dissipated and several elected representatives elsewhere in Ireland had refused to assist the CCORI.

**Figure 6.1** Recruitment meeting in Cork, *IL*, 8 October 1915. Courtesy of the National Library of Ireland.

These gatherings were not unique to Cork, as in Sligo a hugely popular recruitment meeting took place in April. The Irish Guards were present 'and received an enthusiastic reception from thousands of people who had collected at the railway station and along the route to the Town Hall. Several of the streets were decorated with flags and banners, and outside the Town hall were the flags of the Allies.'[125] Sometime between 18 and 30 September, another meeting took place.[126] As in Cork, a cross-section of people attended, and while they may have been attracted to the event because of the musical entertainment provided by the military band, it is significant that they are there at all so late in 1915 given how unfavourable the recruitment campaign had allegedly become by this period.

In Britain, Adrian Gregory has argued that 'the continual local activity' of promoting recruitment at a grassroots level 'created an atmosphere where volunteering was seen as the appropriate act' even if 'the results were sometimes disappointing'. There was an aspect of recruiting meetings that was 'reminiscent of a religious revival', as platforms were established where speakers would appeal to the conscience of a listener, laying out in detail the terrible consequences of a German victory. Men were then asked to 'attest' and those who did so were applauded by the crowd.[127] Recruitment meetings in Ireland bore strong resemblances, as recruiters emphasized the 'noble', 'valorous' and 'brave' traditions of the Irish regiments, which volunteers were perceived to have epitomized.[128] At a Limerick recruiting demonstration, one Protestant, Mr Gubbins, toasted the largely Catholic regiment, the Irish Guards, some members of which were present, and declared to applause that they were gathered 'to do honour to some of Ireland's noble sons'.[129] In Tuam, where Protestant and Catholic higher clergymen attended, speakers claimed that 'they were only asked as free men to do their duty'.[130] German atrocities in Belgium were often referred to, as were those outrages closer to home, such as the torpedoing of the *RMS Lusitania*. Some speakers used tragedies to make the case that this was 'Ireland's war'.[131] Even though Nationalist MPs were hesitant to become 'recruiters for John Bull', almost all of them engaged in 'Hun bashing' when they discoursed on the war, thus reinforcing the perception of German wrongdoing.[132]

In Britain, 'most recruiting meetings made play of the political unity of the locality, with Conservative, Liberal and Labour representatives making speeches in turn'.[133] This was also the case in Ireland, as in March 1915, *The Freeman's Journal* reported the ongoing recruitment campaign in Ulster under the headline 'Northern Recruiting Campaign – Nationalists and Unionists Fraternize'.[134] At a meeting in Newtownhamilton, Co. Armagh, speakers included a Catholic priest, a Belgian cleric (a refugee in Ireland), a Presbyterian minister, a prominent nationalist and unionist, and two INVs who were recovering from wounds received at the front.[135] When this group spoke in Bessbrook, 'the meeting was met with "mottoes of welcome everywhere"'.[136] At a similar event in Newry, Co. Down, the nationalist St Joseph's Brass and Reed Band and the unionist Postley Row Flute Band played each other through their respective districts, having spent the day 'fraternizing together'.[137]

In many places, political differences were no barrier to integrating in these public demonstrations of support for the war effort and the 'higher unity' which occurred in recruitment meetings in Ulster was replicated in the South. In Dundalk, Co. Louth, 'a number of important men and clergymen of different denominations occupied seats on a [recruiting] platform' in April 1915.[138] In urban Meath, the Lord Lieutenant, Sir Nugent Everard, and the Catholic chemist, John Timmon, spoke at almost all of the recruitment meetings, and they were backed by local politicians, the gentry, MPs, clergy and local businessmen – a wide spectrum of middle and upper-class Protestant and Catholic opinion.[139] In Tuam, Co. Galway, the Anglican landlord, Cecil Henry JP, presided at a recruitment demonstration alongside 'his Grace, the Archbishop of Tuam [the Catholic, John Healy], and the Dean of Tuam [the Anglican, John Geddes]'.[140] In Enniscorthy, Co. Wexford, over 2,000 people attended a recruitment meeting in June, while in nearby Newtownbarry, 500 people attended a similar event.[141] 'On the platform were representatives of all sections of politics and religion, including the parish priest and the rector.'[142]

Gregory has argued that the German invasion of Belgium was often cited as a means of enticing men to enlist in Britain, but while the average Briton was sorry for the Belgian people, he was 'not prepared to risk his life to avenge their violation'. A potential recruit 'had to be made to understand that the threat was to his own home'.[143] Recruiters in Ireland used similar methods to convince men to sign up to avenge Belgium. Some recruiting posters asked, 'Is Ireland to share Belgium's fate?'[144] At a recruitment meeting in Sligo, speakers paid tribute to Sligo men who had fallen but encouraged more to enlist as 'otherwise Ireland will be like Belgium'.[145] Fear of invasion was widely expressed in speeches. In Tuam, recruiters emphasized the 'great debt of gratitude' they owed to Belgium for stopping the German army.[146] In November 1915, Fr William Burke spoke at a recruitment meeting in Cahir, Tipperary, stating that 'we are now, to my mind, confronted with the most serious crisis that has occurred for three hundred years – since Cromwell made preparation at Bristol for the invasion of Ireland'. His reference to England's oppression of Ireland, an episode in nationalist history that evoked horror and anger, was used as an analogy to describe Germany's actions in France and Belgium, demonstrating how serious Burke believed the German threat to be: 'Don't think it is England's fight only. As sure as England goes down we will go down, too (applause).'[147]

The perceived German threat was therefore one reason why many middle-class Catholics, and Southern Protestants, publicly aligned themselves with their ally, Britain. As Pennell has argued, 'Many [Irish] people understood the war as a conflict between ideals, and whatever doubts people had about Britain, they believed that in comparison to Prussian militarism, Britain was fighting to uphold peaceful civilization.'[148] This was reflected in gatherings in aid of the war effort. On 4 January 1915, a cross-community concert was held for the 'Children's League of Pity' in Cork, a forerunner to the national Society for the Prevention of Cruelty to Children, at which several middle-class women attended, including, for example, Amy Mary Crosbie, the Catholic wife of a surgeon, and Eileen Maltby, a Dublin Protestant.[149] The concert was presided over by Ellen Harrington, a Catholic married to a chemist.[150] *Irish Life* reported that 'the Hall was brilliantly decorated with evergreens and flags. Huge Union Jacks were hung at the back of the platform which formed the stage'.[151] Songs were sung that reinforced support for Britain, as Violet Foley, a Catholic teenager and solicitor's daughter, sang 'Your King and Country Want You'.[152] Solidarity with the other Allies was also expressed, as a tea garden represented Belgium, while the Protestant, Kathleen Spiers, a 'commercial agent's' daughter, manned a sweet stall representing France.[153] A similar event was held in the Engineers' Hall at Dawson Street, Dublin, where children were entered into a fashion competition, 'the colouring to be that of our Allies'.[154] The winner was the Catholic Dorothy Martin, who dressed in the Belgian colours, while second prize was awarded to Maureen Coffey, a Catholic barrister's daughter who dressed as France.[155]

Even in the west of Ireland, Catholics identified with Britain. In Ballinrobe, Co. Mayo (3,267 Catholics: 112 Protestants), two concerts were held for the Hollymount and Ballinrobe BRCS in January 1915 (662 Catholics and 67 Protestants lived in Hollymount DED).[156] 'The attendance was large; some hundreds of people being unable to gain admission.'[157] Committee members included the Anglicans, Mrs Lyndsey-Fitzpatrick and Mrs Blosse Lynch, and the Catholic Kirwan sisters (the daughters of a solicitor).[158] They acted in a play entitled 'Britannia with Her Allies and Young Soldiers', dressing as the Allies as shown in Figure 6.2.

The name of the play and the elevated position accorded Britannia implies that the participants had named Britain the most significant ally, dressing Britain in white: a colour traditionally associated with innocence and purity, which may have represented Britain's assumed purity in its defence of the Allies' ideals. Britain was represented by a Catholic, Maud Quinlan, a doctor's wife, while Ireland was represented as a peasant by Miss Kirwan (also a Catholic).[159] During the play,

TABLEAUX AND CHORUS OF THE ALLIES.

From Left to Right—RUSSIA, MISS BROOKE; IRELAND, MISS KIRWAN; BELGIUM, MISS DENISE DALY; BRITANNIA, MRS. QUINLAN; SERVIA, MISS BLASCHECK; JAPAN, MISS TURNLY; FRANCE, MISS KIRWAN.

**Figure 6.2** Protestant and Catholic Irish women dressed as the Allies in Ballinrobe, Co. Mayo, *IL*, 29 January 1915. Courtesy of the National Library of Ireland.

Quinlan sang 'Here's to the Day' and the chorus was taken up by France (Miss Kirwan, most likely Florence Kirwan, the sister of Francis Mary Kirwan who represented Ireland), Belgium (Denise Daly, a landlord's daughter), Ireland (Florence Kirwan), Japan (Miss Turnley), Russia (the Anglican, Miss Brooke) and Serbia (an Anglican, Mary Blascheck).[160] Other participants demonstrated the centrality of the nursing services and the dominions to their understanding of the Allied war effort, since Miss Blosse Lynch appeared in the uniform of a Red Cross nurse 'and several little boys in the uniforms of the various branches of the home and colonial services, completed a very pretty scene'.[161]

Many Catholics paid tribute to Britain's stand in the war during the first wartime St Patrick's Day. *The Irish Times* recorded that the 'largest crowd on record' gathered in Cork and 'the processions through the streets included a large number of soldiers in khaki, who wore the shamrock profusely, and were cheered all along the route'. In the evening, 'the Roman Catholic and Protestant bishops expressed the sentiment that Ireland was now irrevocably identified with England in the great struggle for European freedom'. A similar friendly cross-community celebration took place in Limerick, where 'nearly all the young soldiers of the Royal Army Medical Corps wore the shamrock. ... The Union Jack floated from the flagstaff on the tower of St. Mary's Cathedral.' In Strabane, Co. Tyrone, nationalists identified with Britain and linked it to the 'noble cause of the Allies' and 'the Home Rule settlement', declaring that Ireland 'should do her duty to the Empire of which she was a part. ... These words were greeted with great enthusiasm. In the parade, Union Jacks were carried, a thing unknown before in a St Patrick's Day demonstration.'[162]

Indeed, one reason behind some nationalists' public support for the British war effort was because they believed that Home Rule would come into operation at the end of the conflict. Some historians have argued that nationalists saw the fate of the Home Rule bill as their primary concern in assisting the British war effort, which is why nationalist support for the war was supposedly weak, as Home Rule never came into operation.[163] By contrast, the passage of the bill was an incentive for some nationalists to join up, as on 5 January 1916, the Catholic, Michael Lavelle, declared at a recruiting meeting for the Connaught Rangers (his son held a commission with them) that

> he had been an old Fenian and Rebel, but he had seen that by the action of the Irish party and the good sense of the English government, a change had been brought about. Forty years ago they were slaves; today they were free men (applause) and I for one ... have determined that I will do what the Irish leader said we should do. England deserves our loyalty and our cooperation in this war.[164]

Three days before the Rising, Clare County Council praised the IPP. The Catholic chairman, P. J. Linnane, proposed a resolution in favour of recruitment and to 'not go back on the policy of Mr Redmond when they were on the point of being a "nation once again" (applause)'.[165] Much support for the Irish Party can actually be found after the passage of Home Rule, despite its association with recruitment. As Alvin Jackson has argued, this was particularly evident in January 1916 when the party was perceived to have stopped the application of conscription to Ireland following the passage of the Military Service Act 1916, as public bodies such as urban and district councils (Ennis, Galway, Listowel, Limerick No. 2 and Kildysart), boards of guardians (Navan, Tuam, Ennis) and others thanked the party, reflecting its relative vitality before Easter 1916.[166]

Thus a cross-section of Catholics backed the British and Allied war efforts in the period before the Rising, and Ireland's nationalists, as elsewhere in the Empire, entered the conflict in the spirit of a Home Rule nation. However, the Rising and London's subsequent treatment of nationalist Ireland reinvigorated the political question and threatened the 'unity' forged on the back of the war effort, causing many Catholics to question the 'purity' of Britain's stand 'in defence of small nations' and further politicizing the issue of recruitment.

## Politics, conscription and recruitment, 1916–18

The Easter Rising in April 1916 and the executions of the rebel leaders in May helped to change the political face of modern Ireland. At key locations in Dublin, and a handful of less significant places outside of the capital, rebels fought the British army for six days, killing approximately 450 people (most of them civilians), injuring 2,614, and causing widespread damage to buildings. F. S. L. Lyons has argued that London's exaggerated reaction to the Rising, which took the form of mass arrests, secret court martials and the long drawn-out execution of sixteen rebels, shocked and turned many nationalists to separatist nationalism. Moreover, mass internment of Irish men suspected of advanced nationalist activity in the months and years that followed sustained and fostered dissatisfaction with Westminster.[167] Historians have recently acknowledged that the Great War created the context in which the Rising could take place; indeed, it is hard to imagine the event having taken place if it had not been for the abnormal conditions of world war.[168] Emigration virtually came to a halt, thus keeping within Ireland the young people who were inclined to be anti-establishment and who in former years would have been the most likely group to have emigrated.[169] During the rebellion, some revolutionaries even dug trenches around St Stephen's Green, reflecting the context of world war.[170]

The Rising reinvigorated the contentious political debate in Ireland, ending the party truce which had prevailed since the passage of Home Rule.[171] Following the insurrection, Lloyd George proposed to enact self-government for Ireland with the exclusion of Ulster, thus invalidating the un-partitioned bill which had been placed on the statute book in September 1914. Jackson has argued that 'this was decisive in the fortunes of the Home Rule movement in Ireland'. It injected 'massive torpor' into the IPP, and 'there was no avalanche-like collapse of the party because until mid-1917, there was no well-organized alternative'.[172] Recent research has also argued that the party's failure seemed almost inevitable after the Rising.[173] Yet Jackson has argued that it was not guaranteed from the outset, and this was demonstrated in October 1916, when numerous groups and associations sent the IPP resolutions of confidence and protests against conscription following revived discussion about compulsion in nationalist circles. Some of these groups included Clare and Croom county and district councils, boards of guardians (Tipperary, Rathkeale, Loughrea, Croom, Kilrush, Kilmallock) and UIL branches (Limerick, Limerick Young Ireland, Newcastle, Fohenagh, North Galway, Castlemahon and East Limerick), which still comprised the bulk of nationalist political activists in Ireland during this period.[174] In Carlow, for example, RIC reports for January 1917 state that the combined membership of organizations affiliated to the IPP was 3,198 while the combined membership of nationalist societies aligned with more radical nationalist persuasions was 373.[175] Similarly in Cavan, the combined membership of IPP-affiliated organizations was 13,003 while membership of independent associations was 1,874.[176] In Co. Clare, 4,950 people were affiliated to the INV and UIL while 463 persons were members of Sinn Féin and the Irish Volunteers. In Cork County, the split was 8,276 IPP-affiliated persons versus 2,097 independent nationalists.[177]

The IPP's resilience may have been related to the political situation. The Irish Convention, which sat from July 1917 until March 1918 to settle the Irish question via a representative conference of nationalists and unionists, was 'not a failure from the outset' though it is often characterized as such. Jackson has argued that there was 'a degree of political fertility' within the Ulster Unionist camp, whose intransigence to any non-partitioned settlement of the Irish question 'was not guaranteed'. Irish Unionists also made a dramatic shift in their position in November 1917 which broke the political deadlock, and 3 January 1918 was the most likely day when an agreement between the parties was possible.[178]

Popular responses to the Irish Convention have yet to be scrutinized, but the growth of a rival party, Sinn Féin, was unquestionable, and it refused to take part in the Convention, which 'granted the proceedings with an air of unreality'.[179] By July 1917, advanced nationalists had won two by-elections, though in one of these, South Longford, the radical candidate's majority over the IPP candidate was only 32 in a poll of 2,954. There was much sympathy among nationalists for the executed rebels, as £137,808 was raised for their families between May 1916 and the end of 1919 through the INAVDF.[180] Some sympathizers, such as Archbishop Walsh of Dublin, assisted war-relief schemes as well (see, for example, pp. 72, 89), suggesting that there was no contradiction in contributing to causes which, sometime after the war, became aligned with different nationalist political persuasions. However, by October 1917 advanced nationalism had grown in Ireland. Disparate radicals consolidated under the banner of Sinn Féin. The party was thus ready for the unexpected challenge that emerged the following year.[181]

That challenge was the proposed implementation of conscription because of the worsening situation on the Western Front. Following Russia's collapse, hundreds of thousands of German troops and artillery were freed from the east, and on the 21 March 1918, half a million German infantry and ten thousand German artillery pieces attacked a seventy-mile section of front held by the British Third and Fifth Armies. As Gregory has noted, 'It was the greatest single offensive operation of the First World War'. By the end of the day, each army had suffered 40,000 casualties – the single bloodiest day of the war – and the traumatic assault continued for two months.

The German rapid advancement created an emergency for Britain, as the prospect of losing the war was imminent for the first time since 1914, and Gregory has argued that the authorities' decision to introduce conscription in Ireland was necessary in order to placate British public opinion. By April 1918, the British people were 'conscripted, tired, hungry, intermittently bombed, and more than a little war weary'. Many British people thought that the Irish had shirked their military responsibilities, using the conflict as an opportunity to become more prosperous. As the amended military service bill of 1918 increased the age range of British men that were called up (previously the bill could conscript men aged 18 to 41; now it raised the age limit to 50), Ireland had to be included in the measure to sell the amended bill to the British people and to prevent outrage at home, despite the fact that the authorities recognized that Irish troops would not be forthcoming.[182]

Ireland's protest against conscription was tremendous. Hundreds of thousands of nationalists backed by the Catholic Church demonstrated their hostility through demonstrations, petitions to Irish, British and American representatives and a massive £250,000 anti-conscription fund which the Catholic hierarchy inaugurated and which people at home and abroad amassed over a four-month period. Nationalist feeling against compulsion, which had permeated civil society since 1915, was virulent, and the IPP's inability to stop the government effectively made it redundant.[183] Colin Reid has argued that it heralded the death knell of the IPP while Paul Bew has claimed that it gave the radicals a further boost against an ailing Irish Party, as it ended the political neutrality which had existed between the Catholic Church and Sinn Féin.[184]

The nationalist protest against conscription has been widely interpreted as evidence of anti-war sentiment.[185] But was the protest against enforced military service actually a protest against the war? Most of the arguments against conscription rested on political hostility towards Westminster rather than the war itself. Considering each issue in turn – attitudes towards Westminster and attitudes towards the war effort – reveals a level of complexity in the nationalist protest that has been missed in the historiography. It illuminates an alternative multi-layered history of the Irish Catholic relationship with the war effort in the final months of the conflict that differs from the orthodox histories.

The decision to conscript Ireland struck at the heart of the Irish nationalist movement and violated the central argument that had been at the centre of the decades-long campaign for self-government. Nationalists believed that the general 'will' of the Irish people resided in Ireland – not Westminster – and that consent was the basis for any legitimate mobilization of human and economic resources.[186] This principle had underlined successive nationalist campaigns for self-government, as most Catholics believed that only Irish people had the right to govern themselves – and, by extension, to conscript their own, if such a need were to arise. When London proposed to introduce conscription in Ireland at a time when nationalists felt alienated from the government due to the delayed implementation of Home Rule, the memory of the Dublin rebels' executions, internment, martial law and other perceptibly draconian policies – not to mention their severe losses in the war, largely but not exclusively in the British Forces – the great majority felt that the government had violated their civil and national liberties and had broken its 'social contract' with nationalist Ireland. Moreover, the principle of consent was at the heart of the crisis. For decades, nationalists had believed that the 'general will' of the Irish people belonged in Dublin, not Westminster, hence the lengthy campaign to restore the Irish parliament, and this feeling was more visceral in the aftermath of the Easter rebellion and reinvigorated political question. By conscripting Ireland, Westminster, a perceived foreign government, had negated the consent of the Irish people. Violating perceived civil and, most importantly, national liberties, nationalists rebelled against the bill. Frustration towards Westminster was therefore palpable.

This was reflected within Catholic circles. The standing committee of the Irish bishops issued a resolution which protested against the 'conscription o[f] Ireland without the consent of the Irish people'. Similarly, when a representative conference of nationalists was held at the Mansion House to inaugurate an anti-conscription appeal at which the Catholic hierarchy, Sinn Féin, the IPP, Labour Party and

prominent individuals attended, a resolution was drawn up which implied that
Westminster had trespassed on the rights of Ireland's nationhood:

> Taking our stand on Ireland's separate and distinct nationhood and affirming
> the principle of liberty that the governments of nations derive their just powers
> from the consent of the governed, we deny the right of the British government,
> or any external authority, to impose compulsory service in Ireland against the
> clearly expressed will of the Irish people.[187]

When the viceroy, Lord French, announced at the end of May 1918 that Dublin
Castle would resume voluntary recruiting in Ireland in an attempt to raise 50,000
men by 1 October 1918, a scheme that was inaugurated in light of nationalist
Ireland's hostility to compulsion[188] (and more pertinently, because of the urgent
need for men at the front), many Catholics were unreceptive, and exhibited their
exasperation with Westminster by refusing to engage in the scheme. The voluntary
recruitment initiative was undertaken by the Irish Recruiting Council (IRC),
whose members comprised Protestant and Catholic elites.[189] Several elected
representatives refused to let the IRC speak in their districts, including Dublin
County Council, Rathmines County Council, Roscommon Town Commissioners
and Athy Urban Council.[190] Others, such as Carlow County Council, ignored the
IRC's appeal, taking 'no action'.[191] When Clare County Council received the IRC's
request to speak to them, they marked it 'read', as did others, finding it 'scandalous
and insulting' to be asked to promote recruitment.[192] These included Newcastle
West Town Commissioners, who 'followed the course generally adopted through
the country' by marking the communication 'read'.[193] In some places where the
IRC did speak, such as in Galway in July 1918, the *Connacht Tribune* noted that
'barely a quorum' attended and young men heckled the speakers.[194]

The extent to which Westminster itself was at the crux of grievances was evident
in quarters where the IRC was allowed to speak. Most of the hostility expressed at
these meetings rested upon London's treatment of Ireland rather than the war itself.
When hecklers interrupted recruiters at Kingstown, for example, they did so with
questions such as 'What about Ireland?', 'Let the men in jail out (applause)', 'What
about the Irish Republic? (applause)', as well as 'And Home Rule (applause)'.[195]
Cheers and counter cheers were raised when 'a portion of the audience began
to sing the 'Soldier's Song' and another sang 'Rule Britannia' and 'God save the
King'.[196] Similarly at an IRC meeting in Galway, hecklers interrupted recruiters
shouting "'Up Redmond", "Up King George" and "Up de Valera"'.[197] In Limerick,
these taunts resulted in the termination of one meeting because recruiters were
'shouted down'.[198] Nationalists used recruitment meetings as vehicles to express
disaffection towards London, making the recruiting platform a stage upon which
they openly contested Westminster's actions in Ireland and aired their support
for self-government (even if the nature of that self-government differed among
individuals).

Sinn Féin supporters had already adopted this tactic prior to the conscription
crisis, such as in June 1917, when the Nationalist MP, Captain Stephen Gwynn,

was hit with eggs while speaking at a recruitment meeting in Castlebar, Co. Mayo, by men wearing Sinn Féin badges.[199] This was a radically different response to when he had been carried on the shoulders of a crowd at a recruiting meeting in nearby Galway in October 1914 (on this occasion, the crowd followed Gwynn in repeating 'God Save the King' and 'God Save Ireland' and sang the Marseillaise).[200] Other examples can be found of recruitment meetings being terminated due to the speakers being heckled or shouted down, though the vast majority of protests occurred after April 1918.[201]

However, when attitudes towards the war itself are considered – something which, in post-April 1918 Ireland, was hard to distinguish from attitudes towards Westminster – it is clear that support for prosecuting the war against Germany had not changed. Nationalists conceived of recruitment (now associated with Britain's treatment of nationalist Ireland and heavily associated with conscription) and voluntary enlistment (which remained in Ireland's control) as separate and distinct things, though the lines were in fact blurred and stayed blurred until the end of the war. When the government declared that it would resume voluntary recruiting in Ireland, the radically inclined *Irish Independent* welcomed the proposal on the basis of its support for the Allies and that it would remove the threat of conscription, which was ideologically linked to the IRC's appeal for recruits:

> If an effort at voluntary recruiting could rid us of the conscription menace, we, and we believe, a large section of Irishmen would welcome that development. No one objects to voluntary enlistment, and if voluntary recruits can be found we shall be glad, and shall wish the campaign all success.

It made these comments in the same editorial as it enthused about the Catholic troops at the front, dwelling upon the actions of the 16th (Irish) Division at Guillemont and Ginchy and hoping that 'Irish recruits will enlist in their thousands [adding to] the proud acclaim of the nation whose martial fame they were so brilliantly vindicating'.[202]

However, when details of the voluntary recruiting initiative were announced, the IRC's scheme was not free from 'the conscription menace' after all. Lord French declared that if voluntary recruiting failed in Ireland, 'conscription will certainly be applied without delay'.[203] Nationalists consequently received the proposal with mixed feelings. The *Irish Independent* was annoyed that the threat of conscription remained and felt that it would prevent Irish men from joining up, which it strongly endorsed.[204] The nationalist *Dundalk Democrat* declared, 'Let the Government drop conscription, the shadow which is the greatest obstacle to voluntary recruiting.' It encouraged readers to 'follow in the footsteps' of the Nationalist MPs, Willie Redmond and Tom Kettle, 'in lending their aid in the fight against Prussian aggression in Europe'.[205] Even the Protestant organ, the *Church of Ireland Gazette*, felt that the government should recall its conscription policy if voluntary recruiting were to be a success.[206] The scheme's misleading nature was so apparent that the satirical British magazine, *Punch*, had an Irish cartoon with the headline: 'Voluntary Conscription'.[207]

The debates within Galway Urban Council illuminate some of the complexity which permeated discussions about recruitment and the IRC's scheme in late 1918 Ireland, the difficulty in separating military support for the war effort from Westminster's actions and the ambiguity in the government's policy to encourage voluntary enlistment while underpinning that policy with the threat of conscription. Martin Redington, an accountant, thought that 'it was a nice way they [the IRC] were going about it', a sentiment shared by Michael Crowley, a grocer and wine merchant, who stated that 'we are not soldiers, and we should not interfere with men who are inclined to go'.[208] Yet Martin Moloney, another grocer and wine merchant, felt that the IRC 'are not encouraging it'.[209] He declared that 'after all the betrayals of the past, the country had been once more betrayed after the Convention report'. He had been looking forward to the Convention's outcome, stating that it had 'raised great hopes ... but in place of a Home Rule bill we got as the result of the Convention – conscription!'[210] This comment was in reference to a statement made by Lloyd George, who had indirectly tied the Convention's results to compulsion, as he announced both in the same speech in parliament, provoking horror from Nationalist MPs in attendance.[211]

However, Moloney's hostility towards the IRC and recruitment was not a reflection of his attitude towards the Allied war effort, which was quite distinct and perceived as such. He declared that his son was fighting in the American Army and that 'his own sympathies were entirely with the Allies' but noted the 'impossible position' for Ireland to be asked 'to fight for liberty elsewhere when she was denied liberty at home'.[212] John Cunningham, a farmer and shopkeeper, also revealed his support for the Allied war effort but could not support the IRC's plan for domestic political reasons.[213] He declared that 'we are not interfering with them [potential Irish recruits], but England is not encouraging this country to assist in putting down the war'. For these four middle-class Catholics, there was fundamentally no problem about voluntary enlistment, but London had compromised the means of encouraging Irish men to join up.[214]

These attitudes were reflected elsewhere. In Monaghan County Council, the nationalist representatives collectively agreed with the chairman, the Catholic Thomas Toal, when he said:

> He was sure none of them was against voluntary recruiting. ... But they were asked to form themselves into recruiting agents for the British [g]overnment and after what had taken place in the past, he, for one, could not see his way to do any such thing for a British [g]overnment which had so shamefully broken its word with regard to this country.

Conversely in Westmeath County Council, James J. Coen JP, the Catholic chairman and a 'brewers' agent', believed that the council should let the IRC speak because voluntary enlistment would rid Ireland of the conscription threat and would help the Allies: 'He was asking them to support themselves, to support Ireland. They were in the most critical stage of the War at present and they had to ask themselves what they were going to do to save their own country and its liberty.'[215]

Despite these complications, the IRC enjoyed some success in its appeal, which was remarkable given the depth of feeling about Ireland's right to self-government and the frustration which many nationalists felt towards London. From August to November 1918, 9,845 Irish men enlisted in the British forces compared to 5,812 during the previous six months – a 154 per cent increase on the average number of recruits secured per month.[216] This was even though the IRC's 'recruitment campaign became fully operational only in September, due to financial wrangling and bureaucratic delay'.[217] Most recruits joined the navy and the air force rather than the infantry, a circumstance which was likely due to the well-known horrors of trench warfare which were acknowledged in 1918. In Britain, the legacy of hand-to-hand combat stretched into the Second World War when enlistees predominantly joined the navy, air force, artillery and army support services – 'the "clean" arms of the services' – because of the horrors their fathers had experienced in the First World War trenches.[218]

Importantly, these recruits were predominantly Catholics. Lucey has argued that the average monthly recruitment rate for Cork (89,193 of the 101,302 men in urban Cork were Catholics) from June to November 1918 was higher than that from August 1915 to January 1916.[219] 160 men enlisted in this period of 1918 compared with 144 men during the same months of 1916.[220] The response of the Catholic South prompted one Protestant recruiter in Monaghan to claim that 'Waterford, Limerick and Sligo are miles ahead of Co. Monaghan'. The recruiter 'found this difficult to understand considering the high percentage of Protestants in Monaghan (7,932 Catholics: 2,497 Protestants) compared to the other counties named'.[221]

Would the IRC's appeal have enjoyed more success had it not been tied to conscription? This is one possibility because the principle of voluntary enlistment would have been maintained. However, in the context of the times, the appeal would have only ever had limited success due to nationalist feeling towards Westminster in late 1918. In addition to these political complications was a much greater deterrent that overshadowed the prospect of both voluntary enlistment and recruitment. A pervasive war-weariness had developed across Ireland since 1915 due to the conflict itself, as successive Allied offensives had failed to break the deadlock on the Western Front, and no end to the conflict was in sight. The stress and strain of four long years of war was apparent in public morale, much as it was in Britain, where 'the strains of war were creating a widespread sense of gloom'.[222]

This affected Protestants as well as Catholics. On 1 January 1916, John Bennett, a Protestant businessman from Cork, wrote in his diary that 'the new year begins in gloom after a week of rain and heavy gales. Contemplation of our losses during the past year and of the high hopes entertained a year ago of victory or at least material progress towards victory extinguished in disaster'.[223] His pessimism was still apparent in December 1917 – the low-point in public morale in wartime Britain – as Bennett wrote, 'Once more the end of the year sees the war position unfavourable to the [A]llies'.[224] When the Protestant chaplain, John Redmond, who coincidentally had the same name as the Nationalist leader, was home on leave in Belfast during late December 1916, he reflected in his diary, 'When I arrived I found a great wave of depression and pessimism passing over the country. I fought against it in public and in private.'[225] Catholics also became weary of the never-ending carnage, as on 3 March 1917, the headline of the *Connacht Tribune* read 'Will the war end this year?'[226] Around Christmas, its editorial reflected the pessimism which Reverend Redmond had witnessed: 'Merry Christmas. Is it a cruel jest?'[227] It expected two more years of war and believed that for 'the civilian populations ... the strain will become intolerable.'[228] The Catholic author, Katharine Tynan, revealed how war-weariness had affected Irish civilians by 1918. That year, she compiled her memoirs and found it 'intensely depressing' to look back on her accounts written in wartime because of

> the prophecies that never came true: the rumours that were so soon dissipated: perhaps, above all, the fact that these were written down in ignorance of how the war should still be dragging on, slaying and torturing, after three and a half years had gone by, make the reading of these notes a dreary business.[229]

The never-ending slaughter affected recruitment rates. Long before the conscription crisis took place, recruitment in Ireland had been declining (see Chapter 2, Table 2.1). This was not unique to Ireland but was a trend replicated throughout Britain and the Dominions. The biggest decline in Ireland happened between February 1915 and February 1916, when over 50 per cent fewer recruits joined up. At no other point during the conflict was there a similar rate of decline in recruitment.[230] Declining recruitment rates at an international scale was the reason why Britain, Canada, Australia and New Zealand felt forced to introduce the policy of military compulsion: a policy that, outside of wartime, was anathema to the broad Liberal tradition adopted in both Britain and the Dominions and one that marked Britain out from its continental neighbours for whom conscription was a peacetime policy as well. It is thus doubtful that any voluntary enlistment initiative would have successfully combatted the war-weariness that was embedded throughout the British world (including Ireland) in the latter years of the war.

RIC recruiting returns for early 1917 in largely Protestant areas of Ulster – areas which were still loyal to the Empire's war effort and untroubled by the divisive effects of the Dublin rebellion – are indicative of the systemic war-weariness which had infiltrated Irish society since 1915, permeating even 'loyal' areas of the country. In Armagh (21,854 Protestants: 12,625 Catholics), recruitment was 'very poor' in January, and in Monaghan, it was 'at a standstill' in February.[231] In Antrim (329,769 Protestants: 111,091 Catholics) during the month of January 1917, 'recruiting for the army [was] at a complete standstill', and this was the same in Down (32,065 Protestants: 14,677 Catholics).[232] As Fitzpatrick has argued, the risks of being maimed or killed were well known by the end of 1915, and these were strong incentives not to enlist.[233] Wages had also increased in Ireland after the initial months of war, and farmers were offered considerable profits for their produce.[234] Irish men of both creeds, particularly those in agricultural areas, thus had strong incentives not to enlist, and these incentives were all the more powerful for the Catholic population who felt betrayed by London time and again throughout 1918.

That the IRC's appeal was successful at all is striking in light of the many barriers to recruitment which existed in Ireland. These barriers had a profound effect on the success of voluntary enlistment, the principle of which was still backed by many Catholics though the means through which it could be realized had become highly contentious and closely tied to the issue of self-government. For those men that did enlist, it is likely that no single reason could account for why they joined up, but a crucial motivator was the higher cause that had brought Ireland and several other nations into the war in August 1914 and which many Irish people still believed in four costly years later.

## A righteous defence

Catholic support for the Allied war effort – particularly among the middle classes though by no means exclusive to them – endured because many people were convinced by the Allied cause and believed that Germany was in the wrong. In wartime 1914, a new moral order was created in Britain whereby civilians rallied around a national cause to uphold justice, civilization and liberty.[235] These values framed the Allied war effort and became central to the Irish Catholic understanding of the conflict as well. In May 1915, Longford Urban District Council issued a declaration on behalf of the 'Townspeople of Longford' to the 5th (Service) Battalion Royal Irish Regiment, a New Army unit which had been stationed there for seven months. It referred to the men's 'valour, public spirit and patriotism', commending the moral reasons that had prompted them to fight for the Allies:

> Called into existence as you have been by the perils of our Country and a duty to civilization, we desire to express our acknowledgement of the magnificent spirit you have displayed. … Leaving Longford as you do today, we beg to assure you that you carry with you the cordial good wishes and affectionate regard of the people.[236]

Longford people's patriotism was based upon higher principles which were believed to underline the Allied war effort. By mid-1915, the morality of the war was firmly embedded within the Irish Catholic psyche as it was within the populations of other belligerents, wherein people understood the conflict in terms of 'defensive patriotism', believing that their soldiers were defending their territories from unwarranted aggression.[237] This was demonstrated in Longford and was also expressed in Galway when 'an enormous assemblage' of people turned out to welcome the Irish Guards in April 1915. 'The meeting was one of the largest held at Eyre Square since the old Land League days,' and the morality of the Allied cause was the centrepiece around which the gathering revolved.[238] Galway Urban Council declared on behalf of a cross-section of organizations – including council representatives, labour supporters, UIL and INV members, the local Anglo-Irish families, medics, bank officials, clerics (including Monsignor John Hynes, University College Galway's Dean of Residence), state representatives, the RIC and military officers – that the Irish Guards deserved support 'on account of the splendid part it has been, and is, taking, in the defence of freedom and civilization'.[239]

In 1915, the United Kingdom appeared to be fighting in defence of these higher values and as the section 'Home Rule, recruitment and Britain, 1914-16' above has outlined, many Catholics identified with Britain in that year, believing that it was the most significant Ally in the fight against unwarranted German 'aggression'. With Home Rule on the statute book and the expectation that the measure would come into law, there was little reason to question Britain's cause. The extent to which this perception changed after the executions of the Dublin rebels is hard to gauge, but it certainly changed after the conscription crisis and after Lloyd George scuppered the Home Rule Act. Britain was perceived to have compromised its standing in the Allied war effort and much exasperation towards London rested upon how far it was thought to have strayed from the international moral cause.

This was apparent in the protest against conscription, as nationalists compared Westminster's actions with those of Germany. From as soon as the crisis began, headlines such as 'Prussianism in Ireland' and 'the crowning folly of British Junkerdom' aligned Britain's actions with the negatively perceived military strategy of the Germans, and the nationalist press of all persuasions in Cork expressed similar sentiments.[240] For Patrick O'Donnell, the Bishop of Raphoe, conscription equalled 'oppression … its authors [Westminster] flagrantly contradict in our case their own propositions on behalf of freedom. They themselves seek to force on you what they denounce in others on the continent of Europe.'[241] At a large meeting of Catholics in Tuam to welcome Archbishop Thomas Gilmartin, the prelate expressed irony at how Ireland 'was threatened with conscription to fight for the freedom of small nations' yet he revealed his support for voluntary enlistment when he suggested that the government 'would do better if they dropped the threat of conscription'.[242]

In May 1918 when seventy-three men and women were arrested as part of the so-called 'German plot' – an alleged republican conspiracy to side with Germany which Bew has called 'an intelligence fiasco' – nationalists were further alienated from Westminster.[243] Moreover, they were incredulous that Britain had claimed that nationalist Ireland was in league with the German enemy. The *Independent* stated, 'Without any reservation we can declare that we are not pro-German, and that we can have no sympathy with a Power which has stamped with iron heel on the small nations whose territory it has invaded, and which has outraged humanity by its ruthless submarine warfare.'[244] The *Connacht Tribune* was seriously offended and hoped 'that Britain will be speedily compelled to make good the terrible indictment that she has promulgated against these Irishmen or else confess herself a mere political trickster before the world'.[245] It is significant that even unionist organs were uncomfortable with the government's attempt to align nationalism with Germany. The *Church of Ireland Gazette* declared that 'the Irish people are not and never have been pro-German'.[246]

As a result, some Catholics began to question whether Britain was a worthy Ally after all (an attitude which in itself was based on thinking of Ireland as a nation freely involved in the war, rather than as part of a centralized United Kingdom). In August 1918, Joseph O'Neill, a Catholic farmer and member of Westmeath County Council, declared that 'if England was fighting now for the rights of small nations, why were Irishmen pulled out of their beds at night, deported, etc., without any charge against them? If the Government had given Ireland Dominion Home Rule it would have been different.'[247] In Kildimo, Limerick, 'a largely attended meeting' was held 'to protest against the arrest and deportation of Irishmen by the "Protectors of Small Nationalities"'. The attendees declared that 'we regard the militarist Government responsible for the deed as enemies of human liberty'.[248] Similarly, when the *Connacht Tribune* considered the arrest of Irish men over the German plot, it believed that Britain had violated its moral stance in the war: 'The arrest of our countrymen on the charge of complicity with Germany is only one of the many cowardly subterfuges adopted by the "protector of small nationalities" to dragoon Irishmen into revolt whenever a great wrong was about to be inflicted on her.'[249]

Britain's actions in Ireland had corrupted its moral standing as a virtuous Ally. It could no longer claim to be defending the ideals of liberty and civilization (let alone the mantra, 'in defence of small nations') while simultaneously oppressing the Irish at home. This sentiment bubbled over following the conscription crisis. It generated uncertainty in nationalist circles about the morality of the British war effort, which consequently impacted nationalists' ability to support the Allied war effort. Catholic Ireland's only means of militarily contributing to the fight through the regiments and battalions that it could historically call its own had been through Britain. Since April 1918, however, Britain's war effort had become associated with the political future of Ireland, which made Ireland's war effort – bound up as it was with Britain – a politicized, complicated entity that was no longer a simple matter of supporting the Allies.

Yet despite these difficulties, at no point did most people lose support for the Allied cause and the international effort to defeat Germany. This was reflected in civil society in a number of ways, one of which was through support rendered to Irish servicemen. Irish Catholic troops regularly departed for the front in the months which followed the Rising and their decision to fight for the Allies was endorsed by many people at home, just as it had been in earlier periods, though at times the domestic political situation interfered with attitudes towards serving soldiers, bound up as they were with the mix of feelings towards recruitment, Westminster and Britain's role in the war, which had been tainted at some stage after the Rising and more evidently after April 1918. On 29 November 1916, the *Limerick Leader* reported that the Catholic P. E. Kenneally JP, the chairman of Ennis Urban Council and a member of Clare County Council, had joined the RMF with the well-respected local man, Major Larry Roche, who during that week had 'forwarded to the boys [at the front] over 200 hurleys to encourage the National game and keep the lads at it'.[250] Their 'example was followed by several others, and on Monday last a big number of recruits, headed by Mr Kenneally, left Ennis for the Curragh. They were seen-off by a large crowd and given a hearty god-speed'.[251] This battalion had been stationed in Galway before the authorities moved the remaining Irish units to England because they feared that Sinn Féinism might compromise the loyalty of Irish servicemen.[252] Before the Munsters left Galway in November 1917, the *Connacht Tribune* reported that 'during their brief stay here, they apparently made many friends, as the approaches to the station were crowded with people anxious to see them off'.[253]

Irish soldiers and chaplains regularly returned home on leave. On these visits they were generally welcomed, as moral support existed within the communities from which they came. When Sergeant C. Roche returned to Newcastle West in Limerick in November 1916, the *Limerick Leader* reported that 'his many friends in Newcastle West gave him a hearty reception home and a God speed on his return journey'.[254] When two Ballina men returned home on leave who were presumed killed in action, the *Western People* reported 'rejoicing' within the local community. That month, the newspaper noted that 600 certificates were presented in the local Town Hall to relatives of men on active service from Ballina, Crossmolina and Killala.[255] In March 1917, a similar event happened in Navan, Co. Meath, when 80 certificates were handed out, and in Cork, 430 certificates were issued in May.[256] In August 1918 in Queen's County (Laois), before Fr J. S. Kellett departed for the front, he was 'presented with a cheque by a number of his friends in the district on his volunteering for service as military chaplain'.[257] Similarly when Fr Francis Browne, the nephew of the Bishop of Cloyne, returned home in March 1918 (he was granted leave in order to receive the Military Cross from the King), he wrote to his provincial superior that 'my uncle was awfully good to me. He brought me away in his little car to Kerry for three days. Just the two of us together.' The influential bishop did not express anxiety regarding his nephew's war service during the three days they had spent together, and there is no hint in the letters written by Jesuit chaplains to the Dublin province that their families questioned their decision to assist the Allies.[258]

However, instances can be found where Irish soldiers on leave were targeted by Sinn Féin supporters and individuals who could no longer differentiate between the war effort and the political future of Ireland. In July 1916, Lieutenant-Colonel W. S. Caulfield received a complaint from the RIC about one of his men, a Private Gorhan who had been involved in a brawl in Ballsbridge, Dublin, when home on leave. When asked about the offence, Gorhan replied that 'a man shouted out to me "You b---- soldier" to which I replied "you dirty coward, why don't you join up?". He then struck me and I, in self defence, laid him out Sorr [*sic*]'.[259] When the Capuchin priest and republican, Dominic O'Connor, enlisted as a military chaplain, he had to explain his decision to his family:

> I know well you were surprised that I became a chaplain and there was no one that heard it that wasn't. Well someone had to do the work and when those who had done all the recruiting were too cowardly to go there was nothing left except to have us who were anti-recruiters go and help the souls of the soldiers the others had sent out.[260]

O'Connor's decision to become a chaplain was based upon religious considerations but his concern was for the souls of Irish servicemen, many of whom were Home Rulers. O'Connor revealed that they were still good Irish men in his eyes when he told his sister sometime around April 1918: 'In the meantime pray for me and my men of Ireland, please.'[261] O'Connor was later imprisoned for one year and was sent to America by the Church because of his republican convictions. He also ministered to the Cork Lord Mayor, Terence MacSwiney, when he died on hunger strike in 1920. His example reveals that even ardent republicans could make a distinction between Irish troops fighting in the British forces and the British state in the final year of the conflict, something which many could or would not be able to make in the years 1919–23.

Schools and universities remained loci of moral support for members on active service, though they often illuminated the fault-lines which had developed between Catholics who wished to assist the Allies and those who sought to win Irish self-government first. The 1917 edition of *The Belvederian* told readers that 'our magazine is strictly non-political. ... There are in the pages that follow reflections of the views of such opposite parties as those whose sympathies are represented by the motto, "Help to win the war," and those whose doctrine is "Ireland before all."' The magazine catered for the divergent opinions of its readers, as it published articles about radicals such as Joseph Plunkett, a past pupil and executed rebel, as well as Irish officers, such as Jack Anderson and Private John Doyle.[262] It did not stop publishing obituaries of Irish men killed in action, adding fifteen names to the deceased in its 1918 edition, though these obituaries were shorter, leaving less room for interpretation.[263] Other institutions revealed their enduring support for the Irish troops when they offered 'honorary war degrees' for serving members, which University College Galway did in November 1917 and University College Dublin copied in January 1918.[264]

Another way in which civil society demonstrated its enduring support for the war effort was through humanitarianism. When wounded Irish men came home, individuals and groups went out of their way to care for these men and their dependants. On 8 December 1916, Canon P. Lee presided at Abbeyfeale Old Age Pensions Committee which considered pension applications. 'It was decided to make a further appeal to the military authorities to reconsider their [position] in respecting the claim for maintenance of Mr Martin Kennelly, whose son had been wounded in action. The case was considered a most deserving one.'[265] Some employers such as Murphy's, the Catholic brewing dynasty in Cork, considered how to help employees who had been wounded in action. On 25 January 1917, the executives considered the case of William Murray, a 'former cellar clerk now sergt [sergeant] in the Munsters' who had been at Ginchy. They wrote in the minutes, 'He took a wound in head ... was healed ... give him a gratuity of £5.'[266] Similarly on 14 April 1917, a meeting was held by the 'Approved Societies' Association' in the Mansion House, Dublin, to discuss Irish civil society's position towards discharged soldiers, sailors and nurses. Several organizations attended which straddled a cross-section of society including creed (Catholic Girls' Society; Dublin Protestant Society; Union Friendly Society), the labouring classes

(Irish Drapers' Assistants; Flax Roughers, Belfast; Meath Labour Union; Limerick Workers), region (the Great Southern and Western Railway; Great Northern Railway; Roscommon County Society) and women's associations (the WNHA; Nurses' Insurance Society).[267] All had employees in the war. They considered the treasury's 'treatment ... in respect of wounded soldiers ... scandalous' and claimed that it was 'worse for nurses'. The organizations had spent funds looking after their male and female employees because the government was failing to provide for the sick and wounded.[268] Irish civil society thus took the onus upon itself to care for their wounded sailors, soldiers and nurses when the state was perceived to have neglected its duties.

Above all, many Catholics from different backgrounds remained supportive of the other Allies after Britain's fall from grace. While London's actions had invariably made support for the British war effort a political question about Irish self-government and Ireland's right to liberty, the higher values that had propelled the Irish to back the war in the first place – values including freedom, liberty, civilization and justice, values which the American president, Woodrow Wilson, had rebranded as a war for democracy and national self-determination upon America's entry into the war in 1917 and values which the Irish-American community by and large supported, as Michael S. Neiberg has shown – were values that the other Allies continued to uphold and which the Irish in Ireland and elsewhere continued to support.[269] Taking Belgium as an example, from the outset, 'Belgium was viewed more as victim than as partner' because it played an integral role in helping the Irish to understand why Ireland was at war (a situation which closely resembled the British experience).[270] As outlined in Chapter 3, Catholic Ireland had an important historic connection to 'little Catholic Belgium', whose resistance and determination to retrieve its liberty resonated with nationalists because of their own situation. Anger against the larger German aggressor trampling upon a smaller Catholic state paralleled their own historic experience with England, thus investing the Allied war in 'defence of small nations' with personal relevance.[271]

When Belgian refugees arrived in Ireland in 1914, Irish Catholics sourced Belgian symbolism to welcome them, which was 'a striking visual demonstration of Ireland's support for a collaborative war with Britain to liberate Belgium'.[272] Support for Belgium was displayed throughout the country. In Limerick, the INV marched ahead of the refugees carrying three Belgian flags and sang 'A Nation Once Again ... the chorus being taken up by the crowd'.[273] When sixty-eight refugees arrived in Cork, a concert was held to raise funds for their plight at the Palace Theatre. The venue 'was specially decorated for the occasion, prominently displayed being the Irish and Belgian flags entwined, and surmounted by the Union Jack'.[274] Similarly when refugees arrived in Kildare, 'Belgian flags floated everywhere on the breeze, from windows, lamp posts and gates, with here and there a Union Jack – Celbridge's welcome to the fugitives from German aggression and brutality'.[275]

Even during the period when Britain's moral standing was questioned, sympathy for Belgium's plight endured. On 31 March 1917, the Belgian Refugees' Committee announced that 600 refugees remained in Ireland, half of whom were financially supported by generous individuals, who were largely Irish Catholic as Chapter 3 has shown (the other half made use of public funds).[276] Large turnouts of people witnessed the refugees' departure in February 1919, and these gatherings were friendly. Some Belgians flew the British colours upon leaving Ireland, as the Union Flag was the one under which Irish soldiers, both Protestant and Catholic, had fought to liberate Belgium. Though the political situation had worsened nationalist Ireland's relationship with Westminster, making many hostile to British symbolism, this flag still represented for the refugees the liberty which Ireland had helped to secure for them.[277]

Catholic Ireland's support for Belgium in each and every year of the war was considered to have been great. In his Lenten pastoral of 1914, Cardinal Mercier, the Archbishop of Mechelen and Primate of Belgium, referred to the generosity of Ireland as well as the other nations of England, Scotland, France, Holland, the United States and Canada, who mobilized to financially assist the Belgians.[278] In July 1919, the Belgian legation in London presented Cardinal Logue with a prestigious diploma (*Grand Officer de l'Ordre de la Couronne*) on behalf of the Belgian government. (He also received the insignia of the Belgian Order.) The *Irish Catholic Directory* printed that 'it is specially stated that this distinction has been conferred on his eminence in recognition of the kindness shown to the Belgians in this country during the war'.[279] In the decades following the conflict, some advanced nationalists would remember this time differently, as Monsignor Curran told the BMH in 1952 that Archbishop Walsh 'discountenanced the support of those Belgians who fled from their country and has always regarded them as the least deserving of support ... the Belgians who came across are, in perhaps most cases, worthless and worse-than worthless'.[280]

Belgium was not the only country that the Irish assisted, though the arrival of hundreds of Belgian refugees and Ireland's historic links with little Catholic Belgium made the nature of that support different in kind to that rendered to the other Allies. On 10 November 1916, the Vatican newspaper, *Osservatore Romano*, declared that Irish Catholics had contributed over 290,000 francs to help Polish War Victims since November 1915 – fourth most generous among all the nations that contributed to Poland's plight. Ireland's total was 'almost double that of England, and more than a fourth of the United States subscription', an impressive amount given the disparities in population and wealth between the three countries.[281]

'Flag days' (a method of fundraising for the war effort in which miniature flags were sold, usually at the price of one penny) were regularly held to render financial assistance to the Allies. These were especially common in 1915 when public morale was higher. In September 1915, a collection was held in Limerick for the Russian Red Cross. *Irish Life* reported that it was 'a very successful one, thousands of tiny Russian flags being sold in support of the fund, and the contributions in several instances being on a generous scale. All the lady collectors wore the Russian colours'.[282] Similarly, in Dublin city and county, £1,283 11s 3d was raised for Italy in November 1915 and 'in all the thoroughfares of the city ... collectors were present in large numbers tendering their miniature flag and badges for sale, and the day had not gone very far when every pedestrian one met seemed to be decorated with

Italy's national colours – indeed, it was the exception to see a passer-by without a badge or flag'.[283] An Anglo-Russian flag day was also scheduled for 25 May 1916 but was postponed due to the Easter Rising, and a flag day for an Irish ward in 'the Anglo-Russian' hospital was proposed to take place in June 1917, though the Russian Revolution made it slip from memory.[284]

France was a popular nation for the Irish to support. In July 1915, a flag day was held for the country in Dublin and *Irish Life* reported

> All over the city the tri-colour was in evidence, while draperies of red, white and blue adorned many shop windows, while an army of flag sellers numbering about fifteen hundred plied a busy trade in selling miniature French flags and models of the celebrated 75[mm] guns of the French artillery, which reproduced in metal, were seen suspended by tricolour ribbon from the buttonholes of most men's coats.[285]

Pennell has argued that 'there had always been feelings of friendship towards France in the country, stemming from … the Franco-Prussian War of 1870-1871'.[286] *Irish Life* made this clear in the comment 'Irish sympathy with France is no sentiment of recent growth and to most Irish people the Entente Cordiale is a sacred bond'.[287] The historic relationship between nationalist Catholic Ireland and France was made further apparent in April and May 1915, when prominent constitutional nationalists visited Paris where they were received by influential French deputies, clerics and President Raymond Poincaré.[288] The Irish delegates 'spoke of the ancient bond and enthusiastic sympathy between Ireland and France who is defending, with the help of her Allies, civilization, liberty and right, which are threatened by the most oppressive tyranny in history'. Both the Irish and French representatives dwelt upon their shared 'common race' and 'Celtic character', prompting Poincaré to declare that 'history has tightened the bonds of relationship between Ireland and France, and each century as it passed has united us more closely (applause)'.[289]

Though it has been suggested that support for France waned in Ireland following the rise in radical nationalism,[290] little distinction can actually be found between attitudes towards the French after Easter 1916 and those which had prevailed before. In mid-1917, two fundraisers were held for the French Red Cross in Cork and Dublin. The radical-leaning *Irish Independent* encouraged readers to donate even though it speculated that its largely Catholic readership was fatigued by flag days, having contributed heavily to the Allied cause:

> The novelty of flag days has worn off, and possibly there have been too many of them during the past couple of years. … But even those who think so will not object to a French flag day in aid of the French Red Cross Society. … On historical and sentimental grounds alone an appeal made to Irishmen on behalf of a French charity is sure of generous support at any time.[291]

£219 11s 2d was raised in Cork city and county for the French, which was more than the £160 raised for 'wounded and captured Royal Munster Fusiliers' in December 1915 and more than the £150 raised that month for Irish soldiers in Cork.[292]

In October 1916 when prominent French bishops visited Maynooth (the national seminary for Irish Catholic priests), they were 'enthusiastically welcomed' by the Catholic hierarchy, all of whom endorsed the visit apart from the pacifists, archbishops Walsh and O'Dwyer, who saw it for the thinly veiled recruitment exercise which in fact it was. The visit was an attempt by the French to scope out the possibility of securing Irish troops for the French forces in light of the volatile political situation that had been created between Ireland and Britain, which the French felt may deter Irish men from joining up. Cardinal Logue declared that 'they have come here specially to renew the ties which have bound Catholic Ireland to Catholic France for centuries past' and made his support for the French war effort clear in the comment: 'They are fighting a great battle for the Faith and for their people in that great country, France.'[293] At least two French missions to Ireland were attempted in 1916 and after the conscription crisis of 1918, with the aim of securing troops for the French Army. They were ultimately unsuccessful, mainly because they were not put into operation (and ironically because senior Ulster Protestants, such as General Sir Henry Wilson, protested against the notion of Irish men fighting under a French flag, which therefore killed the authorities' plan)[294], but it is also unlikely that non-clerics would have felt the same degree of historical affinity to France as religious elites such as Logue, particularly in a period where recruitment had fallen across Europe and elsewhere.

When America entered the war in April 1917, it provided a morale booster for war-weary Irish Catholics, especially because the conflict was going badly for the Allies. The Russian Revolution was underway, mutinies within the French army were occurring and Italy would soon suffer a major defeat at Caporetto. America's entry into the conflict thus offered a chance to shorten the war and secure a victory for the cause of liberty that underlined Allied discourse. Throughout Catholic Ireland, congratulations were expressed that America had joined the Allied campaign. Galway Urban Council unanimously congratulated America 'on coming in to assist the Allies (hear, hear)'.[295] As America had been the most recent home for Irish Catholic emigrants, the nationalist *Connacht Tribune* reported that 'many mothers in the west [of Ireland now had] sons serving in the United States army', a major incentive for western Catholics to remain committed to the Allied cause.[296] This was a setback for republicans such as Monsignor Curran, who believed that America's support for the Allies compromised the advanced nationalist identification with Germany. However, he suggested republican support for the Germans was not very strong to begin with and that republicans were in fact more supportive of the Allies, in the comment, 'But as they [republicans] were pro-German only to the extent that they were fighting England, they soon discovered that they could still maintain their anti-British outlook and were only concerned with the progress of the Yankees in France.'[297]

The freedom which America was perceived to represent and which was central to the Allies' cause resonated with Catholic-nationalist ideas and traditions. Some individuals wrote letters to the press about America and the war as 'a life and death struggle between the forces of democracy on the one side and tyranny on the other'.[298] In Cork during late 1918 and early 1919, Catholics strongly identified with the United States even though Cork Corporation, which controlled much of the local administration, was against London in this period, revealing how nationalists could simultaneously be against the government and supportive of the Allied war effort. In September 1917, the Corporation's minutes record that it was appalled by the treatment of Irish internees 'at the hands of the militarists, who, at present[,] usurps [*sic*] the powers of government in this country, whilst they hypocritically masquerade before the Nations of the World, as the "Champions of small nationalities".'[299] However, the Corporation's alienation from Westminster was made up by its support for the American war effort, renaming Great George's Street and Great George's Street West 'Washington Street ... as a compliment to America's proposal of Irish-American brigades or for Irishmen to join the American army'.[300]

The Irish Catholic response to the German peace proposal of December 1916 further reveals that the majority of Irish sympathies were with the Allies despite frustration towards Westminster. Some Catholics, such as J. O'Donoghue, no longer trusted England but still considered Germany to be the 'enemy'. He wanted to know the details of Germany's offer and hoped that the Allies would not be 'influenced unduly in their decision by the views of the English press'.[301] Pacifists and those exasperated with the never-ending conflict, such as one Fr Murphy from Limerick, hoped that the gesture would be accepted, 'lest there be no humanity left to fight for'.[302] However, the vast majority of Catholics rejected the German offer. Though they wanted the war to end, their notion of peace was bound up with an Allied victory.

This attitude was not exclusive to Ireland but was in fact common throughout many of the Allied nations. In France, Rousseau and Becker have argued that the French increasingly desired peace, but they did not want to lose the war even though they were tired of it dragging on, and these sentiments were not contradictory.[303] Similarly in Britain, most people desired what Gregory has termed a 'victorious peace'.[304] Catholic Ireland was no different in how it desired the war to end. Following the German peace offer, the conservative-nationalist organ, *The Connaught Telegraph*, declared that 'if we are to have a peace that will leave Germany unhumiliated, the countless lives sacrificed and the billions of money squandered will have been in vain'.[305] The nationalist *Kildare Observer* denounced Germany, concluding that 'the peace for which the spirits of our murdered sons calls out is not of German manufacture'.[306] The radically inclined *Independent* believed that only the Allies could bring peace to the world: 'The war must be ended by a peace which will possess every inherent guarantee of permanence. Unless they can assure themselves of that the Allies cannot agree to negotiate'.[307]

This conception of peace-through-victory had been expressed by Cardinal Logue during the visit of the Irish Canadian Rangers in January 1917, when he declared in a sermon that 'we are longing for peace ... but it must be a stable peace, and it must be a permanent peace'.[308] It had also underlined Archbishop Crozier's sermon to the men, and when the Australian press reported the Armagh visit, two messages were taken from their orations: that the Rangers were defending the Empire's honour and that they were contributing to the achievement of a victorious peace.[309] The conviction that peace could be forged through victory underlined several Lenten pastorals in February 1918, as Thomas Gilmartin, the Bishop of Clonfert, prayed for 'the numerous sons of the diocese who have given their lives for the belief in the cause of right and liberty' and 'for a lasting peace'.[310] Patrick O'Donnell, the Bishop of Raphoe, stated that the war had been 'in the name of outraged liberty' and implied that the Allied war effort would bring peace to the world: 'War has been declared ... to extend the blessings of freedom and secure its enjoyment among the nations, small as well as great.'[311]

When the end of the war came, the notion that a victorious peace had been secured was widely expressed, as discussed below, and this happened at a time when the influenza epidemic raged across Ireland. Communities were grappling with the disease in many quarters, such as in North Galway, where several deaths had been reported in the villages of Cloonlea, Killalane, Lisavally and Loughrea,[312] and in Belfast, where the Presbyterian John Hutchinson, a Royal Irish Fusilier, found upon his return that 'Belfast was ravaged by it [influenza]. I lost more personal friends in this epidemic than I did in the War.'[313] Bereaved families must have experienced a multitude of emotions when the war ended, though many were thankful than the slaughter had stopped. When the London-born Anglican, Rosamond Stephen, visited the Catholic Mrs Rice in Belfast upon hearing of the Armistice, she found Mrs Rice 'sat by the fire saying "I am very glad. I am very glad"'. However, Stephen doubted that this emotion reflected Rice's feelings in their entirety, as she wrote that 'her [Rice's] son Ownie had been killed in action while another, Jo, was in a lunatic asylum with shell shock'.

Many families were delighted that their relatives would soon be coming home, and Stephen's diaries capture these sentiments as she traversed from house to house in the working-class Catholic districts of west Belfast. 'The first really cheerful house' she visited after hearing of the Armistice was that of one Catholic, Mrs McCorry, who was 'sure her Hugh will be home by Christmas and she will send him down to see me. He is an interned sea man and was torpedoed while going to fetch us some meat from South America.' Many Catholics were simply relieved that their loved ones at the front had made it through the war unscathed, such as one Catholic, Mrs Delany, who jumped out of bed even though she had the 'flu'. She declared to the local baker that 'she could not lie in bed when the war was over' as 'God had blessed "this family"'. Neither her own brothers nor her husband's brothers have been killed, though badly wounded some of them.'[314]

These reactions complemented the widespread acknowledgement that the Allies had won. The nationalist press – the political opinions of which were, by this stage, varied in light of the ebbing fortunes of the IPP and increased electoral support for Sinn Féin – waxed lyrical on the achievement. The single-worded headline of the *Connacht Tribune* was 'Victory'.[315] The *Connaught Telegraph* declared that 'the Allies have saved the world from ... the despised Kaiser' while the *Limerick Leader* hoped that 'better standards of right and justice and civilization will replace those under which the terrible conflict that has drawn to a close was possible'.[316] The *Independent* was delighted that 'tyranny had been overthrown', declaring that 'the Prussian military autocracy can never again be a menace to civilization'.[317]

These attitudes were popularly expressed. Rosamond Stephen was told how factory workers in the local mills had responded to the news:

> The manager came and said the war was over. ... One child waved a handkerchief ... but anyway this handkerchief was waved and it was white and a voice shouted 'Germany's flag' and then they all sang all the war songs they knew, and they were quite mad, and the foreman sent them home because of course no one was going to work any more. But it was all the height of good temper.[318]

The colour white, emblematic of a desire to surrender or to forge a truce, reflected how local people in this Belfast mill interpreted the Armistice. Elsewhere, knowledge that Germany had been defeated and that the Allies had prevailed provoked widespread enthusiasm and a relief that the war was coming to an end. The Irish Guards chaplain, Francis Browne, wrote to Fr Nolan: 'Isn't it grand to think that the end has come, and come so well for our side; please God it will come for us *at home* soon, and equally well. Here all is excitement and rejoicing'[319] RIC inspectors reported the delight of townspeople in Kilkenny ('including the Sinn Feiners, who did not however demonstrate their joy as others did'), Galway West, Leitrim, Mayo (though when a Union Flag was hung outside the house of one loyalist to celebrate, 'it was removed and burned ... by some advanced and youthful Sinn Feiners'), Roscommon, Clare, Kerry, Tipperary and Cork (where the Allied flags were displayed).[320] In many places, inspectors noted that people were especially relieved that the conscription threat had ended, thus removing the fear that the 'will' of the Irish people would be compromised by Westminster. Prelates interpreted the victory as a means to implement everlasting peace. The hierarchy proposed a resolution thanking God for stopping the 'cruel, destructive war' and put its faith in the Allied statesmen who had assembled at Versailles to ensure that world war would never happen again: 'It is to be hoped, however, that the wisdom and zeal of those statesmen, in whose hands the destinies of so many peoples rest, will be able to evolve order and harmony from chaos thus establishing a general, just and enduring peace.'[321]

The Allied victory even reinvigorated the spontaneous phenomenon of 'unity' that had occurred in August 1914. As before, this was particularly evident in Ulster. In Newry Co. Down, 'all the local Unionist and Nationalist bands, marched triumphantly through Hill Street to Kildare Street, where the victorious termination of the war was fittingly celebrated. The flags of the Allies were borne in the procession, patriotic songs were sung at intervals, and scenes of the greatest enthusiasm prevailed.'[322] The RIC inspector for Down declared that 'general rejoicings' occurred and that 'the great majority of all creeds and classes were delighted'.[323] Similarly in Fermanagh, the 'thoroughly Protestant and Conservative paper', the *Fermanagh Times*, reported, 'Orange and Green at Blacklion: Celebrate Conclusion of the War: Nationalist and Unionist Bands unite: Enthusiastic Scenes'.[324] RIC reports confirm that 'Nationalists took part with Unionists in the peace rejoicings'.[325] In Bailieboro (Bailieborough), east Cavan, scenes of 'unbounded enthusiasm' prevailed. 'Cheers were given for President Wilson and

King George, also for the Ulster and Irish Divisions, the British navy, Mr Lloyd George, and Major Willie Redmond, who gave his life for the cause of right and freedom.'[326] Yet in less than one month, East Cavan nationalists returned the Sinn Féin candidate, Arthur Griffith, unopposed to Westminster, revealing that more radical political allegiances were reconciled with support for the Allied cause and those constitutional nationalists who had assisted it until at least the end of the war.

Many Irish people thus continued to support the Allies when the political question was reinvigorated because they believed in the higher principles that underlined the Allied cause. Germany was fundamentally thought to have been in the wrong, an attitude which was cemented by mid-1915, and while Britain appeared to be on the side of 'right' until at least May 1916, London's treatment of nationalist Ireland after this date corrupted its moral standing in a war for 'freedom' and 'liberty'. London's 'Prussian-like' actions towards nationalist Ireland (particularly in 1918) heralded Britain's fall from grace in the eyes of nationalists, corrupting the notion of recruitment: the primary means through which Irish Catholics could contribute to the war effort at a time when recruitment was already a challenge for the authorities in Ireland, Britain and elsewhere. While dissatisfaction mounted against Westminster and military support for the British war effort became more of an issue about Ireland rather than about the war itself, Catholics continued to support the other Allies because it was in this Alliance that the bulk of their allegiances lay. Thus when the war ended, Irish Protestants and Catholics celebrated the 'victorious peace' together despite their domestic political differences because, in this respect, they had been on the same side in an international cause ever since the conflict began.

## Chapter 7

## CONCLUSION: IRELAND'S WAR?

On 28 June 1919, exactly five years after the assassination of Archduke Franz Ferdinand in Sarajevo, Bosnia, which ignited the series of interlocking events that led to the outbreak of European hostilities, the state of war between Germany and the Allied Powers formally came to an end. The Treaty of Versailles, one of several peace treaties signed by the Allied and Central Powers following the Armistice of November 1918, was undoubtedly the most significant treaty that was signed in the aftermath of the Great War.[1] For both Britain and Ireland, Germany had been the absolute enemy, a perception embedded in both public and political psyche since 1914, and news that Germany had accepted full responsibility for all loss and damage during the war was welcomed in Dublin. On 29 June, 101 rounds of blank ammunition were fired at regular intervals at every artillery station across the country. Union Flags flew from the windows of leading business establishments and private homes in the capital, while in the suburbs flags were 'hung from almost every house in some avenues and terraces'. Many soldiers celebrated on the streets, bedecked in small Union Flags or 'twisted red, white and blue ribbons around their caps, while the colours were also worn largely by members of the fair sex'. There was no doubt in Ireland's capital that the victory achieved in November 1918 was very much Ireland's victory as well.

By 10.00 pm, however, a different atmosphere pervaded the city. Outside Trinity College Dublin, members of the crowd snatched the Union Flags from those holding them and 'set them on fire, to the accompaniment of cheers for the Irish Republic and its President'. 'The Soldier's Song', the republican anthem, was sung alongside that of labour, 'The Red Flag'. Some civilians who objected to the celebrations came to blows with soldiers at the corner of Henry Street and Sackville Street (the capital's main thoroughfare), while one officer, Major Anderson, was dragged from his car and beaten with hurling sticks, sustaining cuts and bruises.[2] The War of Independence had begun and the Great War would, for the next few years, take a back seat as domestic politics violently overtook the international. But this was not the case for long. The Irish had been too involved and had voluntarily given so much in the earlier conflict, to have relegated the war to the past.

This book began with a photograph of interwar remembrance in Cork city in 1925. It asked the question, how could so many people turn out to mourn their war dead in towns and villages across Ireland when Catholics had supposedly turned their backs on the Allied war effort during the conflict itself? Through examining the attitudes and behaviour of the Irish who assisted the war effort on both the home front and across the British Dominions, it is clear that one major reason why many Catholics and Protestants turned out for the unveiling of the Cork war memorial was because they had consistently supported the Allied campaign for the duration of the conflict, even when domestic politics came to the fore. That Catholics participated alongside Irish Protestants despite the excesses of 1919–23 reflected the fact that the Great War was an all-Irish war effort – one that inspired a level of cross-confessional collaboration on a scale unimaginable in pre-war Ireland.

Both contingent events as well as imagined scenarios shaped Irish reactions to the war. In wartime 1914, participation in battles along the Western Front and the arrival of Belgian refugees helped to make the conflict real, but it was the destruction of the *Lusitania* in May 1915 which legitimized the claims of opinion shapers that Germany was the absolute enemy that had to be defeated. Historians have paid most attention to 1916 because of the Rising and the catastrophic impact of the Battle of the Somme, but 1915 was in some ways more significant in developing attitudes towards the international conflict: it cemented Germany's status as the ultimate despotic power (a perception that remained remarkably fixed until the end of the war) and the losses of the 10th (Irish) Division on the shores of Suvla Bay sealed the commitment to the cause of the Allies for a cross-section of the Irish population – one that stretched beyond Ulster and included both Catholics and Protestants. Both groups participated in recruitment drives, succouring victims of war, fundraising for the Allies and giving moral support to their men who joined up. The Ireland of 1915, as well as wartime 1914, was much more united in a common purpose than it would be at any other point in the twentieth century.

Of course, for such unity to have affected domestic politics, it would have needed to resolve the seemingly intractable question of Ulster, which Fanning and others have shown to have been virtually impossible, but this book has also raised some interesting reflections on the high politics of the time.[3] Both in nationalist Ireland and in diasporic communities, the outburst of enthusiasm for the passage of Home Rule in 1914 revealed that many Irish Catholics felt that their decades-long struggle for self-government had finally been successful. Nationalist dissonance could be quelled with the belief that Home Rule would come into operation – and by the groundswell of support for the Allies – and the Ireland of September 1914 to April 1916 effectively acted as if Home Rule were in place, albeit in the strange and abnormal context of world war.

This raises the important point of whether Irish responses to the war changed significantly after the Rising and conscription crisis of 1918, a period which included the executions of the rebel leaders, mass internment by the government and the reinvigoration of the political question. Though rural Ireland's recruitment rates lagged in comparison with parts of Britain – a trend that was not true of urban Ireland, at least until the introduction of conscription in Britain in 1916 – its commitment to agricultural production for the war effort was high, particularly in 1917 and 1918 when the Irish felt especially threatened by German submarine warfare. Fear of a second Great Famine, an imagined (but not totally unrealistic) danger that was discussed in apocalyptic terms by the Catholic Church and opinion shapers, was transmitted by the press and word of mouth, and inspired a tillage campaign that stood out in terms of productivity and participation within the United Kingdom. Rural society took the defence of Ireland seriously; the low recruitment rates do not reflect the attitudes of people whose primary relationship to the war effort was agricultural.

Nationally, however, recruitment rates declined from early 1915 onwards (as they did in Britain, Canada, Australia and elsewhere), but rose again in August to November 1918, when the Allies most needed support, and in these months, recruitment was actually stronger in largely Catholic counties than in loyalist parts of Ulster. As Gavin Hughes has shown, Irish soldiers in the British army continued to operate with a high commitment to their objective after the Rising and no widespread weakness in morale was evident.[4] For the civilian population, the voluntary war effort on the home front remained consistently strong at a national level, strengthening each and every year of the war and noticeably when the demands of the front required greater resource. No single trend can explain the Irish war experience, but there is no obvious trend to indicate a causal link between support for the war effort and political change within nationalism.

Of course, after April 1918 Ireland was a different country to what it had been in 1915. From that month, the primacy of domestic politics was writ large in every aspect of society. The conscription controversy became a catalyst for moderate nationalists to support advanced nationalist disaffection with Westminster (facilitated, no doubt, by London's scuppering of the Home Rule Act and, moreover, by violating the central principle of consent that had underlined successive nationalist movements). This consequently had an impact on the war effort, particularly in the realm of recruitment. For much of the war, the issue had held more complicated connotations in Ireland than in Britain or elsewhere due to the uneasy historic relationship between Ireland and the government, but after the conscription crisis it became wholly entwined with London's treatment of nationalist Ireland, and it was difficult to separate one from the other. Indeed, it was virtually impossible to disentangle the conscription controversy from the issue of recruitment in 1918. Contradictory opinions and confusion reigned across the country about how Ireland could assist the Allies when recruitment to the regiments and divisions that could historically be called 'Irish' was now a heavily politicized domestic political issue, as much as an international necessity.

Nonetheless, recruitment rates still rose later that year and other trends continued seemingly unhindered to the end of the war, despite domestic politics. Though support for Sinn Fein grew for many reasons – including revulsion against London's repressive policies, rejection of conscription and the obsolescence of the IPP party machine – endorsement for the war effort continued in parts of Catholic Ireland. A considerable degree of stability and continuity thus underlined Ireland's war effort to an extent that has gone unacknowledged.

Why did Catholic support for the war effort not decline more precipitously following the rise in radical nationalism? If, as a number of historians have argued, political preferences among nationalists and support for the war effort were indeed related, one explanation might seek to explain the continuation of support via the six seats won by the IPP in the 1918 general election. However, as this book has demonstrated enduring support for the war effort in counties where Sinn Féin candidates were elected (including Cork, Cavan, and Galway), this explanation does not hold up. Similarly, a historian might look at the uncontested seats in which Sinn Féin candidates won, as the absence of electoral competition might cast doubt on the strength of popular support for the Sinn Féin party, though McConnel, Pašeta and others have convincingly shown that there were many good reasons why the IPP didn't stand in these constituencies, including, among others, the decay of the Party's electoral machine, the fact that it was ill-prepared for the election, having had no major nationalist rival for almost its entire period of existence, and the loss of credibility of the old men with the new electorate.[5] In comparison to Sinn Féin, 'the party had a mountain to climb as it prepared for the general election'.[6]

More interestingly still are the findings that have emerged from Pašeta's research on Irish Nationalist women. Pašeta has shown that in 1918, women made up 40 per cent of the electorate in Dublin, 39 per cent in Belfast and 39 per cent in Cork.[7] The historic hostility which John Redmond had to the cause of suffrage, the IPP's desire to put the national question above women's right to vote and the indifference which the party had to allowing women to fundraise and propagandize on its behalf were major barriers in an election in which the Representation of the People Act 1918 gave the vote to all women over the age of thirty who met certain property qualifications. This was rather different to Sinn Féin, who supported female suffrage, fielding the candidate who became the first female MP in Great Britain. Pašeta's findings – some of the most interesting new history to emerge on this important election – complicate the notion that the election was essentially a referendum on Home Rule versus a Republic. Though these issues were of course important, the stance of Irish political parties towards the cause of suffrage can no longer be ignored in an election that brought about the greatest measure of democracy since the Reform Acts of 1867–8 and 1884.

But other explanations for enduring support for the war effort present themselves which are not reliant on the Unionist/Nationalist divide and the respective nationalist parties' stance towards female suffrage. As we have seen, the expectation that Home Rule would come into operation was one motivation that helped to sustain Ireland throughout a large part of the conflict, and though the question of self-government became more complicated after the Rising, Ireland was too heavily involved in the war on a voluntary basis to abandon its troops, most of whom were civilians from the same stock as the men and women who stayed at home. This is an extremely important point which transcends any attempt to explain enduring support by elections and electoral politics. As in Britain (until 1916), Ireland's war effort was qualitatively different from that of the continent because it was a volunteer effort; unlike Britain, which was forced to impose conscription on two occasions, Ireland avoided the measure even when it was passed in 1918, and this book has shown that the Irish were proud of their voluntary contribution throughout the duration of the conflict. Incidentally, the notion of conscription in Ireland was closely associated with the notion of 'liberty', as it was in Australia, Canada, New Zealand and South Africa. Those who opposed conscription did so in the name of 'liberty', while governments often attempted to justify conscription as a measure that would defend 'liberty'.[8] In this respect the Irish protest was typical, rather than unusual, in the wider British world.

Ireland's voluntary contribution was in aid of values that were of personal relevance to Irish people, values for which the Allies were supposedly fighting. Jeffery has noted that the 'big words' of civilization, freedom, small nations, liberty, democracy and duty had 'real meaning' in 1914, and this book has demonstrated that these words continued to have meaning thereafter, more so when Germany came to embody the ultimate despot and America entered the conflict on the side of 'freedom' and 'democracy'. No amount of advanced nationalist protest or appeals to 'our gallant allies in Europe' could shift this perception; even a rebellion on the home front and Westminster's harsh response could not compel the bulk of nationalists to switch their allegiances – for as long as the war continued – in what they regarded not as a British war but as a wider international struggle in which Irish men and women across the British Empire and, from 1917, in America, were involved.

In Ireland, important social and economic benefits also limited the revolutionary impact of advanced nationalist action. As Fitzpatrick has argued, Ireland had profited from the war, which stimulated external demand on farming and manufacturing. Cormac Ó Gráda and others have also reminded us that the government had improved the old-age pension and other social benefits, while Taylor has shown the extent of the benefits enjoyed by the considerably large cross-section of society directly associated with the forces (including veterans and surviving family members).[9] Though extreme poverty was the norm for the unskilled urban worker, in rural Ireland, 'the reforms of 1882-1903 had dealt with the issue of land hunger – probably the single most revolutionary question elsewhere in wartime Europe'. Farmers could therefore defend what they had already secured, as they did in the 1917 tillage campaign, unlike their counterparts in countries such as the Russian Empire and Italy.[10] Advanced nationalists, therefore, had few grounds upon which to change moderate perceptions surrounding the war; even during the conscription crisis, their protests could only rest on the government's treatment of nationalist Ireland rather than on the legitimacy of the international struggle.

This book has argued that the Irish-Catholic war experience can only be properly understood when the nation state is transcended and Ireland's response to the conflict is situated within the complicated transnational and international setting in which it actually occurred. The Irish diaspora was heavily involved in the conflict, and among settlers within the Empire, Ireland and Irishness were central to their war efforts. Large numbers of first- and second-generation diasporic Irish men were present at the front, and these men have not been taken into account when assessing Irish recruitment returns, which is an omission for a country that had emigration as a fact of life. This book has unfortunately not engaged with the contributions of diasporic Irish women, but it goes without saying that Irish women must have been involved in the war efforts of the Dominions for those efforts to have been so successful. Among diasporic men, Ireland and Irishness were present in the imagination of the troops who evoked nostalgic and cultural attachments to the 'mother country', and this was especially apparent on St Patrick's Day, which was a transnational celebration and an inclusive day for both Protestants and Catholics to celebrate their shared cross-confessional Irishness through the gift-giving of shamrocks. Irish heritage brought some diasporic soldiers from Canada and Australia to the 'mother country', and these soldiers were enthusiastically welcomed by the Irish in Ireland, demonstrating that ties of heritage and nationality could overwhelm the uneasy political relationship which many nationalists had with the Empire.

Across the United Kingdom, there were differences between how cities, towns, regions and individuals experienced the war.[11] As in Britain, urban Ireland experienced the bulk of war-related activities, and this book has demonstrated how Cork and Dublin outstripped Belfast in some war-related efforts. For the western and south-western seaboard, the Great War was also a naval war, as communities were forced to manage the consequences of German submarine warfare, including attacks on Irish shipping. The Irish countryside was isolated from many of these things, but it was rural Ireland on which the burden of cultivating more food fell. No single experience can describe wartime Ireland, and though there were many variations between how different regions, towns and localities responded, the overarching similarity was that support rather than ambivalence characterized the country's response.

That support was given by both Protestants and Catholics. They cooperated to give their troops a good send-off and, in the case of the Irish-Canadian Rangers, welcomed them upon their 'return' to the 'mother country'; they worked together to succour refugees and wounded men; they joined forces in recruitment meetings so as to attract the greatest spectrum of potential recruits for an international cause they both believed in; they produced more food when Ireland was at risk of famine, framing the task as a 'national duty' despite their different political conceptions of nationhood; and even when domestic political divisions had deepened due to their divergent attitudes towards conscription, they still celebrated the conclusion of the war together because on the 11 November 1918, both groups believed that a 'victorious peace' had been won after more than four long bloody years of war in which Irish people of all backgrounds had suffered.

In this regard, the Great War was indeed 'Ireland's war'. The 'inclusive' tone struck at commemorative events held to remember the conflict in recent years – something which has been criticized by historians – had a basis in the war years themselves, as people developed an inclusive patriotism during the war years. From 1914 to 1918, Ireland's war effort was truly national, the 'property' of both Protestants and Catholics. When it ceased to be viewed as such is another question.

# Chapter 8

## EPILOGUE: BEYOND AMNESIA

If Ireland's war effort was 'owned' by Protestants and Catholics when the Armistice of 1918 was announced, when did Catholics lose 'possession' of the memory of the war effort? There is no single answer to this question, but it is clear that there was no mass amnesia in the years that followed the conflict.

As in Britain, waves of veterans returned to Ireland from early 1919, most of whom soon found themselves unemployed. As Gregory has argued, unemployed men and unemployed servicemen were 'close to synonymous' in the immediate post-war period.[1] In Ireland, 46 per cent of Irish ex-servicemen were drawing the out-of-work donation in November 1919, as opposed to only 10 per cent in Britain – a proportion that was lower in Ulster and even higher for Munster.[2] These veterans found themselves in the throes of the Anglo-Irish War, and the entity in which they had served with distinction in France and Flanders was now, for republicans and many others, considered the enemy.

Much has been written on the subject of veterans returning to a politically 'changed' Ireland, and there is no need to recount the main arguments here, except to note that some historians have claimed that ex-servicemen were viewed with suspicion upon their return to Ireland, so much so that the IRA targeted them during the War of Independence.[3] This was especially the case for West Cork according to Peter Hart, where ex-soldiers (as well as Protestants, 'tinkers' and tramps) made up a sizeable proportion of those killed by the IRA – a finding that has triggered tremendous historical debate and controversy ever since Hart's book was published.[4] Hart's findings and those of other scholars have helped to generate a popular view that veterans were considered traitors upon their return from the war, as evidenced in the recent centenary with newspaper headlines such as 'Ireland's first World War veterans: Shunned, ostracized, murdered'.[5]

Other historians have debated the notion that veterans were unwelcome upon their return to Ireland. For example, John Borgonovo in his research on Co. Cork has questioned the narrative of persecution and argued that there was no antagonism between the IRA and veterans.[6] More recently, Taylor has demonstrated that ex-servicemen were integrated and accommodated within the new Irish Free State. Throughout the interwar period, they were considered to be citizens of the new Irish state, even if their claims were treated differently by the interwar governments of Cumann na nGaedheal and Fianna Fáil.[7] This view is supported by Shannon Monaghan, who has gone as far as to say that veterans were popularly supported in the 1920s and early 1930s, serving as vehicles through which the Free State 'cemented its stability and defined its independence and obligations in the international and domestic arenas'.[8]

The findings of this book tend to support the conclusion that veterans were not immediately viewed as 'enemies of the people' upon their return from the war, at least in urban centres among moderate nationalists. As there was no mass aversion towards the war effort among the middle classes or indeed among sections of the urban working-class after 1916 – or even after the conscription crisis of 1918 – there was no reason for veterans to be considered traitors to their country by the majority of people who stayed at home, though of course exceptions can probably be found. How these attitudes changed in the months and years following November 1918 is a question for further research, as little is known about the lives of veterans after the war or how they transitioned to life under the new Irish Free State. The existing historiography of commemoration, however, suggests that it took some time for the wider Catholic population to publicly jettison the memory of 1914–18.

During the Anglo-Irish War, Jane Leonard has argued that there was little urge to mark the anniversary of the Armistice in what was an atmosphere of violence and intimidation, though some forms of remembrance did occur. The multi-volume edition of *Ireland's Memorial Records*, published in 1923, embodied the sense of Irish unity in the war, as Harry Clarke (a Catholic tasked with illustrating the records) chose both Protestant and Catholic themes to make the work inclusive.[9] The records also put forward the disputed figure of 49,000 Irish military casualties; though it is now clear that this figure was incorrect, it did contain the names of Irish men who had served and died while serving in both Irish and non-Irish regiments, a fact that would be later forgotten or disputed by historians. Remembrance was also engaged in by the public. In 1919 in line with a Papal decree, mass for the war-dead was said in every Roman Catholic Church throughout Ireland. In Dublin city, all work and traffic ceased to observe the two minutes' silence that London had decreed in October to be a fitting way to mark the first anniversary, and groups such as Comrades of the Great War took part in parades of remembrance.[10] Contemporary newspapers reveal that commemoration was even more widespread in the capital in 1919 than Leonard has noted, as thousands of people congregated at College Green, which became Dublin's commemorative centre for the next few years. The silence was also observed in parts of Belfast, Derry, Cork, Limerick, Newry, Drogheda and elsewhere, though in 1920 the Anglo-Irish War put a stop to many public demonstrations.[11] Indeed, commemoration of the 1914–18 war could not be divorced from the political context in which the country now found itself. In Athlone, for example, the two minutes' silence was enforced on the public by the Black and Tans, the British-recruited soldiers who assisted the Crown Forces serving in Ireland during the Anglo-Irish War, ascribing a new set of meanings to remembrance that were more about the current turbulent relationship with Westminster than about Irish commemoration of the Great War.[12]

Leonard suggests that the lack of desire to publicly commemorate the Great War in the volatile context of 1919–21 appeared to continue during the civil war of 1922–23, yet evidence exists which complicates this view. Around 2,000 soldiers reportedly took part in the Remembrance Day parade in Cork in 1923, all of whom wore poppies to commemorate the war dead. After services in their respective churches (the newly elected president of the Irish Free State, W. T. Cosgrave, was among the Catholic congregation), Protestants and Catholics marched together along the main streets until the march concluded at the South Mall. This was not dissimilar to the cross-confessional response in the town of Enniskillen, Northern Ireland. In the capital, requiem mass was said for the souls of the war dead in Catholic and Protestant churches.[13] It is not known how widespread these commemorative acts were and what the public response to them was, but these examples do suggest a more nuanced picture of remembrance during the turbulent years of 1919–23. Remembrance could still be inclusive despite the violent and polarized political situation.

During the civil war it is well known that many veterans participated on both sides of the conflict. Some ex-soldiers, such as Tom Barry, joined the anti-Treaty forces, while a considerable number of ex-servicemen joined the pro-Treaty Irish Free State Army. Peter Cottrell has estimated that by May 1923 the army contained 58,000 men, and one-fifth of its officers and half its other ranks were Irish ex-servicemen.[14] No doubt this reflected the endemic lack of employment in Ireland, but whether one joined the anti or pro-Treaty forces must have reflected the different views that Irish civilians – whether ex-servicemen or not – held regarding Ireland's political future.

Though Remembrance Day parades were the most visible form of remembrance, they were not the only medium of commemoration in Ireland. At a private level remembrance took a different form, as family members who had died in the conflict were remembered first and foremost by their absence and by personal mementos and artefacts which remained within the home. Those with wounds and injuries sustained in the war would also find it hard to forget the war as loss, pain and disability took their own trajectories of remembrance that bore little correlation with the wars of 1919–23. Indeed, *The Irish Times* remarked on the continued suffering of veterans who attended the Catholic mass in Blackrock in 1923, as 'men with still bandaged wounds, useless arms in slings', as well as those who couldn't walk, were much in evidence.[15]

In the 1920s there was a proliferation of memorials in villages, towns and cities across Ireland as there was in Britain, creating a landscape of remembrance across the United Kingdom.[16] These memorials served as artefacts of memory, since Westminster had decided during the war that corpses would not be repatriated due to the sheer numbers of the deceased and the logistical and moral dilemmas raised by repatriation.[17] In Bray, Co. Wicklow, a 17-feet high Celtic Cross was erected in 1920 – one of the earliest Great War memorials built in Ireland – and 'the pre-Reformation origins of the cross's design facilitated its use by both Catholic[s] and Protestants'.[18] Other memorials soon sprung up in towns and villages across the island of Ireland and drew on different symbols and imagery, reflecting the influence of local desires. It is noteworthy how large many of them were and that they were placed in prominent locations. In Cork, for example, a memorial representing a single soldier with his head bowed was unveiled on 17 March 1925 on the South Mall, one of the main thoroughfares in the city, as captured in Figure 1.1; the entire monument formed of three granite squares was 20 feet in height and contained the inscription 'Lest we forget'. That year in the border county of Longford, the town council granted a permanent site in Market Square in the town centre for a 20-feet high Celtic Cross carved from limestone, which had been quarried locally. (This can be seen in Chapter 1, Figure 1.3.[19]) In Sligo in 1928, Sligo Corporation approved the construction of the war memorial in the town centre, but at the last minute it was discovered that the site stood above a main town drain. After some discussion, another site was found and a Celtic cross built from Irish limestone was erected with the inscription 'In Glorious Memory of the Men of the Town and County of Sligo, who gave their lives in the Great War, 1914-1918'.[20] That year in Nenagh, Co. Tipperary, a 'very large congregation' attended the St. Mary's of the Rosary Catholic Church (including relatives and friends of those killed in the war) before a 16-foot memorial was unveiled in the centre of the town at Wolfe Tone Terrace.[21]

These memorials reflected local and regional efforts to commemorate local sacrifice and were in addition to the national war memorial built at Islandbridge outside Dublin city centre, which was eventually completed in 1937 though only officially opened in 1988.[22] This picture of local remembrance in Ireland does not appear 'out of place' with the wider desire to commemorate the war dead in villages, towns and cities across interwar Britain, France and elsewhere, yet there are two striking differences.[23] The size and prominence accorded these memorials is at odds with the memorialization of the Great War in Southern Ireland today. Some memorials, such as that in Cork, were significantly scaled down in size in later years, but we do not know when. Secondly, historians have by and large neglected these demonstrations of post-war commemoration and inter-communal solidarity in their analyses of revolutionary and post-revolutionary Ireland. This is not in itself strange, as the Irish struggle to achieve independence and to clarify its understanding of what it meant to be Irish has understandably received considerable attention by historians, but the absence of these organized projects of commemoration from the historical record is striking in light of their apparent popularity in interwar Ireland.[24] In the 1920s it is clear that remembrance of the war was being actively expressed in many towns, not eradicated, even if some of the discussions around building the memorials reflected evolving views towards the meaning of the 1914–18 war.

Who wanted these memorials? Can they be explained by the enduring influence of the Irish elite – both Protestant and Catholic – in post-Independent Ireland? Major Bryan Cooper TD, Senator William Hickie, Viscount Powerscourt, John Horgan and the Earl of Granard were just some of the prominent men involved in the unveiling ceremonies. Their influence must have been of consequence, but it would have been of little consequence had not the projects had the support of the wider public, and though this deserves a study in itself, it is easy to find evidence in contemporary sources to indicate that remembrance had popular support. Indeed, as a result of peacetime conditions, a new space had opened in which to publicly remember the war dead after 1923, and displays of remembrance were much more obvious and widespread at a local and national level.

Mass attendance was the norm at Armistice Day ceremonies in Dublin for most of the 1920s and even for part of the 1930s. Films produced by British Pathé reveal dense crowds at Remembrance Day ceremonies in each and every year that a film was taken (1924, 1925, 1926, 1928 and 1930). Large numbers of poppies were sold on these occasions (in Dublin alone, 150,000 poppies were sold in 1923; over 500,000 were sold there in 1924[25]). Though sustained study would be necessary to establish the precise extent and continuity of such phenomena, there is evidence of popular support at Remembrance Day events across the Southern Provinces throughout the 1920s. Just to quote a few more examples, in 1923 in Carrick-on-Shannon, Co. Leitrim, both Catholic and Protestant Churches marked the hour of 11.00 am. The silence was observed in the town and 'poppies were generally worn', sold by ex-servicemen. Three years later, Remembrance Day was still marked by a 'large number of ex-servicemen' who attended a Requiem Mass at St. Mary's Catholic Church and afterwards processed through the town.[26] In Castlerea, Co. Roscommon, in 1923, mass for the dead was celebrated in the Catholic Church at which there was a large congregation including children from both the Marist Brothers and Convent Schools. Other public demonstrations took place this year in towns such as Fermoy, Loughrea, Nenagh and Longford.[27] These displays were often cross-confessional in Southern Ireland, reflecting a continuation of the joint sacrifice rendered – and suffering endured – by both Protestants and Catholics during the war itself. In Longford, 1,000 people reportedly travelled from around the county to attend the unveiling of the memorial in 1925.[28] In Roscrea, Tipperary, 'the largest body of men yet seen' took part in the ceremony in 1928, marching to the Roman Catholic, Methodist and Church of Ireland churches.[29] These examples do not reflect the actions of a country that had turned its back on the war, even if there were delays, debates and disagreements over the meaning of remembrance that reflected the radically different political contexts of both the Free State and Northern Ireland.

It was only when Fianna Fáil came to power in 1932 that the new Free State government actively dissociated itself from the conflict – a process that was intensified by the hostility that arose out of the economic war with Great Britain, which was 'not conducive' to the republican government helping the veterans.[30] At some stage, participation in Armistice Day ceremonies declined: a process helped by IRA attacks on Remembrance Day events, the declining influence of ex-servicemen, rampant emigration especially among war widows, unemployed veterans and their wives and the emergence of a new generation that had grown up and had no direct memory of the war.[31] When exactly these changes happened is another important area for future research, but from 1929 they most likely occurred as part of a wider paradigm shift in attitudes towards the conflict. In Britain, for example, the war began to be dismissed as a folly and by the end of the 1930s was no longer conceived in the language of stopping German aggression. This attitude was expressed most eloquently by the war poets, whose disenchantment with the conflict contributed to a discursive turn whereby commemoration and memory of the war became 'an object lesson in peace' – a lesson that was part of both the Conservative and Labour governments' policy of building constructive peace in Europe.[32]

Whether this wider shift in the memory of the war affected Ireland is not known, but as Taylor notes, even throughout the 1930s the memory of – and issues that resulted from – the Great War didn't go away. Eamon de Valera, the Fianna Fáil leader, never appeared hostile to the claims of veterans and recognized them as 'equal citizens of the state' (just not citizens that were to be given special privileges on account of their war service).[33] With the outbreak of the Second World War, de Valera banned public commemoration of the 1914–18 conflict; after the war of 1939–45, the earlier conflict could no longer be remembered outside of the context of Irish neutrality and sovereignty, and public remembrance must have fizzled out in the South, though when exactly is not yet known.

In the North, the history is even less clear. From the first day of the Battle of the Somme, the unionist association with the Great War was virtually cemented, and remembrance of the conflict became part of the unionist creation myth that marked out 'Ulster' (and now the new territory of Northern Ireland) as separate from the rest of the island. The main war memorial for Belfast, for example, was located within the grounds of the Protestant-dominated council offices at City Hall, and the unveiling of the cenotaph in 1929 was 'almost exclusively a Protestant affair'.[34] As Nationalists (almost wholly Catholic) boycotted the new Northern Ireland parliament and 'every other state body' upon the opening of parliament on 22 June 1921, the place of the war in northern Catholic memory is difficult to ascertain.[35] At any rate, some anomalies emerge from contemporary sources, which suggest that the inclusivity exhibited during the war years did not completely disappear in all places for some time despite the absence of Catholics within the new administration. In Dungannon, for example, cross-confessional remembrance was part of the Armistice Day celebrations in both 1924 and 1927.[36]

Indeed, it would seem that for a large part of the interwar period the Great War never really disappeared from Irish popular memory. Its eventual repossession by both religious groups across the island of Ireland came only three generations later. It was reflected during the centenary of the Armistice on 11 November 2018. Both Protestants and Catholics took part in wreath-laying ceremonies, commemorative religious services and many other forms of remembrance that reflected the reclaiming of a conflict which, it is now recognized, was central to the history of Ireland, whether nationalist or unionist (and which, as Chapter 2 has noted, has also become an important political tool in the project of peace-building). In Enniskillen, commemorative services started before dawn when representatives from the four main Christian churches in the town were given commemorative lanterns by the Queen's representative in Fermanagh, Viscount Brookeborough. Later that day the mixed clergy attended a joint ceremony in St Michael's Catholic Church to remember the fallen. One thousand people reportedly attended with a further 1,000 gathered outside; after the service, the clergy processed to the grounds of St Macartin's Church of Ireland Cathedral where they used their lanterns to jointly light a beacon to symbolize their shared loss and unity in remembrance.[37] At Glasnevin cemetery in Dublin, which contains the graves of 207 men and women who served in the British Armed Forces during both world wars, President Michael D. Higgins spoke of the 'common humanity' shared by all those who fought in the conflict, and five Victoria Cross commemorative plaques were unveiled and dedicated to five soldiers who had demonstrated extreme bravery during the conflict of 1914–18. Wreath-laying ceremonies took place elsewhere in Belfast, Enniskillen, Cork, Limerick, Sligo, Kilkenny, Westmeath, Galway and Tipperary, which reflected the widespread change in attitudes towards the conflict across Ireland, as discussed in Chapter 2.[38] However, as in 1919 and in the years that followed, feelings were still mixed in nationalist communities about a conflict that cannot be easily reconciled with domestic politics, as minor acts of vandalism and the decision to not report the centenary reflected an enduring uneasiness with its memory.[39]

The Great War continues to simultaneously unite and divide the Irish, but the inclusive tone struck at the centenary had, as this book has shown, a basis in the war years themselves. How this might change in light of changing attitudes towards Europe across the United Kingdom, coupled with a worrying return to some of the polarized rhetoric surrounding identity in Northern Ireland, is part of the ongoing history of the Great War's long shadow.

# NOTES

## Chapter 1

1　Peter Hart, *The I.R.A. and Its Enemies: Violence and Community in Cork, 1916-1923* (Oxford, 1998), p. 51.

2　William H. Kautt, *Ambushes and Armour: The Irish Rebellion 1919-21* (Dublin, 2010), p. 156.

3　*The Cork Examiner*, 18 March 1925 (hereafter, *CE*).

4　Paul Taylor, *Heroes or Traitors? Experiences of Southern Irish Soldiers Returning from the Great War 1919-1939* (London, 2015), p. 9. It is unclear whether Taylor arrived at this figure by deriving population data from the 1911 or 1926 census of Ireland, as his footnotes are unclear. In any case, it assumes that recruits from Cork county enlisted in Cork city. My own attempt at estimating the proportion of men that served in the war provides slightly different results. Using Taylor's figure of 10,106 enlistments and expressing it as a proportion of the total male population in Cork city and county, as recorded in the printed 1911 census of Ireland, reveals that 5.12 per cent of the 197,516 men from the county and city of Cork joined up: an even higher proportion for urban areas from where the bulk of recruits likely hailed (8 per cent of the 126,295 males that resided in the thirteen 'civic' areas in Cork in 1911). These figures assume that there was no population change in Cork between 1911 and 1917 (which there was) and assume that men of all ages and conditions could enlist (which they could not). These numbers should thus be interpreted as guides rather than as facts. *His Majesty's Stationery Office, Census of Ireland, 1911 Area, Houses, and Population: also the ages, civil or conjugal condition, occupations, birthplaces, religion, and education of the people. Province of Munster, County of Cork* (London, 1912), pp. vii, 45, hereafter *1911 Census, Munster, Cork*.

5　*The Irish Times*, 23 September 1924 (hereafter *IT*); Taylor, *Heroes or Traitors?* p. 12.

6　Gerry White and Brendan O'Shea (eds.), *A Great Sacrifice: Cork Servicemen Who Died in the Great War* (Cork, 2010), p. 5.

7　Anne Dolan, *Commemorating the Irish Civil War: History and Memory, 1923-2000* (Cambridge, 2003).

8　Protestants are comprised of Episcopalians (hereafter cited as Anglican or Episcopalian), Presbyterians, Methodists and All Other Denominations; *1911 Census, Munster, Cork*, p. vii. The numbers listed here do not include the seventy-nine people from the county and city who refused to state their religion.

9　Donal Hall, *The Unreturned Army: County Louth Dead in the Great War, 1914-1918* (Dublin, 2005), p. 15.

10　Population returns cited are for Dundalk and Drogheda Urban. *1911 Census, Leinster, Louth*, p. v.

11　Hall, *Unreturned Army*, pp. 17, 24; *World War I and Nationalist Politics in County Louth, 1914–1920* (Dublin, 2005), pp. 51-5.

12   Returns cited are for Kilrush Urban. *1911 Census, Munster, Clare*, pp. vi, 118.

13   Martin Staunton, 'The Royal Munster Fusiliers in the Great War 1914-19', unpublished
     MA thesis, University College Dublin (hereafter UCD), 1986), pp. 13, 9.

14   British Pathé, 'Dublin Remembers 1923'. 'Armistice Day – Dublin 1924'. 'Armistice
     Day in Dublin – 1925'. 'Day of Remembrance Aka Ireland 1930'. 'Remembrance Day –
     Bray 1924'. Available at https://www.britishpathe.com (accessed 07.07.18).

15   Dolan, *Commemorating the Irish Civil War*, pp. 10, 136. Also see Jane Leonard, 'The
     Twinge of Memory: Armistice Day and Remembrance Sunday in Dublin since 1919',
     in Richard English and Graham Walker (eds.), *Unionism in Modern Ireland: New
     Perspectives on Politics and Culture* (Basingstoke, 1996), pp. 99–114.

16   I've borrowed this concept from David Reynolds, *The Long Shadow: The Great War
     and the Twentieth Century* (London, 2013).

17   Catriona Pennell, *A Kingdom United: Popular Reponses to the Outbreak of the First
     World War in Britain and Ireland* (Oxford, 2012), pp. vii, 1.

18   Pennell, *Kingdom United*, p. 6.

19   Jose Harris, 'Introduction: Civil Society in British History: Paradigm or Peculiarity?'
     in Jose Harris (ed.), *Civil Society in British History: Ideas, Identities, Institutions*
     (Oxford, 2003), pp. 1–12.

20   For instance, between 1911 and 1926, the Protestant population of Ireland declined
     by 33.5%; almost a third of Irish Protestants emigrated from the Free State in those
     years. Dennis Kennedy, *The Widening Gulf: Northern Attitudes to the Independent Irish
     State, 1919–49* (Belfast, 1988), pp. 151–2; Charles Townshend, *Ireland: The Twentieth
     Century* (London, 1999), p. 126.

21   Pennell, *Kingdom United*, p. 9.

22   Fintan Lane (ed.), *Politics, Society and the Middle Class in Modern Ireland*
     (Basingstoke, 2010), p. 1.

23   Ian D'Alton, 'A Protestant Paper for a Protestant People: The Irish Times and the
     Southern Irish Minority', *Irish Communications Review*, 12 (2010), pp. 65–73, 65.

24   Senia Pašeta, *Before the Revolution: Nationalism, Social Change and Ireland's Catholic
     Elite, 1879-1922* (Cork, 1999), p. 1.

25   Pennell, *Kingdom United*, pp. 6–7. For studies on crowd behaviour, see Eric J.
     Hobsbawm, 'The Machine Breakers', in Eric J. Hobsbawm (ed.), *Labouring Men:
     Studies in the History of Labour* (London, 1986), pp. 7–26; George F. E. Rudé, *The
     Crowd in History: A Study of Popular Disturbances in France and England, 1730-1848*
     (London, 1981, revised ed.); Edward Palmer Thompson, *The Making of the English
     Working Class* (London, 1963); Mark Harrison, *Crowds and History: Mass Phenomena
     in English Towns, 1790–1835* (Cambridge, 1988).

26   Pennell, *Kingdom United*, pp. 6–7.

27   Kerby A. Miller, *Emigrants and Exiles: Ireland and the Irish Exodus to North America*
     (New York and Oxford, 1985), p. 365.

28   Joseph P. Finnan, *John Redmond and Irish Unity 1912–1918* (New York, 2004), p. 155.

29   Miller, *Emigrants and Exiles*, p. 346.

30   White and O'Shea, *Great Sacrifice*, pp. 512–13.

31   The exact figure is 320,518, and it includes total US deaths in combat, other deaths
     and wounded. It does not include the 4,120 US servicemen who were captured and
     listed as missing in action. For further information, see John Chambers (ed.), *The
     Oxford Companion to American Military History* (New York, 2000), p. 849.

32   White and O'Shea, *Great Sacrifice*, pp. 5, 165–508.

33  Kevin Kenny (ed.), *Ireland and the British Empire* (Oxford, 2004); Colin Barr, "'Imperium in Imperio": Irish Episcopal Imperialism in the Nineteenth Century', *The English Historical Review*, CXXIII, 502 (2008), pp. 611–50; Michael Silvestri, *Ireland and India: Nationalism, Empire and Memory* (Basingstoke, 2009); Santanu Das (ed.), *Race, Empire and First World War Writing* (Cambridge, 2011); Barry Crosbie, *Irish Imperial Networks: Migration, Social Communication and Exchange in Nineteenth-Century India* (Cambridge, 2012).

34  See, for example, the various arguments put forward in Enda Delaney, 'Migration and Diaspora', in Alvin Jackson (ed.), *The Oxford Handbook of Modern Irish History* (Oxford, 2015), pp. 126–47.

35  Mark McGowan, *The Waning of the Green: Catholics, the Irish, and Identity in Toronto, 1887-1922* (Montreal and London, 1999), p. 8. For more information regarding defining ethnicity, see Wsevolod W. Isajiw, *Definitions of Ethnicity* (Toronto, 1979), pp. 4–6, 12–15, 19–22.

36  Patrick O'Farrell, *The Irish in Australia: 1788 to the Present* (Kensington, NSW, 1993), p. 148.

37  Christopher M. Clark, *The Sleepwalkers: How Europe Went to War in 1914* (New York, 2012), pp. xxix–xxxi.

38  Pennell, *Kingdom United*, p. 1.

39  Adrian Bingham, 'The Digitization of Newspaper Archives: Opportunities and Challenges for Historians', *Twentieth Century British History*, 21.2 (June 2010), pp. 225–31.

40  Ibid., p. 6.

41  These include *Limerick Leader* (hereafter *LL*), *Connacht Tribune* (hereafter *CT*), *The Anglo-Celt* (hereafter *AC*), *CE* and *The Freeman's Journal* (hereafter *FJ*).

42  Colum Kenny, 'Tom Grehan: Advertising Pioneer and Newspaperman', in Mark O'Brien and Kevin Rafter (eds.), *Independent Newspapers: A History* (Dublin, 2012), p. 59.

43  *The Connaught Telegraph*, *Newry Reporter* (hereafter *NR*), *Cork Free Press*, and *The Clare Journal and Ennis Advertiser* (hereafter *CJ*).

44  *The Kildare Observer*, *Leitrim Observer* (hereafter *LO*), *Longford Leader*, *Meath Chronicle*, *Nenagh Guardian*, *The Irish News and Belfast Morning News* (hereafter *IN*), *Ulster Herald* and *Westmeath Examiner*.

45  Paul Bew, 'Moderate Nationalism and the Irish Revolution, 1916-1923', *Historical Journal*, 42.3 (1999), pp. 729–49.

46  *The Argus*, *The Catholic Press*, *The Mercury*, and *The Register*. For a full list, see the bibliography.

47  D'Alton, 'A Protestant Paper', p. 65.

48  Pennell, *Kingdom United*, p. 7.

49  Adrian Gregory, *The Last Great War: British Society and the First World War* (Cambridge, 2008), p. 66.

50  The National Archives (NA), 'Ireland: Dublin Castle reports', CO904/167/1, press censorship reports.

51  Pašeta, *Before the Revolution*.

52  These include the University College Cork journal, *The Quarryman*, and the elite Catholic private school serials, *The Clongownian* and *The Belvederian*.

53  Robert Fitzroy Foster, *Vivid Faces: The Revolutionary Generation in Ireland, 1890-1923* (London, 2014), p. 307.

## Chapter 2

1  Reynolds, *Long Shadow*, p. 404.
2  Francis Xavier Martin, '1916 – Myth, Fact and Mystery', *Studia Hibernica*, 7 (1967), pp. 7–126, cited in Keith Jeffery, 'Irish Varieties of Great War Commemoration', in John Horne and Edward Madigan (eds.), *Towards Commemoration: Ireland in War and Revolution, 1912-23* (Dublin, 2013), p. 117.
3  Leonard, 'The Twinge of Memory'.
4  Patrick Lynch, 'The Irish Soldiers and Sailors Land Trust', unpublished MLitt thesis (UCD, 2009).
5  Dolan, *Commemorating the Irish Civil War*.
6  Taylor, *Heroes or Traitors*.
7  Jeffery, 'Irish Varieties', p. 119.
8  Philip Orr, *The Road to the Somme: Men of the Ulster Division Tell Their Story* (Belfast, 1987).
9  For more information see B. Graham and P. Shirlow, 'The Battle of the Somme in Ulster memory and identity', *Political Geography*, 21.7 (2002), pp. 881–904; Richard Grayson, 'The Place of the First World War in Contemporary Irish Republicanism in Northern Ireland', *Irish Political Studies*, 25.3 (2010), pp. 325–45.
10  Philip Orr, *Field of Bones: An Irish Division at Gallipoli* (Dublin, 2006), p. 17. For further information see Terence Denman, 'The 10th (Irish) Division 1914-15: A Study in Military and Political Interaction', *Irish Sword*, XVII.66 (1987), pp. 16–25.
11  Terence Denman, 'Sir Lawrence Parsons and the Raising of the 16th (Irish) Division, 1914-15', *Irish Sword*, 17 (1987), pp. 90–104 and *Ireland's Unknown Soldiers: The 16th (Irish) Division in the Great War, 1914-1918* (Dublin, 1992).
12  David Fitzpatrick, 'Militarism in Ireland, 1900-1922', in Thomas Bartlett and Keith Jeffery (eds.), *A Military History of Ireland* (Cambridge, 1996), pp. 386–9; also see 'Ireland and the Great War', in Thomas Bartlett (ed.), *The Cambridge History of Ireland, Volume IV 1880 to the Present* (Cambridge, 2018), pp. 223–57.
13  Neil Richardson, *According to Their Lights: Stories of Irishmen in the British Army, Easter 1916* (Dublin, 2015), p. 7. Taylor suggests that 62,000 men came from Ulster, *Heroes or Traitors*, pp. 8–9.
14  John Horne, 'Foreword', in John Horne (ed.), *Our War: Ireland and the Great War* (Dublin, 2008), p. ix; Reynolds, *Long Shadow*, p. 404.
15  Reynolds, ibid.
16  Keith Jeffery, *Ireland and the Great War* (Cambridge, 2000), p. 3.
17  RTE News, 'President McAleese visits Gallipoli', 24 March 2010. Available at http://www.rte.ie/news/2010/0324/129080-turkey/ (accessed 24.03.10).
18  Keith Jeffery, 'Gallipoli and Ireland', in Jenny McLeod (ed.), *Gallipoli: Making History* (London, 2004), pp. 98–109, 98; Stuart Ward, 'Parallel Lives, Poles Apart: Commemorating Gallipoli in Ireland and Australia', in John Horne and Edward Madigan (eds.), *Towards Commemoration: Ireland in War and Revolution, 1912-1923* (Dublin, 2013), pp. 29–37, 30.
19  For more on the ANZAC tradition, see Graham Seal, *Great Anzac Stories: The Men and Women Who Created the Digger Legend* (Crows Nest, NSW, 2013).
20  Ward, 'Parallel Lives', p. 30.
21  BBC News, 'Queen lays wreath on Republic of Ireland state visit', 17 May 2011. Available at http://www.bbc.co.uk/news/world-europe-13425722 (accessed 23.07.18).

22 BBC News, 'Queen and Martin McGuinness shake hands', 27 June 2012; 'Martin McGuinness toasts Queen at Windsor Castle state banquet', 8 April 2014. Available at http://www.bbc.co.uk/news/uk-northern-ireland-18607911 and http://www.bbc.co.uk /news/uk-northern-ireland-26948080 (accessed 23.07.18).

23 *IT*, 10 November 2014; Jeffery, 'Irish Varieties', p. 118. RTE, 'Taoiseach wears Shamrock Poppy in Dáil', 7 November 2017. Available at https://www.rte.ie/news/p olitics/2017/1107/918220-shamrock-poppy (accessed 07.07.18).

24 Jay Winter, *Sites of Memory, Sites of Mourning: The Great War in European Cultural History* (Cambridge, 1995); Maureen Healy, *Vienna and the Fall of the Habsburg Empire: Total War and Everyday Life in World War One* (Cambridge, 2004); Jay Winter and Jean-Louis Robert (eds.), *Capital Cities at War: Paris, London, Berlin, 1914-1919*, 2 vols. (Cambridge, 1997, 2007); John Horne, *State, Society and Mobilization in Europe during the First World War* (Cambridge, 1997).

25 Gregory and Pašeta, *Ireland and the Great War*; Horne, *Our War*; Horne and Madigan, *Towards Commemoration*.

26 Michael Snape and Edward Madigan, *The Clergy in Khaki: New Perspectives on British Army Chaplaincy in the First World War* (Surrey, 2013).

27 Jérôme aan de Wiel, *The Catholic Church in Ireland, 1914-1918: War and Politics* (Dublin, 2003).

28 David Fitzpatrick, *Politics and Irish Life, 1913-1921: Provincial Experiences of War and Revolution* (Dublin, 1977); Dermot Lucey, 'Cork Public Opinion and the First World War', unpublished MA thesis (University College Cork (hereafter UCC), 1972); William Henry, *Galway and the Great War* (Cork, 2006), and *Forgotten Heroes: Galway Soldiers of the Great War 1914-1918* (Cork, 2007); Padraig Yeates, *A City in Wartime: Dublin 1919-21* (Dublin, 2011); Colin Cousins, *Armagh and the Great War* (Dublin, 2011); Grayson, *Belfast Boys*.

29 Catriona Pennell, 'Going to War', in John Horne (ed.), *Our War: Ireland and the Great War* (Dublin, 2008), pp. 35–62 and *Kingdom United*.

30 Pennell, *Kingdom United*, pp. 163–97.

31 John Horne, 'Our War, Our History', in John Horne (ed.), *Our War: Ireland and the Great War* (Dublin, 2008), p. 3.

32 F. S. L. Lyons, *The Irish Parliamentary Party, 1890-1910* (London, 1951), p. 264; E. Rumpf and A. C. Hepburn, *Nationalism and Socialism in Twentieth-Century Ireland* (Liverpool, 1977), p. 8; Tom Garvin, *The Evolution of Irish Nationalist Politics* (New York, 1981), p. 99; Fergus J. M. Campbell, *Land and Revolution: Nationalist Politics in the West of Ireland 1891-1921* (Oxford, 2005). For the IPP's 'out-of-touchness' with an emerging 'Irish-Ireland', see Patrick O'Farrell, *Ireland's English Question: Anglo-Irish Relations, 1534-1970* (London, 1971), p. 258 and John Hutchinson, *The Dynamics of Cultural Nationalism: The Gaelic Revival and the Creation of the Irish Nation State* (London, 1987), p. 4. For Redmond's imperial affinities, see James McConnel, 'John Redmond and Irish Catholic Loyalism', *The English Historical Review*, 125.512 (February 2010), pp. 83–111 and for the most recent sophisticated analysis of the party's demise, see James McConnel, *The Irish Parliamentary Party and the Third Home Rule Crisis* (Dublin, 2013).

33 Michael Wheatley, *Nationalism and the Irish Party: Provincial Ireland 1910-1916* (Oxford, 2005), p. 5; Fitzpatrick, *Politics*, pp. 94–8 and *The Two Irelands, 1912-1939* (Oxford, 1998), pp. 17–18; Patrick Maume, *The Long Gestation: Irish Nationalist Life, 1891-1918* (Dublin, 1999), p. 77.

34  Ronan Fanning, *Fatal Path: British Government and Irish Revolution 1910-1922* (London, 2013), p. 133.
35  For more information, see Alvin Jackson, *Home Rule: An Irish History, 1800-2000* (London, 2003). On the UVF, see Timothy Bowman, *Carson's Army: The Ulster Volunteer Force, 1910-22* (Manchester, 2012).
36  Finnan, *John Redmond*, pp. 79–118; Pennell, *Kingdom United*, p. 177.
37  David Howie and Josephine Howie, 'Irish Recruiting and the Home Rule Crisis of August-September 1914', in Michael Dockrill and David French (eds.), *Strategy and Intelligence: British Policy during the First World War* (London, 1996), p. 22; Ben Novick, 'The Arming of Ireland: Gun Running and the Great War, 1914-1916', in Adrian Gregory and Senia Pašeta (eds.), *Ireland and the Great War: 'A War To Unite Us All?'* (Manchester, 2002), p. 99; Pennell, *Kingdom United*, p. 195.
38  Wheatley, *Nationalism*, pp. 222–3.
39  Thomas Bartlett, *Ireland: A History* (Cambridge, 2010), p. 376.
40  David Fitzpatrick, '"The Logic of Collective Sacrifice": Ireland and the British Army, 1914-1918', *Historical Journal*, 38 (1995), pp. 1028–9.
41  Peter Karsten, 'Irish Soldiers in the British Army, 1792-1922: Suborned or Subordinate?' *Journal of Social History*, 17.1 (Autumn, 1983), p. 47.
42  Wheatley, *Nationalism*, p. 214.
43  Fitzpatrick, *Politics*, pp. 63–4; Campbell, *Land and Revolution*, p. 203; Wheatley, *Nationalism*, p. 214; *II, IT*, 5 April 1915.
44  Wheatley, *Nationalism*, pp. 220, 222–3.
45  Pennell, *Kingdom United*, p. 183.
46  Ibid., p. 184.
47  Ibid., pp. 183–9; Terence Denman, '"The Red Livery of Shame": The Campaign against Army Recruitment in Ireland, 1899-1914', *Irish Historical Studies*, 29.114 (November, 1994), pp. 208–33; Benjamin Z. Novick, 'DORA, Suppression, and Nationalist Propaganda in Ireland, 1914-1915', *New Hibernia Review*, 1.4 (1997), pp. 41–57; Tim Bowman, 'The Irish Recruiting Campaign and Anti-Recruiting Campaigns, 1914-1918', in Bertrand Taithe and Tim Thornton (eds.), *Propaganda: Political Rhetoric and Identity, 1300-2000* (Glouchestershire, 1999), pp. 223–38.
48  McConnel, *The Irish Parliamentary Party*, p. 299.
49  Paul Bew, *Ideology and the Irish Question: Ulster Unionism and Irish Nationalism, 1912-1916* (Oxford and New York, 1994), p. 122. The Fenians were members of the nineteenth-century revolutionary nationalist organizations, the Fenian Brotherhood and IRB, which were precursors to later republican movements. For more information, see Brian Jenkins, *The Fenian Problem: Insurgency and Terrorism in a Liberal State* (Liverpool, 2009).
50  Wheatley, *Nationalism*, p. 2.
51  Martin Pugh, *Electoral Reform in War and Peace, 1906-18* (London, 1978), pp. 119, 121.
52  James McConnel, 'Recruiting Sergeants for John Bull? Irish Nationalist MPs and Enlistment during the Early Months of the Great War', *War in History*, 14.4 (2007), pp. 414–15.
53  Pugh, *Electoral Reform*, pp. 119, 121.
54  McConnel, 'Recruiting Sergeants', p. 416.
55  For further information on Redmond, see Terence Denman, *A Lonely Grave: The Life and Death of William Redmond* (Dublin, 1995).

56  Colin Reid, *The Lost Ireland of Stephen Gwynn: Irish Constitutional Nationalism and Cultural Politics, 1864-1950* (Manchester, 2011), pp. 126–49.

57  Timothy Bowman, 'Composing Divisions: The Recruitment of Ulster and National Volunteers into the British Army in 1914', *Causeway*, 2.1 (1995), esp. pp. 26–7, cited in Pennell, *Kingdom United*, pp. 177, 193.

58  Fitzpatrick, *Politics*, p. 112; Bew, *Ideology*, p. 380; Tom Garvin, *1922: The Birth of Irish Democracy* (Dublin, 1996), pp. 24–5.

59  McConnel, 'Recruiting Sergeants', p. 419.

60  J. Finnan, '"Let Irishmen Come Together In The Trenches": John Redmond and Irish Party Policy in the Great War 1914-1918', *Irish Sword*, XXII (2000), p. 185; McConnel, 'Recruiting Sergeants', p. 420.

61  McConnel, 'Recruiting Sergeants', p. 424; Charles Townshend, *Easter 1916: The Irish Rebellion* (London, 2005), p. 60.

62  Fanning, *Fatal Path*, p. 149.

63  Colin Reid, 'Stephen Gwynn and the Failure of Constitutional Nationalism in Ireland, 1919-1921', *The Historical Journal*, 53.3 (2010), p. 724; Michael Laffan, *The Partition of Ireland* (Dundalk, 1983), pp. 49–60.

64  Townshend, *Easter 1916*, p. 60.

65  Reid, *Lost Ireland*, p. 158; Caoimhe Nic Dháibhéid, 'The Irish National Aid Association and the Radicalization of Public Opinion in Ireland, 1916-1918', *The Historical Journal*, 55 (2012), p. 706.

66  Reid, *Lost Ireland*, pp. 161–5.

67  Thomas Hennessey, *Dividing Ireland : World War One and Partition* (London, 1998); David George Boyce, '"That Party Politics Should Divide Our Tents": Nationalism, Unionism and the First World War', in Adrian Gregory and Senia Pašeta (eds.), *Ireland and the Great War: 'A War To Unite Us All?'* (Manchester, 2002), pp. 190–216.

68  McConnel, 'Recruiting Sergeants', p. 420.

69  Wheatley, *Nationalism*, p. 264; McConnel, *The Irish Parliamentary Party*, p. 306.

70  Foster, *Vivid Faces*, p. 264.

71  Charles Townshend, *The Republic: The Fight for Irish Independence, 1918-1923* (London, 2013), p. 13.

72  Bowman, *Carson's Army*, p. 175.

73  The Commonwealth War Graves Commission website shows the following returns for men who had a listed affiliation to, or that were buried in, the towns of Kilrush, Co. Clare (16 men), Dundalk, Co. Louth (22 men) and Clonmel, Co. Tipperary (29 men). Only four of the 16 men linked to Kilrush served in a unit with an Irish designation (1 Royal Irish Regiment; 3 Royal Munster Fusiliers); six out of the 22 men from Dundalk (2 Royal Irish Fusiliers, 1 Royal Irish Regiment, 1 Connaught Rangers, 1 Royal Dublin Fusiliers, 1 Royal Irish Rifles); and 16 from Clonmel (3 Royal Dublin Fusiliers, 8 Royal Irish Regiment, 2 Royal Munster Fusiliers, 1 Irish Guard, 1 Royal Inniskilling Fusiliers, 1 Leinster Regiment). Non-Irish units that were popular included the Highland Light Infantry (3 men, Kilrush; 1 man, Clonmel) and the Royal Field Artillery (1 man, Kilrush; 7 men, Dundalk; 2 men, Clonmel).

74  Thomas Bartlett and Keith Jeffery, 'An Irish Military Tradition?' in Thomas Bartlett and Keith Jeffery (eds.), *A Military History of Ireland* (Cambridge, 1996), p. 8.

75  McConnel, 'Recruiting Sergeants', p. 418; Denman, 'Red Livery', pp. 212–14.

76  Denman, 'Red Livery', pp. 214–15. For further information, see Fitzpatrick, 'Militarism', p. 379.

77  Jeffery, *Ireland*, pp. 10.

78  John Grigg, 'Nobility and War: The Unselfish Commitment', *Encounter* (March 1990), pp. 21–7; Brian Bond, 'British "Anti-War" Writers and Their Critics', in Hugh Cecil and Peter H. Liddle, *Facing Armageddon: the First World War Experienced* (London, 1996), pp. 817–30; Trevor Wilson, *The Myriad Faces of War: Britain and the Great War, 1914-1918* (Cambridge, 1986), pp. 851–3.

79  Senia Pašeta, 'Thomas Kettle: "An Irish Soldier in the Army of Europe?"' in Adrian Gregory and Senia Pašeta (eds.), *Ireland and the Great War: 'A War To Unite Us All?'* (Manchester, 2002), pp. 8–27.

80  Pennell, *Kingdom United*, p. 179; Jeffery, *Ireland*, pp. 10–12; Pašeta, 'Thomas Kettle', p. 10.

81  Fitzpatrick, 'The Logic of Collective Sacrifice', p. 1027; Karsten, 'Irish Soldiers in the British Army', p. 37.

82  Gardiner Mitchell, *'Three Cheers for the Derrys!' A History of the 10th Royal Inniskilling Fusiliers in the 1914-18 War* (Derry, 1991), p. 3.

83  Thomas Dooley, *Irishmen or English Soldiers: The Times and World of a Southern Irish Man (1876-1916) Enlisting in the British Army during the First World War* (Liverpool, 1995), p. 124.

84  Richard Grayson, *Belfast Boys: How Unionists and Nationalists Fought and Died Together in the First World War* (London, 2009), p. 10.

85  Fitzpatrick, 'The Logic of Collective Sacrifice', p. 1023.

86  David Fitzpatrick, 'Home Front and Everyday Life', in John Horne (ed.), *Our War: Ireland and the Great War* (Dublin, 2008), p. 134; Jeffery, *Ireland*, p. 20.

87  Fitzpatrick, 'The Logic of Collective Sacrifice', pp. 1027–9.

88  Jeffery, *Ireland*, p. 20.

89  Fitzpatrick, 'Home Front', p. 134; Pennell, *Kingdom United*, pp. 3–6.

90  Pennell, *Kingdom United*, p. 52. Peter Simkins states that 478,893 men joined the Army between 4 August and 12 September, 301,971 of which enlisted in the fortnight after 30 August, *Kitchener's Army: The Raising of the New Armies, 1914-16* (Manchester, 1988), p. 75.

91  Fitzpatrick, 'Home Front', p. 134.

92  Pennell, *Kingdom United*, p. 192.

93  Fitzpatrick, 'Home Front', p. 137.

94  Keith Jeffery, *1916 A Global History* (London, 2015), p. 110.

95  Jeffery, *Ireland*, p. 6.

96  O'Farrell, *Irish in Australia*, p. 254; Robin B. Burns, 'The Montreal Irish and the Great War', *CCHA Historical Studies*, 52 (1985), p. 74.

97  Paul Bew, *Ireland: The Politics of Enmity 1789-2006* (Oxford, 2007), p. 389.

98  Jeffery, *Ireland*, pp. 6–9.

99  Cousins, *Armagh*, p. 52.

100  Reid, *Lost Ireland*, p. 161.

101  Jeffery, *Ireland*, p. 8.

102  Simkins, *Kitchener's Army*, pp. 104–6, 127.

103  Eileen Reilly, 'Women and Voluntary War Work', in Adrian Gregory and Senia Pašeta (eds.), *Ireland and the Great War: 'A War to Unite Us All'?* (Manchester, 2002), pp. 49–72, pp. 63–5.

104  Roy Stokes, *Death in the Irish Sea: The Sinking of the RMS Leinster* (Cork, 1998); Liam Nolan and John E. Nolan, *Secret Victory: Ireland and the War at Sea, 1914-1918* (Cork, 2009).

105  De Wiel, *Catholic Church*, p. 27.

## Chapter 3

1   Margaret Downes, 'The Civilian Voluntary Aid Effort', in David Fitzpatrick, *Ireland and the First World War* (Dublin, 1988), pp. 27–37; Reilly, 'Women', pp. 49–72; Yvonne McEwen, *It's a Long Way to Tipperary: British and Irish Nurses in the Great War* (Dunfermline, 2006); Catriona Clear, 'Fewer Ladies: More Women', in J. Horne (ed.), *Our War: Ireland and the Great War* (Dublin, 2008), pp. 157–80; Cousins, *Armagh*, pp. 135–77 and Pennell, *Kingdom United*, pp. 168–71.

2   British Red Cross (BRCS), 2003/37, Thekla Bowser, *The Story of British V.A.D. Work in the Great War* (London, 1917).

3   Reilly, 'Women', pp. 50–1.

4   Trevor West, 'Plunkett, Sir Horace Curzon', *Dictionary of Irish Biography* (hereafter *DIB*). Available at http://dib.cambridge.org/viewReadPage.do?articleId=a7385 (accessed 23.07.18).

5   Diarmaid Ferriter, *The Transformation of Ireland, 1900-2000* (London, 2004), p. 68.

6   Reilly, 'Women', p. 66.

7   Elizabeth Mary Margaret Burke-Plunkett Fingall, *Seventy Years Young, Memories of Elizabeth, Countess of Fingall, Told to Pamela Hinkson* (London, 1937), p. 361.

8   *Irish Life* (hereafter *IL*), 21 January, 20 October 1916; *CT*, 26 September 1914.

9   See for instance her efforts to appeal to *IL* readers: 15, 22, 29 January 1915; 12, 19 February 1915; 5, 12, 26 March 1915.

10  Lord and Lady Aberdeen, *'We Twa': Reminiscences of Lord and Lady Aberdeen* (London, 1925), pp. 229–30; *IT*, 11 August 1914; *Church of Ireland Gazette*, 25 September 1914.

11  *IT*, 11 August 1914. Cathy Hayes, 'Lumsden, Sir John', *DIB*. Robert D. Marshall, 'O'Shaughnessy, Sir Thomas Lopdell', *DIB*.

12  *IT*, 7 August 1914. Lawrence William White and Aideen Foley, 'Ormsby, Sir Lambert Hepenstal', *DIB*; Helen Andrews, 'Horne, Sir Andrew John', *DIB*. Available at http://dib .cambridge.org/viewReadPage.do?articleId=a4103 (accessed 23.07.18); 1911 census, Conway Dwyer household.

13  Maria O'Brien, 'Wingfield, Mervyn Edward 7th Viscount Powerscourt', *DIB*; 'Irish Masonic History and the Jewels of Irish Freemasonry'. Available at http://www.iris hmasonichistory.com/the-rw-provincial-grand-lodge-of-the-midland-counties--provi ncial-grand-masters-jewel.html (accessed 07.07.18); CWGC, 'Weldon, Sir Anthony Arthur'. Available at http://www.cwgc.org/find-war-dead/casualty/662834/WELDO N,%20SIR%20ANTHONY%20ARTHUR (accessed 07.07.18).

14  1911 census, Edgar Anderson household. Patrick Maume, 'Murphy, William Martin', *DIB*.

15  Ibid., Nicholas Donnelly household. Also see C. J. Woods, 'Donnelly, Nicholas', *DIB*.

16  Lucey, 'Cork Public Opinion', p. 56.

17  *IT*, 11 August 1914. The Irish Volunteers Voluntary Aid Association counted among its membership Arthur James Francis Plunkett, 11th Earl of Fingall who joined the 7th Battalion Leinster Regiment alongside Nationalist MPs, Stephen Gwynn and Thomas Kettle (see Lieutenant-Colonel Frederick Ernest Whitton, *The History of the Prince of Wales's Leinster Regiment (Royal Canadians) - Volume 2* (Aldershot, 1924), reprint Uckfield, 2004, p. 196); Jenico Preston JP, the 15th Viscount Gormanston who was deputy lieutenant for Co. Meath (see The Peerage, 'Joseph Preston, 15th Viscount Gormanston', Available at http://www.thepeerage.com/p7569.htm#i75687); Charles Grattan-Bellew, 4th Baronet who joined the King's Royal Rifle Corps and

was decorated with the Military Cross in 1918 (see The Peerage, 'Lt.-Col Sir Charles Christopher Grattan-Bellew, 4th Bt'. Available at http://www.thepeerage.com/p425 54.htm#i425539 (accessed 07.07.18); William Gerald Dease JP, a landlord (see 1911 census, William Gerald Dease household); and Henry Harrison, later captain of the Royal Irish Regiment and future member of the Irish Dominion League under Horace Plunkett. His father had stood as a Liberal MP for Belfast (see Owen McGee, 'Harrison, Henry', *DIB*).

18  *IT*, 11 August 1914; 1911 census, Sam H. Bolton household.

19  Aberdeen, '*We Twa*', pp. 229–30; Senia Pašeta, *Irish Nationalist Women, 1900-1918* (Cambridge, 2013), p. 150.

20  Diane Urquhart, *Women in Ulster Politics, 1890-1940* (Dublin, 2000). I am grateful to Senia Pašeta for this information.

21  *IT*, 11 August 1914.

22  For more on Walsh, the 'rogue bishop', see de Wiel, *Catholic Church*, pp. 54–62, 89–94, and Thomas J. Morrissey, *William J. Walsh, Archbishop of Dublin, 1841-1921: No Uncertain Voice* (Dublin, 2000).

23  BMH, WS 687, Monsignor M. J. Curran, p. 13.

24  *IT*, 12 May 1915; *FJ*, 17 October 1918.

25  Troy R. E. Paddock, *A Call to Arms: Propaganda, Public Opinion and Newspapers in the Great War* (London, 2004), pp. 29–30; Gregory, *Last Great War*, pp. 50–5.

26  Pennell, *Kingdom United*, p. 179.

27  De Wiel, *Catholic Church*, p. 27; also cited in *The Irish Catholic Directory and Almanac for 1916* (Dublin, 1916), p. 504.

28  Pennell, *Kingdom United*, p. 194.

29  *Irish Independent* (hereafter *II*), 23 October 1914; *Leitrim Observer*, 24 October 1914.

30  Pennell, *Kingdom United*, p. 170; Lucey, 'Cork Public Opinion', p. 59.

31  Elís Ward, 'A Big Show-Off to Show What We Can Do: Ireland and the Hungarian Refugee Crisis', *Irish Studies in International Affairs*, 7 (1996), pp. 131–41.

32  *II*, 21 October 1914; *IT*, 21 October 1914.

33  *LL*, 23 December 1914; Population returns cited are for Celbridge DED, *1911 Census, Leinster, Kildare*, pp. 17, 89. Urban Limerick includes the city of Limerick, Newcastle Urban, and Rathkeale, *1911 Census, Munster, Limerick*, pp. 3, 5, 157.

34   *FJ*, 21 November 1914. *1911 Census, Connaught, Sligo*.

35  *II*, 29 September, 21 October 1914; *IT*, 3 October 1914.

36  Lucey, 'Cork Public Opinion', p. 59; Galway, *CT*, 27 May 1916; Co. Wicklow, *II*, 3 November 1914; Co. Kildare, *FJ*, 20 November 1914; Co. Limerick, *LL*, 14 February 1916; and in Killaloe (Co. Clare), Cashel (Co. Tipperary), Co. Waterford, Killiney and Ballybrack (Co. Dublin), Dromore (Co. Down), Belfast (Co. Antrim), and Co. Meath, IJA, ADMN/3/7/(1), 'Letters to the Irish Jesuit Provincial, Fr Thomas V. Nolan SJ', document entitled 'Visite aux refugees Belges'.

37  1911 census, Annie Dooley household; IJA, ADMN/3/7/(1), letter from Annie Dooley to Fr Nolan, 22 October 1914; Maggie Mallan to Nolan, 21 October 1914.

38  IJA, ADMN/3/7/(1), letter from the Ballybrack and Killiney Belgian Refugee Committee to Nolan, 24 October 1914.

39  Ibid., May Dooley to Nolan, 25 October 1914.

40  Ibid., F. Mulligan to Nolan, 27 October 1914. 1911 census, F. Mulligan household.

41  Ibid., Anne McHugh to Nolan, 26 October 1914; Mary E. Morrissey to Nolan, 27 October 1914; Sarah Corcoran to Nolan, 4 November 1914; Marian Moynihan

to Nolan, 14 November 1914; Edward Hanrahan to Nolan, 24 October 1914; M. Wangelist [*sic*] to Nolan, 2 October 1914.

42 Ibid., John Hamill to Nolan, 25 October 1914. 1911 census, Marianne Hamill household.

43 Pennell, *Kingdom United*, p. 135.

44 Mary Purcell, *To Africa with Love: The Life of Mother Mary Martin, Foundress of the Medical Missionaries of Mary* (Dublin, 1987), p. 18.

45 BRCS, Arch 1080, *Reports by the Joint War Committee and the Joint War Finance Committee of the British Red Cross Society and the Order of St. John of Jerusalem in England on Voluntary Aid rendered to the Sick and Wounded at Home and Abroad and to British Prisoners of War, 1914–1919: With Appendices* (London, 1921) (hereafter, *JWC*), pp. 728–30; for a complete list, visit The Long Long Trail, 'Military Hospitals in the British Isles, 1914-1918'. Available at http://www.longlongtrail.co.uk/soldiers/a-sol diers-life-1914-1918/the-evacuation-chain-for-wounded-and-sick-soldiers/military -hospitals-in-the-british-isles-1914-1918/ (accessed 07.07.18).

46 For the full list, see The Long Long Trail.

47 C. J. Woods, 'Cosgrave, Ephraim MacDowel', *DIB*. 1911 census, Conway Dwyer household.

48 Aberdeen, '*We Twa*', p. 235. 1911 census, Lorcan George Sherlock household.

49 Aberdeen, '*We Twa*', p. 236.

50 Reilly, 'Women', pp. 49–72, 56–8.

51 Reilly, 'Women', p. 58; Aberdeen, '*We Twa*', p. 238.

52 *IL*, 5 February 1915.

53 1911 census, William Fry household; *IL*, 18 January 1918.

54 Aberdeen, '*We Twa*', p. 238. 1911 census, James Moran household and Charles Maurice Jones household (Lady Aberdeen incorrectly calls him C. J. Jones).

55 *IL*, 22 January 1915.

56 *IL*, 5 February 1915. National Library of Ireland (NLI): Papers of John Redmond Part III.i.18 '1915', MS 15,261/2, 10 February 1915. 1911 census, Martin O'Byrne household.

57 *IL*, 19 February 1915. Patrick Maume, 'Esmonde, Sir Thomas Henry Grattan', *DIB*. Thomas Esmonde was a baronet, landowner, politician and a descendant of the famous Henry Grattan. His family had a long tradition of military service and was part of the Irish Catholic elite. His son, John, joined the navy in the war and was killed at Jutland in 1916.

58 Frances Clarke, 'Hinkson (née Tynan) Katharine', *DIB*.

59 Katharine Tynan, *The Years of The Shadow* (London, 1919), p. 169.

60 Reilly, 'Women', p. 58; Tynan, *Years of the Shadow*, p. 169.

61 *JWC*, p. 726.

62 Aberdeen, '*We Twa*', pp. 231–3.

63 *JWC*, p. 727.

64 Tynan, *Years of the Shadow*, pp. 174–5.

65 Elisabeth Shipton, *Female Tommies: The Frontline Women of the First World War* (Glouchestershire, 2014), p. 69.

66 Ibid., p. 35.

67 *IL*, 30 July 1915, 21 January 1916.

68 Ibid., 21 January 1916.

69 1911 census.

70 *JWC*, p. 727; 'The Long Long Trail'. *IL*, 26 January 1916.

71 *JWC*, p. 727. Ratio of nurses to Catholic nurses in Cork (1,043: 810); Louth (147: 127); Kildare (223: 146); Kilkenny (175: 156); Meath (217: 178); Westmeath (156: 126); Wicklow (228: 149); Wexford (233: 196); Waterford (267: 227) and Queen's County (258: 212). Information taken from 1911 census.

72 *IL*, 21, 26 January 1916, 11 February 1916; *CJ*, 17 June, 30 September, 20 December 1915.

73 *IL*, 26 January 1916.

74 All men with the surname 'Minch' who lived in Kildare in 1911 were Catholic; *FJ*, 20 November 1914.

75 1911 census, Josephine Lawless household and Charles Wisdom Hely household; IJA, ADMN/3/7/(2) 'Letters to the Irish Jesuit Provincial, Fr Thomas V. Nolan SJ', letters to Nolan from the Local Government Board in Dublin, 17 and 20 October 1914; Philippa M. Lawless to Nolan, 31 October 1914.

76 1911 census, Patrick James Byrne household.

77 Ibid., Arnold J. de le Poer Power and Kathleen A. E. Cleeve households.

78 Ibid., Johanna Cooney and Barclay Joseph Clibborn households. All men with the name W. H. Smith who resided in Tipperary were listed as Anglicans. It is possible that the Annie and Mary Cooney listed were the Catholic daughters of Patrick Cooney, a farmer who lived in rural Castletown, but an assumption has been made that the women listed were those who lived with Johanna Cooney because they resided in Clonmel East Urban and the VAD was operating in an urban centre, *IL*, 26 January 1916.

79 Thomas Hennessey, 'The Evolution of Ulster Protestant Identity in the Twentieth Century: Nations and Patriotism', in M. A. Busteed, F. Neal, and J. Tonge (eds.), *Irish Protestant Identities* (Manchester, 2009), pp. 260–1, 266.

80 Reilly, 'Women', p. 67.

81 Purcell, *Africa*, p. 26–7.

82 Patrick M. Geoghegan, 'Fitzmaurice, Henry Charles Keith Petty', *DIB*; *IL*, 19 November 1915, 21 January 1916.

83 *IL*, 1 September 1916. All single females with the surname 'Kearon' and 'Page' residing in Wicklow in 1911 were Protestants. 1911 census, Robert Philpot household. All females with the surname 'McGovern' (there were no listings for the abbreviated spelling of 'M'Govern') in Wicklow in 1911 were Catholic, as were all females with the surname 'Linehan' with one exception: a Baptist in Dublin who would have been fifteen years' old by the time this photograph was taken and thus can be eliminated on account of her age. Similarly, all married females with the surname 'O'Reilly' in Wicklow were Catholic.

84 *IL*, 18 February 1916. 1911 census, Helen Butterfield and James Michael Gallagher households.

85 *IL*, 17 August 1917.

86 There were no men with the initials 'C. E. Doran' living in Tipperary in 1911. The only man with these initials lived in Skibbereen, Cork in 1911. As all other C. Dorans living in Ireland were Catholic except one, who can be excluded on the basis of age, Mrs Doran must have been a Catholic. All women with the surname 'Corby' who lived in 1911 were Catholic. All single women with the surname 'Moloney' who lived in Tipperary were Catholic. 1911 census, Charles Edward Doran, David McKinley, Josephine Rachael Butler Lowe households. All single females living in Tipperary with the surname Trayer are Anglican. However, they are too young to have been the woman pictured in the photograph. As all other single females living elsewhere in

Ireland in 1911 with the surname Trayer were Anglican, she was presumably one of these.

87 *IL*, 12 October 1917.

88 All men living in Kerry in 1911 with the surname 'Fitzgerald' are Catholic except one. He has been excluded on the basis that he was a single labourer in 1911. All women living in Kerry with the surnames 'Whelan' and 'Quill' were Catholic. (There is one Anglican with the surname 'Quill' who would have been aged sixty-two when the photograph was taken and too old to have been the woman pictured here.)

89 1911 census, Abraham Addison Hargrave household.

90 *IL*, 12 October 1917.

91 1911 census, Cecilia Mary Plunkett and Gerald Stanley Caldecott households. In the census, Vivienne is listed as Vivian and lived in Slane (Co. Meath).

92 Ibid., Bernard O'Kelly household.

93 Yeates, *A City in Wartime*, p. 13.

94 *JWC*, p. 729; *IL*, 26 January 1916. VADs can be found in Queenstown, Youghal, Bandon and Cork city. The religious distribution of these towns was Queenstown Urban (6,976 Catholics: 1,233 Protestants), Youghal Urban County District (5,059 Catholics: 589 Protestants), Bandon (2,434 Catholics: 688 Protestants) and Cork city (67,814 Catholics: 8,830 Protestants). In Antrim, the three VAD detachments were established in Larne Urban (1,880 Catholics: 5,313 Protestants), Portrush Urban (275 Catholics: 1,743 Protestants) and Lisburn Urban (2,979 Catholics: 9,042 Protestants), *1911 Census, Munster, Cork*, pp. vii, 45; and *Ulster, Antrim*, pp. vi, 132.

95 *JWC*, p. 726.

96 'The Long Long Trail'; *IL*, 22 January, 5 February 1915; *JWC*, pp. 727–8.

97 *IL*, 13 October 1916.

98 *CE*, 7 January 1916. 1911 census, Arthur Ryan household.

99 *LL*, 27 December 1916, 5 January 1917.

100 DCA, Royal Dublin Fusiliers Archive, Monica Roberts Collection, Volume 2 RDFA/001, location reference g1/01/157, letter from Private Christopher Fox to Monica Roberts, 28 December 1916. 1911 census, Thomas Regan household.

101 *IL*, 13 October 1916. The Daniel Kelly listed was probably a merchant draper who lived in Tipperary Urban.

102 *CE*, 7 January 1916. All men with the initials 'J. Heffernan' who lived in Tipperary in 1911 were Catholics.

103 Casgliad y Werin Cymru: People's Collection Wales, 'Canon Basil Chastel de Boinville', item/24558. 1911 census, George Hugh Chetwood Townsend household.

104 *CE*, 7 January 1916.

105 Jim Shanahan, 'O'Brien, Sir Timothy Carew', *DIB*.

106 Purcell, *Africa*, p. 18.

107 Winter, *Sites of Memory*.

108 Purcell, *Africa*, p. 23. Trinity College Dublin, 'A Family at War: The Diary of Mary Martin, 1 January – 25 May 1916'. Available at http://dh.tcd.ie/martindiary/site/index.xml (accessed 08.07.18).

109 Purcell, *Africa*, pp. 24, 27.

110 *JWC*, p. 726.

111 DDA, Francis Gleeson Papers, WWI Diaries and Letters, P101/1-31, P101/12, letter from Elizabeth Meaney to Fr Gleeson, 23 December 1917.

112 *JWC*, p. 726.

113   *NR*, 22 August 1914. Returns listed are for Newry Urban. *1911 Census, Ulster, Down*, p. vi.

114   1911 census, Arthur McCann and Alexander Gartlan households. All married females living in Newry in 1911 with the surname 'Mullan' were Catholic, as were all single females with the surname 'Murray'.

115   Ibid., Adelaide Swanzy, George John Slipper, and Rowland Wade households.

116   Fitzpatrick, *Politics*, pp. 63–4; Wheatley, *Nationalism*, pp. 201–6; Pennell, *Kingdom United*, p. 178.

117   *The Derry Standard*, 18 December 1914. Newtownstewart was listed as Newtown Stewart in the census, part of Strabane No. 1 Rural District. *1911 Census, Ulster, Tyrone*, p. 131.

118   *NR*, 5 December 1914.

119   Cousins, *Armagh*, pp. 91–2. In 1911, all men with the initials 'J. Edwards' who lived in Armagh were Protestant. Getz lived with the family of another teacher, the Anglican James Wightman, who taught science. James Alexander Wightman household.

120   Cousins, *Armagh*, pp. 31–2, 74–6.

121   De Wiel, *Catholic Church*, pp. 28–30.

122   IJA, ADMN/3/7/(1), Lawless to Nolan, 2 November 1914.

123   Ibid., F. W. Cotter and J. O'Neill to Nolan, 11 November 1914.

124   Ibid., Cotter to Nolan, 16 November 1914.

125   *IL*, 19 February 1915.

126   Linde Lunney, 'Pirrie, Margaret Montgomery Viscountess Pirrie Carlisle', *DIB*; David Murphy, 'Dill, Sir John Greer', *DIB*; Diarmaid Ferriter, 'Hamilton, Thomas', *DIB*; for more information on Robert Meyer see David John Owen, *History of Belfast* (Belfast, 1921), p. viii.

127   1911 census, James McKeown household.

128   Ibid., Charles James Stuart and Adam McMeekin households. In the census, Vivienne is named 'Marguerita Elisabeth Vivienne Stuart'.

129   Grayson, *Belfast Boys*.

130   Bew, *Ideology*.

131   *1911 Census, Ulster, Cavan*, p. vi; *The Irish Post and Weekly Telegraph for Cavan and the Midlands* (hereafter, *IP*), 5 September 1914.

132   Reilly, 'Women', p. 63.

133   Peter Berresford Ellis, 'Tom Lough, the forgotten radical', *Islington Tribune*, 13 November 2009.

134   Reilly, 'Women', pp. 63–4.

135   *IP*, 3 October 1914; *AC*, 3 October 1914.

136   Reilly, 'Women', pp. 63–5. Though the religious composition of these schools cannot be stated for certain, assumptions have been made. There were 1,084 people living in Ballymachugh DED in 1911, 332 of which were Protestant, *1911 Census, Ulster, Cavan*, p. 96. A website outlining the history of the village tends to imply that the primary school located in the area was Anglican. See National Inventory of Architectural Heritage, 'Main Record: County Cavan'. Available at http://www.buildingsofireland.ie/niah/search.jsp?type=record&county=CV&regno=40403715 (accessed 08.07.18). In 1911, 149 people lived in the townland of Crosserlough where Aghakee school was located (148 of them were Catholic). The religious distribution thus tends to suggest that a school located there was Catholic.

137   1911 census, Travers Robert Blackley household.

138  *IP*, 5 June 1915.

139  Fitzpatrick, *Politics*, p. 109, Peter Martin, "'Dulce et Decorum': Irish Nobles and the Great War, 1914-19', in Adrian Gregory and Senia Pašeta (eds.), *Ireland and the Great War: 'A War To Unite Us All?'* (Manchester, 2002), p. 43; Campbell, *Land*, p. 203; Thomas Martin, *The Kingdom in the Empire: A Portrait of Kerry during World War One* (Dublin, 2006), p. 38.

140  *IP*, 19 February 1916.

141  Ibid., 2 September 1916. 1911 census, Keith Robert Collis Hallowes and Thomas Francis Berry household.

142  Population returns cited are for Belturbet Urban, Virginia Urban, Killashandra DED and Ballyconnell DED. *1911 Census, Ulster, Cavan*, pp. 91, 93, 96, 99.

143  *IP*, 2 September 1916.

144  1911 census, John Clarke household.

145  Ibid., William Finlay and Peter Levins households.

146  Ibid., William John Fegan household. All single females with the surname 'Vance' who lived in Cavan in 1911 were Anglican.

147  *IP*, 5 August 1916.

148  *AC*, 30 December 1916. 1911 census, Andrew McCarren and Joseph Patrick Gannon households.

149  *IP*, 13 January 1917.

150  *IT*, 3 November 1916, 11 August, 7 December 1917; *IP*, 19 January 1918.

151  Population figures and religious returns taken from the 1911 digital census.

152  Their populations were Cavan Urban (2,310 Catholics: 651 Protestants), Belturbet (956 Catholics: 415 Protestants), Killashandra (1,216 Catholics: 408 Protestants), Ballyconnell (905 Catholics: 340), Cootehill Urban (1,200 Catholics: 350 Protestants) and Virginia (2,473 Catholics: 249 Protestants) *1911 Census, Ulster, Cavan*, pp. 91, 93, 99.

153  *IT*, 26 October 1918.

154  *JWC*, p. 727.

155  Castlepollard Town (population: 612) was located in Kinturk DED. There are no religious returns listed for the town. The composition of the DED would suggest that the town was largely Catholic (963 Catholics: 104 Protestants), *1911 Census, Leinster, Westmeath*, p. 97.

156  *AC*, 23 November 1918.

157  *IT*, 12, 26 July 1918, 29 January 1919.

158  NLI: Diary of Mrs Augustine Henry for the period June 1916 to July 1919, dealing with the First World War. Mainly newscuttings, Royal College of Science Sub-Depot, *Third Annual Report of the Sphagnum Department of the Irish War Hospital Supply Organisation* (Dublin, n/d), p. 3 (hereafter RCS), MS 7988.

159  *JWC*, p. 727; *IL*, 12 July 1918.

160  William Murphy, 'Green, Alice Sophia Amelia Stopford', *DIB*.

161  Thomas Pakenham, 'Henry, Augustine', *DIB*.

162  Clara Cullen, *The World Upturning: Elsie Henry's Irish Wartime Diaries, 1913-1919* (Dublin, 2013).

163  RCS, *Annual Report*, p. 9.

164  *IL*, 26 July 1918.

165  RCS, *Annual Report*, pp. 16–18.

166  Ibid., pp. 10–11.

167  Cullen, *World Upturning*, p. 186.

168 These figures are taken from the online census and include farmers from Kilgarvan in the Lisselton DED as well as Kilgarvan DED.

169 There were six women with the surname 'Constable' who lived in Ireland in 1911, one of whom was Protestant, but as this Constable would have been aged fifty-two in 1917, it is unlikely that she was the woman Henry describes. Elsewhere in her diaries, Henry mentions that the Constable family was involved in 'art'. Only one individual in the census had a connection to art and that was the Catholic, Patrick Constable from Limerick, who was an 'unemployed painter'. His daughter, Bridget, would have been aged thirteen in 1917 and seems a good fit for Henry's description of typical moss-pickers. The only Anglican named Margaret Shea who lived in Kerry was the mother of a wealthy hotel proprietor and magistrate and was thus unlikely to have been the poorer labourer described by Henry. 1911 census, Jack Francis Shea household.

170 Cullen, *World Upturning*, p. 186. Returns for Kenmare town taken from online census.

171 All single females living in Skibbereen with the surname 'O'Donovan' were Catholic, as were all females living in Clare (indeed, across all of Ireland) in 1911. It is likely that the war-worker was Ellen O'Halloran from Killofin, Co. Clare (1911 census, Simon O'Halloran household). There were five women named Annie Smith living in Cootehill, Cavan, in 1911, where this war-worker was from. One was Anglican and married. She can be excluded on this basis, as the war-worker was listed as 'Miss Annie Smith' and therefore must have been single and thus Catholic. All women with the surname 'McMenamin' living in Donegal in 1911 were Catholics. The war-worker lived in Glenties and only one woman can be found with this surname from this village: Mary Anne McMenamin, 1911 census, Annie Furey household.

172 1911 census, Mary Martin household. There were three women living in Dublin with the initials 'M. Carberry'. All were Catholic. 1911 census, George Fletcher household.

173 Ibid., Harriet Emily Reed household and William Arthur Winter household.

174 Diary entry 23 February 1916, cited in Cullen, *World Upturning*, p. 137; RCS, *Annual Report*, p. 8. The exact number of moss dressings, dysentery pads and rest cushions was 905,653. RCS, *Annual Report*, pp. 16–17.

175 *JWC*, p. 727; *IL*, 12 July 1918.

176 RCS, *Annual Report*, pp. 8, 16–17.

177 Ibid., p. 9.

178 Ibid., pp. 7–8.

179 Cullen, *World Upturning*, p. 185.

180 *JWC*, p. 725.

181 *AC*, 19 January 1918, *FJ*, 25 January 1918; *AC*, 6 November 1915. Population returns cited are for Clones Urban. *1911 Census, Ulster, Monaghan*, p. 86.

182 *AC*, 22 January 1916; *LO*, 3 November 1917. Population returns cited are for Carrick-on-Shannon DED and Drumsna DED. *1911 Census, Connaught, Leitrim*.

183 *FJ*, 27 November 1917. Drogheda Town no longer appeared as an electoral district after the census of 1901. The returns given are for Drogheda Urban, *1911 Census, Leinster, Louth*, p. 62.

184 *LL*, 21 January 1916, 23 September 1918. The population returns given are for the city of Limerick (also recorded as Limerick County Borough), *1911 Census, Munster, Limerick*, pp. vii, 45.

185 *JWC*, p. 726.

186 *CT*, 3 June 1916, 1 June 1918.

187 *IT*, 14 May 1919.
188 *The Weekly Irish Times*, 18 December 1915; also reported in the *IT*, 13 December 1915. The subsequent flag days were reported in *IL*, 21 November 1916, 22 June 1917.
189 *JWC*, p. 726.

## Chapter 4

1 Patrick O'Sullivan, *The Lusitania: Unravelling the Mysteries* (Staplehurst, 2000), p. 48.
2 There is no mention of the war at sea in Gregory and Pašeta, *Ireland* or in Horne and Madigan, *Towards Commemoration*. Only Jeffery and Fitzpatrick have briefly referred to it, Jeffery, *Ireland*, pp. 31–2; Fitzpatrick, 'Home Front', p. 137.
3 Fitzpatrick, ibid.
4 Pennell, *Kingdom United*, p. 175.
5 Lucey, 'Cork Public Opinion', p. 67.
6 White and O'Shea, *Great Sacrifice*, p. 37.
7 *CJ*, 27 May 1915; 1911 census, Josef Fehrenbach and Francis Esch households.
8 Daniela L. Caglioti, 'Aliens and Internal Enemies: Internment Practices, Economic Exclusion and Property Rights during the First World War', *Journal of Modern European History*, 12.4 (2014), pp. 448–59.
9 Cited in David Hennessy, 'Ireland and the First World War: A Cork Perspective', unpublished MPhil thesis (NUI Cork, 2004), p. 53.
10 Ben Novick, 'The Advanced Nationalist Response to Atrocities Propaganda, 1914-1918', in Lawrence W. McBride (ed.), *Images, Icons and the Irish Nationalist Imagination* (Dublin, 1999), pp. 135–7; Pennell, *Kingdom United*, p. 174.
11 *II*, 11 September 1914.
12 Five thousand and ninety-nine persons lived in the County Electoral Division of Askeaton. One thousand and sixty-eight lived in the parish of Askeaton (1,036 were Catholics). *Census of Ireland, 1911, Munster*, pp. 2, 119.
13 *LL*, 7 February 1916. For speculation regarding whether Zeppelins could reach Ireland, see these editorials: *CT*, 5 January 1916; *The Church of Ireland Gazette*, 4 February 1916.
14 *II*, 18 May, 11 August, 1915; *CT*, 5 January 1916; *LL*, 26 April 1916.
15 *CT*, 5 January 1916.
16 Peter H. Wilson, 'The Origins of Prussian Militarism', *History Today*, 51.5 (2001). Available at http://www.historytoday.com/peter-h-wilson/origins-prussian-milit arism (accessed 08.07.18).
17 Nolan, *Secret Victory*, p. 7.
18 Ibid., p. 41.
19 O'Sullivan, *Lusitania*, pp. 26–9.
20 Ibid., p. 49.
21 Ibid., p. 13.
22 Ibid., p. 53.
23 *CT*, 6 February 1915.
24 O'Sullivan, *Lusitania*, p. 29.
25 Ibid., p. 28.
26 *CT*, 3 April 1915.
27 Ibid., 8 May 1915.
28 *IT*, 28 April 1915; *II*, 29, 30 April 1915.

29 *II*, 30 April 1915.
30 International Committee of the Red Cross, 'Convention (IV) respecting the Laws and Customs of War on Land and its annex: Regulations concerning the Laws and Customs of War on Land: The Hague, 18 October 1907', *International Peace Conference. The Hague. Official Record.*
31 O'Sullivan, *Lusitania*, pp. 67–8.
32 Jeffery mentions the ship's demise but does not discuss its impact on Irish opinion, *Ireland*, p. 32; there is no mention of the tragedy in Gregory and Pašeta, *Ireland*.
33 Novick, Advanced Nationalist, p. 147.
34 *Nenagh Guardian*, 8 May 1915; *CT, Connaught Telegraph, AC, The Kerryman, Longford Leader, Ulster Herald, Westmeath Examiner, LO, Nenagh Guardian* 15 May 1915; *LL*, 21 May 1915; *The Kildare Observer*, 29 May 1915.
35 *CE*, 8 May 1915.
36 *IT*, 8 May 1915.
37 *II*, 8 May 1915.
38 Novick, 'Advanced Nationalist', p. 141.
39 *IT*, 8 May 1915.
40 *LL*, 10 May 1915.
41 *CJ*, 10 May 1915.
42 *CT*, 8 May 1915.
43 O'Sullivan, *Lusitania*, p. 89.
44 *Census of Ireland, 1911, Munster, Cork*, pp. 183, 188. These figures include both men and women.
45 *CT*, 15 May 1915; also cited in O'Sullivan, *Lusitania*, p. 89.
46 *CE*, quoted in Lucey, 'Cork Public Opinion', p. 63; *II*, 8 May 1915.
47 Margarita Cappock, 'Lane, Sir Hugh Percy', *DIB*.
48 *II*, 10 May 1915; *IT*, 8, 10 May 1915.
49 Fingall, *Seventy Years Young*, p. 268.
50 *CT*, 8, 15, 22 May 1915.
51 *AC, Ulster Herald*, 15 May 1915.
52 *IT*, 8 May 1915; *AC, The Kerryman, Ulster Herald*, 15 May 1915.
53 *II*, 10 May 1915. Also see the comments of one Miss Lee from Cavan, *AC*, 15 May 1915.
54 *The Kerryman*, 15 May 1915.
55 O'Sullivan, *Lusitania*, p. 81.
56 *CE*, 12 May 1915.
57 CCCA, Bennetts of Ballinacurra Collection, B609/9/A/58, John H. Bennett Diaries and Related Items, 1881–1935, notebook, 'Some Notes in Diary Form on the Great War, Aug 4 1914 to Nov 11 1918'.
58 National Army Museum (NAM), MS. 7608-40, Charles Brett, 'Recollections of C. A. Brett', p. 5.
59 O'Sullivan, *Lusitania*, p. 81.
60 *CE*, 12 May 1915.
61 Nicoletta F. Gullace, '*The Blood of Our Sons': Men, Women and the Renegotiation of British Citizenship During the Great War* (New York, 2002), esp. pp. 17–33.
62 Charles Emelius Lauriat, *The Lusitania's Last Voyage: Being a Narrative of the Torpedoing and Sinking of the R.M.S. Lusitania by a German Submarine off the Irish Coast, May 7, 1915* (New York, 1915), pp. 7, 42.
63 A selection of sympathetic resolutions can be found in the minutes of Cork Harbour Board, Cork Corporation, Cork City Regiment National Volunteers, Cork Recruiting

Committee, Cork Union, Cork Incorporated Chamber of Commerce and Shipping, Queenstown Urban Council, Cork City Executive UIL, and Bantry Board of Guardians, *II*, 15 May 1915; Midleton and Fermoy Board of Guardians, *IT*, 10 May 1915.

64  *II*, 11 May 1915.
65  O' Sullivan, *Lusitania*, p. 82.
66  *II*, 11 May 1915.
67  UIL Westport, *II*, 15 May 1915; Parke Branch UIL in Mayo, *Connaught Telegraph*, 19 June 1915; Louth Urban Council, *IT*, 18 May 1915; Tralee Urban District Council, Tralee and Fenit Pier and Harbour Commissioners, *The Kerryman*, 22 May 1915; Limerick Board of Guardians, *II*, 19 May 1915; Ennis Board of Guardians, *CJ*, 20 May 1915; Kilrush Board of Guardians, *CJ*, 10 June 1915; the Dublin Railway Clerks' Association, *IT*, 17 May 1915; Kiltimagh Teachers' Association, *CT*, 22 May 1915; Kildare Working Men's Association, *Kildare Observer*, 22 May 1915; Dublin Public Libraries Committee for the City of Dublin, *IT*, 4 June 1915 and Clare Committee of Agriculture, *CJ*, 10 June 1915.
68  *LL*, 19 May 1915. 1911 census, Cornelius Quilligan household.
69  *CJ*, 20 May 1915; *LL*, 29 November 1916. All men with the surname Kenneally or Kennealy living in Clare (and in all of Ireland) in 1911 were Catholic.
70  *CT*, 15 May 1915.
71  *IT*, 8 May 1915.
72  *IT*, 17 June 1915; Nic Dháibhéid, 'The Irish National Aid Association', p. 709.
73  *II*, 13, 15 May 1915. 1911 census, Lambert Hefenstall Ormsby household.
74  *IT*, 12 May 1915.
75  Novick, 'Advanced Nationalist'.
76  Staunton, 'The Royal Munster Fusiliers', p. 63.
77  *CT*, 15 May 1915.
78  *AC*, 15 May 1915.
79  Brett, 'Recollections', p. 5.
80  Oonagh Walsh, *An Englishwoman in Belfast: Rosamond Stephen's Record of the Great War* (Cork, 2000), p. 31.
81  *Connaught Telegraph*, 22 May 1915.
82  *LL*, 5 April 1916.
83  Fitzpatrick, 'Home Front', p. 137.
84  For more on the Famine and its resonance throughout modern Irish history, see Cormac Ó Gráda, *Black '47 and Beyond: The Great Irish Famine in History, Economy, and Memory* (Princeton, 1999); Christine Kinealy, *This Great Calamity: The Irish Famine 1845-52* (Dublin, 1994; repr. 2006) and *The Great Famine: Impact, Ideology and Rebellion* (Basingstoke, 2002).
85  *FJ*, 19, 20 February 1917.
86  *AC*, 10 February 1917.
87  *LL*, 8 January 1917.
88  *AC*, 24 February 1917.
89  *II*, 19 February 1917.
90  *FJ*, 19, 20 February 1917.
91  *II*, 7 December 1916.
92  Ibid., 12 December 1916.
93  *Longford Leader*, 18 November 1916; *CT*, 16 December 1916; *II*, 20 January 1917; *Longford Leader*, 10 March 1917.

94  *IT*, 12 January 1917.

95  *FJ*, 20 February 1917.

96  *II*, 20 January 1917.

97  *CT*, 23 December 1916.

98  *FJ*, 8 June 1917, 11 January, 5 February, 27 September 1918.

99  Ibid., 12 May 1917.

100  Ibid., 30 August 1917.

101  Ibid., 16 May, 25 September 1917; 1 January 1918.

102  *II*, 5 February 1917; *CT*, 2 February 1917.

103  *II*, 7 December 1916; 3, 9, 15 January, 16 March 1917.

104  Ibid., 3 January 1917.

105  *LL*, 19, 24 January 1917; *II*, 12 December 1916; 26, 27 January 1917.

106  *II*, 12 December 1916.

107  Ibid., 16 March 1917.

108  *FJ*, 19 February 1917.

109  The branches were Abbeyfeale and East Limerick, *LL*, 24, 26 January 1917; Clontuskert and Moylough, *CT*, 16 March 1918; Ballintemple and Killgarry, *AC*, 24 February 1917; North Longford, *Longford Leader*, 20 January 1917.

110  *LL*, 8 January 1917.

111  Ibid., 12 January 1917.

112  Bew, *Ideology*, pp. 131–7, 140, 146, 149; Wheatley, *Nationalism*, p. 264; McConnel, *The Irish Parliamentary Party*, p. 306; Foster, *Vivid Faces*, p. 264.

113  *II*, 6 January 1917. Also see Jeffery, *Ireland*, p. 31.

114  For more on the land question in Irish politics, see Robert Fitzroy Foster, *Modern Ireland 1600-1972* (London, 1989), pp. 373–99; for the west of Ireland in wartime, see Campbell, *Land and Revolution*.

115  *II*, 9 January 1917. 1911 census, Robert Massy Dawson Sanders household.

116  *II*, 20, 23 January 1917.

117  *LL*, 2 February 1917.

118  *II*, 15 January 1917.

119  Ibid., 19 February 1917.

120  *CT*, 16 December 1916.

121  1911 census, James J. Coen, Robert Downes and John David Fetherstonhaugh households. Two men resided in Westmeath who held the initials 'A. E. Gray' and both were Anglican. They included Alexander Gray, the local RIC inspector, and Arthur Gray, a farmer. Give that the former resided in Mullingar Urban and this was an agricultural concern, the man at the meeting was probably Arthur Gray.

122  *IT*, 26 January 1917.

123  Ibid., 13, 22 January 1917. 1911 census, Henry Powell Bridge household.

124  James Loughlin, 'Russell, Sir Thomas Wallace', *DIB*.

125  *II*, 6 March 1917; 1911 census, Frederick V. Devere household.

126  *II*, 15 January 1917.

127  *II*, 13, 17 March 1917.

128  Oliver Coogan, *Politics and War in Meath 1913-23* (Meath, 1983), p. 66.

129  Cited in Cullen, *World Upturning*, p. 180. For more on Fletcher's Red Cross work, see Aberdeen, '*We Twa*', pp. 224–43.

130  *II*, 17 May, 29 June 1917.

131  Ibid., 27 March 1917.

132  Ibid., 29 June 1917.

133 Ibid., 19 July 1917. Jane Ridley, 'Lindsay, David Alexander Edward, Twenty-Seventh Earl of Crawford and Tenth Earl of Balcarres (1871–1940)', *Oxford Dictionary of National Biography* (hereafter *Oxford DNB*).

134 *II*, 29 November 1917; *CT*, 15 February 1918.

135 *II*, 3 November 1917.

136 For example, articles related to the Battle of Jutland in the North Sea contribute to the frequency with which 'submarine' is reported. Similarly, the popularity of 'Republic' is partly the result of non-Irish articles such as 'Republic for Bavaria', 'A German Republic Inevitable' and 'French Republic'.

137 Pennell, *Kingdom United*, p. 192.

138 Nolan, *Secret Victory*, p. 228.

139 *1911 Census, Munster, County and City of Cork*, p. vi. Population returns listed are for Queenstown Urban.

140 Nolan, *Secret Victory*, p. 230.

141 Ibid., pp. 230–2.

142 IWM, doc. 12333, Private Papers of Captain G. W. Nightingale, MC, letter from G. W. Nightingale to his mother, 3 June 1917.

143 Josephus Daniels, *Our Navy at War* (New York, 1922), p. 361.

144 Nolan, *Secret Victory*, pp. 230–2.

145 Elting Elmore Morison, *Admiral Sims and the Modern American Navy* (Boston, 1942), cited in Nolan, *Secret Victory*, p. 228.

146 *Census of Ireland, 1911, Munster*, County and City of Cork, p. 45.

147 Lucey 'Cork Public Opinion', p. 119; *CE*, 26 September 1918.

148 Lucey, 'Cork Public Opinion', p. 119.

149 *CT*, 24 March 1917.

150 Ibid., 2 June 1917.

151 Ibid., 15 June 1918.

152 Ibid., 2 June 1917.

153 Stokes, *Death*, p. 61.

154 The deceased were Edward MacDermott, Joseph Flaherty, Thomas Hopkins, Coleman Feeney, Tim Keady, Peter Folan, Messrs Flaherty, and the brothers, Edward and Patrick Lee.

155 *CT*, 29 December 1917.

156 Carna was located in the DED, Knockboy, which had 1,880 Catholics out of 1,897 persons. *Census of Ireland, 1911, Connaught, Galway*, pp. 25, 190. All inhabitants are listed as Catholic on the online census.

157 *CT*, 15 June 1918.

158 *II*, 8 June 1918.

159 *CT*, 15 June 1918; *II*, 8 June 1918.

160 *CT*, 13 July 1918.

161 Nolan, *Secret Victory*, p. 261.

162 Stokes, *Death*, pp. 24–5.

163 Nolan, *Secret Victory*, pp. 267, 277.

164 Fingall, *Seventy Years Young*, p. 364.

165 The *IT* reported 580 killed on 11 October 1918. The *CT* reported 527 deaths on 12 October 1918 while the *II* reported 451 victims on 11 October 1918; Stokes, *Death*, p. 1.

166 *FJ*, 11 October 1918.

167 *LL*, 11 October 1918; *CT*, 12 October 1918.

168 *II*, 11 October 1918.

169 *IT*, 11 October 1918.
170 Figures cited are for Kingstown Urban, *1911 Census, Leinster, County of Dublin*, p. 3.
171 *Cork Constitution*, 11 January 1919, cited in Lucey, *Cork Public Opinion*, p. 120.
172 BMH, WS 1438, Christopher Moran (IRA Fingal), p. 11; WS 371, Robert Holland (IRB member and IRA Dublin), p. 36; WS 1558, Frank McGrath (Commandant IRA Tipperary), p. 156.
173 Stokes, *Death*, p. 1.
174 Lucey, *Cork Public Opinion*, p. 120.
175 *II*, *IT*, 12 October 1918.
176 *IT*, 11 October 1918.
177 *II*, 12 October 1918.
178 *IT*, 11 October 1918.
179 *II*, 14 October 1918.
180 Ibid., 12 October 1918.
181 Ibid., 11 October 1918.
182 Ibid., 12 October 1918.
183 *IT*, 12 October 1918.
184 *II*, 12 October 1918.
185 Ibid., 12, 14, 15, 16, 18, 19 October 1918.
186 Ibid., 18 October 1918.
187 *AC*, 19 October 1918.
188 *II*, 18 October 1918.
189 Philip Lecane, *Torpedoed! The RMS Leinster Disaster* (Cornwall, 2005), p. 86.
190 *CT*, 19 October 1918.
191 A selection of these include Derry Harbour Board, Croom District Council, Clare Asylum Managing Committee, Louth Co. Council, *II*, 15 October 1918; Galway Harbour Commissioners, *CT*, 19 October 1918; and Carrickmacross Guardians, *AC*, 26 October 1918.
192 *CT*, 19 October 1918.
193 Hennessy, 'Ireland and the First World War', p. 151.
194 *II*, 12 October 1918.
195 There were thirteen men with the surname 'Young' living in Galway in 1911, all of whom were Protestant. None had the initials J. S. Only two men in Ireland had these initials in 1911. Neither seems a suitable match.
196 *CT*, 19 October 1918. All men with the initials 'T. McDonagh' or 'McDonogh' living in Galway in 1911 were Catholic.
197 *The Irish Catholic Directory and Almanac for 1919* (Dublin, 1919), pp. 523–4; *AC*, 19 October 1918.
198 *FJ*, *II*, 11 October 1918.
199 *FJ*, 12 October 1918.
200 *AC*, 19 October 1918. For further information on Devlin, see James Loughlin, 'Joseph Devlin', *DIB*.
201 *FJ*, 17 October 1918.
202 *II*, 17 October 1918; the *IT* had established its own appeal before the Lord Mayor's. Following the Mayor's intervention, it made clear that subscriptions should now be sent to the 'national' appeal, *IT*, 16 October 1918.
203 De Wiel, *Catholic Church*, p. 225.
204 *FJ*, 17 October 1918.
205 Nic Dháibhéid, 'Irish National Aid', p. 709.

206  For more information on Walsh, see Morrissey, *William J. Walsh*.
207  Nic Dháibhéid, 'Irish National Aid'.
208  *FJ*, 17 October 1918.
209  *II*, 11 October 1918.
210  All men with the surname 'Kennedy' who lived in Kingstown in 1911 were Catholic. Only one had the initials 'J. J. Kennedy': James Joseph Kennedy, an undertaker and proprietor of his own business. 1911 census, James Joseph Kennedy household.
211  *II*, 15 October 1918. All men with the surname 'Rochford' who lived in Kingstown in 1911 were Catholic. Only one had the initials 'C. Rochford'. There were forty-two men who lived in Kingstown in 1911 with the surname 'O'Brien'; three were Anglican. Two can be eliminated on the basis of age, as they were aged one and three years in 1911. The only potential Anglican candidate was a gardener and domestic servant who does not fit the professional background to have been a member of the affluent Kingstown County Council, so O'Brien must have been a Catholic. 1911 census, Christopher Rochford household.
212  *LL*, 18 October 1918.

## Chapter 5

1  Keith Jeffery (ed.), *An Irish Empire?: Aspects of Ireland and the British Empire* (Manchester, 1996); Kenny, *Ireland and the British Empire* and 'Irish Emigrations in a Comparative Perspective', in Eugenio F. Biagini and Mary E. Daly (eds.), *The Cambridge Social History of Modern Ireland* (Cambridge, 2017), pp. 405–22; Barr, '"Imperium in Imperio"', pp. 611–50.
2  There is no mention of the diaspora in Gregory and Pašeta, *Ireland* and Horne, *Our War*. Works that have explored specific Irish settler groups in wartime include Myles Dungan, *Distant Drums: Irish Soldiers in Foreign Armies* (Belfast, 1993); John Sheen, *Tyneside Irish: 24th, 25th & 26th & 27th (Service) Battalions of the Northumberland Fusiliers: A History of the Tyneside Irish Brigade Raised in the North East in World War One* (Barnsley, 2010) and Jeff Kildea, *Anzacs and Ireland* (Cork, 2007); Committee of the Irish National War Memorial, *Ireland's Memorial Records, 1914-1918: Being the Names of Irishmen Who Fell in the Great European War, 1914-1918* (1923).
3  The title of this section is borrowed from Paul Bew in his study of constitutional nationalists during the Irish Revolution in the article, 'Moderate Nationalism'.
4  Donald Harman Akenson, *The Irish Diaspora: A Primer* (Toronto, 1997), pp. 261–3.
5  Margaret Conrad, *A Concise History of Canada* (New York, 2012), p. 108.
6  Akenson, *Irish diaspora*, p. 102.
7  O'Farrell, *Irish in Australia*, p. 63.
8  Thomas A. O'Donoghue, *Upholding the Faith: The Process of Education in Catholic Schools in Australia, 1922-1965* (New York, 2001), pp. 113–31; Australian Bureau of Statistics, *Australian Historical Population Statistics, Data cube Excel Spreadsheet* (Canberra, 2008), cat. no. 3105.0.65.001.
9  Akenson, *Irish Diaspora*, p. 106.
10  Jeff Kildea, *Tearing the Fabric: Sectarianism in Australia, 1910 to 1925* (Sydney, 2002), p. 1.

11 McGowan, *Waning*, p. 8; Akenson, *Irish Diaspora*, p. 262.
12 Akenson, *Irish Diaspora*, p. 262. Concordia University, 'The Irish in Quebec: Fast Facts'. Available at https://www.concordia.ca/artsci/irish-studies/foundation/irish-in-quebec.html (accessed 09.07.18).
13 Burns, 'Montreal Irish', pp. 77–8.
14 O'Farrell, *Irish in Australia*, pp. 86, 89, 155–6.
15 Debate exists regarding how 'nationalistic' settlers were. For arguments suggesting that settlers lost their interest in Irish nationalism, see Gerald Stortz, 'The Catholic Church and Irish Nationalism in Toronto, 1850-1900', in Robert O'Driscoll and Lorna Reynolds (eds.), *The Untold Story: The Irish in Canada* (Toronto, 1988), pp. 871–2 and McGowan, *Waning*, p. 7. For the opposite, see Mary Hickman, 'Alternative Historiographies of the Irish in Britain: A Critique of the Segregation/Assimilation Model', in Roger Swift and Sheridan Gilley (eds.), *The Irish in Victorian Britain: The Local Dimension* (Dublin, 1999), pp. 236–53.
16 Patrick O'Farrell, *The Catholic Church and Community in Australia: A History* (West Melbourne, 1977).
17 For further reading, see Dáire Keogh and Albert McDonnell, *Cardinal Paul Cullen and His World* (Dublin, 2011) and Oliver Rafferty, *The Church, the State, and the Fenian Threat, 1861-75* (Houndmills, 1999).
18 O'Farrell, *The Catholic Church*, p. 143.
19 Robert McLaughlin, *Irish-Canadian Conflict and the Struggle for Irish Independence, 1912-1925* (Toronto, 2013), p. 62.
20 O'Farrell, *Irish in Australia*, pp. 143–4; McLaughlin, *Irish Canadian Conflict*, p. 62.
21 Alan O'Day, *Irish Home Rule, 1867-1921* (Manchester, 1998); Jackson, *Home Rule*.
22 Finnan, *John Redmond*, p. 157.
23 NLI: MS 15,235/1, Papers of John Redmond, Part III.iii.1., Overseas Series: Australia, 1900–1907; MS 15,235/2, Part III.iii.2., Overseas Series: Canada, 1897–1915; MS 15,235/3 Part III.iii.3., Overseas Series: New Zealand, 1902–1907; MS 15,236/1 Part III.iii.5, Overseas Series: South Africa, 1894–1917; MS 15,236/1 Part III.iii.7., Overseas Series: United States, 1891–1917.
24 Loughlin, 'Joseph Devlin'.
25 Michael Cottrell, 'John Joseph Leddy and the Battle for the Soul of the Catholic Church in the West', *CCHA Historical Studies*, 61 (1995), pp. 41–51.
26 Burns, 'Montreal Irish', p. 69.
27 Letters can be found from Laurier to Redmond in November 1908 and April 1912. Extracts from Laurier's speeches delivered in Canada regarding Irish Home Rule can also be found in Redmond's papers. See the items in the following collections: MS 15,235/2 1897–1915, Section III.iii.2; and MS 15,279/3 [1904], Canada, Section VI, news cuttings concerning John Redmond's political career.
28 Hansard, Great Britain, Parliamentary Debates, Commons, Fifth Series, Colonial Office, Vol. 28, 20 July 1911, Mr Hamar Greenwood, cc 1377-95, cc 1390-91.
29 O'Farrell, *Irish in Australia*; McLaughlin, *Irish-Canadian Conflict*.
30 Cited in McConnel, *The Irish Parliamentary Party*, p. 262.
31 Finnan, *John Redmond*, esp. chapter 5, pp. 154–92.
32 IJA/MSSN/AUST. The schools included St Patrick's (Melbourne), St Francis Xavier College (Kew, Melbourne), St Aloysius (Dunedin, New Zealand), St Aloysius College (Sydney), St Ignatius College (Riverview, Sydney), St Louis (Claremont, Western Australia) and Newman College (University of Melbourne).

33  Patrick O'Farrell, *Letters from Irish Australia 1825-1929* (Sydney, 1984); Miller, *Emigrants and Exiles*; David Fitzpatrick, *Oceans of Consolation: Personal Accounts of Irish Migration to Australia* (London, 1994).

34  Bruce Pennay, 'Meagher, John (1836–1920)', *Australian DB. CE*, 10 August 1914. For the meeting of the Catholic Federation, see *The Freeman's Journal (Sydney)*, 13 August 1914 (hereafter *FJ (Sydney)*).

35  *The Catholic Press (Sydney)*, 13 August 1914, p. 24.

36  'P. J. McDermott. His death', *The Catholic Press*, 16 November 1922; T. P. Boland, 'Duhig, Sir James (1871-1965)', Betty Crouchley, 'Murphy, Peter (1853-1925)', Carolyn Nolan, 'Beirne, Thomas Charles (1860-1949)', *Australian DB*; *The Catholic Press (Sydney)*, 13 August 1914, p. 24.

37  Burns, 'Montreal Irish', p. 68.

38  T. P. O'Connor to C. Murphy, 11 August 1914, quoted in Burns, 'Montreal Irish', p. 69.

39  Adrian Ciani, '"An Imperialist Irishman": Bishop Michael Fallon, the Diocese of London and the Great War', *CCHA Historical Studies*, 74 (2008), pp. 73–94; D. H. Akenson, *The Irish in Ontario: A Study in Rural History* (Kingston and Montreal, 1984), pp. 4, 25–6.

40  Elaine McFarland, '"How the Irish Paid Their Debt": Irish Catholics in Scotland and Voluntary Enlistment, August 1914-July 1915', *The Scottish Historical Review*, 82, 214, part 2 (Oct., 2003), p. 272.

41  NLI: MS 15,257/4, Papers of John Redmond, Part III.i.17, Correspondence of John Redmond, chronological series, 1914-1915, letter from Thomas J. Kenny to John Redmond, 5 August 1914.

42  Burns, 'Montreal Irish', p. 68.

43  Roger Duhamel, *The Regiments and Corps of the Canadian Army* (Ottawa, 1964), p. 197.

44  McFarland, '"How the Irish Paid Their Debt"', p. 272.

45  For further information, see Tim Cook, *Clio's Warriors: Canadian Historians and the Writing of the World Wars* (Vancouver, 2011); Joan Beaumont, *Broken Nation: Australians in the Great War* (Crows Nest, A, 2013).

46  Fitzpatrick, 'Home Front', p. 134.

47  Shipton, *Female Tommies*.

48  Sarah Glassford and Amy J. Shaw, *A Sisterhood of Suffering and Service: Women and Girls of Canada and Newfoundland during the First World War* (Vancouver, 2012).

49  *II*, 22 September 1914. Theodore D. Regehr, 'Shaughnessy, Thomas George 1st Baron Shaughnessy', *Dictionary of Canadian Biography* (hereafter *Canadian DB*).

50  *The Montreal Gazette* (hereafter *MG*), 19 September 1914.

51  Fanning, *Fatal Path*.

52  *FJ (Sydney)*, 24 September 1914.

53  O'Farrell, *Irish in Australia*, p. 173.

54  *FJ (Sydney)*, 29 October 1914.

55  *FJ (Sydney)*, 24 September 1914.

56  NLI: MS 15,257/4, Papers of John Redmond, Part III.i.17, Correspondence of John Redmond, chronological series, 1914–1915, letter from Thomas J. Kenny to John Redmond, 5 August 1914.

57  *AC*, 14 November 1914; *IT*, 19 October 1914.

58  *AC*, 14 November 1914; *II*, 9 November 1914. The figure of 5,000 and 6,000 nationalists was reported by the *FJ*, 9 November 1914.

59  O'Farrell, *Irish in Australia*; Akenson, *Irish in Ontario*.

60  McGowan, *Waning*, p. 5.

61  O'Farrell, *Irish in Australia*, p. 174.

62  Carolyn Lambert, 'This Sacred Feeling: Patriotism, Nation-Building and the Catholic Church in Newfoundland, 1850-1914', in Colin Barr and Hilary M. Carey (eds.), *Religion and Greater Ireland: Christianity and Irish Global Networks 1750-1950* (Montreal, 2015), pp. 124–42.

63  Ciani, '"An Imperialist Irishman"', p. 88. For further information on Doherty, see Hector Charlesworth (ed.), *A Cyclopaedia of Canadian Biography* (Toronto, 1919), p. 156.

64  Ciani, '"An Imperialist Irishman"', p. 73.

65  *MG*, 27 June 1916.

66  For more on the Australian conscription crisis, see Kildea, 'Australian Catholics', pp. 298–313. For further information about Mannix, see Patrick Mannix, *The Belligerent Prelate: An Alliance between Archbishop Daniel Mannix and Eamon de Valera* (Newcastle upon Tyne, 2013).

67  Neville Kingsley Meaney, *Australia and World Crisis, 1914-1923* (Sydney, 2009), p. 207.

68  De Wiel, *Catholic Church*, pp. 246–54, 249.

69  James Griffin, 'Wren, John (1871–1953)', *Australian DB*.

70  Jeff Kildea, 'Australian Catholics and Conscription in the Great War', *The Journal of Religious History*, 26.3 (October, 2002), p. 313.

71  All of the following sources are taken from the *Australian DB*. Patrick O'Farrell, 'Kelly, Michael (1850–1940)'; D. F. Bourke, 'Clune, Patrick Joseph (1864–1935)'; Mary Nicholls, 'Delany, Patrick (1853–1926)'; M. French, 'O'Reily, John (1846–1915)'; Ruth Schumann, 'Spence, Robert William (1860–1934)'; T. P. Boland, 'Duhig, Sir James (1871–1965)'; John N. Molony, 'Carr, Thomas Joseph (1839–1917)'; James Griffin, 'Mannix, Daniel (1864–1963)'; K. M. Manning, 'Dunne, John (1845–1919)'; W. G. McMinn, 'Dwyer, Patrick Vincent (1858–1931)'; McMinn, 'Dwyer, Joseph Wilfrid (1869–1939)'; V. E. Callaghan, 'Gibney, Matthew (1835–1925)'; Frances O'Kane Hale, 'Higgins, Joseph (1838–1915)'; and Griffin, 'Phelan, Patrick (1856–1925)'.

72  *LL*, 20 November 1916, 24 January 1917; *FJ*, 11 January 1918.

73  *LL*, 13 October 1916.

74  Bourke, 'Clune, Patrick Joseph', *Australian DB*.

75  *FJ (Sydney)*, 13 August 1914.

76  Catholic Archdiocese of Sydney (CAS), pastoral letters series 9/027, 'Deeds of administration pastoral letters 1913, 1914 and 1915-1916', Archbishop Michael Kelly pastoral letters 20 December 1914 and Lent 1916.

77  *The Catholic Press*, 28 June 1917.

78  Bede Nairn, 'Meagher, Richard Denis (Dick) (1866–1931)', *Australian DB*; IJA/MSSN/AUST.

79  *The Catholic Press*, 28 June 1917.

80  CAS, pastoral letters series 9/027, 'Deeds of administration pastoral letters 1915-1916', Archbishop Michael Kelly, letter dated 6 October 1916.

81  John K. A. Farrell, 'Michael Francis Fallon Bishop of London Ontario – Canada 1909-1931: The Man and His Controversies', *CCHA Study Sessions*, 35 (1968), pp. 73, 78–9.

82  Ciani, '"An Imperialist Irishman"', pp. 81–2.

83  J. M. Bumsted, 'Davies, Sir Louis Henry', *Canadian DB*; quoted in Burns, 'Montreal Irish', p. 72.

84 *The Catholic Press*, 28 June 1917.

85 Ciani, '"An Imperialist Irishman"', p. 77.

86 *MG*, 27 April 1916.

87 O'Farrell, *Irish in Australia*; Burns, 'Montreal Irish'; McLaughlin, *Irish Canadian Conflict*.

88 Burns, 'Montreal Irish'; for the rebellion, see the following reports: *MG*, 25, 26, 28, 29 April 1916.

89 *MG*, 13, 18 May 1916.

90 For more information on the German mission, see Reinhard R. Doerries, *Prelude to the Easter Rising: Sir Roger Casement in Imperial Germany* (London, 2000).

91 *MG*, 2, 3, 10, 11, 12, 13, 15, 18 May, 12 June 1916.

92 O'Farrell, *Irish in Australia*, p. 265; McLaughlin, *Irish Canadian Conflict*, p. 99.

93 DDA, Papers of Archbishop William Walsh [Laity 1916], Letter to Archbishop Walsh from Montreal citizens, 26 June 1916.

94 Nic Dháibhéid, 'Irish National Aid', pp. 705–29.

95 O'Farrell, *Irish in Australia*, p. 266.

96 Ibid., pp. 259, 265, 274–8.

97 Ibid., p. 254.

98 McLaughlin, *Irish Canadian Conflict*, p. 109.

99 *MG*, 12 June 1916.

100 Burns, 'Montreal Irish', p. 74.

101 For more information on Canadian losses, see Geoffrey Hayes and Andrew Iarocci (eds.), *Vimy Ridge: A Canadian Reassessment* (Ontario, 2007).

102 Burns, 'Montreal Irish', p. 67.

103 Jackson, *Home Rule*, p. 201.

104 De Wiel, *Catholic Church*, p. 253.

105 O'Farrell, *Irish in Australia*, pp. 271–2.

106 Kildea, 'Australian Catholics', esp. pp. 306 ff.

107 Sidney John Roderick Noel, *Politics in Newfoundland* (Toronto, 1971), p. 135.

108 Burns, 'Montreal Irish', p. 80.

109 C. J. Doherty, *The Military Service Act* (Ottawa, 1917), p. 32.

110 In Australia, for example, Redmond's claim was printed in *The Argus*, *The Sydney Morning Herald*, *The Brisbane Courier*, *Examiner* (Launceston, Tasmania), *The Register*, *The Mercury*, *The West Australian*, *The Ballarat Courier*, *Warwick Examiner and Times*, *Zeehan and Dundas Herald*, *Bendigo Advertiser*, 29 January 1917.

111 *IT*, 1 August 2014.

112 Kildea, *Anzacs and Ireland*, pp. 80, 249–50.

113 McGowan, *Waning*, pp. 257, 397.

114 Lambert, 'This Sacred Feeling'.

115 *FJ*, 14 December 1914.

116 McFarland, '"How the Irish Paid Their Debt"', p. 261.

117 IJA, CHP 25, 1–62, 'Letters from military chaplains to the Irish Jesuit Provincial, T. V. Nolan SJ', Fr Henry Gill Papers, letter from Fr Henry Gill to Rev. T. V. Nolan SJ, 4 December 1914.

118 Tom and Seamus Burnell, *The Wicklow War Dead* (Dublin, 2009), pp. 160–2.

119 *FJ*, 17 November 1914.

120 *LL*, 3 November 1916.

121 *The Mungret Annual*, July 1915, IV, 4, p. 380.

122  The Irish-Australian Jesuits included Frs. Michael Bergin, William Gwynn, Joseph
     Hearn, Patrick Tighe, Edward Sydes and F. X. O'Brien. From the Irish Province,
     chaplains who were killed included John Gwynn (12 October 1915), William Doyle
     (17 August 1917), Michael Bergin (12 October 1917) and John Fitzgibbon (18
     September 1918). Austin Hartigan (16 July 1916) and Edward Sydes (15 November
     1918) died from illness. In the English Province, Irish Jesuits killed in the conflict
     included Timothy Carey (Limerick) and Walter Montagu (Cromore, Portstewart,
     Co. Derry). While no Irish Jesuit served in the CEF, Jerome O'Mahony did serve
     in the 5th Canadian General Hospital in Salonika as part of the Mediterranean
     Expeditionary Force during 1916–17. For more information, see Damien Burke,
     'Irish Jesuit Chaplains in the First World War', *Studies: An Irish Quarterly Review*,
     104.414 (2015), pp. 167–75.
123  IJA, CHP 25, 1–62, 'Letters from military chaplains to the Irish Jesuit Provincial,
     T. V. Nolan SJ', Fr McCann Papers, letter from Fr McCann to Fr T. V. Nolan SJ, 27
     March 1917.
124  *CT*, 13 April 1917.
125  Tom Burnell and Margaret Gilbert, *The Wexford War Dead* (Dublin, 2009),
     pp. 260–1. 1911 census, Michael James O'Connor household.
126  Tom Burnell, *The Carlow War Dead: A History of the Casualties of the Great War*
     (Dublin, 2011), pp. 62–3.
127  1911 census, William Doyle household.
128  Mark Cronin, *Blackpool in the First World War: A Cork Suburb and Ireland's Great
     War 1914-1918* (Cork, 2014), p. 17.
129  *MG*, 22 April 1916. These regiments were the Royal Irish Rifles, the Irish Guards, the
     London Irish Rifles, the Connaught Rangers and the North Irish Horse.
130  British Military Badges, 'L55/174 - Tyneside Irish Regiment Cap Badge'. Available at
     http://britishmilitarybadges.co.uk/products/l55174---tyneside-irish-regiment-cap
     -badge.html (accessed 26.07.18).
131  Burns, 'Montreal Irish', p. 71.
132  Robert Craig Brown, 'Hughes, Sir Samuel', *Canadian DB*.
133  Cited in Burns, 'Montreal Irish', p. 72.
134  These religious distributions reflect those of the resident settler-Irish populations
     rather than the entire populations of Quebec and Ontario; for more information on
     Redmondism, see Bew, *Ideology*, pp. 119–52.
135  Kildea, 'Irish Anzacs', p. 4.
136  Hennessey, *Dividing Ireland*; McLaughlin, *Irish Canadian Conflict*, p. 87; Reynolds,
     *Long Shadow*, p. 23.
137  IJA, MSSN/AUST/300-MSSN/AUST 310, 'Australian Mission', letter from Fr Patrick
     F. Tighe to Reverend T. V. Nolan SJ, 7 December 1915.
138  AWM, 3862, Typescript extracts of the diary of Sergeant J. J. Makin, 21st Battalion
     Australian Imperial Force, World War 1914–18, Item 2 of 2.
139  O'Farrell, *Irish in Australia*, p. 174.
140  IJA, CHP 1/9 (9–12), letter from Fr Francis Browne to the Jesuit, Fr T. V. Nolan SJ,
     15 March 1916.
141  IWM, doc. 1776, Private Papers of Major T. D. McCarthy, 17 March 1916.
142  James Wilson, *Up the Micks! An Illustrated History of the Irish Guards* (Barnsley,
     2016), p. 18.
143  1911 census, James Bannon household.

144 AWM, 1DRL/0087, Papers of Gunner John Stanley Bannon and Nicholas Bannon, 'Extracts from letters of Gnr. J. S. Bannon', n/d.

145 NAM, Ms. 7670-61-1, 3 vols, Noel E. Drury, 'My War Diary, 1914-1918', vol. 1, pp. 22–3, 25. A shillelagh was a stick of wood, usually blackthorn or oak.

146 IWM, 14391, T. S. P. Martin, Private Papers of Lieutenant T. S. P. Martin, document entitled 'St Patrick's Day in Egypt'.

147 Armagh County Museum, *'Faugh-a-Ballagh' The Regimental Gazette of The Royal Irish Fusiliers*, XV.80 (October 1914–October 1916), p. 25.

148 1911 census, Thomas Campbell household. Gleeson was one of twelve children from an Irish-speaking Catholic family in rural Tipperary. For more information, see Niall Cummins '"Defend them with their lives": The Political and Spiritual Role of Irish Roman Catholic priests in the British Army 1914-1918', unpublished BA thesis (Trinity College Dublin, 2013), p. 10.

149 *IL*, 20 August 1915, pp. 279–80. 1911 census, Courtenay Moore household.

150 Benedict Anderson, *Imagined Communities: Reflections on the Origin and Spread of Nationalism* (London, 1983).

151 David Feldman, 'Jews and the British Empire, c1900', *History Workshop Journal*, 63.1 (2007), pp. 70–89.

152 The village is recorded as 'Liscasey' in *1911 Census, Munster, Clare*, p. 128.

153 AWM, file 89/1795, Papers of Sergeant D. Scanlon, conflict W1, letter from unnamed family member to John, 27 December 1916.

154 Ibid., letter from Daniel Scanlon to his nephew from Codford, England, 28 January 1917.

155 Ibid., letter from Daniel Scanlon to his niece, Violet, 21 December 1916.

156 E. H. H. Green, 'Law, Andrew Bonar (1858-1923), businessman and prime minister', *Oxford DNB*.

157 Burns, 'Montreal Irish', p. 75.

158 McConnel, *The Irish Parliamentary Party*, p. 306; Townshend, *The Republic*, p. 13; Foster, *Vivid Faces*, p. 264.

159 Robert Kee, *The Green Flag: A History of Irish Nationalism* (London, 2000), p. 591.

160 Conor Mulvagh, 'Sit, act, and vote: the political evolution of the Irish Parliamentary Party at Westminster, 1900-1918', unpublished DPhil thesis (University College Dublin, 2012).

161 Fanning, *Fatal Path*, p. 149.

162 Kee, *Green Flag*, pp. 596–7.

163 Paddy Lysaght, 'Limerick's Bacon Factories', *Old Limerick Journal*, 15 (1980), pp. 10–12.

164 Cousins, *Armagh*, p. 15.

165 Ibid., pp. 13–17.

166 Crosbie, *Irish Imperial Networks*, p. 43 ff; W. A. Maguire, *Belfast: A History* (Lancaster, 2009); Yeates, *A City in Wartime*.

167 Cronin, *Blackpool*, p. 6.

168 Staunton, 'Royal Munster Fusiliers'.

169 Cousins, *Armagh*, p. 16.

170 Dermot Keogh, *Jews in Twentieth-Century Ireland: Refugees, Anti-Semitism and the Holocaust* (Cork, 1998), pp. 26 ff.

171 NA, CO904/102, 'Inspector-General's monthly confidential report for January 1917, together with county inspectors' reports for same period', January–April 1917.

172 BMH, WS 687, Monsignor M. Curran, p. 183.

173 *II*, 2 January 1917; *Nenagh News, IT*, 6 January 1917; *Northern Whig* (hereafter *NW*), *IN*, 10 January 1917; *LO, AC, Nenagh News, LL* 13 January 1917.

174 *LL*, 15 January 1917.

175 *CE*, 30 January 1917.

176 *II*, 26 January 1917.

177 *IT*, 10 January 1917.

178 *NW*, 12 January 1917.

179 *IT*, 10 January 1917.

180 Ibid., 12 January 1917.

181 *LL*, 19 January 1917.

182 *NW*, 19 January 1917.

183 *CE*, 16 January 1917.

184 Dermot and Ann Keogh, *Bertram Windle, the Honan Bequest and the Modernisation of University College Cork, 1904-1919* (Cork, 2010); 1911 census, Francis Levis and Simon Spiro households. Bridget Hourican, 'Horgan, John Joseph', *DIB*. All men living in Cork in 1911 with the initials 'D. Buckley' were Catholics.

185 *IT*, 26 January 1917.

186 A. M. Drysdale, *Canada to Ireland: The Visit of the 'Duchess of Connaught's Own'* (London, 1917), pp. 5–6; *IT*, 27 January 1917.

187 *IT*, 26 January 1917.

188 *LL*, 25 April 1917; *CT*, 14 July 1917.

189 DCA, Volume 2 RDFA/001, location reference g1/01/157, letter from Private Christopher Fox to Monica Roberts, 31 January 1917.

190 *The Toronto World*, 27 January 1917; *The Argus* (Melbourne), 29 January 1917; *The Mercury* (Hobart), 29 January 1917; *Zeehan and Dundas Herald* (West coast Tasmania), 29 January 1917. Also see *The Sydney Morning Herald*, 29 January 1917.

191 For more information see R. B. McDowell, *The Irish Convention, 1917-18* (London, 1970).

192 James Ashe, *The Work before the Irish Convention: A Final Plea for Lasting Conciliation* (Dublin, 1917); *IL*, 8 June 1917.

193 *IL*, 22 June 1917; West, 'Plunkett'; C. J. Woods, 'Gill, Thomas Patrick, *DIB*.

194 Townshend, *Easter 1916*, p. 75.

195 Bryan Mahon, 'Introduction', in Bryan Cooper, *The Tenth (Irish) Division in Gallipoli* (Dublin, 1918), pp. xv–xvii. He later became an Irish senator and prominent advocate for the Irish ex-servicemen's movement.

196 Henry Hanna, *The Pals at Suvla Bay: Being the Record of 'D' Company of the 7th Royal Dublin Fusiliers* (Dublin, 1917), pp. 133–4, 141.

197 1911 census, Alexander Fisher household. *NR*, 14 November 1918.

198 *IT*, 2 August 1918; *IL*, 30 August 1918; *NR*, 6 June, 14 November 1918.

199 Brian M. Walker (ed.), *Parliamentary Election Results in Ireland, 1801-1922* (Dublin, 1978), p. 187.

200 *NR*, 30 November 1918.

201 *NW*, 18 January 1917; 1911 census, William Gallagher and Edward Cowan households. All Patrick O'Neills living in Armagh in 1911 were Catholic except one: a farm labourer.

202 1911 census, James Wilkins and Hans Garmany Leeman households.

203 *IT, NW*, 18 January 1917.

204 *NW*, 29 January 1917.

205 Burns, 'Montreal Irish', p. 71.

206 *MG*, 14 April 1916.

207 *The Irish Canadian Rangers* (Montreal, 1916), p. 24; Kevin James, 'The Saint Patrick's Society of Montreal: Ethno-religious Realignment in a Nineteenth-Century National Society', unpublished MA thesis (McGill, 1997).

208 *II*, 29 January 1917; *The Times* (London), 30 January 1917; *MG*, 1 February 1917. *The Argus, The West Australian, The Register, The Queensland Times, Leader* (NSW), 23 October 1916.

209 *Kilmore Free Press*, 2 November 1916.

210 *The Mercury*, 23 October 1916.

211 *Watchman*, 26 October 1916.

212 *II*, 29 January 1917.

213 For more on Crozier, see Andrew Scholes, *The Church of Ireland and the Third Home Rule Bill* (Dublin, 2010), p. 11.

214 For more information see F. S. L. Lyons, *Culture and Anarchy in Ireland 1890-1939* (Oxford, 1979); Hutchinson, *The Dynamics of Cultural Nationalism*.

215 *II*, 29 January 1917.

216 *IT, II*, 29 January 1917.

217 De Wiel, *Catholic Church*, pp. 166–7.

218 Barr, '"Imperium in Imperio"'. Also see *Ireland's Empire: The Roman Catholic Church in the English-Speaking World, 1829-1914* (Cambridge, 2020).

219 *II*, 29 January 1917.

220 *IT*, 29 January 1917.

221 NA, CO904/102, 'Inspector-General's monthly confidential report for January 1917, together with county inspectors' reports for same period', report for Armagh County.

222 *The Toronto World*, 29 January 1917. Australian newspapers that reported the visit to Armagh included *The Mercury, The Ararat Advertiser, The Ballarat Courier, Bendigo Advertiser, Kalgoorlie Miner, Port Pirie Recorder and North Western Mail, Mount Alexander Mail, Hamilton Spectator*, 30 January 1917; *Western Argus*, 6 February 1917; *The Muswellbrook Chronicle*, 7 February 1917.

223 *IT*, 30 January 1917. 1911 census, Ellen Tiernan and Patrick Dempsey households. For more on McCullagh, see 'Rt. Hon. Sir Crawford McCullagh', *Biographies of Members of the Northern Ireland House of Commons*. Available at http://www.election.demon.co.uk/stormont/biographies.html (accessed 23.07.18).

224 *IT*, 30 January 1917.

225 *NW*, 29 January 1917.

226 *Belfast Telegraph* cited in *MG*, 30 January 1917. The newspaper's proprietor was Robert Hugh Hanley Baird.

227 *NW*, 29 January 1917.

228 *MG*, 30 January 1917.

229 *NW*, 29 January 1917.

230 *The Times* (London), 30 January 1917.

231 *Belfast Evening Telegraph, IN, The Frontier Town, NW*, 31 January 1917. *NW* reprinted the *Frontier Town's* comments.

232 *II*, 30 January 1917.

233 NA, CO904/102, 'Inspector-General's monthly confidential report for January 1917, together with county inspectors' reports for same period', report for Belfast City.

234 *Examiner*, 29 January 1917; *The Argus, The Sydney Morning Herald, The Brisbane Courier, The West Australian, The North Western Advocate and the Emu Bay Times, The Mercury, The Advertiser, Kalgoorlie Miner, The Queensland Times*, 31 January 1917; *Townsville Daily Bulletin, The Northern Miner*, 1 February 1917.

235  *IT*, 12 January 1917.

236  The Peerage, 'James Francis Bernard, 4th Earl of Bandon'. Available at http://
www.thepeerage.com/p7513.htm#c75127 (accessed 10.07.18). Patrick Maume,
'Brodrick, William St John Fremantle', *DIB*.

237  1911 census, Richard Henry Tilson, Arthur Frederick Sharman-Crawford, Thomas
Clifford Butterfield, Kate McNamara, and James George Crosbie households. For
more on Horgan, see Reid, *Lost Ireland*, p. 162. For the other attendees, see *IT*, 12
January 1917.

238  NA, CO904/102, 'Inspector-General's monthly confidential report for January
1917, together with county inspectors' reports for same period', report for Cork
City.

239  *II, IT*, 31 January 1917.

240  *MG*, 1 February 1917.

241  *Quebec Telegraph*, 1 February 1917.

242  *IT*, 31 January 1917.

243  National Film Board of Canada (NFB), 'The Irish Canadian Rangers Visit to Ireland'.
Available at http://www3.nfb.ca/ww1/postwar-film.php?id=538101 (accessed
26.02.14, link no longer working). I contacted the NFB and was told that there is
no archival code for the film and that 'the film is likely being preserved in the NFB's
vaults, but it is no longer commercially available' (email from author to NFB client
services, 12.07.18).

244  NA, CO904/167/1, Press Censorship reports taken from Dublin Castle.

245  BMH: WS 687, Monsignor M. Curran, p. 183.

246  NA, CO904/102, Inspector General to Dublin Castle, in 'Inspector-General's monthly
confidential report for January 1917, together with county inspectors' reports for
same period', pp. 6–7.

247  Population returns cited are for Limerick County Borough. *1911 Census, Munster,
Limerick*, pp. viii, 3.

248  De Wiel, *Catholic Church*, pp. 62–77. For further information on O'Dwyer, see
Thomas J. Morrissey, *Bishop Edward Thomas O'Dwyer of Limerick, 1842-1917*
(Dublin, 2003).

249  *The New York Times*, 18 June 1916.

250  De Wiel, *Catholic Church*, p. 106.

251  *LL*, 19 February 1917.

252  *IT*, 18 January 1917; *LL*, 19 January 1917; *II*, 2 February 1917. 1911 census, James
Quin, Sir Francis Edgar Kearney and William Mont Kidd households.

253  *IT*, 18 January 1917.

254  Andrew Murphy, *Ireland, Reading and Cultural Nationalism, 1790-1930: Bringing the
Nation to Book* (Cambridge, 2018), p. 148.

255  *LL*, 30 March 1963. For more information on musical bands and nationalism in
Limerick, see Tadhg Moloney, *Limerick Constitutional Nationalism, 1898-1918:
Change and Continuity* (Newcastle, 2010), p. 22.

256  *IT*, 2 February 1917.

257  NA, CO904/102, Inspector General to Dublin Castle in 'Inspector-General's monthly
confidential report for January 1917, together with county inspectors' reports for
same period', pp. 6–7.

258  *LL*, 5 February 1917.

259  David George Boyce, *Decolonisation and the British Empire, 1775-1997* (Basingstoke,
1999); McConnel, *The Irish Parliamentary Party*, p. 265.

260 De Wiel, *Catholic Church*, p. 167. The officers were Major Campbell Stuart and
    Captain W. J. Shaughnessy. Shaughnessy was a second generation Irish-Canadian
    whose father was the knighted Chairman of the Canadian Pacific Railway. See
    Regehr, 'Shaughnessy', *Canadian DB*.
261 *Irishman*, 6, 13, 20, 27 January 1917; *Leader*, 6, 13, 20, 27 January, 3 February 1917;
    *The Phoenix*, 6, 13, 20, 27 January, 3 February 1917; *Irish Citizen*, January and
    February, 1917; *Claidheamh Soluis*, 3 February 1917; *The Factionist*, 27 January, 15
    February 1917; *New Ireland*, 6, 13, 20, 27 January, 3 February 1917.
262 For more on the radical press during the war, see Ben Novick, *Conceiving Revolution:
    Irish Nationalist Propaganda during the First World War* (Dublin, 2001).
263 Harrison, *Crowds and History*, p. 4.
264 *FJ*, 10 January 1917.
265 *IT*, 1 February 1917.
266 *IT*, 24 January 1917.
267 *IT*, 3 February 1917.

## Chapter 6

1  Wheatley, *Nationalism*, p. 264; McConnel, *The Irish Parliamentary Party*, p. 306;
   Foster, *Vivid Faces*, p. 264; Townshend, *The Republic*, p. 13.
2  Jeffery, *Ireland*, p. 49; Pašeta, *Irish Nationalist Women*, p. 212; Foster, *Vivid Faces*,
   pp. 217, 224–5. For more on Irish radicals and their relationship with Germany, see
   Doerries, *Prelude*.
3  Pennell, *Kingdom United*.
4  Pennell, 'Going to War', p. 38.
5  Ibid., p. 39.
6  Fitzpatrick, *Politics*, pp. 63–4; Martin, 'Dulce et Decorum', pp. 28–48.
7  *NR*, 6 August 1914.
8  Cousins, *Armagh*, pp. 72–3.
9  Ibid., p. 73; *II*, 6 August 1914.
10 Pennell, *Kingdom United*, pp. 160–2; Jeffrey Verhey, '"War Enthusiasm": Volunteers,
   Departing Soldiers, and Victory Celebrations', in Michael S. Neiberg (ed.), *World War
   I Reader* (New York and London, 2007), pp. 148–57.
11 Martin, 'Dulce et Decorum', p. 43.
12 Fitzpatrick, *Politics*, p. 109.
13 *FJ*, 14 November 1914. Returns are taken from the online 1911 census of Ireland,
   as the printed edition does not list the specific occupations of persons engaged in
   national or local government in Mayo.
14 *CT*, 16 January 1915. Population returns cited are for Athenry DED. For more on
   the Irish Guards, see Rudyard Kipling, *The Irish Guards in the Great War: The Second
   Battalion* (Staplehurst, 1923, repr. 1993).
15 *CT*, 7 January 1916. *1911 Census, Connaught, Galway*, pp. 5, 199.
16 Lucey, 'Cork Public Opinion', p. 51.
17 *II*, 6 August 1914.
18 1911 census, Patrick Carroll Hickey household.
19 All men who lived in Clare whose surname was Lillis in 1911 were listed as
   Roman Catholics in the census of Ireland. An assumption has been made that this
   representative was Thomas Lillis by virtue of his position in local life.

20  *LL*, 12 May 1915. All men who lived in Clare whose surname was Doherty in 1911 were listed as Catholics.

21  *CJ*, 9 March 1916.

22  Charlotte Bennett, 'For God, Country, and Empire? New Zealand and Irish Boys in Elite Secondary Education, 1914-1918', unpublished DPhil thesis (University of Oxford, 2018).

23  *The Belvederian*, IV.1 (summer, 1915).

24  Pašeta, *Before the Revolution*, p. 62; Howie, 'Irish Recruiting and the Home Rule Crisis', p. 22.

25  NLI, MS 15,177/3, Papers of John Redmond, 'Correspondence with Denis J. Coffey', letter from Denis J. Coffey to John Redmond, 7 April 1915.

26  NLI, MS 15,177/3, memo from War Office to Denis J. Coffey, 12 June 1915.

27  These included ten members of staff, 478 students, one surgeon who worked at the Dublin Castle Red Cross Hospital and a surgeon who was serving on the *RMS Lusitania* before its demise on 7 May 1915. At the time of publication, forty-three members of the amalgamated National University of Ireland had been killed during the conflict. The National University of Ireland, *War List: Roll of Honour* (Dublin, 1919), pp. 3–39.

28  UCC, 'Record of students past and present engaged in the war: distinctions gained, deaths: record of the College War Guild, Sphagnum Depot, books for Munsters' soldiers fund, 1914-1919' (Cork, 1919); The National University of Ireland, *War List*, pp. 30–8.

29  1911 census, Patrick J. McNamara and Thomas Linehan households.

30  *The Quarryman*, February 1915, p. 61.

31  Ibid., April 1915, p. 93.

32  1911 census, Bertram Coghill Alan Windle household. Keogh, *Bertram Windle* (Windle's involvement in the war isn't discussed, nor is how the conflict impacted UCC).

33  *The Quarryman*, February 1916, p. 59.

34  Ibid., March 1916, p. 89.

35  Fergus J. M. Campbell, 'The Social Dynamics of Nationalist Politics in the West of Ireland, 1898-1918', *Past & Present*, 182 (February, 2004), pp. 175–209, 184.

36  *CT*, 15 May 1915. 1911 census, Ralph B. Mahon household.

37  Forty-eight members served in the Royal Army Medical Corps and related medical services. A high proportion of UCC and UCD students also assisted the medical services. The National University of Ireland, *War List*, pp. 39–42.

38  *CT*, 3 October 1914. 1911 census, Alexander Anderson household. For more on Anderson, see Patricia M. Byrne, 'Anderson, Alexander', *DIB*.

39  *CT*, 5 January 1916.

40  Henry, *Galway*, pp. 125–6.

41  Lyn MacDonald, *1915: The Death of Innocence* (London, 1993). For more on the 'short-war illusion' and the tension between how military planners and the public conceived of the war's duration, see David Stevenson, *1914-1918: The History of the First World War* (London, 2005).

42  Karsten, 'Suborned or Subordinate?' pp. 31–64.

43  For more about the Munsters in the battles of late 1914, see Jessie Louisa Moore Rickard, *Story of the Munsters at Etreux, Festubert, Rue Du Bois and Hulloch* (London, 1918).

44 The Royal Irish Rifles had eight officers killed in action, seven wounded and one reported missing, as well as 49 wounded men from the ranks. The Royal Dublin Fusiliers suffered 106 wounded men while the Royal Irish Regiment had 46 casualties, *II*, 18, 31 May 1915.

45 NA, W095/4310, 'War Diary 86th Brigade, January 1915 to February 1916, 1st RDF in '86 Infantry Brigade: Headquarters; War Diaries for Jan 1916 not included. Reported ...'. Report by Captain G.W. Geddes, 1st RMF.

46 *II*, 21 May 1915.

47 Alan Osborn (n/d), 'The Diary of Sergeant Denis Joseph Moriarty, No 8308, 1st Royal Munster Fusiliers, 86th Brigade, 29th Division, Expeditionary Force', 1, 8 May 1915. Available at http://ww1.osborn.ws/a-gallipoli-diary (accessed 12.07.18).

48 *II*, 21 May 1915.

49 IWM, doc. 12333, Private Papers of Captain G. W. Nightingale MC, letter from Captain G. W. Nightingale to his mother, 22 May 1915.

50 *II*, 21 May 1915.

51 Orr, *Field of Bones*; Cooper, *The Tenth*.

52 Fitzpatrick, 'Militarism', p. 390; Hanna, *The Pals*.

53 See, for example, David Bilton, *The Trench: The Full Story of the 1st Hull Pals: A History of the 10th (1st Hull) Battalion, East Yorkshire Regiment, 1914-1918* (Barnsley, 2002); Michael Stedman, *Manchester Pals: 16th, 17th, 18th, 19th, 20th, 21st, 22nd & 23rd Battalions of the Manchester Regiment: A History of the Two Manchester Brigades* (Barnsley, 2004); Michael Stedman, *The Somme 1916: & Other Experiences of the Salford Pals: A History of the 15th, 16th, 19th & 20th Battalions Lancashire Fusiliers 1914-1919: A History of the Salford Brigade* (Barnsley, 2006).

54 Fitzpatrick, 'Militarism', p. 390. See, for example, Grayson, *Belfast Boys*; Brett, 'Recollections of C. A. Brett', pp. 2, 7; Hanna, *The Pals*, pp. 131–4; Rev. H. C. Foster, *At Antwerp and the Dardanelles* (London, 1918), p. 11.

55 *IT*, 1 May 1915.

56 Hanna, *The Pals*, p. 31.

57 *II*, 1 May 1915.

58 Ibid., 16 May 1915.

59 Ibid., 14 May 1915.

60 *II*, 20, 23, 25, 26, 27, 28, 30, 31 August 1915; 1, 4, 6, 7 September 1915.

61 IWM, doc. 12333, Private Papers of Captain G. W. Nightingale MC, personal diary entry, n/d/, p. 8.

62 Michael Hickey, *Gallipoli* (London, 1995). Forward p. xi. Also see [no author], 'The Continuity of Learning in Gallipoli'. Available at http://www.greatwar.ie/wp-content/uploads/2016/03/Article-on-learning-in-Gallipoli-forThe-Gallipolian.pdf (accessed 14.07.18), pp. 1–27, 4.

63 John Gibney, 'PALS – The Irish at Gallipoli', *History Ireland*, 23. 3 (2015).

64 David H. Campbell, *Forward the Rifles: The War Diary of an Irish Soldier, 1914-1918* (Dublin, 2009), p. 7. Population and religious returns for Coombe, Merchants Quay DED, were not available in the printed census so have been taken from the digital edition.

65 Tynan, *Years of the Shadow*, p. 178.

66 Fingall, *Seventy Years Young*, p. 360.

67 Campbell, *Forward the Rifles*, pp. 59, 81.

68 Pašeta, 'Thomas Kettle', p. 17.

69  Ward, 'Parallel Lives', p. 35. For more information, see RTE Century Ireland, 'Guides Hill 60 and Croke Park'. Available at https://gallipoli.rte.ie/guides/hill-60-and-croke-park/ (accessed 14.07.18).

70  Tom Johnstone, *Orange, Green and Khaki: The Story of the Irish Regiments in the Great War, 1914-18* (Dublin, 1992), p. 152. This figure does not include non-Irish soldiers, nor does it include Irish soldiers serving in foreign armies, such as the AIF.

71  Ward, 'Parallel Lives', pp. 34–5.

72  Tynan, *Years of the Shadow*, p. 178.

73  NLI, MS 15,190/3, Papers of John Redmond, III.ii. T. P. Gill, letter from the Earl of Granard to T. P. Gill, 12 August 1915; 1911 census, Thomas Patrick Gill household; MS 15,261/9, 'Memorandum of a conversation with the Reverend Father Murphy, Catholic chaplain with the 10th (Irish) Division, just returned from Gallipoli', 10 November 1915.

74  *II*, 6 March 1916.

75  *FJ*, *II*, 6 March 1916.

76  Ward, 'Parallel Lives', p. 34.

77  NLI, MS 15,190/3, letter from the Earl of Granard to T. P. Gill, 12 August 1915.

78  Wanderers' Rugby Club, Dublin, Club House Minute Book [no reference], Committee Report for the year 1915.

79  Ward, 'Parallel Lives'; Michael MacDonagh, *The Irish at the Front* (London, 1916); S. Parnell Kerr, *What the Irish Regiments Have Done* (London, 1916); Cooper, *The Tenth*.

80  *II*, 25 May 1915.

81  *IT*, 4 September 1915.

82  *FJ*, 6 March 1916; *II*, 6 March 1916.

83  *FJ*, 6 March 1916.

84  *II*, 6 March 1916.

85  *FJ*, 6 March 1916.

86  *LL*, 4 February 1916.

87  Sentiments that dwelt on "pride" and "glory in heroic circumstances" were common in many of the letters written by Jesuit military chaplains during the war, and these sentiments were often linked to the Catholic faith.

88  IJA, ADMN 3/7/(2), 'Letters to the provincial superior, T. V. Nolan SJ', letter from Robert Kane, the secretary of the Clongowes Union, to T. V. Nolan, 3 November 1915.

89  1911 census, Conel W. O'Donel Long Alexander household.

90  *The Quarryman* (December, 1915), p. 5.

91  Pašeta, *Before the Revolution*.

92  Wheatley, *Nationalism*, pp. 206, 262–3.

93  *II*, 19 September 1914.

94  *CE*, 19 September 1914.

95  *II*, 21 September 1914. The 'All for Ireland' League was a Munster-based political party established by William O'Brien. It aimed to achieve 'conference, conciliation and consent' within Irish politics, reconciling Irish unionists to an All-Ireland parliamentary settlement. It was an 'irritant' rather than a 'threat' to the IPP, capturing eight seats in the general elections of January and December 1910. Jackson, *Home Rule*, p. 94.

96  *CE*, 19 September 1914.

97  *II*, 21 September 1914.

98  Ibid., 19, 22, 24 September 1914; *CT*, 19 September 1914.

99  *II*, 22 September 1914.

100  Ibid., 22, 24 September 1914.

101  Ibid., 19, 22, 24 September 1914.

102  Belfast Executive UIL, Mid-Armagh Executive of UIL, *II*, 19 September 1914; Dublin UIL and Cork City Executive UIL, *II*, 24 September 1914; Mid Tipperary Executive UIL, Athlone Young Ireland Branch, UIL, Longford District and Urban UIL, *II*, 22 September 1914.

103  Cork City and County AOH, *CE*, 19 September 1914; Galway AOH, *CT*, 10 October 1914; Strokestown AOH, Midleton AOH, Swinford AOH, *II*, 22 September 1914.

104  Drogheda Harbour Commissioners, *II*, 24 September 1914; Lisburn Catholic Club, *II*, 24 September 1914; Limerick Corporation, *II*, 19 September 1914; East Limerick Executive, *CE*, 30 September 1914; Clonakilty Nationalists, *CE*, 19 September 1914; Nationalists of Inns Quay Ward, *II*, 20 September 1914; Louth Nationalists, *II*, 22 September 1914; Miss M. O'Farrell, President Loughrea Volunteer Nursing Corps, *CT*, 3 October 1914.

105  John Privilege, *Michael Logue and the Catholic Church in Ireland, 1879-1925* (Manchester, 2009), p. 92.

106  *II*, 22 September 1914; *CE*, 30 September 1914.

107  *CE*, 19 September 1914.

108  *II*, 20 September 1914.

109  De Wiel, *Catholic Church*, p. 49; *II*, 20, 22 September 1914.

110  *CE*, 19 September 1914.

111  *II*, 20 September 1914.

112  Bew, *Ideology*, p. 122; Wheatley, *Nationalism*, pp. 222–3; Townshend, *Easter 1916*, p. 60; McConnel, 'Recruiting Sergeants', p. 424 and *The Irish Parliamentary Party*, pp. 298–9.

113  Coogan, *Politics*, pp. 61–2; *CJ*, 20 May, 10 June 1915.

114  *IT*, 29 September 1915.

115  Coogan, *Politics*, p. 62.

116  *II*, 1 June 1915.

117  II, 6 August 1915. 1911 census, Edward Kelly household.

118  1911 census, Charles Lacy, Margaret M. Timmon, and John Spicer households.

119  1911 census, Martin McDonagh household.

120  Henry, *Forgotten Heroes*, p. 21.

121  All men with the initials M. Hogan living in Mayo in 1911 were Catholic; 1911 census, Denis Fay household), *IT*, 20 March 1916; Tom Burnell, *The Offaly War Dead* (Dublin, 2010), p. 7.

122  *IT*, 15 March 1915; *IL*, 19 March 1915. 67,814 of the 76,673 persons who lived in the city of Cork were Catholic. *1911 Census, Munster, County and City of Cork*, pp. vi, vii.

123  *IL*, 19 March 1915.

124  1911 census, Hyacinth A. Pelly, David Thos. Barry and Conel W. O'Donel Long Alexander households.

125  *IT*, 27 April 1915. The religious returns for Sligo Urban are not listed in the printed 1911 census, which returns 11,163 persons residing in the DED, Sligo Urban. The online census, which returns 11,167 persons for the DED, Sligo Urban, returns 9,261 Roman Catholics out of this total. *1911 Census, Connaught, Sligo*, p. vi.

126  *IL*, 8 October 1915.

127  Gregory, *Last Great War*, p. 75.

128  *CT*, 11 March 1915.

129 The speaker was either Francis Gubbins JP, an Episcopalian, or Blakeney Gubbins, an Anglican and factory manager, as there were no other men called Gubbins of influential standing in Limerick in the 1911 census.

130 *CT*, 15 May 1915.

131 This was the case for recruitment meetings in Cavan, *IL*, 2 April 1915; Sligo, *IT*, 27 April 1915; Tuam, *CT*, 15 May 1915; and Donabate, Co. Dublin, *II*, 17 May 1915.

132 McConnel, 'Recruiting Sergeants', pp. 416–17.

133 Gregory, *Last Great War*, p. 75.

134 *FJ*, 29 March 1915.

135 The town of Newtownhamilton (also listed as Newtown Hamilton in the printed 1911 census) had a population of 612 persons in 1911. There is no record of the town's religious distribution. The parish of Newtownhamilton had 2,810 persons (1,496 were Catholics). The DED returns 1,369 persons (1,378 on the online census). Of these, the online census states 474 were Catholics, *1911 Census, Ulster, Armagh*, p. 73.

136 Bessbrook Town had 2,888 persons listed in printed 1911 census. There is no record of the religious distribution of the town. Only 285 persons are returned in the online 1911 census, 27 of whom were Catholic, *1911 Census, Ulster, Armagh*, p. 2.

137 Cousins, *Armagh*, p. 39. The county district of Newry Urban and county electoral division of Newry had 11,963 persons living there in 1911. There is no record of the religious distribution of this district. The parish returns for the part of Newry that was in Co. Down listed 16,345 persons, 11,129 of whom were Catholics. The parish returns for the part of Newry that was in Co. Armagh listed 2,113 persons, 1,225 of whom were Catholics. *1911 Census, Ulster, Down*, p. 115, and *Ulster, Armagh*, p. 73.

138 *IL*, 2 April 1915.

139 Coogan, *Politics*, p. 62. 1911 census, Nugent Talbot Everard household.

140 At this time, Patrick Maume has noted that Healy was quite sick having suffered a stroke in 1913. A second stroke in 1916 reduced him to 'senility'. See Maume, 'Healy, John', *DIB*. 1911 census, John Geddes household; *CT*, 15 May 1915. In 1911, 2,980 persons resided in Tuam Town. No religious distribution returns are listed. *1911 Census, Connaught, Galway*, p. 2.

141 The population of Enniscorthy County Electoral Division in 1911 was 7,991, 5,495 of whom resided in Enniscorthy Urban. There is no religious distribution listed for either area. However, the online census of Ireland returns 5,557 persons for Enniscorthy Urban, 5,026 of whom were Catholics. A total of 884 persons resided in Newtownbarry Town as listed in printed 1911 census. The online census returns 964 persons, 828 of whom were Catholics *1911 Census, Leinster, Wexford*, pp. 2, 17.

142 *IT*, 5 June 1915.

143 Gregory, *Last Great War*, p. 77.

144 *IT*, 20 March 1915.

145 Ibid., 27 April 1915.

146 *CT*, 15 May 1915.

147 *CJ*, 22 November 1915.

148 Pennell, *Kingdom United*, p. 179.

149 1911 census, Amy Mary Crosbie and Sarah Maltby households.

150 Ibid., Ignatius E. Harrington household.

151 *IL*, 15 January 1915.

152 1911 census, James Foley household.

153 Ibid., John Spiers household.

154 *IL*, 15 January 1915.

155 1911 census, Alfred Coffey household. There were four children living in Dublin in 1911 with the name Dorothy Martin, three of whom were Catholic. The only Anglican with this name can be eliminated, as she was born in 1911 and therefore would have been too young to have participated in the competition.
156 *1911 Census, Connaught, Mayo*, pp. 3, 123, 143.
157 *IL*, 29 January 1915.
158 1911 census, Robert Blosse Lynch and Timothy F. Kirwan households.
159 1911 census, Patrick J. Quinlan household.
160 Ibid., John Archer Daly households. 1901 census, William Persse household. There were eighteen single females with the surname, 'Brooke', living in Ireland in 1911, five of whom were Catholics. However, three can be excluded on the basis that they were too old to have been the women in this photograph (they were aged fifty, forty-four and forty-eight in 1911), while the two remaining do not fit the socio-economic profile of the other war-workers in this event (one was a domestic servant while the other was a dress maker). Unfortunately Miss Turnley cannot be identified.
161 *IL*, 29 January 1915.
162 *IT*, 8 March 1915.
163 Howie, 'Irish Recruiting and the Home Rule Crisis', p. 22; Novick, 'The Arming of Ireland', pp. 94–112.
164 *CT*, 5 January 1916.
165 *LL*, 21 April 1916.
166 Jackson, *Home Rule*, pp. 172, 150. Some other bodies which thanked Redmond and his acolytes for stopping conscription included UIL and AOH associations (Galway, Young Ireland Limerick branch, Tuam, Ashford Newcastle West, Abbeyfeale, Limerick Hibernians and Shanagolden Hibernians), *CT*, 5, 15 January 1916; *LL*, 7, 24, 26, 28 January, 18 February 1916.
167 F. S. L. Lyons, 'The New Nationalism, 1916-18', in J. R. Hill (ed.), *A New History of Ireland, Volume VI: Ireland Under the Union II, 1870-1921* (Oxford, 1996), pp. 224–39.
168 Keith Jeffery, 'The First World War and the Rising: Mode, Moment and Memory', in G. Doherty and D. Keogh (eds.), *1916: The Long Revolution* (Cork, 2007), pp. 86–101; Richard S. Grayson, *Dublin's Great Wars: The First World War, the Easter Rising and the Irish Revolution* (Cambridge, 2018).
169 Foster, *Vivid Faces*.
170 Jeffery, 'The First World War'.
171 Hennessey, *Dividing Ireland*.
172 Jackson, *Home Rule*, p. 171.
173 Conor Mulvagh, *The Irish Parliamentary Party at Westminster, 1900-18* (Manchester, 2016).
174 *LL*, 9, 11, 13, 14, 16, 18, 27, 30 October and 6, 17 November, 15 December 1916.
175 Organizations affiliated to the IPP included the UIL, AOH, INV and INF. Those aligned with more radical nationalist persuasions included the GAA, the Irish Volunteers and independent associations. NA, CO904 files, 'Confidential monthly reports from the district inspectors of Carlow, Cavan, Clare and the County of Cork to Dublin Castle for the month ending January 1917'.
176 IPP-affiliated organizations included the AOH, UIL, INV and INF, while independent-nationalist associations included Sinn Féin, the Town Tenants League, GAA, Gaelic League, Evicted Tenants' Association, Irish Volunteers and the Labour League, ibid.
177 IPP-affiliated organizations included the AOH, INV, Irish National Boy Scouts and UIL, while independent-nationalist associations included the Irish Volunteers,

Gaelic League, GAA, Young Ireland Society, Sinn Fein Society, Land and Labour Association and the Sinn Féin Club, ibid.

178  Jackson, *Home Rule*, pp. 182–5.

179  Reid, *Lost Ireland*, p. 151.

180  Nic Dháibhéid, 'The Irish National Aid Association', p. 714.

181  Jackson, *Home Rule*, p. 179.

182  Adrian Gregory, '"You Might as Well Recruit Germans": British Public Opinion and the Decision to Conscript the Irish in 1918', in Adrian Gregory and Senia Pašeta (eds.), *Ireland and the Great War: 'A War To Unite Us All?'* (Manchester, 2002), pp. 113, 127.

183  Bew, *Ideology*, p. 389.

184  Reid, *Lost Ireland*, pp. 158–9; Bew, *Ideology*, p. 389; Townshend, *The Republic*, p. 13.

185  Foster, *Vivid Faces*, p. 264; Wheatley, *Nationalism*, p. 264; McConnel, *The Irish Parliamentary Party*, p. 306.

186  Marianne Elliot, *Partners in Revolution: The United Irishmen and France* (New Haven and London, 1982), pp. 10, 16, 26–8, 32–3, 47; Richard English, *Irish Freedom: The History of Nationalism in Ireland* (London, 2006).

187  *Irish Catholic Directory ... 1919*, p. 511.

188  Reid, *Lost Ireland*, p. 161.

189  They included the Protestant and unionist, Sir Maurice Dockrell; an Evangelical Christian from Belfast, Henry McLaughlin; a Catholic lawyer, A. M. Sullivan (who had incidentally defended Roger Casement during his trial for treason in 1916) and Gwynn. Pauric J. Dempsey and Shaun Boylan, 'Dockrell, Sir Maurice Edward', *DIB*; 1911 census, Henry McLaughlin household; Frank Callanan, 'Sullivan, Alexander Martin', *DIB*.

190  *IT*, 26 July, 8, 12 August 1918.

191  Ibid., 15 August 1918.

192  *LL*, 28 August 1918.

193  Ibid., 14 August 1918.

194  *CT*, 20 July 1918.

195  *FJ*, 1 October 1918.

196  Ibid., 1 October 1918.

197  *CT*, 5 October 1918.

198  *FJ*, 28 September 1918.

199  *CT*, 9 June 1917.

200  Ibid., 3 October 1914.

201  *IT*, 20 July 1918; *FJ*, 28 September, 1 October 1918; *CT*, 5 October 1918.

202  *II*, 20 May 1918.

203  These words were highlighted in bold print in the *Independent*, 20 May 1918.

204  Ibid., 20 May 1918.

205  *Dundalk Democrat*, cited in the *LL*, 9 October 1918.

206  *Church of Ireland Gazette*, 31 May 1918.

207  Cited in *II*, 20 May 1918.

208  1911 census, Martin Stephen Redington and Michael Crowley, households.

209  Ibid., Martin Moloney household.

210  *CT*, 20 July 1918.

211  On 9 April 1918, Lloyd George declared in the Commons that 'the Government will, by Order in Council, put the Act: [military service] into immediate operation … Without delay. Meanwhile, we intend to invite Parliament to pass a measure of

self-government in Ireland'. When pressured by Nationalist MPs, the prime minister revealed that the Convention's results would not actually come into operation at all, as he stated that the report was 'not such as to justify the Government in saying that it [r]epresents "substantial agreement". That means that the Government must accept the responsibility of submitting to Parliament, with such guidance as the Convention's Report affords, such proposals for the establishment of self-government in Ireland,' Hansard Great Britain Parliamentary Debates, Commons, Fifth Series, Vol. 104, cc1357-64, The Prime Minister, 1361–2, 09 April 1918.

212  *CT*, 13 July 1918.

213  There were seventy-nine men living in Galway in 1911 with the name 'John Cunningham'. All but one was Catholic, and he can be excluded because he was born in 1911. It is possible that the member cited was not the John Cunningham referred to in the sources, as the proposed candidate lived outside of Galway North in 1911. However, his profession was listed as a 'County Councillor' in the 1911 census.

214  *CT*, 13 July 1918.

215  *AC*, 3 August 1918. 1911 census, Thomas Toal and James J. Coen households.

216  Cousins, *Armagh*, p. 52.

217  Reid, *Lost Ireland*, p. 161.

218  Daniel Todman, *The Great War: Myth and Memory* (London, 2005), p. 27.

219  Urban Cork is defined here as the principal towns within the county of Cork. It includes Cork County Borough, several urban county districts and other principal towns, some of which have populations under 2,000 persons, *1911 Census, Munster, Cork*, p. 45.

220  Lucey, 'Cork Public Opinion', p. 71.

221  Cited in Terence A. Dooley, 'County Monaghan, 1914-1918: Recruitment, the Rise of Sinn Fein and the Partition Crisis', *Clogher Record*, 16.2 (1998), p. 146. Religious returns for urban Monaghan are derived from collating the number of Catholics and Protestants in the four urban districts of Monaghan. *1911 Census, Ulster, Monaghan*, pp. vi, 86.

222  Gregory, *Last Great War*, p. 213.

223  CCCA, B609/9/A/34, diary 1916, 1 January 1916.

224  Ibid., diary 1917, n/d December 1917; Gregory, *Last Great War*, p. 213.

225  Somme Heritage Centre (SHC), E1774, War diary of Rev. John Redmond, 1 January 1917.

226  *CT*, 3 March 1917.

227  *CT*, 22 December 1917.

228  Ibid., 29 December 1917.

229  Tynan, *Years of the Shadow*, p. 146.

230  Jeffery, *Ireland*, pp. 6–8.

231  NA, CO904 files, RIC inspector reports on the conditions of Armagh in January 1917; Dooley, 'County Monaghan', p. 146. Returns given are for urban Armagh. *1911 Census, Ulster, Armagh*, pp. vi, 82.

232  NA, CO904 files, RIC inspector reports on the conditions of Antrim and Down in January 1917. Returns for urban Antrim include the city of Belfast. *1911 Census, Ulster, Antrim*, pp. vi, 131; *City of Belfast*, p. vi; *Down*, pp. vi, 129.

233  Fitzpatrick, 'Home Front', p. 134.

234  Jeffery, *Ireland*, p. 31.

235  Pennell, *Kingdom United*, pp. 72–83.

236 IWM, document 9494, 'Longford District Council address to 5th battalion Royal Irish Regiment, First World War'.

237 Stéphane Audoin-Rouzeau and Annette Becker, *1914-1918 : Understanding the Great War*, trans. Catherine Temerson (London, 2002), p. 107.

238 The Land League was a political organization in the late nineteenth century which aimed to abolish landlordism in Ireland and enable tenant farmers to own the land they cultivated. For further information, see Foster, *Modern Ireland*, pp. 373–99.

239 *CT*, 1 May, 24 April 1915.

240 Ibid., 13 April 1918; Lucey, 'Cork Public Opinion', pp. 104–7.

241 Archive of the Archdiocese of Armagh (AAA), Cardinal Michael Logue Political Folders 6-11, ARCH 9/3/1-18, letter from Bishop O'Donnell to Cardinal Logue, n/d.

242 *The Tuam Herald*, 17 August 1918.

243 Bew, *Ireland*, p. 388.

244 *II*, 20 May 1918.

245 *CT*, 25 May 1918.

246 *Church of Ireland Gazette*, 24 May 1918.

247 *Westmeath Examiner*, 31 August 1918.

248 *LL*, 21 June 1918.

249 *CT*, 25 May 1918.

250 All men with the surname 'Kenneally' living in Clare (and indeed in all of Ireland) in 1911 were Catholic. The 'national' game was hurling, a sport revived by the GAA in the late nineteenth century as part of its effort to promote 'native Irish games', which were bathed in imagined notions of Irishness. For more information, see Paul Rouse, *Sport & Ireland: A History* (Oxford, 2015), pp. 3, 177–81.

251 *LL*, 29 November 1916.

252 Staunton, 'Royal Munster Fusiliers', pp. 201–2.

253 *CT*, 10 November 1917.

254 *LL*, 1 December 1916.

255 *Western People*, June 1917.

256 Coogan, *Politics*, p. 64; Staunton, 'Royal Munster Fusiliers', p. 64.

257 *II*, 12 August 1918.

258 IJA, CHP 1/9 (49), Fr Francis Browne collection, letter from Fr Francis Browne to Fr T. V. Nolan SJ, 8 March 1918.

259 IWM, 14237, Private Papers of Lieutenant-Colonel W. S. Caulfield, p. 183.

260 ICPA, CA/IR/1/5/1-5, 2, Fr Dominic O'Connor collection, letter from Fr Dominic O'Connor to his sister, Sister Constantine O'Connor, n/d.

261 Ibid., 1, letter from Fr Dominic O'Connor to his sister, Sister Constantine O'Connor, n/d but an assumption has been made that it must have been written in April 1918.

262 *The Belvederian* [1917].

263 Ibid., [1918].

264 *CT*, 10 November 1917; DDA, Archbishop William Walsh papers, Memo from University College Dublin Students' Representative Council to Archbishop William Walsh, n/d but sent sometime after 25 January 1918.

265 *LL*, 8 December 1916.

266 UCC, BL/BC/MB/204, Murphy's Brewery Minutes, 30 September 1916–17 February 1917, 25 January 1917.

267 The Women's National Health Association appeared at this meeting under the name *Sláinte* (health), which was the title of the organization's magazine.

268 *IT*, 14 April 1917.

269 Michel S. Neiberg, "'I Want Citizens' Clothes": Irish and German-Americans Respond to War, 1914-1917', in Gearóid Barry, Enrico Dal Lago and Róisín Healy (eds.), *Small Nations and Colonial Peripheries in World War I* (Leiden and Boston, 2016), pp. 37–53.

270 Pennell, *Kingdom United*, p. 68.

271 Ibid., p. 179.

272 Ibid., p. 170.

273 *LL*, 23 December 1914.

274 Pennell, *Kingdom United*, p. 170; Lucey, 'Cork Public Opinion', p. 59.

275 *The Kildare Observer*, 24 October 1914.

276 *II*, 21 January 1918.

277 *IL*, 21 February 1919.

278 AAA, Irish Dioceses Pastoral Letters ARCH 9/3/2, *Pastoral Letter of His Eminence Cardinal Mercier Archbishop of Malines, Primate of Belgium, Christmas 1914* (London, 1914), p. 27.

279 *Irish Catholic Directory and Almanac for 1920* (Dublin, 1920), p. 509.

280 BMH, WS687, Monsignor M. J. Curran, p. 13.

281 Ireland's contribution was beaten by Germany (including the Polish Provinces), the United States and Austria (also including the Polish Provinces). Only three countries other than those mentioned contributed more than 100,000 francs, *Irish Catholic Directory and Almanac for 1918* (Dublin, 1918), p. 498.

282 *IL*, 24 September 1915.

283 Ibid., 5 November 1915.

284 Ibid., 11 April 1916.

285 *IL*, 14 July 1915.

286 Pennell, *Kingdom United*, p. 179.

287 *IL*, 14 July 1915.

288 Irish representatives included T. P. O'Connor (who went in place of John Redmond), Joseph Devlin MP, James Gallagher (the Lord Mayor of Dublin), T. J. Condon MP (Mayor of Clonmel Borough Council, Tipperary), J. Donovan MP (secretary of the INV), John Dillon Nugent (secretary of the AOH and member of the provisional committee of the INV. For more, see Marie Coleman, 'Nugent, John Dillon', *DIB*), Hugh Law MP (an IPP representative who served as secretariat of the Ministry of Munitions in London from 1915 to 1916 and later in the Ministry of Reconstruction in 1918. See Coleman, 'Law, Hugh Alexander', *DIB*), Thomas Scanlan MP (MP for North Sligo and joint secretary of the IPP. See Adam Pole, 'Scanlan, Thomas', *DIB*), T. J. Hanna (secretary to Redmond) and Fr John Mullan (provincial superior of the Passionist Order). Some of the French deputies who received them included Cardinal Leon Adolphe Amette (the Archbishop of Paris), Mr Georges Leygues (who later became president of France in 1920), Léon Bourgeois (former president of France 1895–6 and later president of the Council of the League of Nations, for which he won the Nobel Peace Prize in 1920. At the time of the visit he was president of a senate committee on foreign affairs), René Viviani (the French prime minister), and Théophile Delcassé (minister for foreign affairs) as well as several other representatives of the war ministry. The British ambassador to France, Sir Francis Bertie, was also present.

289 DDA, Archbishop William Walsh papers, Laity [1914] 378/1, booklet entitled 'Perception in Paris of the Irish members of parliament by the French deputies', 30 April and 1 May 1915.

290  De Wiel, *Catholic Church*, p. 150.

291  *II*, 19 May 1917.

292  *The Weekly Irish Times*, 18 December 1915; also reported in the *IT*, 13 December 1915. The second flag day was reported in *IL*, 21 November 1916 and the third, *IL*, 22 June 1917.

293  *The Irish Catholic Directory … 1917*, p. 528–9. The French bishops who visited Ireland included Monseigneur Touchet (Bishop of Orleans), Monseigneur Lenfant (Bishop of Digne), Monseigneur Batiffol (canon of Notre Dame de Paris) and Monseigneur L'Abbé Flynn (parish priest of Suresnes in the diocese of Paris).

294  For further information, see de Wiel, *Catholic Church*, pp. 128–52, 304–24.

295  *CT*, 19 May 1917.

296  Ibid., 31 August 1918.

297  BMH, WS687, p. 86.

298  *FJ*, 31 September 1918.

299  Hennessy, 'Ireland and the First World War', p. 126.

300  Lucey, 'Cork Public Opinion', p. 118.

301  *II*, 16 December 1916.

302  *LL*, 29 December 1916.

303  Audoin-Rouzeau and Becker, *1914-1918*, p. 108.

304  Gregory, *Last Great War*, p. 269.

305  *Connaught Telegraph*, 16 December 1916.

306  *The Kildare Observer*, 23 December 1916.

307  *II*, 13 December 1916.

308  *Irish Catholic Directory … 1918*, p. 506.

309  *The Mercury*, *The Ararat Advertiser* (Victoria), *The Ballarat Courier*, *Bendigo Advertiser*, *Kalgoorlie Miner*, *Port Pirie Recorder* and *North Western Mail* (South Australia), *Mount Alexander Mail* (Victoria), *Hamilton Spectator* (Victoria), 30 January 1917; *Western Argus* (Kalgoorlie), 6 February 1917; *The Muswellbrook Chronicle*, 7 February 1917.

310  *CT*, 11 February 1918.

311  *IT*, 11 February 1918.

312  *CT*, 16 November 1918.

313  John Hutchinson, *The early Reminiscences of a Royal Irish Rifleman 1917-1919* (Belfast, 1986), p. 43.

314  Walsh, *An Englishwoman*, p. 75.

315  *CT*, 16 November 1918.

316  *The Connaught Telegraph*, 16 November 1918; *LL*, 11 November 1918.

317  *II*, 12 November 1918.

318  Walsh, *An Englishwoman*, pp. 77–8.

319  IJA, CHP 1/9 (65), Fr Francis Browne papers, letter from Fr Francis Browne to Fr T. V. Nolan SJ, 13 November 1918; emphasis in original.

320  NA, CO904 files, Inspector General's Monthly Report for November 1918.

321  AAA, Cardinal Michael Logue papers, Hierarchy-meetings-pastoral addresses ARCH 9/3, Meetings of the Hierarchy 1882-1920, Resolution of the Irish Hierarchy regarding the Armistice of 1918, p. 2.

322  *NR*, 14 November 1918.

323  NA, CO904 files, RIC Inspector report for Co. Down for the month November 1918.

324  *Newspaper Press Directory* (London, 1918), p. 202; *The Fermanagh Times*, 21 November 1918.

325 NA, CO904 files, RIC Inspector report for Co. Fermanagh for the month November 1918.
326 *IP*, 16 November 1918.


## Chapter 7

1 For more on the Treaty of Versailles, see Margaret MacMillan, *Peacemakers: The Paris Conference of 1919 and Its Attempt to End War* (London, 2001).
2 *IT*, 30 June 1919.
3 Fanning, *Fatal Path*.
4 Gavin Hughes, *Fighting Irish: The Irish Regiments in the First World War* (Dublin, 2015).
5 James McConnel, 'The Franchise Factor in the Defeat of the Irish Parliamentary Party, 1885-1918', *Historical Journal*, 27.2 (2004), pp. 355-77, 359, 371-3.
6 Pašeta, *Irish Nationalist Women*, p. 250.
7 Ibid.
8 See, for example, Neville Kingsley Meaney, *Australia and World Crisis, 1914-1923: A History of Australian Defence and Foreign Policy, 1901-23: Volume 2* (Sydney, 2009), p. 7.
9 Fitzpatrick, 'Ireland and the Great War', pp. 223-57; Cormac Ó Gráda, '"The Greatest Blessing of All": The Old-Age Pension in Ireland', *Past & Present*, 175 (May 2002), pp. 124-61; Taylor, *Heroes or Traitors*.
10 Eugenio Biagini, 'Review Article: A Long Way to Tipperary: The Irish in the First World War', *The Historical Journal*, 61.2 (2017), p. 534.
11 Pennell, *Kingdom United*, p. 228.


## Chapter 8

1 Adrian Gregory, *The Silence of Memory: Armistice Day 1919-1946* (Oxford, 1994), p. 54.
2 Hart, *The I.R.A.*, p. 312.
3 See, for example, Joost Augusteijn, *The Irish Revolution 1913-1923* (Basingstoke, 2002); Michael Hopkinson, *The Irish War of Independence* (Dublin, 2002); Townshend, *The Republic*, Marie Coleman, *County Longford and the Irish Revolution 1910-1923* (Dublin, 2003), p. 154. For further discussion in this book, see chapter II, 'Politics and Irish Nationalism'. Also see Leonard, 'The Twinge of Memory', p. 99.
4 Hart, *The I.R.A.*, p. 303. For further information on the controversy, see Ian McBride, 'The Peter Hart Affair in Perspective: History, Ideology, and the Irish Revolution', *The Historical Journal*, 61.1 (2018), pp. 249-71.
5 *IT*, 10 November 2018.
6 John Borgonovo, *Spies, Informers and the 'Anti-Sinn Fein Society': The Intelligence War in Cork City, 1920-1921* (Dublin, 1996).
7 Taylor, *Heroes or Traitors*.
8 Shannon Monaghan, 'Whose Country, Whose Soldiers, Whose Responsibility? First World War Ex-Servicemen and the Development of the Irish Free State, 1923-1939', *Contemporary European History*, 23.1 (2014), pp. 75-94.

9   Marguerite Helmers, *Harry Clarke's War: Illustrations for Ireland's Memorial Records* (Dublin, 2016).

10  Leonard, 'The Twinge of Memory', pp. 99–114. Also see *IT*, 12 November 1919. For more information on London's construction of the two minutes' silence, see Gregory, *Silence*, pp. 8–12.

11  *IT*, 12 November 1919, 1920.

12  See, for example, the threatening notices posted in Athlone, *IT*, 10 November 1920.

13  *IT*, 12 November 1923.

14  Peter Cottrell, *The Irish Civil War 1922–1923* (Oxford, 2008), p. 51.

15  For further information on the nervous disorders which Irish veterans experienced, see Joanna Bourke, 'Shell-Shock, Psychiatry and the Irish Soldier during the First World War', in Adrein Gregory and Senia Pašeta, *Ireland and the Great War: 'A War To Unite Us All?'* (Manchester, 2002), pp. 156–68. *IT*, 12 November 1923.

16  Gregory, *Silence*, pp. 28–31.

17  Johnson, *Ireland*, p. 82.

18  Ibid., p. 98.

19  *Longford Leader*, 29 August 1925, cited in Johnson, ibid., p. 100.

20  Johnson, *Ireland*, p. 105.

21  *Nenagh Guardian*, 17 November 1928.

22  Ibid., p. 109; The Office of Public Works, 'The Irish National War Memorial Gardens', document entitled 'Conservation Management Plan'. Available at http://phoenixp ark.ie/wp-content/uploads/2017/08/WM-CMP-PDF.compressed-1.pdf (accessed 14.12.18).

23  Gregory, *Silence*; Leonard V. Smith, Stéphane Audoin-Rouzeau and Annette Becker, *France and the Great War* (Cambridge, 2012), pp. 162 ff.

24  The notable exceptions are from scholars who have explicitly investigated post-war remembrance, including Leonard, 'The Twinge of Memory' and Johnson, *Ireland*.

25  Leonard, 'The Twinge of Memory', p. 102.

26  *LO*, 15 November 1924; *Munster Express*, 19 November 1926.

27  *LO*, 15 November 1924.

28  *Longford Leader*, 29 August 1925, cited in Johnson, ibid., p. 100.

29  *Nenagh Guardian*, 17 November 1928.

30  Taylor, *Heroes or Traitors*, p. 184.

31  Leonard, 'The Twinge of Memory', p. 103.

32  For more information on this change in attitude towards the war, see Paul Fussell, *The Great War and Modern Memory* (Oxford, 1975). Also see Gregory, *Silence*, pp. 118–42.

33  Taylor, *Heroes or Traitors*, pp. 171–219.

34  Johnson, *Ireland*, p. 107; Jeffery, *Ireland*, p. 132.

35  Marianne Elliot, *The Catholics of Ulster* (London, 2000), p. 383.

36  *IT*, 15 November 1924, *The Belfast Newsletter*, 8 November 1927.

37  Diocese of Clogher, 'Enniskillen Hosts Special Events to Mark the Centenary of the Ending of First World War'. Available at http://clogher.anglican.org/News/newseve nt.php?id=734 (accessed 14.12.18).

38  RTE, 'Events around Ireland Mark Centenary of Armistice Day'. Available at https://www.rte.ie/news/ireland/2018/1111/1010146-world-war-one-commemoration/ (accessed 14.12.18).

39  See, for example, 'Woman charged with criminal damage after wreaths thrown in river', *NR*, 5 December 2018. The newspaper also did not report on remembrance services in the town.

# BIBLIOGRAPHY

## *I. Manuscripts*

Owing to the large amount of material consulted during the research for this book I will only list the archives, not the individual collections. Specific references to the individual items are listed in full in the notes.

### *Australia*

Australian War Memorial, Canberra (AWM)
Catholic Archdiocese of Sydney (CAS)

### *England*

Imperial War Museum (IWM)
National Archives (NA)
National Army Museum (NAM)
The British Red Cross Society (BRCS)

### *Ireland*

Archive of the Archdiocese of Armagh (AAA)
Armagh County Museum
Bureau of Military History, Online Archive (BMH)
Cork City and County Archives (CCCA)
Dublin City Archives (DCA)
Dublin Diocesan Archives (DDA)
Irish Capuchin Provincial Archives (ICPA)
Irish Jesuit Archives (IJA)
National Library of Ireland (NLI)
Somme Heritage Centre (SHC)
The Wanderers' Rugby Club
University College Cork (UCC)

## *II. Newspapers and Periodicals*

### America

*New York Times*

## Australia

*Bendigo Advertiser*
*Examiner*
*Hamilton Spectator*
*Kalgoorlie Miner*
*Kilmore Free Press*
*Leader*
*Melbourne Advocate*
*Mount Alexander Mail*
*Port Pirie Recorder and North Western Mail*
*The Advertiser*
*The Ararat Advertiser*
*The Argus*
*The Ballarat Courier*
*The Brisbane Courier*
*The Catholic Press*
*The Freeman's Journal*
*The Mercury*
*The Muswellbrook Chronicle*
*The North Western Advocate and the Emu Bay Times*
*The Northern Miner*
*The Queensland Times*
*The Register*
*The Sydney Morning Herald*
*The West Australian*
*Townsville Daily Bulletin*
*Warwick Examiner and Times*
*Watchman*
*Western Argus*
*Zeehan and Dundas Herald*

## Canada

*New Freeman*
*Quebec Telegraph*
*The Catholic Register*
*The Globe*
*The Montreal Gazette*
*The Toronto World*

## England

*Punch*
*The Illustrated London News*
*The Times*

## Ireland

*Belfast Evening Telegraph*
*Claidheamh Soluis*

*Connacht Tribune*
*Cork Constitution*
*Cork Free Press*
*Dundalk Democrat*
*Irishman*
*Irish Citizen*
*Irish Independent*
*Irish Life*
*Leitrim Observer*
*Limerick Leader*
*Leader*
*Longford Leader*
*Meath Chronicle*
*Munster Express*
*Nenagh Guardian*
*Nenagh News*
*New Ireland*
*Newry Reporter*
*Northern Whig*
*The Anglo-Celt*
*The Belfast Newsletter*
*The Belvederian*
*The Church of Ireland Gazette*
*The Clare Champion*
*The Clongownian*
*The Clare Journal and Ennis Advertiser*
*The Connaught Telegraph*
*The Cork Examiner*
*The Derry Standard*
*The Factionist*
*The Fermanagh Times*
*The Freeman's Journal*
*The Frontier Town*
*The Irish News and Belfast Morning News*
*The Irish Post and Weekly Telegraph for Cavan and the Midlands*
*The Irish Times*
*The Kerryman*
*The Kildare Observer*
*The Mungret Annual*
*The Phoenix*
*The Quarryman*
*The Tuam Herald*
*The Weekly Irish Times*
*Ulster Herald*
*Western People*
*Westmeath Examiner*

## III. Official Publications

Australian Bureau of Statistics, *Australian Historical Population Statistics*. Available at
    http://www.abs.gov.au/AUSSTATS/abs@.nsf/DetailsPage/3105.0.65.0012008?Open
    Document (accessed 23.07.18).
Committee of the Irish National War Memorial (1923), *Ireland's Memorial Records,
    1914–1918: Being the Names of Irishmen Who Fell in the Great European War,
    1914–1918*, Dublin: Maunsel and Roberts.
Hansard, HC, vol. 28, cols. 1377–95, 20 July 1911; vol. 104, cols. 1357–64, 9 April 1918.
    Available at https://www.parliament.uk/ (accessed 22.08.19).
His Majesty's Stationery Office (1912), *Census of Ireland, 1911: Registrar General of Births,
    Deaths and Marriages*, 8 vols, London: His Majesty's Stationery Office.
International Committee of the Red Cross, *International Peace Conference. The
    Hague. Official Record*. Available at https://www.icrc.org/ihl/INTRO/195
    (accessed 08.07.18).
Joint War Committee of the British Red Cross Society and the Order of St. John of
    Jerusalem in England (1921), *Reports by the Joint War Committee and the Joint War
    Finance Committee of the British Red Cross Society and the Order of St. John of Jerusalem
    in England on Voluntary Aid rendered to the Sick and Wounded at Home and Abroad and
    to British Prisoners of War, 1914–1919: With Appendices*, London: H. M. S. O.
Newspaper Press Directory (1918), *Newspaper Press Directory*, London: Benn Bros.
The Army Council (1921), *General Annual Reports on the British Army (Including the
    Territorial Force from the Date of Embodiment) for the Period from 1st October, 1913, to
    30th September, 1919*, London: His Majesty's Stationery Office.
The Irish Catholic Directory (1916–1920), *The Irish Catholic Directory and Almanac*,
    Dublin: James Duffy and Co.
The National University of Ireland (1919), *War List: Roll of Honour*, Dublin: Alex. Thom & Co
    (Limited).

## IV. Published Primary Sources

Aberdeen, Lord and Lady Aberdeen (1925), *'We Twa': Reminiscences of Lord and Lady
    Aberdeen*, London: W. Collins Sons & Co. Ltd.
Ashe, James (1917), *The Work Before the Irish Convention: A Final Plea for Lasting
    Conciliation*, Dublin: Cahill.
Bowser, Thekla (1917), *The Story of British V.A.D. Work in the Great War*, London:
    Andrew Melrose Ltd, reprinted 2003, Imperial War Museum: Dept of Printed Books.
Campbell, David Henry (2009), *Forward the Rifles: The War Diary of an Irish Soldier,
    1914–1918*, Dublin: Nonsuch.
Cooper, Bryan (1918), *The Tenth (Irish) Division in Gallipoli*, reprinted 1993, Dublin: Irish
    Academic Press.
Cullen, Clara (2013), *The World Upturning: Elsie Henry's Irish Wartime Diaries, 1913–1919*,
    Dublin: Merrion.
Daniels, Josephus (1922), *Our Navy at War*, New York: George H. Doran.
Doherty, Charles J. (1917), *The Military Service Act, 1917*, Ottawa: The King's Printer.
Drysdale, A. M. (1917), *Canada to Ireland: The Visit of the 'Duchess of Connaught's Own'*,
    London: T. Fisher Unwin.

Fingall, Elizabeth Mary Margaret Burke Plunkett (1937), *Seventy Years Young, Memories of Elizabeth, Countess of Fingall, Told to Pamela Hinkson*, London: Collins.

Foster, Rev. H. C. (1918), *At Antwerp and the Dardanelles*, London: Mills & Boon Ltd.

Hanna, Henry K. C. (1917), *The Pals at Suvla Bay: Being the Record of 'D' Company of the 7th Royal Dublin Fusiliers*, Dublin: E. Ponsonby Ltd.

Hutchinson, John (1986), *The Early Reminiscences of a Royal Irish Rifleman 1917–1919*, Belfast: The Royal Irish Rangers.

Kerr, S. Parnell (1916), *What the Irish Regiments Have Done*, London: T. F. Unwin Ltd.

Kipling, Rudyard (1923), *The Irish Guards in the Great War: The Second Battalion*, reprinted 1993, Staplehurst: Spellmount.

Lauriat, Charles Emelius (1915), *The Lusitania's Last Voyage: Being a Narrative of the Torpedoing and Sinking of the R.M.S. Lusitania by a German Submarine off the Irish Coast, May 7, 1915 ... With Illustrations*, Boston and New York: Houghton Mifflin Co.

MacDonagh, Michael (1916), *The Irish at the Front*, London: Hodder and Stoughton.

Morison, Elting Elmore (1942), *Admiral Sims and the Modern American Navy*, New York: Russell & Russell.

Osborne, Alan (1915), The Diary of Sergeant Denis Joseph Moriarty, No 8308, 1st Royal Munster Fusiliers, 86th Brigade, 29th Division, Expeditionary Force. Available at http://ww1.osborn.ws/a-gallipoli-diary (accessed 22.08.19).

Owen, David John (1921), *History of Belfast*, Belfast: W. G. Baird.

Rickard, Jessie Louisa Moore (1918), *Story of the Munsters at Etreux, Festubert, Rue Du Bois and Hulloch*, London: Hodder and Stoughton.

The Irish Canadian Rangers (1916), *The Irish Canadian Rangers*, Montreal: Gazette Printing Co. Ltd.

Tynan, Katharine (1919), *The Years of the Shadow*, London: Constable.

Walsh, Oonagh (2000), *An Englishwoman in Belfast: Rosamond Stephen's Record of the Great War*, Cork: Cork University Press.

Whitton, Lieutenant-Colonel Frederick Ernest (1924), *The History of the Prince of Wales's Leinster Regiment (Royal Canadians) – Volume 2*, Aldershot: Gale & Polden, reprinted 2004, Uckfield: The Naval & Military Press.

## V. Websites

Australian Dictionary of Biography

BBC News

British Military Badges

British Pathé

Biographies of Members of the Northern Ireland House of Commons

Casgliad y Werin Cymru: People's Collection Wales

Commonwealth War Graves Commission

Concordia University

Dictionary of Canadian Biography

Dictionary of Irish Biography

Irish Masonic History and the Jewels of Irish Freemasonry

National Archives of Ireland

National Film Board of Canada

National Inventory of Architectural Heritage

Oxford Dictionary of National Biography
Phoenix Park
RTE Century Ireland
RTE News
The Long Long Trail
The Peerage
Trinity College Dublin


## VI. Secondary Literature

Akenson, Donald Harman (1984), *The Irish in Ontario: A Study in Rural History*, Kingston and Montreal: McGill.

Akenson, Donald Harman (1996), *The Irish Diaspora: A Primer*, Belfast and Toronto: Queen's University Press.

Anderson, Benedict (1983), *Imagined Communities: Reflections on the Origin and Spread of Nationalism*, London: Verso.

Barr, Colin (2008), '"Imperium in Imperio": Irish Episcopal Imperialism in the Nineteenth Century', *The English Historical Review*, CXXIII, 502, pp. 611–50.

Barr, Colin (forthcoming), *Ireland's Empire: The Roman Catholic Church in the English-Speaking World, 1829–1914*, Cambridge: Cambridge University Press.

Bartlett, Thomas (2010), *Ireland: A History*, Cambridge: Cambridge University Press.

Bartlett, Thomas and Keith Jeffery (1996), 'An Irish Military Tradition?' in Thomas Bartlett and Keith Jeffery (eds.), *A Military History of Ireland*, Cambridge: Cambridge University Press, pp. 1–25.

Bew, Paul (1994), *Ideology and the Irish Question: Ulster Unionism and Irish Nationalism, 1912–1916*, Oxford and New York: Clarendon Press.

Bew, Paul (1999), 'Moderate Nationalism and the Irish Revolution, 1916–1923', *Historical Journal*, 42, 3, pp. 729–49.

Bew, Paul (2007), *Ireland: The Politics of Enmity*, Oxford: Oxford University Press.

Biagini, Eugenio (2017), 'Review Article: A Long Way to Tipperary: The Irish in the First World War', *The Historical Journal*, 61, 2, pp. 525–39.

Biagini, Eugenio and Mary E. Daly (eds.) (2017), *The Cambridge Social History of Modern Ireland*, Cambridge: Cambridge University Press.

Bingham, Adrian (2010), 'The Digitization of Newspaper Archives: Opportunities and Challenges for Historians', *Twentieth Century British History*, 21, 2, pp. 225–31.

Bond, Brian (1996), 'British "Anti-War" Writers and Their Critics', in Hugh Cecil and Peter H. Liddle (eds.), *Facing Armageddon: The First World War Experienced*, London: Pen & Sword Select, pp. 817–30.

Borgonovo, John (2006), *Spies, Informers and the 'Anti-Sinn Fein Society': The Intelligence War in Cork City, 1920–1921*, Dublin: Irish Academic Press.

Bourke, Joanna (2002), 'Shell Shock, Psychiatry and the Irish Soldier during the First World War', in Adrian Gregory and Senia Pašeta (eds.), *Ireland and the Great War: 'A War To Unite Us All?'* Manchester: Manchester University Press, pp. 156–68.

Bowman, Timothy (1995), 'Composing Divisions: The Recruitment of Ulster and National Volunteers into the British Army in 1914', *Causeway* 2, 1, pp. 24–9.

Bowman, Timothy (1999), 'The Irish Recruiting Campaign and Anti-Recruiting Campaigns, 1914–1918', in Bertrand Taithe and Tim Thornton (eds.), *Propaganda: Political Rhetoric and Identity, 1300–2000*, Glouchestershire: Sutton Pub, pp. 223–38.

Bowman, Timothy (2012), *Carson's Army: The Ulster Volunteer Force, 1910–22*, Manchester: Manchester University Press.

Boyce, David George (1999), *Decolonisation and the British Empire, 1775–1997*, Basingstoke: Macmillan.

Boyce, David George (2002), '"That Party Politics Should Divide Our Tents": Nationalism, Unionism and the First World War', in Adrian Gregory and Senia Pašeta (eds.), *Ireland and the Great War: 'A War to Unite Us All?'* Manchester: Manchester University Press, pp. 190–216.

Burke, Damien (2015), 'Irish Jesuit Chaplains in the First World War', *Studies: An Irish Quarterly Review*, 104, 414, pp. 167–75.

Burnell, Tom and Seamus, Burnell (2009a), *The Wicklow War Dead*, Dublin: Nonsuch.

Burnell, Tom and Seamus, Burnell (2009b), *The Wexford War Dead*, Dublin: Nonsuch.

Burnell, Tom and Seamus, Burnell (2010), *The Offaly War Dead*, Dublin: Nonsuch.

Burnell, Tom and Seamus, Burnell (2011), *The Carlow War Dead: A History of the Casualties of the Great War*, Dublin: History Press Ireland.

Burns, Robin B. (1985), 'The Montreal Irish and the Great War', *CCHA Historical Studies*, 52, pp. 67–81.

Caglioti, Daniela L. (2014), 'Aliens and Internal Enemies: Internment Practices, Economic Exclusion and Property Rights during the First World War', *Journal of Modern European History*, 12, 4, pp. 448–59.

Campbell, Fergus J. M. (2004), 'The Social Dynamics of Nationalist Politics in the West of Ireland, 1898–1918', *Past & Present*, 182 (February edition), pp. 175–209.

Campbell, Fergus J. M. (2005), *Land and Revolution: Nationalist Politics in the West of Ireland 1891–1921*, Oxford: Oxford University Press.

Chambers, John (ed.) (2000), *The Oxford Companion to American Military History*, New York: Oxford University Press.

Ciani, Adrian (2008), '"An Imperialist Irishman": Bishop Michael Fallon, the Diocese of London and the Great War', *CCHA Historical Studies*, 74, pp. 73–94.

Clark, Christopher M. (2012), *The Sleepwalkers: How Europe went to war in 1914*, New York: Allen Lane.

Clear, Catriona (2008), 'Fewer Ladies: More Women', in John Horne (ed.), *Our War: Ireland and the Great War*, Dublin: Royal Irish Academy, pp. 157–80.

Coleman, Marie (2003), *County Longford and the Irish Revolution 1910–1923*, Dublin: Irish Academic Press.

Conrad, Margaret (2012), *A Concise History of Canada*, New York: Cambridge University Press.

Coogan, Oliver (1983), *Politics and War in Meath 1913–23*, Meath: Dunshaughlin.

Cottrell, Michael (1995), 'John Joseph Leddy and the Battle for the Soul of the Catholic Church in the West', *CCHA Historical Studies*, 61, pp. 41–51.

Cottrell, Peter (2008), *The Irish Civil War 1922–1923*, Oxford: Osprey.

Cronin, Mark (2014), *Blackpool in the First World War: A Cork Suburb and Ireland's Great War 1914–1918*, Cork: Collins Press.

Crosbie, Barry (2012), *Irish Imperial Networks: Migration, Social Communication and Exchange in Nineteenth-Century India*, Cambridge: Cambridge University Press.

Cousins, Colin (2011), *Armagh and the Great War*, Dublin: The History Press.

D'Alton, Ian (2010), 'A Protestant Paper for a Protestant People: The *Irish Times* and the Southern Irish minority', *Irish Communications Review*, 12, (2010), pp. 65–73.

Delaney, Enda (2014), 'Migration and Diaspora', in Alvin Jackson (ed.), *The Oxford Handbook of Modern Irish History*, Oxford: Oxford University Press, pp. 126–47.

Denman, Terence (1987a), 'Sir Lawrence Parsons and the Raising of the 16th (Irish) Division, 1914–15', *Irish Sword*, 17, pp. 90–104.

Denman, Terence (1987b), 'The 10th (Irish) Division 1914-15: A Study in Military and Political Interaction', *Irish Sword*, XVII, 66, pp. 16–25.

Denman, Terence (1992), *Ireland's Unknown Soldiers: The 16th (Irish) Division in the Great War, 1914–1918*, Dublin: Irish Academic Press.

Denman, Terence (1994), '"The Red Livery of Shame": The Campaign against Army Recruitment in Ireland, 1899–1914', *Irish Historical Studies*, 29, 114, pp. 208–33.

Dolan, Anne (2003), *Commemorating the Irish Civil War History and Memory, 1923–2000*, Cambridge: Cambridge University Press.

Dooley, Terence A. M. (1998), 'County Monaghan, 1914–1918: Recruitment, the Rise of Sinn Fein and the Partition Crisis', *Clogher Record: Journal of the Clogher Historical Society*, 16, 2, pp. 144–58.

Dooley, Thomas (1995), *Irishmen or English Soldiers: The Times and World of a Southern Irish Man (1876-1916) Enlisting in the British Army During the First World War*, Liverpool: Liverpool University Press.

Downes, Margaret (1988), 'The Civilian Voluntary Aid Effort', in David Fitzpatrick, *Ireland and the First World War*, Dublin: Trinity History Workshop, pp. 27–37.

Duhamel, Roger (1964), *The Regiments and Corps of the Canadian Army*, Ottawa: The Queen's Printer.

Dungan, Myles (1993), *Distant Drums: Irish Soldiers in Foreign Armies*, Belfast: Appletree.

Elliot, Marianne (1982), *Partners in Revolution: The United Irishmen and France*, New Haven and London: Yale University Press.

Elliot, Marianne (2000), *The Catholics of Ulster*, London: Allen Lane.

English, Richard (2006), *Irish Freedom: The History of Nationalism in Ireland*, London: Macmillan.

Fanning, Ronan (2013), *Fatal Path: British Government and Irish Revolution 1910–1922*, London: Faber and Faber.

Farrell, John K. A. (1968), 'Michael Francis Fallon Bishop of London Ontario – Canada 1909–1931 The Man and His Controversies', *CCHA Study Sessions*, 35, pp. 73–90.

Feldman, David (2007), 'Jews and the British Empire, c1900', *History Workshop Journal*, 63, 1, pp. 70–89.

Ferriter, Diarmaid, (2004) *The Transformation of Ireland, 1900-2000*, London: Profile.

Finnan, Joseph P. (2000), '"Let Irishmen Come Together in the Trenches": John Redmond and Irish Party Policy in the Great War 1914–1918', *Irish Sword*, XXII, pp. 174–92.

Finnan, Joseph P. (2004), *John Redmond and Irish Unity, 1912–1918*, New York: Syracuse University Press.

Fitzpatrick, David (1977), *Politics and Irish Life, 1913–1921: Provincial Experience of War and Revolution*, London: Gill & Macmillan.

Fitzpatrick, David (1994), *Oceans of Consolation: Personal Accounts of Irish Migration to Australia*, New York and London: Cornell University Press.

Fitzpatrick, David (1995), 'The Logic of Collective Sacrifice: Ireland and the British Army, 1914–1918', *Historical Journal*, 38, pp. 1017–30.

Fitzpatrick, David (1996), 'Militarism in Ireland 1900-1922', in Thomas Bartlett and Keith Jeffery (eds.), *A Military History of Ireland*, Cambridge: Cambridge University Press, pp. 379–406.

Fitzpatrick, David (2008), 'Home Front and Everyday Life', in John Horne (ed.), *Our War: Ireland and the Great War*, Dublin: Royal Irish Academy, pp. 131–56.

Fitzpatrick, David (2018), 'Ireland and the Great War', in Thomas Bartlett (ed.), *The Cambridge History of Ireland, Volume IV 1880 to the Present*, Cambridge: Cambridge University Press, pp. 223–57.

Foster, Robert Fitzroy (1989), *Modern Ireland 1600–1972*, London: Penguin.

Foster, Robert Fitzroy (2014), *Vivid Faces: The Revolutionary Generation in Ireland, 1890–1923*, London: Allen Lane.

Garvin, Tom (1996), *The Birth of Irish Democracy*, Dublin: Gill and Macmillan.

Gibney, John (2015), 'PALS – The Irish at Gallipoli', *History Ireland*, 3, 23. Available at https://www.historyireland.com/volume-23/pals-the-irish-at-gallipoli/ (accessed 14.07.18).

Glassford, Sarah and Amy J. Shaw (2012), *A Sisterhood of Suffering and Service: Women and Girls of Canada and Newfoundland during the First World War*, Vancouver: UBC Press.

Graham, Brian and Peter Shirlow (2002), 'The Battle of the Somme in Ulster Memory and Identity', *Political Geography*, 21, 7, pp. 881–904.

Grayson, Richard (2009), *Belfast Boys: How Unionists and Nationalists Fought and Died Together in the Great War*, London and New York: Continuum.

Grayson, Richard (2010), 'The Place of the First World War in Contemporary Irish Republicanism in Northern Ireland', *Irish Political Studies*, 25, 3, pp. 325–45.

Grayson, Richard S. (2018), *Dublin's Great Wars: The First World War, the Easter Rising and the Irish Revolution*, Cambridge: Cambridge University Press.

Gregory, Adrian (1998), *The Silence of Memory: Armistice Day 1919–1946*, Oxford: Berg.

Gregory, Adrian (2002), '"You Might as Well Recruit Germans": British Public Opinion and the Decision to Conscript the Irish in 1918', in Adrian Gregory and Senia Pašeta (eds.), *Ireland and the Great War: 'A War to Unite Us All?'* Manchester: Manchester University Press, pp. 113–32.

Gregory, Adrian (2008), *The Last Great War: British Society and the First World War*, Cambridge: Cambridge University Press.

Gregory, Adrian and Senia Pašeta (eds.) (2002), Ireland and the Great War: 'A War to Unite Us All?' Manchester: Manchester University Press.

Grigg, John (1990), 'Nobility and War: The Unselfish Commitment', *Encounter* 74, 2 (March), pp. 21–7.

Gullace, Nicoletta F. (2002), *'The Blood of Our Sons': Men, Women and the Renegotiation of British Citizenship during the Great War*, New York: Palgrave.

Hall, Donal (2005a), *The Unreturned Army: County Louth Dead in the Great War, 1914–1918*, Dundalk: County Louth Archaeological and Historical Society.

Hall, Donal (2005b), *World War I and Nationalist Politics in County Louth, 1914-1920*, Dublin: Four Courts.

Harris, Jose (2003), 'Introduction: Civil Society in British History: Paradigm or Peculiarity?' in Jose Harris (ed.), *Civil Society in British History: Ideas, Identities, Institutions*, Oxford: Oxford University Press, pp. 1–12.

Harrison, Mark (1988), *Crowds and History: Mass Phenomena in English Towns, 1790–1835*, Cambridge: Cambridge University Press.

Hart, Peter (1998), *The I.R.A. and Its Enemies: Violence and Community in Cork, 1916–1923*, Oxford: Clarendon.

Healy, Maureen (2004), *Vienna and the Fall of the Habsburg Empire: Total War and Everyday Life in World War One*, Cambridge: Cambridge University Press.

Helmers, Marguerite (2016), *Harry Clarke's War: Illustrations for Ireland's Memorial Records*, Dublin: Irish Academic Press.

Hennessey, Thomas (1998), *Dividing Ireland: World War I and Partition*, London: Routledge.

Hennessey, Thomas (2009), 'The Evolution of Ulster Protestant Identity in the Twentieth Century: Nations and Patriotism', in Mervyn A. Busteed, Frank Neal and Jonathan Tonge (eds.), *Irish Protestant Identities*, Manchester: Manchester University Press, pp. 257–69.

Henry, William (2006), *Galway and the Great War*, Cork: Mercier Press.

Henry, William (2007), *Forgotten Heroes: Galway Soldiers of the Great War 1914–1918*, Cork: Mercier Press.

Hickey, Michael (1995), *Gallipoli*, London: John Murray Ltd.

Horne, John (1997), *State, Society and Mobilization in Europe during the First World War*, Cambridge: Cambridge University Press.

Horne, John (2008), 'Foreword' and 'Our War, Our History', in John Horne (ed.), *Our War: Ireland and the Great War*, Dublin: Royal Irish Academy, pp. ix–xv, 1–34.

Horne, John and Edward Madigan (eds.) (2013), *Towards Commemoration: Ireland in War and Revolution, 1912–23*, Dublin: Royal Irish Academy.

Howie, David and Josephine Howie (1996), 'Irish Recruiting and the Home Rule Crisis of August-September 1914', in Michael Dockrill and David French (eds.), *Strategy and Intelligence: British Policy during the First World War*, London: Hambledon Press, pp. 1–22.

Hughes, Gavin (2015), *Fighting Irish: The Irish Regiments in the First World War*, Dublin: Merrion Press.

Jackson, Alvin (2003), *Home Rule: An Irish History, 1800–2000*, London: Weidenfeld & Nicolson.

Jeffery, Keith (1996), 'The Irish Military Tradition and the British Empire', in Keith Jeffery (ed.), *'An Irish Empire?' Aspects of Ireland and the British Empire*, Manchester: Manchester University Press.

Jeffery, Keith (2000), *Ireland and the Great War*, Cambridge: Cambridge University Press.

Jeffery, Keith (2004), 'Gallipoli and Ireland', in Jenny McLeod (ed.), *Gallipoli: Making History*, London: Frank Cass, pp. 98–109.

Jeffery, Keith (2007), 'The First World War and the Rising: Mode, Moment and Memory', in Gabriel Doherty and Dermot Keogh (eds.), *1916: The Long Revolution*, Cork: Mercier Press, pp. 86–101.

Jeffery, Keith (2013), 'Irish Varieties of Great War Commemoration', in John Horne and Edward Madigan (eds.), *Towards Commemoration: Ireland in War and Revolution, 1912–23*, Dublin: Royal Irish Academy, pp. 117–25.

Jeffery, Keith (2015), *1916 A Global History*, London: Bloomsbury.

Johnson, Nuala (2003), *Ireland, the Great War and the Geography of Remembrance*, Cambridge: Cambridge University Press.

Johnstone, Tom (1992), *Orange, Green and Khaki: The Story of the Irish Regiments in the Great War, 1914–18*, Dublin: Gill and Macmillan.

Karsten, Peter (1983), 'Irish Soldiers in the British Army, 1792–1922: Suborned or Subordinate?' *Journal of Social History*, XVII, pp. 31–64.

Kautt, William H. (2010), *Ambushes and Armour: The Irish Rebellion 1919-21*, Dublin: Irish Academic Press.

Kee, Robert (2000), *The Green Flag: A History of Irish Nationalism*, London: Penguin.

Kennedy, Dennis (1988), *The Widening Gulf: Northern Attitudes to the Independent Irish State, 1919-49*, Belfast: Blackstaff.

Kenny, Colum (2012), 'Tom Grehan: Advertising Pioneer and Newspaperman', in Mark O'Brien and Kevin Rafter (eds.), *Independent Newspapers: A History*, Dublin: Four Courts Press, pp. 52–66.

Kenny, Kevin (ed.) (2004), *Ireland and the British Empire*, Oxford: Oxford University Press.

Kenny, Kevin (2017), 'Irish Emigrations in a Comparative Perspective', in Eugenio Biagini and Mary E. Daly (eds.), *The Cambridge Social History of Modern Ireland*, Cambridge: Cambridge University Press.

Keogh, Dáire (1998), *Jews in Twentieth-Century Ireland: Refugees, Anti-Semitism and the Holocaust*, Cork: Cork University Press.

Keogh, Dáire and Albert McDonnell (eds.) (2011), *Cardinal Paul Cullen and His World*, Dublin: Four Courts.

Keogh, Dermot and Ann Keogh (2010), *Bertram Windle, the Honan Bequest and the Modernisation of University College Cork, 1904–1919*, Cork: Cork University Press.

Kildea, Jeff (2002a), 'Australian Catholics and Conscription in the Great War', *The Journal of Religious History*, 26, 3, (October edition), pp. 298–313.

Kildea, Jeff (2002b), *Tearing the Fabric: Sectarianism in Australia, 1910 to 1925*, Sydney: Citadel.

Kildea, Jeff (2007), *Anzacs and Ireland*, Cork: Cork University Press.

Laffan, Michael (1983), *The Partition of Ireland, 1911–25*, Dundalk: Dundalgan Press.

Lambert, Carolyn (2015), 'This Sacred Feeling: Patriotism, Nation-Building and the Catholic Church in Newfoundland, 1850–1914', in Colin Barr and Hilary M. Carey (eds.), *Religion and Greater Ireland: Christianity and Irish Global Networks 1750–1950*, Montreal: McGill-Queen's University Press, pp. 124–42.

Lane, Fintan (ed.) (2010), *Politics, Society and the Middle Class in Modern Ireland*, Basingstoke: Macmillan.

Lecane, Philip (2005), *Torpedoed! The RMS Leinster Disaster*, Cornwall: Periscope Publishing Ltd.

Leonard, Jane (1996), 'The Twinge of Memory: Armistice Day and Remembrance Sunday in Dublin since 1919', in Richard English and Graham Walker (eds.), *Unionism in Modern Ireland: New Perspectives on Politics and Culture*, Basingstoke: Macmillan, pp. 99–114.

Lyons, F. S. L. (1996), 'The New Nationalism, 1916–18', in J. R. Hill (ed.), *A New History of Ireland VI: Ireland under the Union II, 1870-1921*, Oxford: Oxford University Press, pp. 224–39.

Lysaght, Paddy (1980), 'Limerick's Bacon Factories', *Old Limerick Journal*, 15 (1980), pp. 10–12.

MacDonald, Lyn (1993), *1915: The Death of Innocence*, London: Headline.

Maguire, William A. (2009), *Belfast: A History*, Lancaster: Carnegie Publishing.

Martin, Francis Xavier (1967), '1916 – Myth, Fact and Mystery', *Studia Hibernica*, 7, pp. 7–126.

Martin, Peter (2002), '"Dulce et Decorum": Irish Nobles and the Great War, 1914–19', in Adrian Gregory and Senia Pašeta (eds.), *Ireland and the Great War: 'A War to Unite Us All?'* Manchester: Manchester University Press, pp. 28–48.

Martin, Thomas (2006), *The Kingdom in the Empire: A Portrait of Kerry during World War One*, Dublin: Nonsuch.

Matthew, Henry Colin Gray and Brian Harrison (eds.), (2004), *Oxford Dictionary of National Biography: From the Earliest Times to the Year 2000*, revised edition, Oxford: Oxford University Press in association with the British Academy. Available at https://www.oxforddnb.com/.

McConnel, James (2004), 'The Franchise Factor in the Defeat of the Irish Parliamentary Party, 1885–1918', *Historical Journal*, 27, 2, pp. 355–77.

McConnel, James (2007), 'Recruiting Sergeants for John Bull? Irish Nationalist MPs and Enlistment during the Early Months of the Great War', *War in History*, 14, 4, pp. 408–28.

McConnel, James (2010), 'John Redmond and Irish Catholic Loyalism', *English Historical Review*, CXXV, 512, pp. 83–111.

McConnel, James (2013), *The Irish Parliamentary Party and the Third Home Rule Crisis*, Dublin: Four Courts Press.

McEwen, Yvonne (2006), *It's a Long Way to Tipperary: British and Irish Nurses in the Great War*, Dunfermline: Cualann Press.

McFarland, Elaine (2003), '"How the Irish Paid Their Debt": Irish Catholics in Scotland and Voluntary Enlistment, August 1914–July 1915', *The Scottish Historical Review*, 82, 214, part 2 (October edition), pp. 261–84.

McGowan, Mark G. (1999), *The Waning of the Green: Catholics, the Irish, and Identity in Toronto, 1887–1922*, Montreal and London: McGill University Press.

McGuire, James and James Quin (eds.), (2009–2013), *Dictionary of Irish Biography: From the Earliest Times to the Year 2002*, Cambridge: Cambridge University Press: Royal Irish Academy. Available at https://dib.cambridge.org/.

McLaughlin, Robert (2013), *Irish Canadian Conflict and the Struggle for Irish Independence, 1912–1925*, Toronto: University of Toronto Press.

Meaney, Neville Kingsley (2009), *Australia and World Crisis, 1914–1923*, Sydney: Sydney University Press.

Miller, Kerby (1985), *Emigrants and Exiles: Ireland and the Irish Exodus to North America*, New York and Oxford: Oxford University Press.

Mitchell, Gardiner (1991), *'Three Cheers for the Derrys!' A History of the 10th Royal Inniskilling Fusiliers in the 1914–18 War*, Derry: Yes! Publications.

Monaghan, Shannon (2014), 'Whose Country, Whose Soldiers, Whose Responsibility? First World War Ex-Servicemen and the Development of the Irish Free State, 1923–1939', *Contemporary European History*, 23, 1, pp. 75–94.

Morrissey, Thomas J. (2000), *William J. Walsh, Archbishop of Dublin, 1841–1921*, Dublin: Four Courts.

Morrissey, Thomas J. (2003), *Bishop Edward Thomas O'Dwyer of Limerick, 1842–1917*, Dublin: Four Courts.

Mulvagh, Conor (2016), *The Irish Parliamentary Party at Westminster*, Manchester: Manchester University Press.

Murphy, Andrew (2018), *Ireland, Reading and Cultural Nationalism, 1790-1930: Bringing the Nation to Book*, Cambridge: Cambridge University Press.

Nairn, Bede and Geoffrey Serle (eds.) (1979–1986), *Australian Dictionary of Biography*, Melbourne: Melbourne University Press, vols. 7–10.

Neiberg, Michel S. (2016), '"I Want Citizens' Clothes": Irish and German-Americans Respond to War, 1914–1917', in Gearóid Barry, Enrico Dal Lago and Róisín Healy (eds.), *Small Nations and Colonial Peripheries in World War I*, Leiden and Boston: Brill, pp. 37–53.

Nic Dháibhéid, Caoimhe (2012), 'The Irish National Aid Association and the Radicalization of Public Opinion in Ireland, 1916–1918', *The Historical Journal*, 55, pp. 705–29.

Noel, Sidney John Roderick (1971), *Politics in Newfoundland*, Toronto: University of Toronto Press.

Nolan, Liam and John E. Nolan (2009), *Secret Victory: Ireland and the War at Sea, 1914–1918*, Cork: Mercier Press.

Novick, Ben (1997), 'DORA, Suppression, and Nationalist Propaganda in Ireland, 1914–1915', *New Hibernia Review*, 1, 4, pp. 41–57.

Novick, Ben (1999), 'The Advanced Nationalist Response to Atrocities Propaganda, 1914–1918', in Lawrence W. McBride (ed.), *Images, Icons and the Irish Nationalist Imagination*, Dublin: Four Courts, pp. 130–47.

Novick, Ben (2001), *Conceiving Revolution: Irish Nationalist Propaganda during the First World War*, Dublin: Four Courts Press.

Novick, Ben (2002), 'The Arming of Ireland: Gun Running and the Great War, 1914–1916', in Adrian Gregory and Senia Pašeta (eds.), *Ireland and the Great War: 'A War to Unite Us All?'* Manchester: Manchester University Press, pp. 94–112.

O'Donoghue, Thomas (2001), *Upholding The Faith: The Process of Education in Catholic Schools in Australia, 1922–1965*, New York: P. Lang.

O'Farrell, Patrick (1977), *The Catholic Church and Community in Australia: A History*, West Melbourne: Nelson.

O'Farrell, Patrick (1984), *Letters from Irish Australia 1825–1929*, Sydney: New South Wales University Press.

O'Farrell, Patrick (1993), *The Irish in Australia: 1788 to the Present*, Sydney: New South Wales University Press.

Ó Gráda, Cormac (2002), '"The Greatest Blessing of All": The Old-Age Pension in Ireland', *Past & Present*, 175 (May), pp. 124–61.

O'Sullivan, Patrick (2000), *The Lusitania: Unravelling the Mysteries*, Staplehurst: Spellmount.

Orr, Philip (1987), *The Road to the Somme: Men of the Ulster Division Tell Their Story*, Belfast: Blackstaff Press.

Orr, Philip (2006), *Field of Bones: An Irish Division at Gallipoli*, Dublin: The Lilliput Press.

Paddock, Troy R. E. (2004), *A Call to Arms: Propaganda, Public Opinion and Newspapers in the Great War*, London: Praeger Publishers.

Pašeta, Senia (1999), *Before the Revolution: Nationalism, Social Change and Ireland's Catholic Elite, 1879–1922*, Cork: Cork University Press.

Pašeta, Senia (2002), 'Thomas Kettle: "An Irish Soldier in the Army of Europe?"' in Adrian Gregory and Senia Pašeta (eds.), *Ireland and the Great War: 'A War to Unite Us All?'* Manchester: Manchester University Press, pp. 8–27.

Pašeta, Senia (2013), *Irish Nationalist Women, 1900–1918*, Cambridge: Cambridge University Press.

Pennell, Catriona (2008), 'Going to War', in John Horne (ed.), *Our War: Ireland and the Great War*, Dublin: Royal Irish Academy, pp. 35–62.

Pennell, Catriona (2012), *A Kingdom United: Popular Responses to the Outbreak of the First World War in Britain and Ireland*, Oxford: Oxford University Press.

Privilege, John (2009), *Michael Logue and the Catholic Church in Ireland, 1879–1925*, Manchester: Manchester University Press.

Pugh, Martin (1978), *Electoral Reform in War and Peace, 1906–18*, London: Routledge.

Purcell, Mary (1987), *To Africa with Love: The Life of Mother Mary Martin, Foundress of the Medical Missionaries of Mary*, Dublin: Gill and Macmillan.

Reid, Colin (2010), 'Stephen Gwynn and the Failure of Constitutional Nationalism in Ireland, 1919–1921', *The Historical Journal*, 53, 3, pp. 723–45.

Reid, Colin (2011), *The Lost Ireland of Stephen Gwynn: Irish Constitutional Nationalism and Cultural Politics, 1864–1950*, Manchester: Manchester University Press.

Reilly, Eileen (2002), 'Women and Voluntary War Work', in Adrian Gregory and Senia Pašeta (eds.), *Ireland and the Great War: 'A War to Unite Us All?'* Manchester: Manchester University Press, pp. 49–72.

Reynolds, David (2013), *The Long Shadow: The Great War and the Twentieth Century*, London: Simon & Schuster.

Richardson, Neil (2015), *According to Their Lights: Stories of Irishmen in the British Army, Easter 1916*, Dublin: The Collins Press.

Ritchie, John (ed.) (1990), *Australian Dictionary of Biography*, Melbourne: Melbourne University Press, vol. 12.

Rouzeau, Stephane Audoin and Annette Becker (2002), *1914–1918: Understanding the Great War*, trans. Catherine Temerson, London: Profile Books.

Scholes, Andrew (2010), *The Church of Ireland and the Third Home Rule Bill*, Dublin: Irish Academic Press.

Serle, Geoffrey (ed.) (1988), *Australian Dictionary of Biography*, Melbourne: Melbourne University Press, vol. 11.

Shipton, Elisabeth (2014), *Female Tommies: The Frontline Women of the First World War*, Glouchestershire: The History Press.

Simkins, Peter (1988), *Kitchener's Army: The Raising of the New Armies, 1914–16*, Manchester: Manchester University Press.

Smith, Leonard V., Stéphane Audoin-Rouzeau and Annette Becker (2012), *France and the Great War*, Cambridge: Cambridge University Press.

Stokes, Roy (1998), *Death in the Irish Sea: The Sinking of the RMS Leinster*, Cork: Collins Press.

Taylor, Paul (2015), *Heroes or Traitors? Experiences of Southern Irish Soldiers Returning from the Great War 1919–1939*, Liverpool: Liverpool University Press.

Todman, Dan (2005), *The Great War: Myth and Memory*, London: Hambledon and London.

Townshend, Charles (1999), *Ireland: The Twentieth Century*, London: Arnold.

Townshend, Charles (2005), *Easter 1916: The Irish Rebellion*, London: Allen Lane.

Townshend, Charles (2013), *The Republic: The Fight for Irish Independence, 1918–1923*, London: Allen Lane.

Urquhart, Diane (2000), *Women in Ulster Politics, 1890–1940*, Dublin: Irish Academic Press.

Verhey, Jeffrey (2007), '"War Enthusiasm" Volunteers, Departing Soldiers, and Victory Celebrations', in Michael S. Neiberg (ed.), *World War I Reader*, New York and London: New York University Press, pp. 148–57.

Walker, Brian M. (ed.) (1978), *Parliamentary Election Results in Ireland, 1801–1922*, Dublin: Royal Irish Academy.

Ward, Eilís (1996), 'A Big Show-off to Show What We Can Do: Ireland and the Hungarian Refugee Crisis', *Irish Studies in International Affairs*, 7, pp. 131–41.

Ward, Stuart (2013), 'Parallel Lives, Poles Apart: Commemorating Gallipoli in Ireland and Australia', in John Horne and Edward Madigan (eds.), *Towards Commemoration: Ireland in War and Revolution, 1912–1923*, Dublin: Royal Irish Academy, pp. 29–37.

Wheatley, Michael (2005), *Nationalism and the Irish Party: Provincial Ireland 1910–1916*, Oxford: Oxford University Press.

White, Gerry and Brendan O'Shea (eds.) (2010), *A Great Sacrifice: Cork Servicemen Who Died in the Great War*, Cork: Echo Publications.

Wiel, Jérôme aan de (2003), *The Catholic Church in Ireland, 1914–1918: War and Politics*, Dublin: Irish Academic Press.

Wilson, James (2016), *Up the Micks! An Illustrated History of the Irish Guards*, Barnsley: Pen & Sword.

Wilson, Peter H. (2001), 'The Origins of Prussian Militarism', *History Today*, 51, 5.
    Available at http://www.historytoday.com/peter-h-wilson/origins-prussian-militarism
    (accessed 08.07.18).
Wilson, Trevor (1986), *The Myriad Faces of War: Britain and the Great War, 1914–1918*,
    Cambridge: Polity Press.
Winter, Jay M. (1995), *Sites of Memory, Sites of Mourning: The Great War in European
    Cultural History*, Cambridge: Cambridge University Press.
Winter, Jay M. and Jean-Louis Robert (eds.) (1997–2007), *Capital Cities at War: Paris,
    London, Berlin, 1914–1919*, 2 vols, Cambridge: Cambridge University Press.
Yeates, Pádraig (2011), *A City in Wartime: Dublin, 1919–21*, Dublin: Gill & Macmillan.

## VII. Unpublished Theses and Papers

Bennett, Charlotte (2018), 'For God, Country, and Empire? New Zealand and Irish Boys
    in Elite Secondary Education, 1914–1918', unpublished DPhil thesis, University of
    Oxford.
Hennessy, David (2004), 'Ireland and the First World War: A Cork Perspective',
    unpublished MPhil thesis, National University of Ireland, University College Cork.
James, Kevin (1997), 'The Saint Patrick's Society of Montreal: Ethno-religious Realignment
    in a Nineteenth-Century National Society', unpublished MA thesis, McGill University,
    Montreal.
Lucey, Dermot (1972), 'Cork Public Opinion and the First World War', unpublished MA
    thesis, University College Cork.
Lynch, Patrick (2009), 'The Irish Soldiers and Sailors Land Trust', unpublished MLitt
    thesis, University College Dublin.
Mulvagh, Conor (2012), 'Sit, Act, and Vote: The Political Evolution of the Irish
    Parliamentary Party at Westminster, 1900–1918', unpublished DPhil thesis, University
    College Dublin.
Staunton, M. (1986), 'The Royal Munster Fusiliers in the Great War, 1914–19', unpublished
    MA thesis, National University of Ireland, University College Dublin.

# INDEX

Aberdeen, Lady Ishbel    32–4, 37–8
academics and the war effort    52, 116,
    133–4, 140, 143
advanced nationalism, *see also* Sinn Féin
    advanced nationalist press    64–5, 127
    anti-English/British sentiment    54,
        64–5, 82–3, 158–9, 163, 165, 171
    anti-war    5, 22 127, 163–5, 175
    and Germany (*see* Germany)
    and moderate nationalist press    80–1,
        87, 153, 164–6
    women (*see* Cumann na mBan;
        suffrage)
agricultural production
    as national duty    28, 77, 81–3, 90, 139,
        172–3
    tillage schemes    74–9, 81, 89
Alexander, William (Archbishop of
    Armagh)    88
Allies, the    15, 105, 112, 140, 175,
    *see also* Catholic Church; individual
        countries
    discourse    63, 98, 125, 136, 138–40,
        147, 157, 162, 164–5
    flag and visual displays    70, 144,
        146–7, 163–4, 168
    fundraising for    30, 48–9, 56–8 72,
        128, 162–3, 172
    losses at sea    61, 81, 85–6, 90
    nationalist opposition    20, 25, 82, 125,
        138, 159–60
    press support    72, 89, 136, 147, 153,
        165–6
    public support    61, 70–1, 90, 98, 154,
        157, 165, 169
    war-relief    30–1, 39, 131, 159, 164
ambulance associations    32–3, 39, 45, 96
America, *see* United States of America
Ancient Order of Hibernians    93–4, 96,
    141
Anglicans    8, 11, 153, 158, 181, 183

cross-confessional cooperation    49,
    85, 89, 116–17, 119, 145
Anglo-Irish, the    8, 46, 53, 158
Anglo-Irish War    1, 19, 26, 100, 102, 161,
    177–8
anti-war, *see also* advanced nationalism
    activism    20, 25, 54–5, 82
    attitudes    5, 34, 83, 127, 131, 151
Antrim    35, 44, 63, 156
Arklow and Avoca War Hospital Supply
    Depot    41–2
Armagh    114, 141
    cross-confessional cooperation    132,
        145
    Irish-Canadian Rangers    114, 118–19,
        121, 125, 166
    recruitment    145, 156
    refugees in    47–8
    war-relief    53–4, 85, 112
Armenian genocide    139
Armistice Day    167–8, 171
    commemoration of    3–4, 17, 137,
        178–83
Asquith, Herbert (Prime Minister)    24,
    97
Athlone    75, 141, 178
Australia
    Irish diaspora    9, 91–8, 102–6,
        111–12, 123, 176
    recruitment    29, 99, 106–7, 109, 111,
        156, 175
    war effort    19, 99–101, 113, 138, 166
Australian and New Zealand Army Corps
    (ANZAC)    19, 102
Australian Imperial Force (AIF)    100,
    102, 107–9, 111–12
Austria-Hungary    25, 62

Bandon, Lord James Bernard    123
Battalion
    Australian Imperial Force, 21st    111

Australian Imperial Force, 49th   112

Canadian Expeditionary Force, 199th
   (Irish-Canadian Rangers)   109

Canadian Expeditionary Force,
   9th   96

Cheshire, 13th   109

Leinster, 6th   33

Royal Dublin Fusiliers, 1st   135

Royal Dublin Fusiliers, 6th   111, 136

Royal Dublin Fusiliers, 7th   136-7

Royal Irish, 1st and 2nd   32

Royal Irish, 4th (Extra Reserve)   67

Royal Irish, 5th (Service)   157

Royal Irish Fusiliers, 2nd   49

Royal Irish Fusiliers, 5th   136

Royal Irish Rifles, 4th   132

Royal Munster Fusiliers, 1st   46, 83,
   135

Royal Munster Fusiliers, 2nd   112,
   134

Royal Munster Fusiliers, 7th   136

South African Infantry, 5th   108

Belfast
   impact of war   27-8, 75, 89, 167-8
   Irish-Canadian Rangers   114-15,
      121-2, 125, 128
   war-relief   44, 48-9, 85, 162

Belgium   19, 25, 146-7
   Belgian Refugees' Committee   40, 48,
      50, 121, 162
   Catholic Church in Ireland   27, 35
   German atrocities   66, 71, 102, 144
   German invasion   27, 34, 64, 139,
      145-6, 162
   refugees in Ireland   12, 35-7, 47-51,
      98, 145, 163, 172

*Belvederian, The*   133, 161

Bethmann-Hollweg, Theobald von
   (Chancellor of Germany)   64

Black and Tans   1, 178

Boer War   26, 31, 111, 117, 127

Bonar Law, Andrew   79, 113

Borden, Robert (Prime Minister of
   Canada)   99, 109, 113

Brigade
   Field Artillery, 2nd (Australian
      Imperial Force)   111
   Tyneside Irish   108-9

Britain, *see also* United Kingdom

military service acts   29, 148, 150-4,
   156 (*see also* conscription)

recruitment   22-30, 68, 108, 142-5,
   155, 173

shipping losses   61, 63, 82-5

Union Flag (*see* Union Flag)

as unworthy Ally   15, 138, 158-9, 162,
   165-6, 169

war effort   79, 81, 131-2, 134-5, 150,
   155, 157 (*see also* UK countries)

Westminster   9, 12, 21, 23-5, 79, 81,
   94

Westminster, nationalist opposition
   towards   54-5, 151-5, 166-9,
   173, 175, 178-9 (*see also* advanced
   nationalism)

as worthy Ally   5, 20, 146-8

British Empire
   and Catholic Church, Irish   93, 97,
      99, 120
   Catholic Irish loyalty to   14, 58, 94-9,
      103-7, 147
   Home Rule   21, 148
   and Ireland   114, 117-21, 123, 129,
      156, 166
   Irish diaspora   9, 90-1, 108-13, 175-6
      (*see also* individual countries)
   Irish nationalism   22, 26, 99-100,
      103-5, 126-7, 176
   Ulster Unionist loyalty to   58, 121-2

British Legion Society   2

British Red Cross Society (BRCS), *see* Red
   Cross

Browne, James (Bishop of Ferns)   74

Browne, Robert (Bishop of Cloyne)   69,
   74, 139, 142, 160

Butterfield, Thomas (Lord Mayor of
   Cork 1916-18)   41, 66, 115, 123,
   128

Canada
   Irish diaspora   91-5, 98-9, 103-5,
      112, 120, 176
   recruitment   29, 96, 99, 105-9, 121,
      156, 175
   war effort   55, 105-6, 134, 163

Canadian Expeditionary Force
   (CEF)   96, 107-9, 113

Carlow   40, 53, 149, 152

Carr, Thomas (Archbishop of
    Melbourne)   102
Carson, Sir Edward   21, 23–4, 121
Casement, Roger   104
Catholic and Protestant collaboration
    military units   49, 112, 117, 135–6
        (*see also* Irish-Canadian Rangers)
    recruitment   109–10, 117, 134,
        143–5
    remembrance   2–4, 179, 181–3
    shared celebrations   100–1, 111–12,
        131–2, 147–8, 167–9, 176
    war-relief   11, 14, 30–3, 38, 40–4, 85,
        146–7 (*see also* Red Cross; Ulster
        and relevant counties)
Catholic Church   70, 93, 114, *see also*
        Allied countries
    anti-conscription   25, 150–1
    anti-German sentiment   85, 102–3,
        139, 144–6, 158, 165
    hierarchy and war   25, 74, 99, 120,
        138–9, 173 (*see also* individual
        prelates)
    Irish clerics and recruitment   34,
        95–6, 99, 117–18, 138, 145–6, 158
    Irish clerics and war effort   34–5, 40,
        47–8, 52, 85, 95, 111, 125
    lenten pastorals   12, 74, 76, 102, 139,
        163, 167
    lenten pastorals and pacifism   125,
        138
    lenten pastorals and righteousness of
        Allied cause   102, 139, 167
    military chaplains (*see* chaplains)
    remembrance   178, 180–2
    support for Allies   103, 139, 167
        (*see also* the Allies)
Cavan   149, 168, 174
    war effort   49–53
    Women's Patriotic Committee
        (CCWPC)   49–52
censorship   12, 87, 124, 127, 136
centenary, *see* remembrance
chaplains
    letters (*see* letter-writing)
    war service   102, 115, 117, 138, 155,
        160
Cherry, Richard (Chief Justice of
    Ireland)   32

children
    child refugees   35–6, 47
    died at sea   64, 68–9, 89
    at remembrance events   1, 181
    in war-relief   30, 48, 146
Churchill, Winston (First Lord of the
    Admiralty)   63, 134
Church of Ireland, *see* Anglicans
Clare
    anti-recruitment   148–9, 152
    war effort   3, 112–13, 132, 142, 159,
        168
    war-relief   35, 39, 53, 55, 78
Clune, Patrick (Archbishop of
    Perth)   102
Cobh, *see* Queenstown (Cobh)
Coffey, Denis (President of University
    College Dublin)   89, 133
Cohalan, Daniel (Bishop of Cork)   115,
    124
Commonwealth War Graves Commission
    (CWGC)   26
*Connacht Tribune*
    supporting soldiers   132, 160, 165,
        167
    on the war at sea   63, 66, 72, 75, 84–5,
        87
Connaught Rangers   45, 58, 108, 134,
    148
conscription
    1918 conscription crisis   42, 56, 87,
        165, 172–3, 178
    compared with voluntary
        enlistment   29, 142–3, 148, 153–6,
        174
    in the diaspora   99, 102, 106–7, 156,
        175
    fear of   76, 106, 142–3, 149–56
    nationalist opposition   24–5, 89,
        149–51, 158–9, 168, 175–6
constitutional nationalism, *see* moderate
    nationalism
convalescent homes   32, 37, 39
Cork
    anti-war sentiment   82–3
    and the Empire   9, 102, 109, 114
    food production   74–5, 77–8
    Irish-Canadian Rangers   115–16,
        123–5, 128

Irish nationalism 140–1, 149, 158, 165–6, 174, 177
medical relief-work 33, 39, 43–4
refugees 35–6, 162
remembrance 1–4, 171–2, 178–80, 183
the war at sea 61–8, 70, 84–5, 87–8
war effort 132–3, 143–4, 155, 168, 176
war-relief 53, 55, 58, 146–7, 160–1, 164
Cork Western Front Association 1, 4
Cosgrave, Ephraim MacDowell (President of the Royal College of Physicians) 37–8
Council for the Organization of Recruitment in Ireland (CCORI) 142–3
County Cavan Women's Patriotic Committee (CCWPC) 49–52
Crawford, Lord David Lindsay 79
Cromwell, Oliver (memory of) 66, 146
Crozier, John Baptist (Archbishop of Armagh) 89, 119, 166
Cullen, Cardinal Paul 93
Cumann na mBan 33, 141
Cumann na nGaedheal 178
Curran, Monsignor Michael 34, 114–15, 124, 163, 165

Dardanelles 39, 45, 111, 117, 134–40
Suvla Bay 19, 135, 137–8, 172
Delany, Patrick (Archbishop of Hobart) 102
Department of Agriculture and Technical Instruction (DATI) 32, 51, 55, 77–8, 117
Derry 66, 88, 99, 141, 178
war effort 27, 54, 75, 132, 139
Desart, Lord Hamilton Cuffe 78
Devlin, Joseph (MP) 89, 93
Division
Irish, 10th 18–19, 26, 111, 117, 135–8, 172
Irish, 16th 3, 18–19, 23, 26, 44, 153
Ulster, 36th 17–19, 23, 26
Welsh, 38th 26
Doherty, Charles (Minister of Justice, Canada) 99, 107

Dominions, *see also* relevant countries
Dominion forces 9, 12, 91, 108
Irish diaspora 11, 14, 91–8, 105, 176
recruitment (*see* recruitment)
support for Home Rule (*see* Home Rule)
war effort 29, 58–9, 91, 102, 156, 176
Donegal 53, 55, 67, 75, 141
Donnelly, Nicholas (auxiliary bishop of Dublin) 33–4
Down
cross-confessional cooperation 117, 121, 132, 145, 168
war-relief 35, 47–8, 53–4
Drogheda 2, 57, 75–6, 141, 178
Dublin
anti-German sentiment 62
and the Easter Rising 91, 148, 151, 156, 158
and the Empire 94, 99, 103–4, 114
food production 74–6, 78
Irish-Canadian Rangers 114–16, 121, 125, 128
Irish nationalism 140–1, 151, 160, 171, 174
medical aid 32–3, 37–41, 44–6, 161
remembrance 3–4, 17, 178, 180–1, 183
war at sea 67, 71–3, 85, 87–9
war effort 22, 28, 135–8, 152, 163–4, 176
war-relief 35–6, 43, 52–4, 56, 146, 150
Dublin Castle 37, 45, 104, 140, 152
censorship reports 12, 124, 127
Red Cross Hospital (*see* Red Cross)
Dublin rebellion, *see* Easter Rising
Duhig, James (Archbishop of Brisbane) 95, 102
Dundalk 2, 36, 67, 141, 145, 153
Dungannon 75, 141, 182
Dunne, John (Bishop of Bathurst) 102
Dunraven, Lord Windham Wyndham-Quin 112, 125
Dwyer, Joseph Wilfrid (Bishop of Wagga Wagga) 102
Dwyer, Patrick Vincent (Bishop of Maitland) 102

Dwyer, Sir Conway (President of the Royal College of Surgeons)  33, 37

Easter Rising  148–9, *see also* Britain
  effect of Rising  30, 40, 52, 105, 113, 156
  execution of Dublin rebels  23, 91, 100, 104, 151, 158
  memory of  17, 19–20, 137
  before the Rising  11, 14, 148, 164
  and Westminster  54, 113, 149, 175
Edinburgh  37, 95–6, 108
educational institutions  6, 12
  schools  47, 49–50, 133, 139, 161
  Trinity College Dublin  18, 73, 137, 171
  University College Cork  133, 139–40, 143
  University College Dublin  133, 161
  University College Galway  134, 161
Edward VII, King  31
England  62
  historical legacy in Ireland  66, 103–5, 142, 146, 162
  nationalist distrust of  55, 64–5, 73, 154, 159–60, 165–6
  war effort  22, 28, 78, 96, 98
  war losses  62–3, 72, 81, 84
  war-relief  31, 55–7, 89, 163
enlistment, *see* recruitment
Ennis  71–2, 113, 142, 148, 159–60
Enniskillen  17, 75, 132, 179, 182–3
Etreux, Battle of  134

Fallon, Michael (Bishop of London [Ontario])  95, 99, 103
Fermanagh  17, 53, 75, 132, 168, 182
Fianna Fáil  178, 181–2
Finegan, Patrick (Bishop of Kilmore)  49, 74, 77
Fingall, Countess Elizabeth Burke-Plunkett  32, 41–2, 66, 86, 137
fishing industry  66, 84–5, 90
Fitzpatrick, Sir Charles (Chief Justice of the Supreme Court of Canada)  103–4
flag days  58, 163–4
Fogarty, Michael (Bishop of Killaloe)  74, 142

Foley, Patrick (Bishop of Kildare and Leighlin)  74, 76–7, 139, 142
France  163
  experience of war  37, 56, 64, 134, 165–6
  historic relationship with nationalists  23, 37, 146, 164–5
  Irish war-relief for  58, 146–7, 164
  recruitment missions to Ireland  165
French, Sir John (Lord Lieutenant of Ireland)  89, 116, 152–3

Gaelic Athletic Association (GAA)  137
Gaelic language  55, 85, 99, 119, 125
Gaelic League  137
Gallagher, James and Annie (Lord Mayor and mayoress of Dublin)  41, 115–16, 121, 128
Gallipoli, *see* Dardanelles
Galway  167
  food production  75–7
  Irish diaspora  88, 102, 109
  nationalist sentiment  116, 134, 141, 148–9, 152, 174
  recruitment  22, 132, 143, 145, 152–4, 168
  support for soldiers  157, 160–1, 165, 183
  war at sea  71–2, 84–5, 88
  war-relief  32, 35, 40, 53, 58
Gaughran, Laurence (Bishop of Meath)  77
George V, King  98, 152, 169
German plot  158–9
Germany  48, 153, 157, 169, 181
  and advanced nationalists  22, 62, 87, 105
  citizens in Ireland  61–2
  defeat of  20, 166, 168, 171
  German threat  120, 129, 139, 144–6, 150, 172
  invasion of Belgium  27, 34–5, 144–6, 162
  and Irish nationalism  64–5, 104, 131, 158–9, 165–6, 175
  peace proposal  166
  perceived barbarism  15, 63–8, 73, 84–90, 102–3, 134, 145

pro-German sentiments 62, 105, 158, 165
war at sea 14, 30, 61–8, 72–5, 79, 81–90, 176
Gibney, Matthew (Bishop of Perth) 102
Gilmartin, Thomas (Bishop of Clonfert) 74, 139, 142, 158, 167
Ginchy, Battle of 153, 161
Glasgow 37, 96, 98, 108
Granard, Lord Bernard Forbes 138, 180
Griffith, Arthur 62, 169
Guillemont, Battle of 153
Gwynn, Captain Stephen (MP) 23, 89, 134, 152–3

Hague Conventions 64
Hamilton, Sir Ian 138
Harrison, Henry (MP) 33
Harty, John (Archbishop of Cashel) 74, 141–2
Healy, John (Archbishop of Tuam) 139, 145
Henry, Elsie 53–6, 78
Hibernian Australasian Catholic Benefit Society 97, 103
Higgins, Joseph (Bishop of Rockhampton) 102
Higgins, Michael D. (President of Ireland) 19, 183
Hoare, Joseph (Bishop of Ardagh and Clonmacnoise) 74
Home Rule 21, 40, 98, 140, *see also* Irish Parliamentary Party
  compared with submarine 79–81
  diasporic support for 94–9, 104–6, 172
  opposition towards 21, 23–4, 34, 97, 113–14, 117, 121, 140, 149–50
  passage of bill 96–9, 140–2, 173
  and recruitment 104–5, 147–8, 152, 154, 159
  waning fortunes 24–5, 29, 79–80, 105–6, 113–14, 149–52, 154, 158–9
  and war effort 21, 23–5, 95, 97–8
Horgan, John J. 66, 116, 123, 180
hospitals 37–9, 41–6, 53, 55, *see also* Dublin Castle
  charitable donations 34, 37–9, 164
  civilian casualties 67, 88

War Hospital Supply Depots 51–2
  and women 34, 37–9, 41–2, 45–6
House of Commons 95–6, 102
House of Lords 41, 78
Howley, Michael Francis (Archbishop of St. John's [Newfoundland]) 99
Hughes, Billy (Prime Minister of Australia) 100
Hughes, Sam (Minister of Militia and Defence of Canada) 109, 121

influenza 23, 167
interwar period 15, 137, 177–8
  remembrance 2–3, 17, 171, 180, 182
Ireland's Memorial Records 91, 178
Irish-Canadian Rangers 99, 107, 113–14, 166
  and Irish unity 91, 109, 127–9, 176
  recruitment 103, 105, 109
  tour the southern provinces 115–17, 123–6
  tour Ulster 118–22
Irish Convention 117, 149–50, 154
Irish Independent 11, 132
  Irish-Canadian Rangers 115, 120, 123
  war at sea 65, 80, 89
Irish Midlands 22, 33, 66, 72, 140, 143
Irish National Aid Association and Volunteer Dependants' Fund (INAVDF) 72, 89, 104, 150
Irish National Defence Fund 89
Irish National Foresters (INF) 95, 103
Irish National Volunteers (INV) 21–2, 27–8, 70, 145, 158, 162
Irish Parliamentary Party (IPP) 11, 18, 21, 71
  ambivalence to war effort 21–6
  competition from Sinn Féin 74, 113–15, 149–51, 167, 173
  diasporic support 93–7, 104–7
  election losses 20–1, 123, 127, 150, 174
  fundraising for 91, 94, 174
  Home Rule 11, 29, 141–2, 148–9 (*see also* Home Rule)
  MPs in forces 23, 27, 33, 44, 88–9, 102–3, 152–3, 169

newspaper attitudes towards 11, 93,
115, 167
support for war effort 18, 21, 27, 76,
89, 131–2
Irish Recruiting Council (IRC) 152–5,
157
Irish Republican Army (IRA) 17, 19,
177, 181
Irish Sea 63, 81–6, 88
Irish soldiers in the Great War 83
British Army 17–19, 23, 28–9, 108,
160–1, 173
civilian support 44, 58, 160, 164, 177
gift-giving of Shamrocks 111–12,
123, 176
Irish symbolism in the forces 26, 99,
109, 111–12, 147
losses 19, 36, 88, 134–5
*Irish Times, The* 138, 179
Irish-Canadian Rangers 115, 121,
123, 125, 128
supporting war effort 58, 74, 77, 89,
136, 147
war at sea 65–6, 72, 79–80, 87, 89
Irish women 12, 46, 117
in the Dominions 96–7, 176
medical assistance 96, 39, 42,
52–5 (*see also* Voluntary Aid
Detachment)
nurses 32–4, 38–45, 55, 90, 147,
161–2
other war-work 14, 30–1, 39, 44, 47
titled ladies and wives of peers 33,
38, 40–2, 49, 72, 180
wives of academics 48, 55, 133
wives of government officials 32, 41
wives of mayors 41
wives of MPs 49
wives of professionals 40, 47–8, 50–1,
55, 87, 146
wives of servicemen 32
working classes 2–4, 54–5, 59, 71–3,
123, 128, 135, 143, 167
Italy 55, 163–5

Jesuits 12, 36, 94, 103, 108, 111, 160
Jews 36, 112, 114, 116
Johnston, James (Lord Mayor of
Belfast) 115, 122

Joint War Committee 31, 39, 43, *see also*
Red Cross

Kelly, Denis (Bishop of Ross) 74
Kelly, Michael (Archbishop of
Sydney) 12, 102–3
Kenneally, Peter. E. 72, 159
Kerry 160, 168
anti-war-work behaviour 54
war at sea 64, 67, 71–2, 84
war-relief 39–40, 42–3, 53–5, 59, 78
Kettle, Tom (MP) 27, 153
Kildare 142
anti-German sentiment 71, 139, 162,
166
war effort 28, 74–5, 77, 143
war-relief 35, 39–40, 53, 162
Kilkenny 39–40, 67, 102, 109, 183
nationalist sentiment 141, 168
Killanin, Lord Martin Morris 85
King, loyalty to the 98, 140, 146, 169,
176
God Save the King 97, 116, 119,
152–3
King's County (Offaly) 22, 53, 85, 143
Kitchener's New Army 17, 44, 77, 97,
136
Knights of Columbus 94, 103

Laois, *see* Queen's County (Laois)
Laurier, Wilfrid (Prime Minister of
Canada) 94, 99
Leinster House (BRCS meeting) 32–4,
37
Leitrim 22, 75, 168, 181
war-relief 40, 53, 57
letter-writing 96, 138, 141
chaplains in general 12, 51, 108, 111,
160–1, 168
chaplains to parents of soldiers 46,
139
newspapers 10, 66, 74, 77, 125, 165
public 103, 107
relatives 45–6, 94, 112
Liberal Party 23, 97–8, 104, 107, 145
Irish MPs, wives and war effort 49–51,
77
Limerick 62, 102, 108
Armistice 166–7, 178, 183

food production 75–7
Irish-Canadian Rangers 114–15, 121, 125–6, 128
nationalist sentiment 116, 125, 141, 148–9, 152, 159
recruitment 138, 149, 152, 155
support for soldiers 32, 139, 144, 147, 160
war at sea 66, 71, 85, 90
war-relief 32, 35, 39–40, 53, 57, 162–3
linen industry 27, 114
Liverpool 93, 97, 108
Lloyd George, David (Minister for Munitions, Prime Minister of Great Britain) 24, 26, 113, 149, 154, 158, 169
Logue, Cardinal Michael (head of Catholic Church, Ireland) 12, 48, 74, 88, 119, 121, 127, 138–9, 141, 163, 165–6
London 19, 38, 84, 108, 178
London *Times* 63
Longford 141, 150
remembrance 3–4, 180–1
war effort 22, 39, 53, 76, 157
Loos, Battle of 134
lord lieutenant, *see* French, Sir John (Lord Lieutenant of Ireland)
Lough, Mrs E. H. (Thomas) 49–51
Louth 71, 74, 76, 141, 145
war-relief 36, 39, 57
remembrance 2–3
Lusitania 64–74, 85–90, 134, 140, 145, 172

McAleese, Mary (President of Ireland 1997–2011) 19
McCullagh, Crawford (Lord Mayor of Belfast) 48, 121
McGuinness, Martin 19
McHugh, Charles (Bishop of Derry) 139
McKenna, Patrick (Bishop of Clogher) 74, 139
MacRory, Joseph (Bishop of Down and Connor) 121, 139
Malta 41, 45
Mangan, John (Bishop of Kerry) 142

Mannix, Daniel (Archbishop of Melbourne) 99–102, 106
Marne, Battle of 28, 172
Martin, Marie 41, 45–6
Mayo 71
nationalist sentiment 153, 168
recruitment 22, 132, 142–3, 153
war-relief 40, 53, 72, 146–7
Mayo, Countess Geraldine Sarah Bourke 40, 72
Meath 75, 77
recruitment 22, 142, 145
war-relief 35, 39–40, 53, 72, 160, 162
Mediterranean Expeditionary Force (MEF) 136, 138
Melbourne 92–3, 99–100, 102, 123
Mercier, Désiré-Félicien-François-Joseph (Archbishop of Mechelen) 163
Messines, Battle of 19, 102
Methodists 33, 47, 115, 121, 181
Midleton, Lord William St John Brodrick 123
missioner 120
moderate nationalism 1, 11, 25–6, 117–18, 133, 169, 173, *see also* Home Rule
and diaspora 91, 93–8, 102
Monaghan 36, 53, 57, 143, 154–6
Mons, Battle of 28, 172
Montreal 92–3, 95–6, 99, 104–5, 113, 115, 118–19
moss-picking 52–6, 58–9, 78
Munster 27, 77, 116, 177
Murphy, Charles (Secretary of State, Canada) 94–5, 99
Murphy, Fr. 117, 138, 166
Murphy, William Martin 11, 33, 38
musical bands 70, 116, 125, 132, 141, 144–5

national duty as concept 27, 77–8, 82, 89, 176
National Egg Collection Scheme 50–1, 53, 58, 153
Nationalism, *see* advanced nationalism; Irish Parliamentary Party; Ulster
Naughton, Jacob (Bishop of Killala) 74
naval war, *see* war at sea
Navan 78, 143, 148, 160

Neuve Chapelle, Battle of   134
Newcastle   98, 160
Newfoundland   92, 99, 105–6, 108
Newry   47, 117, 132, 145, 168, 178
New South Wales (NSW)   92, 95, 98, 108
newspapers   10–13, 93, 177–8
　anti-German feeling   27, 48, 61–2,
　　73, 134
　Irish diaspora   95, 97, 100, 102–4
　Irish nationalism   122, 125, 127,
　　140–1, 153, 158
　supporting soldiers   112, 115–16,
　　119–23, 136, 138, 160
　tillage campaign   74, 77–9, 173
　war at sea   63–8, 80–1, 84, 86–8
　war effort   35, 38, 47, 49–51, 163,
　　165–7
newspapers and magazines
　Anglo-Celt, The   51, 66, 72
　Argus, The (Melbourne)   123
　Belfast (Evening) Telegraph   121–2
　Catholic Press, The   11, 102–3
　Catholic Register, The (Toronto)   93
　Church of Ireland Gazette, The   11,
　　153, 158
　Clare Champion, The   132
　Clare Journal, The   62, 66
　Connacht Tribune (see Connacht
　　Tribune)
　Connaught Telegraph, The   73, 166–7
　Cork Constitution   61
　Cork Examiner, The   65, 67–8, 115,
　　140
　Derry Standard, The   47
　Dundalk Democrat   153
　Freeman's Journal, The (Dublin)
　　80–1, 87, 89, 99, 132, 138, 145
　Freeman's Journal, The (Sydney)   11,
　　93, 97, 103
　Frontier Town, The   122
　Globe, The   93
　Irish Independent (see Irish
　　Independent)
　Irish Life   38–9, 41–2, 143, 146, 163–4
　Irish News, The   122
　Irish Post, The   50–1
　Irish Times (see Irish Times, The)
　Kerryman, The   67
　Kildare Observer, The   166

　Limerick Leader   66, 73, 77, 115,
　　159–60, 167
　Melbourne Advocate   93
　Montreal Gazette, The   11, 93, 104–5,
　　124
　Newry Reporter   132
　Northern Whig   115, 118, 121–2
　Osservatore Romano (Vatican)   163
　Punch   153
　Quebec Telegraph   124
　Saint John's New Freeman   93
　Ulster Herald   66
New Zealand   29, 93–4, 106, 156, 175
New Zealand Expeditionary Force   33,
　108
Nolan, Fr. Thomas V.   12, 36, 40, 48, 111,
　168
Nursing, see Irish women

O'Callaghan, Dr. Thomas Alphonsus
　(Bishop of Cork)   35
O'Connor, T. P. (MP)   93–5, 98
O'Dea, Thomas (Bishop of Galway,
　Kilmacduagh and Kilfenora)   74,
　88
O'Donnell, Patrick (Bishop of
　Raphoe)   74, 139, 142, 158, 167
O'Dwyer, Edward Thomas (Bishop of
　Limerick)   125, 127, 138–9, 165
Offaly, see King's County (Offaly)
Officers' Training Corps (OTC)   18, 73,
　133
O'Neill, Lawrence (Lord Mayor of
　Dublin)   89
Ontario   92, 94–5, 99, 109
Orange Order   109, 114
O'Reily, John (Archbishop of
　Adelaide)   102
Ormsby, Sir Lambert   33, 72
O'Shaughnessy, Thomas   33
O'Shea, Henry (Lord Mayor of Cork)
　36
Ottoman Empire   135, 139

pacifism   125, 127, 138, 165–6
Pals battalions   96, 136
paramilitary organizations   17–18, 21,
　23, 28
pastorals, see Catholic Church

patriotism
  expressed through war effort   39, 79,
    96, 99, 121, 157
  Ireland   44, 77, 98, 138, 176
Phelan, Patrick (Bishop of Sale)   102
Phillips, John (MP)   22
Plunket, Dr. Benjamin (Bishop of Tuam,
    Killala and Achonry)   85
Plunkett, Joseph   114, 161
Plunkett, Sir Horace   32, 117
Poincaré, Raymond (President of
    France)   98, 164
Poland   30, 163
potato crops   73–6
Power, Lady Talbot   38
Powerscourt, Lord Mervyn and Lady Sybil
    Wingfield   33, 180
Presbyterians   47–8, 111–12, 117–18,
    140, 143, 145
Press, *see* newspapers
Pretty Polly, The (sinking of)   84–5
priests, *see* Catholic Church
prisoners of war (POWs)   46, 58, 104
propaganda   64–5, 68, 72, 77, 109,
    138
Protestant and Catholic unity, *see* Catholic
    and Protestant unity
Protestantism, *see also* relevant
    denominations and Divisions
  cross-confessional cooperation   51,
    55–6, 70, 85, 117, 147
  military chaplains   115, 155
  remembrance   70, 179, 181
Prussian militarism (perceived)   63, 98,
    139, 146, 153, 167

Q ships   63
Quebec   92, 103, 109, 124
Queen Alexandra   31, 111
Queen's County (Laois)   22, 39–40, 53,
    160
Queen Elizabeth II   19
Queenstown (Cobh)   63, 65, 67–9, 74,
    82–5
Quin, Stephen (Mayor of Limerick)   115,
    121, 125

radical nationalism, *see* advanced
    nationalism

recruitment, *see also* Irish-Canadian
    Rangers; relevant countries
  anti-recruitment   5, 22, 25, 152–3,
    159, 169, 173
  authorities (*see* CCORI; IRC)
  clerical opposition towards   34, 138,
    165
  clerical support for   95–6, 99, 117–18,
    145–6, 158, 165
  cross-confessional support for   115,
    134, 143–8, 172, 176
  enlistment versus conscription   25,
    29, 142–3, 148, 153–8, 173
  ideological motivations   27, 35, 67,
    90, 137, 157–60, 175
  Ireland   18–20, 26–30, 38, 49, 132,
    142, 156–7, 172–3
  Irish nationalism   20–5, 148, 152–3,
    155, 158
  of Irish settlers in the
    Dominions   105, 107, 110–11,
    113, 119, 175–6
  and Irish/Unionist insignia   23, 26
    (*see also* Irish soldiers in the Great
    War)
  Nationalist MPs (*see* Irish
    Parliamentary Party)
  peer encouragement   28, 96, 133–4
  propaganda   68, 109–10, 113–14,
    144–5, 165
  reservists   23, 27, 29, 131–2
  voluntary enlistment   30, 90, 142,
    152–8, 175
Red Cross   31
  branches in Ireland   31–4, 37–9,
    42–6, 49–52, 56–8, 117, 145–6,
    163–4
  cross-confessional cooperation   32–3,
    38, 40–3, 51–2, 56–8, 146–7
  Dublin Castle Red Cross
    Hospital   37–8, 45
  fundraising   38, 51–2, 56–8, 146–7,
    163–4
  medical care   37–9, 45–6
  war-relief   31–4, 42–3
Redmond, John (MP)   21, *see also*
    Irish National Volunteers; Irish
    Parliamentary Party
  diasporic support   102–3, 109

encouraging recruitment　49, 128, 133, 152

and Home Rule　21, 24, 105–6, 140–2 (*see also* Home Rule)

Redmondism　25, 65–6, 77, 80, 106, 109–10, 141

support for war effort　34, 38, 121–2

support in Scotland　95–6, 98, 108

Redmond, Maj. Willie (MP)　23, 44, 102–3, 153, 169

Regiments　1, 26, 28, 71, 96, 119, 144, 178

Connaught Rangers　45, 58, 88, 108, 134, 148,

Irish-Canadian Rangers (*see* Irish-Canadian Rangers)

Irish Guards　111, 132, 144, 157–8, 168

Leinster　33, 123

Royal Dublin Fusiliers (RDF)　43–5, 111, 114, 116–17, 123, 134–7, 143

Royal Inniskilling Fusiliers　132

Royal Irish　32, 39, 67–8, 70, 134, 157

Royal Irish Fusiliers　49, 112, 114, 116, 123, 136, 167

Royal Irish Rifles　114, 132, 134

Royal Munster Fusiliers (RMF)　1, 4, 46, 58, 72, 83, 112, 114, 134–6, 143, 159–61, 164

selected others in which Irishmen served　108–9

Winnipeg Rifles, 90th　96

Remembrance, *see* Armistice Day

republican symbolism　1, 116, 171

Richards, Richard Watkins (Lord Mayor of Sydney)　102

RMS Leinster　85–90

Roscommon　127, 141, 168, 181

recruitment　22, 152

war-relief　32, 40, 162

Royal Army Medical Corps (RAMC)　38, 53, 134, 147

Royal College of Physicians　33, 37

Royal College of Science (RCS)　52–6, 78

Royal College of Surgeons　33, 37

Royal Irish Constabulary (RIC)　18, 124–5, 149, 156, 158, 160, 168

Royal Navy　84, 134, 155, 169

Russia　134, 147, 150, 163–5

Ryan, Monsignor Arthur　44, 141–2

sailors　37, 41, 52, 132, 161–2

American sailors　82–4

St Patrick's Day　4, 98, 100, 111–13, 147–8, 176, *see also* Irish Soldiers in the Great War

Scotland　22, 31, 37, 78, 114, 163

sectarianism　47–8, 109, 114

Serbia　27, 111, 147

Shamrocks, *see* Irish soldiers in the Great War

Sherlock, Lorcan (Lord Mayor of Dublin)　37

Sims, William (Admiral)　82–4

Sinn Féin　102, 134, 173, *see also* advanced nationalism

anti-British　3, 62, 82, 160, 168

anti-recruitment　5, 22, 25, 115, 124, 152–3 (*see also* recruitment)

by-election victories　79, 113–14, 127, 150

diasporic response　104–6

general election of 1918　7, 20, 24, 169, 174

growth of　7, 25, 104–5, 124, 149–51

versus Irish Parliamentary Party　58, 74, 80, 113, 149–51, 167

women　41, 174

Sligo　35, 40, 141, 180, 183

recruitment　22, 144–5, 155

Somme, Battle of the　18, 45, 49, 56, 105, 137, 172, 182

Spence, Robert William (Archbishop of Adelaide)　102

sphagnum moss, *see* moss-picking

steamship companies　84, 87, 116

Stephen, Rosamond　72, 167–8

submarine warfare, *see* war at sea

suffrage　5, 40, 174

Suvla Bay, *see* Dardanelles

Sydney　93, 97, 102, 141

tillage schemes, *see* agricultural production

Tipperary　88

food production　75, 77–8

nationalist sentiment　141–2, 149

support for war　146, 168, 180–1, 183

war-relief   32, 35–6, 39–40, 42, 44–5, 53
Titanic   64, 66
Toronto   92–3, 96, 98, 103, 109, 121
Treaty of Versailles   99, 168, 171
Tuam   85, 139, 143–5, 148, 158
Tynan, Katharine   38, 137, 156
Tyrone   141
  war effort   47, 53, 75, 77, 132, 147

U-Boat, *see* war at sea
Ulster, *see also* relevant denominations
  cross-confessional collaboration   70, 77–8, 112, 117–18, 121–3, 132, 168
  cross-confessional war-relief   14, 30, 33–6, 47–52
  Division, 36th (Ulster) (*see* Division)
  in Home Rule debates   6, 20–1, 24, 97, 114, 140, 149, 172 (*see also* Home Rule)
  Irish-Canadian Rangers (*see* Irish-Canadian Rangers)
  nationalist memory of war   17–19
  nationalists   89, 122–3, 132, 145, 147, 149, 154, 168–9, 182–3
  recruitment   18, 23, 26–8, 145, 156, 173
  territory of   8, 14, 47, 168–9, 172, 177, 182
  Unionist remembrance of war   17–18, 20, 182
  Unionists   21, 23, 115, 117, 121, 150, 165 (*see also* unionism)
  Unionist women   33–4, 41–3, 47–9
  war-relief (general)   42–4, 47–9, 52–4, 56
Ulster Volunteer Force (UVF)   21, 27, 33, 95, 132
Ulster Women's Unionist Council (UWUC)   34
Union Flag
  and Allied cause   65, 146–8, 162–3
  desecration of   168, 171
  and Irish-Canadian Rangers   116, 121–5
  use of alongside nationalist flags   1, 120–2, 162
  use of in remembrance   70–1
  use of upon Armistice   171

unionism, *see also* Ulster
  recruitment   23, 26–7, 49, 145
  unionist press   11, 35, 47–8, 50, 61, 65, 79–80, 115, 122, 158
  war-relief   14, 32–5, 40–1, 43, 49–50, 58
United Irish League (UIL)
  and the Irish Parliamentary Party   71, 93, 96, 141, 149
  war effort   76, 88, 108, 158
United Irish League of Great Britain (UILGB)   93, 96, 98, 108
United Kingdom   17, 131, 136, 158–9, 173, 176, 179, *see also* Britain
United States of America
  Irish diaspora   9, 67, 93, 107–8, 120, 175
  and the Lusitania   67–8, 70
  war effort   9, 55, 61, 82–5, 163, 165–6

Varadkar, Leo (Taoiseach)   19
Victoria (Australia)   92–3, 98, 100
Victoria Cross   100, 183
Voluntary Aid Detachments (VADs)   31–2, 38–46, 53, 58

Wales   22, 26, 32, 56–7, 114
Walsh, William (Archbishop of Dublin)   12, 104, 141
  pacifism   34, 114–15, 138, 163, 165
  war-relief   34, 72, 88–9, 150
war at sea, *see also* fishing industry; Germany; Irish Sea; newspapers; relevant counties
  effect on Irish life   73, 75, 79–81, 134, 139, 167, 176
  and feared food shortages   73–9
  in general   61, 63, 81–6, 90, 103
  Lusitania (*see* Lusitania)
  RMS Leinster (*see* RMS Leinster)
  on shaping attitudes towards Germany   65–7, 71–3, 75, 84–5, 87–90
  U-Boat   61, 63, 81–6
war memorials   1–4, 17, 19, 100, 172, 179–82
Waterford   141
  war at sea   63–4
  war effort   35, 39, 41, 78, 155

Waterford, Lady Beatrix Francis
    Petty-Fitzmaurice 41
Western Front 64, 150, 155
Westmeath 62, 159, 183
  war effort 22, 39, 52–3, 76–7, 154
Westminster, *see* Britain
Wexford 103, 109, 141
  war effort 27, 38–9, 53, 78, 145
Wicklow 21, 28, 108, 179
  war-relief 35–6, 39–41, 53
Wilhelm II, Kaiser 66, 73, 90, 167

Wilson, Sir Henry 165
Wilson, Woodrow (President of the
    United States of America) 162,
    168
Women's National Health Association
    (WNHA) 32, 42, 162

Yeats, William Butler 38
Ypres, Battle of 39, 46, 56, 134

Zeppelin 62

Printed in the USA
CPSIA information can be obtained
at www.ICGtesting.com
LVHW010841111223
766169LV00003B/126